Self-Relations in the Psychotherapy Process

Self-Relations
in the
Psychotherapy
Process

Edited by J. Christopher Muran

American Psychological Association
Washington, DC

Published by
American Psychological Association
750 First Street, NE
Washington, DC 20002

Copies may be ordered from
APA Order Department
P.O. Box 92984
Washington, DC 20090-2984

In the U.K., Europe, Africa, and the Middle East, copies may be ordered from
American Psychological Association
3 Henrietta Street
Covent Garden, London
WC2E 8LU England

Typeset in Berkeley Book by EPS Group Inc., Easton, MD

Printer: Automated Graphic Systems, White Plains, MD
Cover Designer: Kathy Keler Graphics, Washington, DC
Production Editor: Amy J. Clarke

The opinions and statements published are the responsibility of the authors, and such opinions and statements do not necessarily represent the policies of the American Psychological Association.

Library of Congress Cataloging-in-Publication Data
Self-relations in the psychotherapy process / edited by J. Christopher Muran.—1st ed.
    p. cm.
    Includes bibliographical references and index.
    ISBN 1-55798-733-5 (cb: acid-free paper)
    1. Self.   2. Psychotherapy.   3. Postmodernism.   I. Muran, J. Christopher.
    RC489.S43 S46 2001
    616.89'14—dc21   00-040164

British Library Cataloguing-in-Publication Data
A CIP record is available from the British Library.

Printed in the United States of America
First Edition

When my son Andrew was barely a toddler, I remember I would often play a game with him in which I would ask "Who's Andrew?" and sometimes follow with "Am I Andrew?" One time, perhaps just for emphasis, Andrew responded, "No, I'm Andrew *now*!" It was around the time I was planning this book project, and I was struck by the postmodern wisdom of his qualification.

To Andrew and his future

Contents

Contributors List

Lewis Aron, PhD, Postdoctoral Program in Psychotherapy and Psychoanalysis, New York University, New York

Sheldon Bach, PhD, private practice, Institute for Psychoanalytic Training and Research, New York Freudian Society, and Postdoctoral Program in Psychotherapy and Psychoanalysis, New York University, New York

Muriel Dimen, PhD, private practice, New York

Leslie S. Greenberg, PhD, Department of Psychology, York University, North York, Ontario, Canada

Jennifer Gregg, BA, Department of Psychology, University of Nevada, Reno

Steven C. Hayes, PhD, Department of Psychology, University of Nevada, Reno

William P. Henry, PhD, Department of Psychology, University of Utah, Salt Lake City

Mardi J. Horowitz, MD, Department of Psychiatry, University of California at San Francisco

Stanley B. Messer, PhD, Graduate School of Applied Psychology, Rutgers University, Piscataway, NJ

J. Christopher Muran, PhD, Beth Israel Medical Center, New York

Stuart A. Pizer, PhD, private practice, Cambridge, MA

Barry Protter, PhD, private practice, New York

Jeremy D. Safran, PhD, Psychology Department, New School for Social Research, New York

Timothy J. Strauman, PhD, Department of Psychiatry, University of Wisconsin, Madison

Zindel V. Segal, PhD, Clarke Institute of Psychiatry, Toronto, Ontario, Canada

C. Seth Warren, PhD, Graduate School of Applied Psychology, Rutgers University, Piscataway, NJ

William J. Whelton, PhD, Department of Psychology, University of Regina, Regina, Saskatchewan, Canada

Preface

The purpose of this book is to present current trends in understanding the self in the context of the psychotherapeutic situation. Traditionally, clinical considerations of the self have tended to espouse a self-contained individualism—a firmly bounded, highly individuated conception of the self. In recent years, however, there have been numerous postmodern challenges to the way the self has been understood. In the clinical setting, we are currently witnessing the emergence of several overlapping trends in the consideration of the self that reflect these challenges. To highlight a few, these include trends toward (a) *contextualism*: the recognition that we are intrinsically embedded in context; (b) *multiplicity*: the idea that we are composed of multiple selves; (c) *intersubjectivity*: the appreciation of subjective relations in our interpersonal encounters; (d) *social constructionism*: the understanding of our selves as social and historical constructions; and (e) *deconstruction*: the process of decentering from such identities as gender and race in our self-constructions.

A number of clinicians, who represent many of these current trends in their work, were invited to consider further postmodernism in their own conceptual language. The intent was to include authors who not only reflect these emergent trends but also represent psychoanalytic, behavioral, cognitive, and humanistic traditions as well as those who have a psychotherapy research emphasis. In addition, the intent was to establish a dialogue among the various contributors by having them discuss each other's respective chapters; specifically, each author provides a brief commentary on one other chapter contribution. The authors comment on a contribution from another tradition or orientation that touches on themes also present in their own work. Most important, the authors orient their discussion to the details of the psychotherapeutic process. In this way, the reader can have a tangible understanding of the application of theory to practice.

The idea for this book was inspired in part by my own frustrations with the field of psychotherapy. To elaborate, my professional life can in a sense be considered a multicultural experience. I have been part of the cognitive–behavioral community as a member of the Association for the Advancement of Behavior Therapy since the late 1980s because of my graduate school, internship, and fellowship training. Since 1990, I have been an active member of the psychotherapy research community primarily through the Society for Psychotherapy Research. In 1993, I entered psychoanalytic training at New York University's postdoctoral program and encountered a third culture. What has been so striking about this experience is how "dissociated" in a sense these communities really are. There seems to be very little open dialogue and a great deal of stereotyping, "strawman" comparisons, and insular or close-minded thinking. In point of fact, you actually see a great deal of this within these communities, among different orientations (e.g., Sullivanians vs. Kohutians, Beckians vs. Ellisians). In addition, I also joined the Society for the Exploration of Psychotherapy Integration in the mid-1990s only to find yet another community that is to some extent separate. In a sense, this can be seen as postmodernism at its worst—fragmented and disconnected. My ambition was to bring together clinicians from diverse traditions, from all these communities, to stimulate an open dialogue regarding similarity and difference, to decenter from the multiple conceptions of the self, and to move toward greater understanding. In this sense, this seems to be postmodernism at its best.

Acknowledgements

I would like to thank all the contributors for participating in this dialogic process and for making it what I believe to be a lively and enlightening one. I would also like to thank a number of people who have been particularly supportive and instrumental in the development of this project: Lewis Aron and Zindel Segal, who were especially facilitative in its construction; Margaret Schlegel, who embraced it with great enthusiasm; Adrian Harris Forman, who thoughtfully and diligently deconstructed it; Arnold Winston, who created an intellectual context that, very simply, made this all possible; Jeremy Safran, who for the last 10 years has challenged me, alternatively as mentor, colleague, and friend; the many colleagues, students, teachers, and patients who shaped my understanding of self and change; and, finally, my family and especially my wife Elisa who helped me to define my thoughts and persist despite my many self-doubts.

Self-Relations in the Psychotherapy Process

CHAPTER 1

An Introduction: Contemporary Constructions and Contexts

J. Christopher Muran

Back in the early 1970s, during the heyday of the variety show on television, a young comedian was introduced in one such show to the audience. He stepped up beside the host and responded to her welcome with "it's great to be here." He then stepped a few feet back and acknowledged, with some surprise, "it's also great to be here." He slid another few feet away and declared, "hey, it's great to be here, too." Finally, he paused and then mused, "and remember how great it was to be over there," looking back to where he once was. Although this was a humorous play on everyday language and expression, it also was an insightful commentary on the multiplicity and continuity of self-experience, and the significance of context.

Perhaps no notion has been more attractive and yet so elusive as the self has been to scholars in the humanities, arts, and sciences since the emergence of modernism from the intellectual context of the Enlightenment and Romantic movement (Taylor, 1989). Modernism essentially comprises the search for truth, for understanding the true nature of reality, and one of its most fundamental assumptions is the idea of the self as self-contained individualism with a rich conscious and unconscious life, "as an autonomous entity, not subject to continuous change or reformation, but a stable and rational being: *res cogitans*, in Cartesian terms" (White & Hellerich, 1998, p. 3). As a number of people have noted (e.g., Cushman, 1995; Smith, 1994), this cultural focus is probably responsible to a great extent for the popularity and proliferation of psychotherapy as a science and profession.

During the latter half of the 20th century, however, the idea of a firmly bounded, unitary self has been greatly challenged (e.g., Anderson, 1997, Gergen, 1991; Sampson, 1989; White & Hellerich, 1998). In his book *Constructing the Self, Constructing America*, for example, Philip Cushman (1995) defined the self as a concept of the individual as articulated by the indigenous psychology of a particular culture, the shared understandings within a cultural group of what it is to be human. According to this definition, one can approach the field of psychotherapy as a world composed of many cultures—from psychoanalysis to cognitive–behavioral to humanistic psychotherapies, from classical perspectives to various contemporary derivations.

At the level of theory, the modern search for the self in psychotherapy has failed to yield a universal truth. What is the self? We seem to have so many terms for it (e.g., *mind, consciousness, personality, character, identity, ego, subjectivity, self-representation, self-schema, self-concept, self-image*) and so many different meanings (e.g., experience or behavior, process or content, substance or structure, descriptive phenomenon or explanatory hypothesis). There seems to be no universal theory of self, no metanarrative, only local theories or narratives. There seems to be no simple discourse that can unify all theories of the self in psychotherapy, but rather multiple discourses, many different Wittgensteinian language games, which are not readily reducible to each other.

At the level of the person, Kenneth Gergen (1991) described the human condition as marked by multiple selves created and re-created in multiple relational contexts. We are continuously engaged in multiple relationships or social realities that pull us in myriad directions and invite us to play such a variety of roles that we are challenged to experience the sense of a single and stable, real self. This has been defined as the postmodern condition.

A Modernist Reading of Postmodernism

What is postmodernism? Like the definition of the self, it can mean different things to different people: "We could speak of postmodernisms" (Rosenau, 1992, p. 15); "there are probably as many forms of postmodernism as there are postmodernists" (Featherstone, 1988, p. 207). Although this may be consistent with the postmodern sensibility, it does make communication and comprehension somewhat impracticable and leaves one always teetering on the brink of collapsing into confusion. In general terms, postmodernism represents a challenge to the fundamental assumptions of modernism, including both the idea of an ultimate truth and the idea of the world as founded on hidden structures. It is antifoundationalism (the attempt to ground thought or inquiry on pregiven principles assumed true) and antiessentialism (the idea that there are pregiven "essences" inside things or people that constitute what they truly are). It has been defined as "incredulity towards metanarratives" (Lyotard, 1984, p. xxv). Instead, it promotes multiple and situationally dependent truths (see Kvale, 1992).

As some (e.g., Rosenau, 1992) have suggested, postmodernism is probably best understood as a correction or critique of modernism, a sensibility that can exist only alongside it, rather than a theory in and of itself. So, to counterbalance the modern emphasis on synthesis and unity, there is the postmodern preference for preserving difference and complexity. In contrast to the modern conception of the self, the postmodern perspective is one that disavows the notion that human beings have any essential or unitary core. There is no basic structure that is the self, no true or real self, but rather a number of selves that are equally real. Each self is constructed out of social encounters that comprise one's relationships, and each requires a social context if it is to exist and become present in experience (Anderson, 1997; Burr, 1995; Cushman, 1995; Gergen, 1991, 1994; White & Hellerich, 1998).

In an effort to "modernize" postmodernism, one useful way of approaching the definition of postmodernism is to reduce it to the less abstract level of the various, highly interdependent themes or theories of reality that have been associated with it. These include (a) constructivism, (b) pluralism, (c) contextualism, (d) relativism, and (e) perspectivism.

From the *constructivist* viewpoint, individuals are constantly and actively constructing their realities. Michael Mahoney (1991) distinguished between two important variants of constructivist theory: (a) *radical constructivism*, which is on the idealist end of the spectrum and suggests that there is no reality beyond our personal experience, and (b) *critical constructivism*, which accepts the existence of an inescapable real world but also recognizes that it can never be directly known. The critical constructivist conceives of the individual as coconstructor of personal realities, emphasizing the interactive relationship with the social environment. Alternatively identified as *social constructionism*, this perspective suggests that all knowledge is coconstructed and thus exists between people, not within them. This theory of reality emphasizes language as a fundamentally social phenomenon, whose relationship to reality is never fixed in meaning (Burr, 1995; see poststructuralism). Thus, the self is considered neither a private possession nor a personal construction but rather a social construction.

The *pluralist* perspective proposes that there is no single theory but rather a plurality of theories with truth claims.[1] It refers to the recognition that we live in a world of multiplicity and changeability, of infinite constructions and reconstructions. "The postmodern condition . . . is marked by a plurality of voices vying for the right to reality" (Gergen, 1991, p. 7). The dominance of a particular voice in a given moment is always subject to change (Lifton, 1993). The self is thus redefined as "an open slate . . . on which persons may inscribe, erase, and rewrite their identities as the ever-shifting, ever-expanding, and incoherent network of relationships invites or permits" (Gergen, 1991, p. 228). As Michel Foucault put it, "do not ask me who I am and do not expect me to remain the same" (quoted in Anderson, 1997, p. xx). Dating the origin of a

---

[1]In addition to the recognition that there is no single, true theory, there is also no single method to determine the truth of a theory. The notion of multiple methods to go along with multiple theories is termed *neopragmatism*(Margolis, 1986).

line of thought can be somewhat of an arbitrary punctuation, but it does seem the idea of multiple selves was at least very present in the latter part of the 19th century, when William James (1890/1981) was describing a self as a "stream of selves." Around the same time, Friedrich Nietzsche (1888/1968) wrote that

> the assumption of one single subject is perhaps unnecessary: perhaps it is just as permissible to assume a multiplicity of subjects, whose interaction and struggle is the basis of our thought and our consciousness in general. . . . My hypothesis: The subject is a multiplicity. (Sec. 409)

A *contextualist* theory of reality suggests that all knowledge or truth claims are intelligible only within their specific context, within a specific time and place.[2] Our constructions are embedded within a social context that has specific cultural and historical referents. Thus, the self functions within a particular historical and cultural configuration, matching and maintaining it (Cushman, 1995; Sampson, 1989). For example, Philip Cushman (1995) described an "empty self" as a post-World War II construction of Western culture that yearns to acquire and consume as a way of compensating for the absence of community, tradition, and shared meaning. This example illustrates contextualism in relatively global terms; it can also imply a more specific focus, a more microanalytic level of analysis, such as a given place and moment for a particular person.

The view of the self as intrinsically embedded in context can at least be traced to the intellectual milieu in Germany during the early part of the 20th century; specifically, to phenomenologists, such as Edmund Husserl; to existentialists, such as Martin Heidegger; and to gestalt psychologists, including Kurt Koffka and Kurt Lewin, who contributed significantly to the development of field theory. For example, Heidegger (1927/1962) suggested the essence of the self is that it has a world; a human being is a "being-in-the-world"; we are always already "thrown" into certain situations.[3,4]

---

[2]The notion of the hermeneutical circle also highlights the contextual nature of knowledge. Accordingly, a fact can be understood only in relation to the larger structure of theory (Messer, Sass, & Woolfolk, 1988).

[3]It seems worth noting here the likeness between the Western notion of contextualism and the Eastern tradition of Zen Buddhism, specifically with its recognition and reverence for wholeness, for the person in his or her natural and social environment, and for the idea that "we start from where we stand in life" (Gard, 1961, p. 15), that we are "there in relationship" (p. 107). To what extent the latter influenced the former is difficult to establish in any definitive sense.

[4]Contextualism also leads naturally to an appreciation of multiculturalism and specifically to differences among diverse cultures regarding the idea of self (e.g., Roland, 1996).

A *relativist* or *relational* theory of reality challenges modern science's causal explanation, suggesting instead a descriptive model of infinitely complex interwoven relationships. Thus the emphasis is more on processes than on structures, on *how* things are related or interact. "A *self* does not amount to much, but no self is an island; each exists in a fabric of relations that is now more complex and mobile than ever before" (Lyotard, 1984, p. 15). *Connectionism* is a related notion, which suggests a network of a large number of units, complexly interconnected with feedback loops, but responding only to local information; thus it is not rule based and governed by a central control or underlying level (Bechtel & Abrahamsen, 1991; Cilliers, 1998). *Intersubjectivity* is another idea that seems based on a relational theory of reality. The term is attributed to critical theorist Jurgen Habermas (1971), who applied it to contrast subject–subject from subject–object relations in human communication. For him, open and free interactive discourse between two subjects can reconcile differences and approximate truth through dialogic consensus. Feminist contributions, such as those by Dorothy Dinnerstein (1976), as well as Martin Buber's (1923/1958) "interhuman" philosophy seem to be parallel perspectives.[5]

What is meant by *perspectivism* is the process of decentering the self and seeing all views as perspectival, interpretive, or constructive. This is more method than theory. It suggests situating the self in a context of heightened self-reflexivity—an openness to the multiplicity of social constructions of one's continuous experience. Gergen (1991) referred to this as a "new self-consciousness." A related method is *deconstruction*. Accordingly, whenever we construct something through language, we are not only identifying what it is (i.e., what is present) but also what it is not (i.e., what is absent). Deconstruction thus involves the recognition of how a construction relies on both presence and absence (Derrida, 1978). Its goal is to undo and reveal all constructions.

Although postmodernism has been presented in a positive light, as a much-needed corrective to modernism—as "modernity without illusions," for example (Elliott & Spezzano, 1996)—there is also a dark side. Postmodernism can be depicted as Janus like. As Pauline Marie Rosenau (1992) distinguished, there is a skeptical position that there is no truth or reality, it is pure illusion, and there is an affirmative position that truth is personal and contextually specific. The former position seems to promote a radical relativism for all knowledge, where everything is fragmented, and anything can go, thus approaching a nihilistic sensibility. The latter position seems to suggest a more practicable perspectivism in that it permits the possibility of dialogue with other discourses

---

[5]Hegel (1807/1969) presented an early example of this thinking when he challenged the Cartesian idea of the self existing in solitary reflection, suggesting instead that the self cannot be known in isolation but only in relation to another.

(or belief systems), such as modernism. Whereas the skeptical position calls for the death of the self, the affirmative one permits the possibility of reconciling multiplicity and unity (Anderson, 1997; White & Hellerich, 1998). Gary Brent Madison (1988) made a similar distinction, using the terms *postmodernist* to refer to the more radical position and *postmodernistic* to refer to the more affirmative position.

M. Brewster Smith (1994) described the postmodern dilemma as involving the metaphors of expansion and depletion: The former is characterized by expanding awareness of multiple possibilities, by a breaking away from the shackles of our social constructions, which permits mutliple identities and prizes change; the latter is characterized by emptiness and depletion, as a loss or absence of community, tradition, and shared meaning (Cushman, 1995). On whatever side of the postmodern fence one stands, postmodernism is a sensibility that requires a tolerance for ambiguity and ambivalence and that provides a challenge to our modern conceptions of personhood, agency, commitment and, of course, reality (Burr, 1995; Smith, 1994). We have become accustomed to thinking of ourselves as having a certain personality with a certain set of beliefs of which we are the principal author. We have also become accustomed to the assumption that we make choices and commitments and take responsibility for the life we have accordingly fashioned. Who am I? What do I believe? What should I do? All these, and then some, are now open to serious question.

The Self in Psychotherapy: Modernism and Postmodernism

It is interesting to see the cultivation of postmodern ideas in a field that was so inspired by the modern spirit as psychotherapy. Perhaps this demonstrates the intrinsic and inextricable relationship of postmodern to modern thought. Perhaps it also suggests that postmodern seeds were already sown in modern conceptions of the self in the psychotherapy literature. What follows is a brief and selective history of clinical conceptions of the self and their application to the psychotherapy process. Depending on what one's selection criteria are, the literature regarding clinical insights on self and change can be quite voluminous. I chose to eschew a more traditional chronological presentation of contributions and decided to organize this section by important thematic developments regarding the self in psychotherapy, to present a sampling of the critical themes and innovations, especially those that reflect the postmodern spirit. Needless to say, as much as is present, there is no doubt much that is absent. I also resolved to resist organizing this historical summary into separate sections by the traditional distinction of the psychoanalytic, cognitive–behavioral, and humanistic psychotherapies, given that these distinctive boundaries have become increasingly permeable. Instead, I present the respective contributions of these traditions within the various themes that I have identified. In a sense, this section should not only lay the groundwork for the rest of this book but also provide a preview of this book's aim: that is, to break down arbitrary boundaries that are maintained more for sociopolitical reasons than for intellectual purposes.

Self as Representational

There has been a long-standing interest in the psychotherapy literature in self-representation, particularly in the psychoanalytic and cognitive traditions. The contributions in this regard have served as a point of departure for all other conceptual developments about the self.

In the psychoanalytic tradition there have been a number of efforts to articulate the relationship of the self to the ego; these conceptions of the self were essentially representational, conceptualizing the self as an object of experience rather than as a subject of experience; the self was a descriptive concept; the explanatory concepts remained the id, ego, and superego. In his redefinition of narcissism, Heinz Hartmann (1958) introduced the notion of self as representation into Freud's (1923) drive/structure model. He distinguished between the ego as mental system and the self as representation within that system and changed the object of narcissistic investment from the ego to the self. His self referred to the content of the mind; it was an internal image, similar to those formed of objects. His self, though, was subordinate to the ego, and thus he remained faithful to Freud's modern ideal of psychotherapeutic change, whereby the ego as master purposefully directs the individual through its integrative functions to a realistic adaptation to the world. In other words, "where id is, ego shall be" (Freud, 1933, p. 80).

Hartmann's contribution to the classical framework paved the way for future theorists, such as Edith Jacobson (1964) and Otto Kernberg (1976, 1982), to propose structures in which the interaction between self and object became of central motivational importance. Kernberg, for example, posited an ego system (or ego identity) that comprises various internalized, bipolar representations synthesized into an integrated sense of self. Each bipolar representation includes a self-representation, other representation, and affective valence; it is an internalization (through introjection and identification) of an interpersonal experience (especially early ones) and serves as a template for ongoing relationships. For him, the self is the sum total of all these representations. Joseph Sandler (e.g., Sandler & Rosenblatt, 1962) also elaborated on Hartmann's contribution with a series of formulations of the "representational world." For him, the representational world is the product of ego functions; self- and object representations are constructed by the ego from external experience, organized within the representational world, and then used to guide adaptive activity. Id impulses become associated with self- and object representations through experience and seek gratification through wishes that involve self- and object images.

Likewise, self-representation has received a great deal of attention in cognitive therapy circles, specifically in terms of the schema concept, which has become the organizing principle or explanatory construct for the cognitive model of human experience and disturbance. Although Albert Ellis (1962) contributed significantly to the development of this model, it was Aaron T. Beck (1967) who first introduced the schema construct in his information-processing model of depression, whereby specific patterns of self-schemas make a person vulnerable to specific stressors. This contribution laid the groundwork for a model that distinguished among cognitive products, processes, and structures (Hollon & Kriss, 1984). Products refer to the resultant expressed thoughts and images that we experience, often out of awareness at an automatic level; these represent overt and covert self-statements, or what Beck called *automatic thoughts*, which are products of various cognitive processes or operations that can seriously distort one's experience of reality. Beck described human disturbance as related to a number of cognitive distortions, systematic errors in logic or misinterpretations of an event, including arbitrary inference, selective abstraction, overgeneralization, magnification–minimization, personalization, and dichotomous thinking. Both Beck and Ellis believed that these products and processes are generated by underlying belief systems that are tacit and have become "structuralized," in a sense, as permanent formations of one's cognitive organization.

Beck (1967) adopted the schema construct from the cognitive sciences to define such belief systems. In so doing, he established the basis for a dialogue between cognitive therapists and cognitive scientists, such as Hazel Markus (1977), Susan Harter (1983), and Tory Higgins (1987), that has led to an enrichment of the cognitive model of the mind (see chapter 11, this volume). Since Beck introduced the self-schema construct, cognitive therapists have increasingly invested their energies in the clinical study of the self (see chapter 11, this volume)—in the areas of depression (e.g., Segal, 1988), anxiety (e.g., Beck, Emery, & Greenberg, 1985), and personality disorders (e.g., Beck, Freeman, & Associates, 1990; Young, 1990). Self-schemas have been generally understood to be "cognitive generalizations about the self, derived from past experience, that organize and guide the processing of self-related information contained in an individual social experience" (Markus, 1977, p. 63). In the evolution of cognitive therapy and practice guidelines, there seems to have been a definite shift in focus from automatic thoughts and self-statements to underlying mechanisms with regard to self-schemas. In a sense, this can be seen as a shift from surface structure to deep structure. Early treatment models concentrated on accessing thoughts at the surface level; challenging their truth or heuristic value; and developing alternative, more adaptive self-statements. Developers of later models turned their attention to the elucidation of underlying beliefs and assumptions.

It is interesting to note that the use of the self-schema construct, and more generally the language of the cognitive sciences, has been embraced by clinical theorists from an object-relational orientation, such as Sydney Blatt (e.g., Blatt & Blass, 1992) and Mardi Horowitz (e.g., 1987; chapter 3, this volume), as well as those from a humanistic–experiential orientation, such as Leslie Greenberg (e.g., Greenberg, Rice, & Elliott, 1995, see chapter 4, this volume). As some have argued (e.g., Horowitz, 1991), one apparent benefit of the application of such a neutral language to clinical theory is that it has fostered more dialogue among diverse orientations and more cross-fertilization (e.g., Segal & Blatt, 1993). For example, both Beck (Clark & Beck, 1991) and Blatt have suggested two kinds of self-schemas: (a) those concerned with agency and self-definition and (b) those concerned with relatedness and communion—a formulation that corresponds with David Bakan's (1966) contribution to human motivation.

Self as Developmental

A developmental view of the self is a perspective taken by clinical theorists from diverse orientations, many of whom are presented in other sections in this chapter. Here I highlight two critical contributions regarding the self as a developmental phenomenon that have had considerable influence on the clinical literature.

Margaret Mahler (1968) provided further elaboration of Hartmann's (1958) self, depicting it as a developmental achievement. Her conception of the process of separation and individuation results in a self with a coherent sense of identity. For Mahler, the infant begins life without a sense of self or of objects in what she described as the autistic stage of development, which is characterized by need and its gratification. By the second month a connection is made between need gratification and the mother, which marks the beginning of the symbiotic stage. Then, through a complex process of differentiation (from the mother), practicing (by exploration of the world), rapprochement (regressing and reuniting with the mother), and finally separation–individuation proper, the child becomes a separate person with a sense of identity. Mahler saw psychopathology as resulting from either failure to negotiate this developmental process or regression to a primordial symbiosis; thus, it is marked by a loss of self. Although Mahler primarily concentrated on development and psychopathology, she did provide a transitional link between Hartmann's reformulation of the drive/structure model and models in which interpersonal conditions are promoted (J.

Greenberg & Mitchell, 1983). Thus, she laid the groundwork for various sem-
inal contributions regarding clinical process and the psychoanalytic process
(Kernberg, 1976; Kohut, 1984, see below for an elaboration; Loewald, 1980;
Pine, 1987, 1990).

Daniel Stern, a student of Mahler, offered a contrasting view of self-
development that has received a great deal of attention in psychotherapeutic
circles (Stern, 1985). He challenged the notion of an autistic and symbiotic
primordial state and instead suggested an epigenetic developmental model in
which the development of self-experience is innately wired and in evidence as
early as the age of 2 months. Stern's self is essentially experiential in nature.
For him, there are four self-experiences that emerge in succession: (a) the emergent self (self in the process of formation), (b) the core self (in the form of self-
agency, self-cohesion, self-affectivity, and self-history), (c) the subjective self (the
discovery of subjectivity as well as intersubjectivity), and (d) the verbal self (self
represented as a narrative). A great number of contemporary analysts, such as
those associated with relational and intersubjective orientations (e.g., Aron,
1996, and chapter 6, this volume; Mitchell, 1988; Stolorow, Brandchaft, &
Atwood, 1987), have embraced Stern's ideas and articulated therapeutic implications, particularly with respect to his subjective self. Stern has also had a
significant impact on cognitive therapists with a developmental orientation (e.g.,
Guidano, 1987, 1991; Mahoney, 1991, see below for an elaboration on both).

Self as Process

In contrast to the treatises of the self as representational structure, there have
been a number of significant contributions in the psychotherapy literature that
have portrayed the self as an active agent in process.[6] In the psychoanalytic
literature, there have been numerous researchers, including as prominent examples Harry Stack Sullivan, Ronald Fairbairn, and John Bowlby, who rejected
the ego psychological focus on the self as subordinate and representational and
posited the self as primary and functional.

Sullivan (1953, 1964) set forth a field theory of personality in which the
self could be considered not in isolation but in relation to another. The self is
what is manifest in the interpersonal field.[7] For Sullivan, the emphasis is on

---

[6]It seems important to at least mention that the view of the self as process, as embedded
in an interpersonal field, is a perspective particularly characteristic of family therapies.
To do justice to that literature, along with the other traditions, seemed to me to be
beyond the scope of this chapter. See Kaslow and Celano (1995) for a brief but comprehensive review of that literature.

[7]Sullivan was especially influenced by the intellectual movement that has been described as the "mosaic of Chicago social science" (Perry, 1964). Most notable of the

interpersonal process. We are what we do, and everything we do that is knowable is done in relation to others (J. Greenberg & Mitchell, 1983). Personality is construed as a patterning of interpersonal situations and can be manifest only in the context of an interpersonal relationship. Thus, he conceptualized the therapeutic process as one involving a "detailed inquiry" and analysis of the patient's interpersonal relations. One of his most important contributions to the psychotherapy process, which logically follows, is the recognition of the therapist as "participant–observer," as embedded in the interpersonal field of the psychotherapeutic process. Over the years, a number of contemporary interpersonal analysts have developed a model of change from Sullivan's original ideas, in which what constitutes change is an enrichment or expansion of self (Ehrenberg, 1992; Levenson, 1992). By increasing the patients' awareness of themselves in relation to others, change does not simply suggest a correction of a distortion but rather an elaboration and clarification of the self.

Ronald Fairbairn (1952) also provided a dramatic revision of Freud's model, but from an object relations perspective. He began with redefining the libido as object seeking. His use of ego is much more akin to traditional uses of self, and his view is not one in which the ego or self is considered a developmental achievement; rather, he envisioned a primary ego in its original wholeness, with its own libidinal energy, seeking relations to external objects. If this drive is not met satisfactorily, the ego splits and establishes compensatory internal objects. Fairbairn described an incorporation process that establishes a psychic structure consisting of a central ego intrinsically tied to the ideal object, which represents the gratifying aspects of the mother, and subsidiary egos tied to internalized objects: the libidinal ego tied to the exciting object, which represents the enticing promise of relatedness, and the antilibidinal ego tied to the rejecting object, or the aspects of the mother experienced as depriving and withholding. The central ego is also the part of the ego that remains available for real relationships in the external world. For Fairbairn, conflict takes places among these three ego-object, structural patterns, and change involves the analyst becoming a good object to help the patient relinquish ties to bad objects, although he did not provide much more detail in this regard.

Closely related to the theories of both Sullivan and Fairbairn is that of John Bowlby (1988), who applied an ethological framework to the self. He understood human experience and behavior in terms of survival function and specifically considered attachment as a biologically prewired goal with survival implications. In this regard, he suggested that attachment to the mother was

---

Chicago intellectuals, which included sociologists and cultural anthropologists, were George Herbert Mead and Robert E. Park, both of whom had spent considerable time studying philosophy in Germany during the early part of the 20th century and, when studying at Harvard, also came under the influence of William James.

primary, not the result of the mother's function as a gratifier of needs. Bowlby considered all human experience with regard to attachment, separation, and loss. According to him, we develop internal working models representing interpersonal interactions relevant to attachment behavior. The development of these models is based on our propensity to organize and coordinate through cognitive processes different action sequences and behavioral patterns that are biologically wired in and guide the pursuit of attachment in relatively flexible ways. Bowlby has applied his attachment model to understanding the experiences of sadness and depression and of anxiety and anger. In contrast, he has written relatively little with regard to the application of attachment theory to the psychoanalytic process, short of discussing the importance of providing a secure base for the patient (Bowlby, 1988). The relevance of attachment theory for understanding the self and change, however, is beginning to receive increasing attention in psychoanalytic circles due in large measure to the recent efforts of Jeremy Holmes (1996) and Peter Fonagy (e.g., Fonagy & Target, 1996).

The notion of the self as process has always been central to the humanistic tradition (L. S. Greenberg & Rice, 1997). Humanistic psychotherapies are essentially field theories that consider the self in context, stressing the interdependent nature of humans. Accordingly, there is no meaningful way to consider the person as an isolate, as apart from the field, especially the interhuman aspects of it. Fritz Perls (1969) particularly emphasized the "contact boundary" between self and world:

> What makes us interested in the world? How come I cannot function, cannot live, just as a kind of autistic organism, completely self-contained? A living organism is an organism which consists of thousands and thousands of processes that require interchange with other media outside the boundary of the organism. (p. 14)

The gestalt tradition by definition is founded on the idea of a pattern or configuration organized by a figure–ground relationship in which the figure is what is salient in experience and is regulated by the needs of the person and the demands of the situation. Meaning is constituted in the relation between figure and ground and is thus always contextualized. "People are defined by their boundaries" (Yontef, 1995, p. 263). The sense of "I" can be established only by "I–thou" or "I–it" contact, indicative of Martin Buber's (1923/1958) influence on this tradition. Humanists with an existential orientation, such as James Bugental (1978) and Irving Yalom (1981), have emphasized the separate, although related, aspect of this contact with the world.

The humanistic view of the self thus is one of continual dynamism, the unending flow of being and experience, without much regard for structure. As described in the person-centered tradition, the self refers not to an internal structure or substance but to the experience of oneself as a whole person in any given moment (Bohart, 1995). The self is formed by an assimilative process of continually interacting with the environment. With each interaction, a new self emerges. As our awareness of our own being and functioning develops, we acquire a sense of self that comprises experiences of our own being and functioning within this environment. This is what Carl Rogers (1961, 1980) referred to as our *developing self-concept*, which is a dynamic process dependent on our perception of our experiences in the world, particularly our perception of how others regard us. To Rogers, we have a need for positive regard, and the extent to which this is satisfied or frustrated shapes our sense of self-regard.

From a humanistic perspective, maladjustment essentially involves a failure or disruption in the individual's ability to evolve ongoingly, the critical feature of which is some breakdown in awareness. In the person-centered tradition, it involves an incongruence between self-concept and experience. It results from a failure to learn from feedback, to be in process, and to focus on the flow of inward experience that provides for the creative resolution of a problem (Rogers, 1951, 1961). In gestalt terms, the human condition is construed as an ongoing process of a need arising and being satisfied, where the emphasis is on the natural self-regulation of the needs of the organism and the demands of the environment (e.g., Yontef, 1995). Self-regulation depends on discriminating figural feelings and needs by means of sensory awareness. Dysfunction occurs when awareness does not develop as needed and the need–satisfaction cycle is interrupted. From an existential perspective (e.g., Bugental, 1978), dysfunction similarly involves awareness-constricting or awareness-distorting ways of defining the self and the world.

Treatment thus involves establishing the necessary conditions in which patients can become aware of their inner and outer realities, their needs and the corresponding demands of the environment, and can restore the process of learning and growth (see chapter 4, this volume). From a person-centered perspective, the process involves providing the appropriate conditions of therapist empathy, positive regard, and congruence and focusing closely on the moment-to-moment flow of a patient's inner track so that patients can become aware of their own perceptions of inner and outer reality and construct new meanings in order to creatively solve their problems (Bohart, 1995). The assumption is that in the appropriate interpersonal context, the patients let go of learned conditions of worth and then are guided by their own actualizing tendency toward growth and autonomy. Eugene Gendlin (1995) described a process of engaging the patient in an experiential search that includes attending to, differentiating, and integrating an inner referent in order to construct meaning and carry one forward. From a gestalt perspective, the emphasis is more on perceptual awareness and evoking an intense experience of what one is talking about. In this regard, the therapist is more directive, by setting experiments to intensify experience and by making the process of the interruption figural, subject to awareness; then the need–satisfaction cycle is restored (see Yontef, 1995). In the existential tradition, the psychotherapeutic process is not as well articulated, perhaps because it is so varied, but in general therapy is also regarded as facilitating greater awareness of construal of self in the world (see Bugental, 1978; Yalom, 1981).

The notion of self as process is relatively newer to the cognitive–behavioral tradition. There are two developmental paths in this regard that are noteworthy. The first concerns the contributions of Vittorio Guidano (1987, 1991), Michael Mahoney (1991), and Jeremy Safran (1998; Safran & Segal, 1990) to the cognitive therapy literature. The three could be readily grouped in their shared sensibility, but I discuss their contributions in separate sections, according to their respective emphases, as I see them. First, I focus on Safran, who challenged the perspective originally presented by Beck and provided a view of the self in interpersonal process. Following in the footsteps of Sullivan, Fairbairn, and Bowlby as well as Stern, Safran defined *interpersonal schemas* as generalized representations of self–other relationships that are abstracted on the basis of interactions with attachment figures and that permit the individual to predict interactions such that the probability of maintaining a relationship with these figures is increased. Thus, they contain procedural knowledge about particular interpersonal events that serves not only the passive processing of an experience but also the active construction of that experience. These schemas include specific information regarding expectancies and strategies for relating to others, which are learned but are stored in memory as a result of an innate propensity to relate to others for the sake of survival. Accordingly, an individual may have different interpersonal schemas for people who play different roles in his or her life (e.g., authority figures, prototypical lovers). Thus, interpersonal schemas can be understood as the building blocks of the self system at large. For Safran, the information contained within such schemas is also represented in expressive-motor form, which orients the individual to the environment, helping him or her adjust continually. According to him, the infant from birth develops memory stores that consist of specific expressive-motor responses, physiological arousal, associated images, and relevant eliciting stimuli. These memory stores serve as the primary templates for emotional experience that are developed and elaborated over time through the process of learning into subtle and idiosyncratic variations.

Safran's contributions represent an important shift from a model of the self as passive processor of information to one as active constructor of information, from an information-processing model to one of a more constructivistic nature. Instead of a vulnerability model of dysfunction, Safran presented a model of dysfunction based on what he called the *cognitive–interpersonal cycle*. Accordingly, an interpersonal schema shapes one's perception of the interpersonal world and leads to cognitive–interpersonal operations that in turn shape the environment in a manner that confirms the schema; thus, a self-perpetuating

cycle emerges. Maladjusted individuals tend to possess rigid and constricting interpersonal schemas that restrict the range of interpersonal behaviors, which pull for similar responses from a range of different people, resulting in a limited range of interpersonal experiences. On the basis of this model, Safran suggested a psychotherapeutic course in which the therapeutic relationship is the vehicle to elucidating cognitive–interpersonal cycles and to challenging maladaptive interpersonal schemas within the individual (see Safran & Muran, 2000). He identified *decentering* (increasing immediate awareness of cognitive–interpersonal operations) and *disconfirmation* (challenging beliefs and expectations implicit to the schema by providing a new interpersonal experience) as central change processes.

The second noteworthy development in the cognitive–behavioral literature has emerged from the behavioral end of the spectrum. It has been described, in contrast to the methodological behaviorism so predominant in behavioral therapies, as a more philosophical form of behaviorism, founded on B. F. Skinner's (1953, 1957) operant theory of learning (Hayes, Follette, & Follette, 1995). Skinner approached the definition of behavior, including verbal behavior, in terms of its function, rather than its form, and articulated a behavioral model based on contingency principles, including "rule-governance," in which behavior is regulated by verbal formulas. He defined *the self* as a functionally unified system of responses that are contextually situated in terms of history of environmental contingencies and specific circumstances in which they currently emerge. This concept of the self leaves open the possibility that any one person might exhibit a number of selves. Skinner's conceptual contributions laid the groundwork for a "contextual functionalism" in behavior theory and therapy, the main proponents of which have been Steven Hayes (e.g., Hayes et al., 1995; chapter 12, this volume) and Robert Kohlenberg (e.g., Kohlenberg & Tsai, 1991). They have used the concepts of verbal behavior and rule governance to address language and meaning in matters such as consciousness, subjectivity, and self. Accordingly, verbal behavior is symbolic (rather than physical) behavior that affects the environment by its linguistic meaning and not just its physical impact. The focus on verbal behavior transforms the behavioral analysis from one investigating the functional relationships among behavioral responses, physical antecedents, and consequences to one investigating the meanings of the antecedents, the meanings of the behaviors, and the meanings of the consequences. As an example of this perspective, Kohlenberg and Tsai (1991) described a model of self-development in which self-referential words such as *I* and *me* first develop under public "stimulus control" and then progressively come under private stimulus control, becoming associated with private experience. Pathologies of self involve a disruption in this developmental process; for example, the lack of development of "I" statements associated with private experience can make one dependent on public cues from others to determine

how one feels. Treatment essentially involves helping clients align their self-statements and the related self-awareness with their private experience. For them, the therapeutic relationship is a critical context for effecting such change. For Hayes, Strosahl, and Wilson (1998; chapter 12, this volume), treatment involves reinterpreting a problematic psychological phenomenon by placing it in a different interpretive context, which invariably alters its meaning. A critical target of this approach is to facilitate self-awareness and the experience of the "observing self" (cf. Deikman, 1982).

Self as Reflexive

William James (1890/1981) presented what many consider the seminal conception of the self. He captured the complexity of the concept, its Janus-like nature as consciousness and as mental structure, as multiplicity of consciousness and unity of identity. He distinguished between the self as "I"—self as subject and observer—and the self as "me"—self as object and observed. A number of clinical theorists have taken up this conception over the years and applied it to understanding the psychotherapeutic process. In a sense, this conception has provided a means to bridge the self as process and the self as representation.

In the interpersonal tradition, evincing the influence of William James (see footnote 7), Sullivan also put forth a reflexive conception by generally describing the self with two distinct referents: the *operational* self and the representational self (Barnett, 1980). The former refers to the processes or operations, including "security operations," that establish and protect the content of the latter and function to minimize anxiety. The *representational* self includes the various beliefs, images, and ideas derived from "reflected appraisals" of significant others. It comprises the "personifications of the self," the various "me–you patterns" of an individual's interpersonal history, including those aspects designated "good me," because they have been met with approval; "bad me," because they have been met with anxiety; and "not me"—dissociated aspects met with dread by a "significant other." Benjamin Wolstein (1974, 1977) elaborated on Sullivan's reflexive conception. He emphasized the dialectical relation between "I" processes and "me" patterns and promoted the use of the therapeutic relationship and the process of "coparticipatory inquiry" to facilitate the patient's experience of his or her "unique" self in the context of an intimate interaction with another, that is, the analyst.

Arnold Modell (1993) is another analyst who attempted to unpack a number of the paradoxes in James's conception, including the structural continuity of the self, its discontinuity in consciousness, and the problem of objectifying the subjective experience of the self, as well as the conception of the self as dependent on social affirmation and as autonomous in generating itself from

within. As one solution, he proposed Gerald Edelman's (1987) neurobiological theory of evolutionary value, according to which value can extend from homeostatic brain functions to the domain of personal interests and meanings. Accordingly, the need to maintain coherence and continuity becomes less dependent on others over time because of the generativity of the "private" self. Modell described the psychotherapeutic process as an interplay between private and shared meanings in patient and therapist constructions.

Irene Fast (1998) has also adopted a Jamesian perspective in her application of the dynamic "I-self" and the imagistic "me-self" in her integration of Piagetian principles and object-relational approaches to psychoanalytic theory. She has referred to all self-activities (such as perceiving, thinking, feeling, and acting) as *selving* to emphasize their dynamic and active nature and proposed that the basic units of the mind are action schemes, or "I-schemes" that represent personally motivated self–nonself interactions and that develop through integration and differentiation. These I-schemes are intimately related with self- and object representations, such that these representations at any given moment reflect the schemes in play. Our representations are defined by the constellation of I-schemes active in a moment and shaped by the I-schemes of past moments. She described the presence of personal agency as basic or primary to selving, as well as the subjective sense of self as a developmental achievement with important implications for understanding psychopathology.

Sheldon Bach (1985, 1994; see chapter 2, this volume) has invoked James's conception by his distinction between subjective awareness and objective self-awareness in his analytic formulation. By *subjective awareness,* he refers to states of mind when we are immersed in thought or act and unaware of ourselves as subject of thought or action. By *objective self-awareness,* he refers to other states of mind when we take our self as object of our thoughts or actions. For Bach, we not only vary switching from one state to the other, but we also vary in developed capacities to flexibly and appropriately switch. John Auerbach and Sydney Blatt (1996) elaborated on Bach's contribution with what they referred to as *self-reflexivity,* which is the capacity to move easily between the subjective and objective selves. Peter Fonagy and his colleagues (e.g., Fonagy & Target, 1996) have also contributed significantly to this discussion with their comparable notion of *reflective functioning,* which emerged from the attachment literature, specifically the work of Mary Main (1991).

In the cognitive literature, Guidano's (1987, 1991) and Mahoney's (1991) formulation of the self highlights self-reflexivity. They depict humans as self-organizing, self-determining agents capable of ongoing growth and differentiation. Their emphasis is more on self as process, without ignoring self as structure. They highlight the role of attachment processes in the emergence of self as subject and as object, and they describe the importance (especially Guidano) of differentiation through self-observation of the continuously unfolding process of circularity between the experiencing "I" and explaining "me." For them, human disturbance represents a "nonviable level of awareness that prevents a coherent assimilation of personal experience" (Guidano, 1991, p. 60). Thus, the therapeutic process reflects "the dynamics of experiential reorganization" (Mahoney, 1991, p. 270) in which new and often more complex core ordering processes emerge and a viable level of awareness is established. Guidano (1991) described a "scene-analysis" psychotherapeutic process in which the therapist "directs" the patient's self-observation by encouraging the patient to zoom in and out and pan a succession of life scenes and to shift his or her point of view from the "why" of experience to the "how." For him, change is an increase of flexibility in assessing and differentiating the experiencing "I" and the explaining "me" of selfhood dynamics.

Self as Nuclear and Integral

Although the idea of the self as nuclear and integral can be seen in cognitive and humanistic theories in terms of the self as a core organizing principle (e.g., L. S. Greenberg et al., 1995; Guidano, 1991), it is a perspective that is particularly well developed in psychoanalytic thought. Beginning with Carl Jung's (1945) notion of an archetypal predisposition to develop an integrated sense of self, a number of analytic theorists from various orientations have conceptualized the self in superordinate terms—as nuclear or core, as integral or cohesive—and the psychoanalytic process as facilitative of this development. George Klein's (1976) contributions exemplify this position. He posited a superordinate need to maintain a coherent and integrated self. Accordingly, we are always trying to maintain and preserve a sense of self or "self-conception." In this regard, we split off or dissociate meaning schemas from self-structure that are in conflict with our self-conception. He termed this process *fractionation*. Another means by which we seek continuity is through identification, which is an assimilative process of schema change in Piagetian terms.

Heinz Kohut (1971, 1977, 1984) has put forth a similar perspective in which the self was not subordinate to the ego of the drive/structure model and not a representational product of ego activity but rather primary, active, and functional. He described a nascent self that requires the participation of others to provide a sense of cohesion, constancy, and resilience. These others are "self-objects" that are not at first differentiated from the self from the infant's perspective but are objectively separate individuals in the child's life, whose functions eventually become incorporated into the child's psychic structure. They attempt to empathically respond to the infant's narcissistic needs and to provide the relational experiences necessary for the development of the self. The needs that infants seek to satisfy are (a) to display developing capabilities and to be admired for them by a "mirroring" selfobject and (b) to form an idealized image of a parental figure, usually the mother, and experience a sense of merger with that image of an "idealized" self-object. One need represents a healthy omnipotence, the other a healthy desire for connectedness. By means of "transmuting internalization," these two types of external object relations are transformed into internal relational configurations that become the structure of the self. The nature of any given self is determined by the content of these two narcissistic configurations and by their relationship to each other. Kohut's depiction of the analytic process is consistent with his relational formulation, as the analyst must serve selfobject functions and provide for the developmental deficit.

Self as Authentic or True

There have also been a number of clinical theorists who have described the notion of an authentic or true self. This is especially evident in writings of those directly influenced by existential thought. For example, a basic premise in the humanistic tradition is that neurosis involves the encumbrance of the authentic self, a loss of autonomy, as a result of the need to maintain a self-concept based on learned conditions of worth; psychotherapy is thus directed toward freeing the individual to pursue his or her inherent potential to grow and to live more authentically (Bugental, 1978; May, 1983; Rogers, 1961; Yalom, 1981).

This premise is also fundamental to the work of analyst Erich Fromm (1941, 1947), who envisioned a true self as a core of potentialities that can be developed. For him, before birth we are at one with nature, completely embedded within the maternal environment. At birth, we begin the process of becoming increasingly aware of our separateness and isolation, which serves as the basis for our developing consciousness. This is both freeing and frightening. We are then faced with the task of finding new attachments. Fromm saw two courses of choice in this regard: one progressive and one regressive. The former involves acceptance of one's separateness and individuation, recognition of responsibility and choice, and an authenticity in selfhood. The latter involves a complex process of self-deception and -disavowal in the service of social conformity in order to overcome aloneness and alienation and to re-establish a state of embeddedness and merger with others. By conforming to familial, societal, and cultural standards and demands, an illusory sense of security is bought at the expense of freedom and individuality (see Horney, 1950, for a comparable conception of authenticity, conformity, and self-alienation). Fromm did not write much about the practice of psychoanalysis, but many of his students have commented on the urgency and commitment he demonstrated in encouraging patients toward a progressive or "productive orientation" (J. Greenberg & Mitchell, 1983).

Winnicott (1958, 1965) was said to be at least indirectly influenced by existentialism (Phillips, 1988). Like Fairbairn (as well as Sullivan), he conceived of personality as structured around the need for maintaining relatedness to caretakers. He did not, however, take on classical theory as directly as Fairbairn but rather developed his own personal idiom. He described a delicate dialectic of contact and differentiation between mother and child, where there is a progression of perfect to "good-enough" mothering, of graduated failure, which permits the incipient self of the infant to emerge (J. Greenberg & Mitchell, 1983). Any impingement by the mother on this delicate development leads to a fragmentation of the child's experience as a split between a "true self" and a "false self." The true self is the source of authenticity in the child, the experience of spontaneity, of feeling real and alive. In fact, Winnicott wrote little about what he meant by true self, in contrast to the false self. The false self results from the mother's failure to provide a "holding environment" for the infant, which would meet his or her spontaneous expressions and needs. As a result, the infant develops strategies of compliance to meet the demands of the mother's behavior and survive them. The false self protects the true self from the environment and provides an illusion of existence shaped by maternal expectations and claims. All humans develop false selves under the most fortuitous conditions. However, under extreme conditions of repeated maternal failures, the true self is so hidden as to seem absent, and there is a pervasive sense of unreality, futility, and lack of vitality. Accordingly, Winnicott saw the function of psychoanalysis as to compensate for maternal failures, "to provide a certain type of environment" (1958, p. 168), to reach the true self and permit it to "go on being."

Self as Multiple and Discrete

The idea of multiple selves was sown early on in humanistic psychotherapies, especially those inspired by Carl Rogers ("[the self] is a fluid and changing process, but at any given moment it is a specific entity"; Meador & Rogers, 1979, p. 147) and interpersonally oriented psychoanalyses, beginning with Harry Stack Sullivan ("for all I know every human being has as many personalities as he has interpersonal relations"; 1964, p. 221). Both Rogers and Sullivan were greatly influenced by William James, largely through George Herbert Mead (1934). Nevertheless, recent years have evidenced a great deal of discussion regarding this idea among clinical theorists from diverse orientations (see special issue of *Journal of Psychotherapy Integration*, September, 1997, vol. 7 no. 3) and a greater appreciation of and more nuanced approach to it.

Over the years there has been a marked shift in emphasis from the content to the process of the analytic situation. This has even been true of the orientations traditionally known to be more interpretive and content focused; for example, Betty Joseph (1986/1989) and Thomas Ogden (1994) from a Kleinian slant and Paul Gray (1994) from an ego psychological slant have drawn attention to the significance of tracking the minute, moment-to-moment shifts in patients' in-session experience. To illustrate, Ogden (1994), influenced by Melanie Klein and Wilfred Bion, described human experience as involving a dialectical interplay of the psychic positions of *autistic–contiguous* (the sensory continuity and integrity of self-experience), *paranoid–schizoid* (experience of self and others as objects), and *depressive* (experience of self and others as subjects). For him, change reflects a shift in this dialectical interplay "such that a more generative and mutually preserving and negating interaction is created" (p. 188).

This development is also evident in the growing trend among relationally oriented analysts toward conceptualizing human experience as consisting of multiple selves or multiple self-states, which possess varying degrees of compatibility with one another (e.g., Bromberg, 1998; Mitchell, 1993; Pizer, 1998). Different self-states become dominant at different times, depending on the focus of the individual's attention. Moreover, different self-states emerge in different relational contexts. This perspective provides a way of viewing the intersection between interpersonal and intrapsychic realms in therapy in terms of the mutual influence of shifting self-states in patient and therapist. Accordingly, each individual experiences a perpetual cycling between different self-states, which in turn evoke complementary self-states in the other (Bach, 1994; Bromberg, 1998). Psychoanalytic feminists, such as Julia Kristeva (1986), Luce Irigaray (1985), Muriel Dimen (1991; see chapter 9, this volume), Jane Flax (1996), and Lynne Layton (1998), to name just a few, have also contributed to this perspective with their consideration of multiple subjectivities and identities in studies of gender.

This perspective suggests the value of attending to the reciprocal changes of self-states in the patient–analyst system during the course of therapy. The transitions or boundaries between self-states vary in seamlessness but are often objectively marked by changes in vocal quality, facial expression, focus and content of verbal reports, emotional involvement, and so forth. As Philip Bromberg (1998) noted, they are also subjectively marked: That is, these shifts can become apparent in the analyst's experience, by a corresponding shift in self-state for the analyst. Thus, as a number have articulated (Bromberg, 1998; Davies, 1996; Mitchell, 1992), psychotherapy can be understood as figuring out who is speaking to whom in a given moment, which patient self is communicating to which therapist self (and vice versa). Stuart Pizer (1998; see chapter 5, this volume) described this process along Winnicottian lines as involving "intersubjective negotiation" whereby patient and therapist ongoingly negotiate what to make of each other.

The notion of multiple selves holds that there is no central executive control in the form of the ego. Consciousness is a function of a coalition of different self-states. It is thus an emergent product of a self-organizing system. The bifurcation of the psychic system into conscious and unconscious is overly simplified and overly static. That which is conscious is that which is attended to. Attention to different self-states in different moments is a function of different stimulus cues, both internal and external. As Stephen Mitchell (1992) described, the self "moves in time rather than exists in space" (p. 9); it has no core, but multiple versions expressed in various states of mind and with different degrees of awareness. Bromberg (1998) described "a view of the self as decentered and the mind as a configuration of shifting, nonlinear, discontinuous states of consciousness in an ongoing dialectic with the healthy illusion of unitary selfhood" (p. 270). Bach (1985, 1994; see chapter 2, this volume), likewise, has paid close attention to multiplicity or, as he has used, alternate states of consciousness, including their rhythmicities and transitions. They each describe an ideal psyche in which the transitions between states are relatively seamless and barely beyond awareness.

Dissociation is basic to the understanding of multiple selves. As Bromberg (1998) noted, dissociation is a healthy, adaptive function of the human mind, a basic process that allows individual self-states to function optimally and that permits a person to maintain personal continuity, coherence, and integrity of the sense of self. "Health is the ability to stand in the spaces between realities without losing any of them—the capacity to feel like one self while being many" (p. 186). The particular configuration of one's self-experience is always selective. At any point in time, certain aspects of self-experience are predominant and others not. It is inevitable that certain aspects of self-experience are out of focal awareness when others are dominant. This dissociative exclusion of aspects of self from focal awareness is a form of selective inattention, similar in nature to Sullivan's understanding of the way in which security operations function. There is a systemic direction of attention away from aspects of self-experience that are assessed as being potentially dangerous. Aspects of self-experience that are dissociated are typically those that have been associated with traumatic experience of one kind or another (Davies, 1996). The relevant trauma can range from physical or sexual abuse at one end of the spectrum to experiences that have involved disruption of relatedness to parents and others of interpersonal significance at the other end. Depending on the nature of a trauma, an aspect of the self can be split off and stranded from awareness in a more extreme sense. Experiencing and accepting the multiplicity of self is part of the change process. Therapy does not entail integrating different parts of the self but rather bringing them into dialogue with each other through awareness.

Despite the long-standing emphasis on process and awareness in the humanistic tradition, recent years have evidenced greater efforts toward defining this treatment focus. For example, Leslie Greenberg, Laura Rice, and Robert Elliott (1995; see chapter 4, this volume) have developed a humanistic model identified as *process–experiential psychotherapy*, which is an integration of person-centered and gestalt therapy with principles drawn from contemporary theories of cognition and emotion. They have provided a more operationally defined account of the cognitive–affective processes involved in several emotional tasks and the relevance of awareness in undertaking such a task. Elaborating on previous humanistic contributions, they describe dysfunction as a failure to explore certain cognitive–affective information and the goal of treatment as to facilitate different classes of cognitive–affective operations in order to foster deeper exploration. They have identified, for example, different patient behaviors as therapeutic markers to guide therapist intervention, two kinds of which they call *self-splits*: the *conflict split* and the *interruptive split*. The former refers to when two parts of the self are in conflict; one part wants "this" and another wants "that." Such splits typically lead to dialogues involving "self-evaluations or self-coercion," to some form of conflict between "shoulds" and "wants." This essentially involves the use of coercive power against the self. In contrast, the interruptive split involves an interruptive activity against the self. In this split, one part of the self interrupts a second part of the self; thus, the individual feels cut off or loses contact with a part of the self (integral to the pursuit of one's needs), which can result in a paralyzed state of confusion, helplessness, and hopelessness. In each case, the therapist's aim is to focus on the split marker and invite the patient to dialogue with the different aspects of the self toward creative resolution.

Self as Intersubjective

Contemporary psychoanalysis, particularly of the relational orientation, has also been marked by the proliferation of perspectives often described as "intersubjective" (see Aron, 1996; and chapter 6, this volume) and sometimes as "subject-relations" (see Kennedy, 1997). These perspectives represent a shift away from viewing the therapeutic relationship in terms of discrete enactments involving transference–countertransference (where the direction of influence is largely from the patient to the therapist and the implication is that what is experienced is distorted and irrational) to viewing the relationship as an ongoing interplay of separate subjectivities.

The notion of intersubjectivity has been introduced by various traditions and applied in a variety of ways. On the basis of his infant research, for example, Stern (1985) described a course of development for children whereby they achieve the capacity to recognize another person as a separate center of subjectivity and with whom a subjective state can be shared. Other infant researchers, such as Beatrice Beebe and Frank Lachmann (1992), have focused on the ways in which the subjective states of mother and child are interpersonally communicated and regulated. The emphasis in their work seems to be more on mutual regulation or influence than on mutual recognition.

With regard to its application to the analytic situation, Robert Stolorow and colleagues (Stolorow, Brandchaft, & Atwood, 1987; Stolorow & Atwood, 1992; Orange, Atwood, & Stolorow, 1997), as well as Joseph Natterson (Natterson & Friedman, 1995) and James Fosshage (1992), have used intersubjectivity in their extension of self psychological theory. They consider it an overarching term to describe the psychological field between patient and therapist, that is, "the interplay between the differently organized subjective worlds" (Stolorow et al., 1987, p. 1), "the reciprocal influence of the conscious and unconscious subjectivities" (Natterson & Friedman, 1995, p. 1) of the two people in the relationship. Similar to Beebe and Lachmann's emphasis, it seems the emphasis here is also on mutual regulation.

Jessica Benjamin's (1988, 1990) notion of intersubjectivity integrates a number of perspectives (Buber, 1923/1958; Dinnerstein, 1976; Habermas, 1971; Hegel, 1969; Winnicott, 1965); she provided a comprehensive view of mutual recognition and regulation in the psychoanalytic situation. One of the central themes in her work follows feminist psychoanalytic criticism and challenges the traditional psychoanalytic view of the mother as an object to the infant's drives and needs. J. Benjamin argued that the child must recognize the mother as a separate subject with her own experiential world, with her own intentions and desires, and that the capacity for such recognition is a developmental achievement. Accordingly, she suggested that the aim of the psychoanalytic inquiry is such that "where objects were, subjects must be" (1990, p. 34). To J. Benjamin, the developmental achievement of subjective recognition is one that is inconsistently maintained, and the analytic situation must invariably involve a dialectic tension between relating to the other as an object and relating to the other as a subject, that the process continually involves the recognition and negation of the other as a separate center of subjectivity.

Ogden (1994) also placed great emphasis on the dialectic nature of this process by introducing his concept of "the analytic third," which represents neither subject nor object but rather an intersubjective, jointly created space between patient and therapist. Other notables, who have similarly attended to the interplay between the subjectivities in the analytic encounter, but along Winnicottian lines, are Christopher Bollas (1989) and Stuart Pizer (1998; chapter 5, this volume). Jay Greenberg's (1995) description of the analytic situation as an *interactive matrix,* in which every moment is shaped by the interaction of the personal beliefs, wishes, needs, and fears of the patient and analyst, shares a similar sensibility. This increased attention to therapist subjectivity is also evident in psychoanalytic circles oriented more toward the classical tradition (e.g., Chused, 1992; Jacobs, 1991; Renik, 1993).

In their review, Leslie Greenberg and Laura Rice (1997) observed an important development with regard to the humanistic view of the self, which involves a shift in emphasis from the traditional view of the self as an active agent motivated by the actualizing tendency toward growth and autonomy to a greater consideration of the self as an interpersonal phenomenon. Although there is a long history in the humanistic tradition of recognizing the importance of genuine contact and interhuman interaction, indicative of the influence of Buber, there has been increasingly more discussion of this and its relevance to the therapeutic relationship. Instead of just describing the real relationship between patient and therapist as a crucial ingredient or ground, there is more discussion of the intersubjective dimension of the psychotherapeutic process (e.g., Bohart, 1995; Bugental & Sterling, 1995). For example, Gary Yontef (1995, 1998) has placed greater emphasis on the I–thou relationship than on the use of technique, making it more figural. There has also been a growing interest in empathy as an intersubjective phenomenon (Bohart & Greenberg, 1997) involving a complex blend of cognitive understanding of and affective resonance with the other.

Self as Illusion or Construction

Jacques Lacan (1981) was one of the first clinical theorists to challenge the modern conception of the self, following a poststructuralist discourse. For him, the "I" of our personal consciousness does not exist outside of linguistic reality. The self as subject is not the speaker of language but rather its creation. In his own words, "I am not a poet, but a poem" (Anderson, 1997, p. 43). He articulated a position that in a sense is consistent with David Hume's (1738/1911) conception of self as illusion and Ludwig Wittgenstein's (1953) conception of self as grammatical fiction and that has been taken up by contemporary constructivists. This idea of the self can also be found in Buddhist psychology, which maintains that the self is an illusion constructed on a moment-by-moment basis and that change is seeing through this illusion and surrendering to just being (see Epstein, 1995, 1998).

Since the 1980s, there has been increasing interest in constructivist epistemology in psychoanalytic circles, as evidenced by the contributions of Donald Spence (1982, 1987), Roy Schafer (1983, 1992), and Barnaby Barratt (1984, 1993). There has also been particular interest in social constructionism, as evidenced by the contributions by Irwin Hoffman (1998), Barry Protter (1985, 1988; chapter 13, this volume), and Donnel Stern (1997). Hoffman, for example, described the individual and social aspects of human experience as interdependent and irreducible to each other and construed them in terms of a dialectical interplay of figure and ground in experience. Accordingly, the analytic situation is one of multiple, fluctuating, complementary figure–ground relationships within each of the participants. The analyst is understood as intimately involved with the patient in a relational struggle that includes various conflicts, themes of mutuality and authority, and multiple potentials of the self.

As yet another example, Stern (1997) presented a perspective that builds on Sullivan's original field theory (and includes as well Joseph Sandler's notion of "role-responsiveness" and Heinrich Racker's idea of unconscious communication), such that the self is seen as invariably embedded in the field of interpersonal relations in which unconscious invitations are ceaselessly being issued and unwittingly responded to in various interpersonal ventures. In this regard, he takes up the notion of multiple selves:

> We are becoming used to the idea that we move in and out of self-states on the basis of our perceptions of the interpersonal world that faces us. But we are less used to the thought that we *are moved* in and out of self-states. (p. 154, emphasis in original)

In fact, we are not so aware of how thoroughly embedded we are in the world around us. Thus, our personal responsibility for the interpersonal field in which we find ourselves (in which we are embedded) is somewhere between the active and the passive. "The field . . . is neither simply the result of our own unconscious internal choices nor a force or filter imposed on us by others. It is both simultaneously" (p. 155). As he went on to describe, "we are always caught in the grip of the field," the clinical implications of which are that "we face the endless task of trying to see the field and climb out of it—and into another one, for there is nowhere else to go" (p. 158).

A constructivist thread has also been spun in the cognitive tradition, beginning with the early contributions of George Kelly (1955). Kelly's model of "person as scientist" depicted humans as actively and ongoingly construing and integrating information from past experience into personal theories, in order to anticipate the future. He described the individual as organizing constructs by contrast into a construct system composed of more abstract superordinate constructs (such as those concerning self-identity) and more specific subordinate structures. Kelly also acknowledged the social embeddedness of the construing process. He described treatment as one in which the therapist helps the patient "design and implement experiments" (p. 941), to test hypotheses or beliefs in terms of various dimensions, such as consistency (e.g., reconciling a specific self-construct with a conflicting behavioral pattern) or predictiveness (e.g., taking a risk and testing a prediction from a particular construal of a situation). Proponents of Kelly's perspective, the most prominent of whom is Robert Neimeyer (1986), have promoted a therapeutic approach that is "technically eclectic but theoretically consistent" (p. 242).

It took some time, however, before constructivist thinking became more central to the dialogue in the cognitive therapy community. The 1980s witnessed a number of challenges to what seemed to be an exclusive interest in the self as representational structure and a rationalist perspective on human experience and change. This has been described as an evolutionary epistemological movement, the chief proponents of which were Guidano and Mahoney (see Safran, 1998, for another proponent; see also Neimeyer & Mahoney, 1995). They especially emphasized several basic assumptions, such as knowledge as an evolutionary process, knowledge as an interactive process, and knowledge development as biased by self-organizing processes (Guidano, 1987). They challenged the traditional split in the cognitive literature of the cognition–affect–behavior relationship and of what is rational and irrational, suggesting instead a view in which emotions are viewed as primitive, powerful, knowing processes and the validity of knowledge is less important than its viability (Mahoney, 1991).

A constructivistic epistemology has also emerged in recent years in the humanistic tradition, which has led to a more dialectically interactive view of self-functioning between biology and culture (Bohart, 1995; Gendlin, 1995; Greenberg & Pascual-Leone, 1995; chapter 4, this volume). Constructivist theorizing has moved the humanistic tradition beyond just a descriptive theory of self-experience to one that includes an explanatory dimension that elucidates what underlies self-experience. In a dialectical constructive view, the self refers to a tacit level of organization that integrates or synthesizes more basic elements of self-experience into a coherent and actualized whole. The self is thus viewed as a community of voices in continuous dialogue (Elliott & Greenberg, 1997). It operates as a dynamic relationship between tacit emotional experience and explicit conceptual knowing, which provides the basis for making sense of our experience and for constructing a narrative of our identity (L. S. Greenberg & Van Balen, 1998).[8]

Trend and Themes in Treatment

In their insightful analysis of the psychoanalytic literature, Jay Greenberg and Stephen Mitchell (1983) recognized two threads of thought regarding the analytic situation. One, which they identified as the *drive model*, sees the patient as entering treatment with self-contained, encapsulated pathogenic conflicts and the goal of treatment as providing insight or knowledge and increasing the power of the ego and its authority over the drives. This thinking is especially in evidence in the ego-psychological orientation. The second thread, which they identified as the *relational model*, sees the analytic situation as inherently dyadic and the goal of treatment as providing a formative interpersonal experience. This thinking is manifest in the interpersonal, object-relational, and self-psychological orientations. The development of this view of therapeutic action has been largely attributed to the seminal thinking of Sandor Ferenczi (Aron &

[8]Constructivist epistemology has also emerged in family therapy. See Gerson (1996) as a noteworthy example.

Harris, 1991), who has influenced both the American interpersonal school and British object relations school through his analyses of prominent figures of these schools, such as Clara Thompson and Michael Balint. Of course, with regard to some orientations, this bifurcation should be understood as a matter of emphasis. It certainly seems, though, that the emphasis on insight was stronger in the earlier days of psychoanalysis than it is now. In contrast, we are witnessing today a strong swing toward seeing therapeutic action as interpersonal experience, as evidenced, for example, by the rediscovery of Ferenczi, the emergence of a "relational" school of thought (e.g., Aron, 1996; Mitchell, 1988), and the increased attention to therapist experience and participation, even by those oriented to the classical tradition (e.g., Jacobs, 1991). As J. Greenberg and Mitchell (1983) observed, psychoanalysis has undergone a significant shift from "solitary reflection" to "relational struggle."

This pendulum swing can also be seen in the cognitive–behavioral and humanistic traditions, where the therapeutic relationship has become more figural. In the cognitive–behavioral tradition, there has been a clear progression from early models, in which change involved educating patients about strategies to correct their thinking and behavior, to the recent contributions, such as those by Safran and Kohlenberg, in which the therapeutic relationship is considered central to change. In the humanistic tradition, even though the therapeutic relationship has received a variety of considerations, from Rogers's heavy emphasis to Perls's light emphasis, there was still a sense that the relationship was considered fertile ground on which the patient as figure could grow. Today, there is increasing reconsideration among humanists of the therapeutic relationship as figural, specifically conceptualizing change as an intersubjective process, as exemplified by Yontef's contributions. This shift in emphasis has also been greatly influenced by various research traditions: for example, developmental research that shows the interactions of mother–infant dyads (e.g., Harter, 1999; Stern, 1985), attachment research that likewise shows the relationship of attachment patterns and growth (e.g., Cassidy & Shaver, 1999; Parkes, Stevenson-Hinde, & Marris, 1991), and psychotherapy research that generates an extensive body of evidence demonstrating the relevance of the therapeutic relationship for change (e.g., Horvath & Greenberg, 1994; Horvath & Symonds, 1991).

What seems to have also emerged over the years is yet another bifurcation of thinking. This has to do with seeing change as correction or expansion, with respect to the provision of both insight and interpersonal experience.[9] By cor-

---

[9]Of course, one could always argue that the expansive orientation implies or includes a correction of sorts as well, but it remains a distinct orientation. A similar argument could be made about insight versus interpersonal experience.

rection through insight, patients are given information or knowledge that corrects or brings under control a way of thinking or behaving. In classical psychoanalysis, this would mean providing an interpretation regarding the patient's behavior that would make what was unconscious conscious and enhance the control of the ego over the id (e.g., Fenischel, 1945). In cognitive therapy, this would mean making patients aware of their cognitive distortions and teaching them more rational responses (e.g., Beck, 1976). By correction through interpersonal experience, patients are in a sense provided with a "corrective emotional experience" (Alexander & French, 1946). This is best exemplified in psychoanalytic models, such as Kohut's (1984), in which the goal of therapeutic action is to remediate developmental deficits.

Considering change as expansion, enrichment, or elaboration suggests the postmodern sensibility. Expansion in awareness seems grounded in a model of the mind as multiple and dissociative. It is a perspective on change that seems to have always been present in the humanistic tradition, from the person-centered (e.g., Rogers, 1951) to the gestalt (e.g., Perls, 1973) to the existential (e.g., Bugental, 1978) orientation. It is a perspective that has its roots in early psychoanalytic ideas sown by Fairbairn and Winnicott, among others (e.g., Ferenczi, 1931), who described the process of splitting of the self and that has been greatly elaborated by contemporary analysts, such as Bach (chapter 2, this volume), Bromberg (1998), Davies (1996), Mitchell (1992, 1993), and Pizer (chapter 5, this volume), to name just a few. In addition, it is a perspective that has begun to receive attention among cognitive–behaviorists (e.g., Guidano, 1991; Hayes, Strosahl, & Wilson, 1998; Linehan, 1993; Muran, 1997; Safran, 1998; Teasdale, Segal, & Williams, 1995).

As for the expansion by interpersonal experience, this is a perspective that can be traced to the interpersonal orientation in psychoanalysis. Specifically, Edgar Levenson (1992) described change as an interpersonal enrichment rather than a developmental correction. It seems evident in current conceptions that articulate an intersubjective model of therapeutic action; for example, Aron (chapter 5) from psychoanalysis, Safran and Muran (chapter 7) from the cognitive tradition, and Yontef from the humanist tradition. By the title of this edited volume, *Self-Relations in the Psychotherapy Process*, my intent was to imply the intrahuman and interhuman experience captured in these "expansive" conceptions of the change process in psychotherapy.

The Plan of the Book

Navigating a path between the extremes of relative nihilism on one side and naive realism on the other is a difficult task, one that has preoccupied many contemporary philosophers of science (e.g., Bernstein, 1983; Margolis, 1986;

Rorty, 1991). Hans-Georg Gadamer (1975; cf. Warnke, 1987) proposed a resolution to this dilemma that provides a framework for conceptualizing this book project. He suggested that our perceptions of reality are always constrained by our preconceptions or prejudices. These preconceptions function as the ground for everything we experience, for without preconceptions new experience is meaningless. The task of understanding, therefore, is one of finding some way of moving beyond our preconceptions so that we are able to move toward apprehending the "things themselves." For Gadamer, this task involved a Socratic process, an open dialogue that can take place in relation to other human beings or to something else (as in the case of textual interpretation). This is a "genuine conversation" in which we recognize our own fallibility and hence are open to the possible truth of other views. Central to this thinking is the notion that dialogue of this type not only allows two people to come to an understanding of one another's positions but also to arrive at a richer, more developed understanding of things as they really are. Thus, truth is both constructed and discovered.

The aim of this book project is to encourage an open dialogue among a plurality of perspectives on a subject that is so central to understanding the human condition and the possibility of change. By confronting other perspectives and coming to understand them, we can clarify both similarities and differences in a more nuanced way and learn to enrich our point of view. We can move to a new, shared understanding of the subject matter. We can create a new truth, a "fusion of horizons" that is more differentiated and articulated than the separate views with which the dialogue began. Toward this end, I have invited a number of clinical theorists who identify themselves with the psychoanalytic, cognitive–behavioral, and humanistic traditions, some of whom are active psychotherapy researchers.

In chapter 2, Sheldon Bach writes about mental functioning as a continual cycling of states of consciousness and shifting between different points of view, which he describes as subjective and objective self-awareness. For him, normality requires some dynamic balance between the ability to freely cycle between alternate states and the necessity of maintaining some integration among these states. He describes the psychoanalytic process as involving reciprocal changes of states of consciousness in both patient and analyst and as facilitating normal cycling and complex integration.

In chapter 3, Mardi J. Horowitz presents his systematic and much-researched approach to pattern recognition that he has called *configurational analysis*, which involves segmentalizing behavior and experience into states of mind. These states, state transitions, or cycles are explained and organized in terms of self and other schemas and role-relationship models. He then applies his model to the formulation, planning, and practice of psychotherapy.

In chapter 4, William Whelton and Leslie Greenberg articulate a process–

experiential approach to the self, according to which the self is understood as constructed and as an ongoing, self-organizing process. They also describe the self as an emergent organization of more basic elements bound together by emotion. For them, constructing the self in psychotherapy involves the processes of identifying, symbolizing, and differentiating various self-experiences. Their view is developed from dynamic systems and dialectical–constructivist theories as well as their own research program.

In chapter 5, Stuart Pizer approaches the notion of multiple selves by making the distinction between a distributed multiple self and a dissociated multiple self. He presents a view of the self as distributively structured among multiple memorial clusters of relational experience, which are maintained to the extent that one is able to negotiate and tolerate paradox. To him, the analyst's role is to build or repair bridges between dissociated islands in the self's memorial system. In his approach, he also makes links to neurobiology and chaos theory.

In chapter 6, Lewis Aron discusses intersubjectivity and self-reflexivity in the analytic situation and explores the relevance of recognizing the subjectivity of the other, as well as the self, to the psychoanalytic process, especially with regard to the patient's exploration of the therapist's subjectivity and the use of self-disclosure.

In chapter 7, Jeremy Safran and I present our view of the therapeutic alliance as a process of intersubjective negotiation. We describe two types of alliance ruptures—confrontation and withdrawal—that reflect different ways of coping with the tension between the dialectically opposed needs for agency and relatedness. We then present two stage-process models that have emerged from our research efforts and that represent the processes and sequences involved in resolving ruptures in the therapeutic alliance.

In chapter 8, Stanley Messer and Seth Warren grapple with what they consider the expanding concept of the modern self, including the so-called postmodern challenges. They suggest, in contrast to the enthusiastic reception by other clinicians, that the postmodern self represents psychopathology because it promotes fragmentation and hyperreflexivity and posits a lack of unity or the existence of an inner core, which for them is a critical achievement in human development and psychotherapy.

In chapter 9, Muriel Dimen approaches the self in psychoanalysis from a deconstructionist perspective on sexuality, gender, and culture. She describes self-experience in terms of complex and shifting relations among multiple contrasts or differences. For her, difference is a paradoxical space that selfhood inhabits, and self-experience consists of transitions between different polarities, such as autonomy and dependence, which are but different moments of the self.

In chapter 10, Timothy Strauman and Zindel Segal provide a perspective on cognitive models of the self, integrating historical and current contributions from the cognitive therapy and social cognition literature, including those grounded in research. They examine the self in psychopathology, particularly with regard to self-evaluation, self-discrepancy, self-regulation, and vulnerability, and then explore implications for various change strategies in cognitive therapy.

In chapter 11, William Henry invokes the structural analysis of social behavior (SASB) model (L. S. Benjamin, 1974) to conceptualize the self as embedded within circumplexes of self–other and self–self relations. The SASB model is a highly researched one that consists of two-dimensional spaces in which interpersonal and introjective processes are conceptualized along the dimensions of interdependence and affiliation. Henry then presents an interpersonal perspective on case formulation and psychotherapy process that is greatly informed by this model.

In chapter 12, Steven Hayes and Jennifer Gregg describe a behavioral analytic view of the self that is based on verbal knowledge, on systematic learning through language in the social community. They consider the self as conceptualized content, as verbal process, and as context. They highlight the importance of self-awareness, experiential avoidance, and self-observation in presenting an approach to the practice of therapy that is grounded in functional contextualism.

In chapter 13, Barry Protter explores three modes of knowing the self in the analytic situation and considers the implications for integrative practice. The three modes include existential or monadic knowing, which is phenomenologic and empathic; contextual or dyadic knowing, which is interpersonal knowledge through dyadically constructed relationships; and narrative or triadic knowing, which entails knowing the other in such a way as to give meaning and coherence to the other's behavior.

The book concludes with a chapter by me, which provides a model of self-relations that is informed by relational psychoanalysis, as well as principles from the behavioral and humanistic traditions, that is also grounded in contemporary theories of cognition and emotion and that aims to be at once both integrative and elaborative.

I invited these authors to contribute to this volume because I felt their theoretical development as reflected by their preceding work positioned them to thoughtfully and creatively consider many of the emergent postmodern trends and themes that have implications for understanding the self in the context of psychotherapy. I have challenged them by focusing their discussions on the details of the psychotherapeutic process and by providing commentary on another author's contribution: someone coming from another tradition or orientation, someone with whom they are not so familiar but with whom they seem to me to share some common ground, so that similarity and difference could be confronted and readily and vividly defined. My hope is to render postmodern thinking and self-conceptions more relevant to the practice of psychotherapy. My hope is also to break down the barriers to communication that seem to me to persist among all these communities or cultures and to establish some dialogue, some enrichment of theory and practice, some fusion of horizons.

References

Alexander, F., & French, T. M. (1946). *Psychoanalytic therapy*. New York: Ronald.

Anderson, W. J. (1997). *The future of the self: Exploring the post-identity society*. New York: Tarcher/Putnam.

Aron, L. (1996). *A meeting of minds: Mutuality in psychoanalysis*. Hillsdale, NJ: Analytic Press.

Aron, L., & Harris, A. (Eds.). (1991). *The legacy of Sandor Ferenczi*. Hillsdale, NJ: Analytic Press.

Auerbach, J., & Blatt, S. (1996). Self-representation in severe psychopathology: The role of reflexive self-awareness. *Psychoanalytic Psychology, 13,* 297–341.

Bach, S. (1985). *Narcissistic states and the therapeutic process*. New York: Aronson.

Bach, S. (1994). *The language of perversion and the language of love*. Northvale, NJ: Aronson.

Bakan, D. (1966). *The duality of human existence*. Boston: Beacon Press.

Barnett, J. (1980). Interpersonal processes, cognition, and the analysis of character. *Contemporary Psychoanalysis, 16,* 397–416.

Barratt, B. (1984). *Psychic reality and psychoanalytic knowing*. Hillsdale, NJ: Analytic Press.

Barratt, B. (1993). *Psychoanalysis and the postmodern impulse*. Baltimore: Johns Hopkins University Press.

Bechtel, W., & Abrahamsen, A. (1991). *Connectionism and the mind: An introduction to parallel processing in networks*. Cambridge, England: Basil Blackwell.

Beck, A. T. (1967). *Depression: Causes and treatment*. Philadelphia: University of Pennsylvania Press.

Beck, A. T. (1976). *Cognitive therapy and the emotional disorders*. New York: International Universities Press.

Beck, A. T., Emery, G., & Greenberg, R. (1985). *Anxiety disorders and phobias: A cognitive perspective*. New York: Basic Books.

Beck, A. T., Freeman, A., & Associates. (1990). *Cognitive therapy of personality disorders*. New York: Guilford Press.

Beebe, B., & Lachmann, F. (1992). The contribution of mother–infant mutual influence to the origins of self- and object representations. In N. J. Skolnick & S. C. Warshaw (Eds.), *Relational perspectives in psychoanalysis* (pp. 83–118). Hillsdale, NJ: Analytic Press.

Benjamin, J. (1988). *The bonds of love.* New York: Pantheon Books.

Benjamin, J. (1990). An outline of intersubjectivity: The development of recognition. *Psychoanalytic Psychology, 7,* 33–46.

Benjamin, L. S. (1974). Structural analysis of social behavior. *Psychological Review, 81,* 392–425.

Bernstein, R. (1983). *Beyond objectivism and relativism.* Philadelphia: University of Pennsylvania Press.

Blatt, S. J., & Blass, R. (1992). Relatedness and self-definition: Two primary dimensions in personality development, psychopathology and psychotherapy. In J. Barron, M. Eagle, & D. Wolitsky (Eds.), *Interface of psychoanalysis and psychology* (pp. 399–435). Washington, DC: American Psychological Association.

Bohart, A. (1995). The person-centered psychotherapies. In A. S. Gurman & S. B. Messer (Eds.), *Essential psychotherapies* (pp. 85–127). New York: Guilford Press.

Bohart, A., & Greenberg, L. S. (Eds.). (1997). *Empathy reconsidered.* Washington, DC: American Psychological Association.

Bollas, C. (1989). *The shadow of the object.* New York: Columbia University Press.

Bowlby, J. (1988). *A secure base.* New York: Basic Books.

Bromberg, P. M. (1998). *Standing in the spaces.* Hillsdale, NJ: Analytic Press.

Buber, M. (1958). *I and thou* (2nd ed., R. G. Smith, Trans.). New York: Scribner. (Original work published 1923)

Bugental, J. (1978). *Psychotherapy and process: The fundamentals of an existential–humanistic approach.* New York: McGraw-Hill.

Bugental, J., & Sterling, M. (1995). Existential-humanistic psychotherapy: New perspectives. In A. S. Gurmer & S. B. Messer (Eds.), *Essential psychotherapies: Theory and practice* (pp. 226–260). New York: Guilford Press.

Burr, V. (1995). *An introduction to social construction.* New York: Routledge.

Cassidy, J., & Shaver, P. R. (1999). *Handbook of attachment: Theory, research, and clinical applications.* New York: Guilford Press.

Chused, J. F. (1992). The patient's perception of the analyst: The hidden transference. *Psychoanalytic Quarterly, 61,* 161–184.

Cilliers, P. (1998). *Complexity and postmodernism: Understanding complex systems.* New York: Routledge.

Clark, D. A., & Beck, A. T. (1991). Personality factors in dysphoria: A psychometric refinement of Beck's Sociotropy–Autonomy Scale. *Journal of Psychopathology and Behavioral Assessment, 13,* 369–388.

Cushman, P. (1995). *Constructing the self, constructing America.* Reading, MA: Addison-Wesley.

Davies, J. M. (1996). Linking the "pre-analytic" with the post-classical: Integration, dissociation, and the multiplicity of unconscious processes. *Contemporary Psychoanalysis, 32,* 553–576.

Deikman, A. J. (1982). *The observing self*. Boston: Beacon Press.

Derrida, J. (1978). *Writing and difference* (A. Bass, Trans.). Chicago: University of Chicago Press.

Dimen, M. (1991). Deconstructing difference: Gender, splitting, and transitional space. *Psychoanalytic Dialogues, 1*, 335–352.

Dinnerstein, D. (1976). *The mermaid and the minotaur*. New York: Harper & Row.

Edelman, G. (1987). *Neural Darwinism: The theory of neuronal group selection*. New York: Basic Books.

Ehrenberg, D. (1992). *The intimate edge*. New York: Norton.

Elliott, A., & Spezzano, C. (1996). Psychoanalysis at its limits: Navigating the postmodern turn. *Psychoanalytic Quarterly, 65*, 52–83.

Elliott, R., & Greenberg, L. S. (1997). Multiple voices in process-experiential therapy: Dialogue between aspects of the self. *Journal of Psychotherapy Integration, 7*, 225–240.

Ellis, A. (1962). *Reason and emotion in psychotherapy*. Secaucus, NJ: Citadel.

Epstein, M. (1995). *Thoughts without a thinker*. New York: Basic Books.

Epstein, M. (1998). *Going to pieces without falling apart*. New York: Broadway.

Fairbairn, W. R. D. (1952). *Psychoanalytic studies of the personality*. London: Tavistock.

Fast, I. (1998). *Selving: A relational theory of self organization*. Hillsdale, NJ: Analytic Press.

Featherstone, M. (1988). In pursuit of the postmodern: An introduction. *Theory, Culture, and Society, 5*, 195–217.

Fenischel, O. (1945). *The psychoanalytic theory of neurosis*. New York: Norton.

Ferenczi, S. (1931). Child analysis in the analysis of adults. In M. Balint (Ed.) & E. Mosbacher (Trans.), *Final contributions to the theory and technique of psychoanalysis* (pp. 126–142). London: Karnac.

Flax, J. (1996). Taking multiplicity seriously: Some consequences for psychoanalytic theorizing and practice. *Contemporary Psychoanalysis, 32*, 577–593.

Fonagy, P., & Target, M. (1996). Playing with reality: I. Theory of mind and the normal development of psychic reality. *International Journal of Psycho-Analysis, 77*, 217–233.

Fosshage, J. (1992). Self psychology: The self and its vicissitudes within the relational matrix. In N. J. Skolnick & S. C. Warshaw (Eds.), *Relational perspectives in psychoanalysis* (pp. 21–42). Hillsdale, NJ: Analytic Press.

Fromm, E. (1941). *Escape from freedom*. New York: Holt, Rinehart & Winston.

Fromm, E. (1947). *A man for himself*. New York: Rinehart.

Freud, S. (1923). The ego and the id. In J. Strachey (Ed.), *The standard edition of the complete psychological works of Sigmund Freud* (Vol. 19, pp. 1–66). London: Hogarth.

Freud, S. (1933). New introductory lectures on psycho-analysis. In J. Strachey (Ed.), *The standard edition of the complete psychological works of Sigmund Freud* (Vol. 22, pp. 1–182). London: Hogarth.

Gadamer, H.-G. (1975). *Truth and method* (G. Barden & J. Cumming, Trans. & Eds.). New York: Seabury.

Gard, R. A. (Ed.). (1961). *Buddhism*. New York: George Braziller.

Gendlin, E. (1995). *Focusing-oriented psychotherapy: A manual of the experiential method*. New York: Guilford Press.

Gergen, K. J. (1991). *The saturated self: Dilemmas of identity in community life*. New York: Basic Books.

Gergen, K. J. (1994). *Realities and relationships: Soundings in social construction*. Cambridge, MA: Harvard University Press.

Gerson, M. J. (1996). *The embedded self: A psychoanalytic guide to family therapy*. Hillsdale, NJ: Analytic Press.

Gray, P. (1994). *The ego and analysis of defense*. Northvale, NJ: Aronson.

Greenberg, J. (1995). Psychoanalytic technique and the interactive matrix. *Psychoanalytic Quarterly, 64,* 1–22.

Greenberg, J., & Mitchell, S. A. (1983). *Object relations in psychoanalytic theory*. Cambridge, MA: Harvard University Press.

Greenberg, L., & Pascual-Leone, J. (1995). A dialectical-constructivist approach to experiential change. In R. Neimeyer & M. Mahoney (Eds.), *Constructivism in psychotherapy* (pp. 169–191). Washington, DC: American Psychological Association.

Greenberg, L. S., & Rice, L. N. (1997). Humanistic approaches to psychotherapy. In P. L. Wachtel & S. B. Messer (Eds.), *Theories of psychotherapy* (pp. 97–129). Washington, DC: American Psychological Association.

Greenberg, L. S., Rice, L. N., & Elliott, R. (1995). *Process–experiential therapy: Facilitating emotional change*. New York: Guilford Press.

Greenberg, L. S., & Van Balen, R. (1998). The theory of experience-centered therapies. In L. S. Greenberg, J. C. Watson, & G. Lietaer (Eds.), *Handbook of experiential psychotherapy* (pp. 28–57). New York: Guilford Press.

Guidano, V. F. (1987). *Complexity of the self*. New York: Guilford Press.

Guidano, V. (1991). *The self in process: Toward a post-rationalist cognitive therapy*. New York: Guilford Press.

Habermas, J. (1971). *Knowledge and human interests* (J. Shapiro, Trans.). Boston: Beacon Press.

Harter, S. (1983). Developmental perspectives on the self-system. In P. H. Mussen (Ed.), *Handbook of child psychology* (Vol. 4, pp. 275–385). New York: Wiley.

Harter, S. (1999). *The construction of the self: A developmental perspective*. New York: Guilford Press.

Hartmann, H. (1958). *Ego psychology and the problem of adaptation*. New York: International Universities Press.

Hayes, S., Follette, W. C., & Follette, V. M. (1995). Behavior therapy: A contextual approach. In A. S. Gurman & S. B. Messer (Eds.), *Essential psychotherapies* (pp. 128–181). New York: Guilford Press.

Hayes, S., Strosahl, K., & Wilson, K. (1998). *Acceptance and commitment therapy*. New York: Guilford Press.

Hegel, G. W. F. (1969). *Phenomenology of spirit*. New York: Oxford University Press. (Original work published 1807)

Heidegger, M. (1962). *Being and time* (J. MacQuarie & E. Robinson, Trans.). New York: Harper & Row. (Original work published 1927)

Higgins, E. T. (1987). Self-discrepancy: A theory relating self and affect. *Psychological Review, 94,* 319–340.

Hoffman, I. Z. (1998). *Ritual and spontaneity in the psychoanalytic process: A dialectical-constructivist view*. Hillsdale, NJ: Analytic Press.

Hollon, S. D., & Kriss, M. R. (1984). Cognitive factors in clinical research and practice. *Clinical Psychology Review, 4,* 35–76.

Holmes, J. (1996). *Attachment, intimacy, autonomy: Using attachment theory in adult psychotherapy*. Northvale, NJ: Aronson.

Horney, K. (1950). *Neurosis and human growth: The struggle toward self-realization*. New York: Norton.

Horowitz, M. J. (1987). *States of mind* (2nd ed.). New York: Plenum Press.

Horowitz, M. J. (Ed.). (1991). *Person schemas and maladaptive interpersonal patterns*. Chicago: University of Chicago Press.

Horvath, A. O., & Greenberg, L. S. (Eds.). (1994). *The working alliance: Theory, research, and practice*. New York: Wiley.

Horvath, A. O., & Symonds, B. D. (1991). Relation between working alliance and outcome in psychotherapy: A meta-analysis. *Journal of Counseling Psychology, 38,* 139–149.

Hume, D. (1911). *A treatise on human nature*. London: Dent/Everyman. (Original work published 1738)

Irigaray, L. (1985). *This sex which is not one* (C. Poter & C. Burke, Trans.). Ithaca, NY: Cornell University Press.

Jacobs, T. (1991). *The use of the self: Countertransference and communication in the analytic setting*. Madison, CT: International Universities Press.

Jacobson, E. (1964). *The self and the object world*. New York: International Universities Press.

James, W. (1981). *The principles of psychology*. Cambridge, MA: Harvard University Press. (Original work published 1890)

Joseph, B. (1989). *Psychic equilibrium and psychic change: Selected papers of Betty Joseph*

(M. Feldman & E. B. Spillius, Eds.; New Library of Psychoanalysis, No. 9). London: Tavistock. (Original written in 1986)

Jung, C. (1945). The relations between the ego and the unconscious. In G. Adler, H. Read, & W. M. McGuire (Eds.), *Collected works of Carl Jung* (Vol. 7, pp. 123–241). Princeton, NJ: Princeton University Press.

Kaslow, N. J., & Celano, M. P. (1995). The family therapies. In A. S. Gurman & S. B. Messer (Eds.), *Essential psychotherapies* (pp. 343–402). New York: Guilford Press.

Kelly, G. A. (1955). *The psychology of personal constructs.* New York: Norton.

Kennedy, R. (1997). On subjective organizations: Toward a theory of subject relations. *Psychoanalytic Dialogues, 7,* 553–581.

Kernberg, O. (1976). *Object relations theory and clinical psychoanalysis.* New York: Aronson.

Kernberg, O. (1982). *Internal world and external reality.* New York: Aronson.

Klein, G. (1976). *Psychoanalytic theory: An exploration of essentials.* New York: International Universities Press.

Kohlenberg, R., & Tsai, M. (1991). *Functional analytic psychotherapy.* New York: Plenum Press.

Kohut, H. (1971). *The analysis of the self.* New York: International Universities Press.

Kohut, H. (1977). *The restoration of the self.* New York: International Universities Press.

Kohut, H. (1984). *How does analysis cure?* Chicago: University of Chicago Press.

Kristeva, J. (1986). *The Kristeva reader: Julia Kristeva* (T. Moi, Ed.). New York: Columbia University Press.

Kvale, S. (1992). *Psychology and postmodernism.* London: Sage.

Lacan, J. (1981). The four fundamental concepts of psychoanalysis (J.-A. Miller, Ed., & A. Sheridan, Trans.). New York: Norton.

Layton, L. (1998). *Who's that girl? Who's that boy?: Clinical practice meets postmodern gender theory.* Northvale, NJ: Aronson.

Levenson, E. (1992). *The purloined self: Interpersonal perspectives in psychoanalysis.* New York: Contemporary Psychoanalysis Books.

Lifton, R. J. (1993). *The protean self: Human resilience in an age of fragmentation.* New York: Basic Books.

Linehan, M. (1993). *Cognitive–behavioral treatment of personality disorder.* New York: Guilford Press.

Loewald, H. (1980). On the therapeutic action of psychoanalysis. *International Journal of Psycho-Analysis, 58,* 463–472.

Lyotard, J. F. (1984). *The postmodern condition: A report on knowledge.* Manchester, England: Manchester University Press.

Madison, G. B. (1988). *The hermeneutics of postmodernity: Figures and themes.* Bloomington: Indiana University Press.

Mahler, M. (1968). *On human symbiosis and the vicissitudes of individuation.* New York: International Universities Press.

Mahoney, M. J. (1991). *Human change processes: The scientific foundations of psychotherapy.* New York: Basic Books.

Main, M. (1991). Metacognitive knowledge, metacognitive monitoring, and singular (coherent) vs. multiple (incoherent) model of attachment: Findings and directions for future research. In C. M. Parkes, J. Stevenson-Hinde, & P. Marris (Eds.), *Attachment across the life cycle* (pp. 127–159). London: Tavistock.

Margolis, J. (1986). *Pragmatism without foundations: Reconciling realism and relativism.* Oxford, England: Basil Blackwell.

Markus, H. (1977). Self-schemata and processing information about the self. *Journal of Personality and Social Psychology, 35,* 63–67.

May, R. (1983). *The discovery of being.* New York: Norton.

Mead, G. H. (1934). *Mind, self, and society from the standpoint of a social behaviorist.* Chicago: University of Chicago Press.

Meador, B. D., & Rogers, C. R. (1979). Person-centered therapy. In R. J. Corsini (Ed.), *Current psychotherapies* (pp. 131–184). Itasca, IL: Peacock.

Messer, S. B., Sass, L. A., & Woolfolk, R. L. (Eds.). (1988). *Hermeneutics and psychological theory: Interpretive perspectives on personality, psychotherapy, and psychopathology.* New Brunswick, NJ: Rutgers University Press.

Mitchell, S. A. (1988). *Relational concepts in psychoanalysis.* Cambridge, MA: Harvard University Press.

Mitchell, S. A. (1992). True selves, false selves, and the ambiguity of authenticity. In N. J. Skolnick & S. C. Warshaw (Eds.), *Relational perspectives in psychoanalysis* (pp. 1–20). Hillsdale, NJ: Analytic Press.

Mitchell, S. A. (1993). *Hope and dread in psychoanalysis.* New York: Basic Books.

Modell, A. H. (1993). *The private self.* Cambridge, MA: Harvard University Press.

Muran, J. C. (1997). Multiple selves and depression. *In-Session: Psychotherapy in Practice, 3,* 53–64.

Natterson, J. M., & Friedman, R. J. (1995). *A primer of clinical intersubjectivity.* Northvale, NJ: Aronson.

Neimeyer, R. A. (1986). Personal construct therapy. In W. Dryden & W. Golden (Eds.), *Cognitive-behavioural approaches to psychotherapy* (pp. 224–260). London: Harper & Row.

Neimeyer, R. A., & Mahoney, M. J. (Eds.). (1995). *Constructivism in psychotherapy.* Washington, DC: American Psychological Association.

Nietzsche, F. (1968). *The will to power* (W. Kaufmann, Trans.). New York: Vintage Books. (Original work published 1888)

Ogden, T. (1994). *Subjects of analysis.* Northvale, NJ: Aronson.

Orange, D. M., Atwood, G. E., & Stolorow, R. D. (1997). *Working intersubjectively: Contextualism in psychoanalytic practice.* Hillsdale, NJ: Analytic Press.

Parkes, M. J., Stevenson-Hinde, J., & Marris, P. (Eds.). (1991). *Attachment across the life cycle.* London: Tavistock/Routledge.

Perls, F. (1969). *Gestalt therapy verbatim.* Moab, UT: Real People.

Perls, F. (1973). *The gestalt approach and eye witness therapy.* Palo Alto, CA: Science & Behavior.

Perry, H. S. (1964). Introduction. In H. S. Sullivan (Ed.), *The fusion of psychiatry and social science* (pp. xii–xxxv). New York: Norton.

Phillips, A. (1988). *Winnicoff.* Cambridge, MA: Harvard University Press.

Pine, F. (1987). *Developmental theory and clinical process.* New Haven, CT: Yale University Press.

Pine, F. (1990). *Drive, ego, object, and self: A synthesis for clinical work.* New York: Basic Books.

Pizer. S. A. (1998). *Building bridges: The negotiation of paradox in psychoanalysis.* Hillsdale, NJ: Analytic Press.

Protter, B. (1985). Toward an emergent psychoanalytic epistemology. *Contemporary Psychoanalysis, 21,* 209–227.

Protter, B. (1988). Ways of knowing in psychoanalysis. *Contemporary Psychoanalysis, 24,* 498–526.

Renik, O. (1993). Analytic interaction: Conceptualizing technique in light of the analyst's irreducible subjectivity. *Psychoanalytic Quarterly, 62,* 553–571.

Rogers, C. R. (1951). *Client-centered therapy.* Boston: Houghton Mifflin.

Rogers, C. (1961). *On becoming a person.* New York: Houghton Mifflin.

Rogers, C. (1980). *A way of being.* New York: Houghton Mifflin.

Roland, A. (1996). The influence of culture on the self and selfobject relationships. *Psychoanalytic Dialogues, 6,* 461–475.

Rorty, R. (1991). *Objectivity, relativism, and truth.* Cambridge, England: Cambridge University Press.

Rosenau, P. M. (1992). *Post-modernism and the social sciences: Insights, inroads, and intrusions.* Princeton, NJ: Princeton University Press.

Safran, J. D. (1998). *Widening the scope of cognitive therapy.* Northvale, NJ: Aronson.

Safran, J. D., & Muran, J. C. (2000). *Negotiating the therapeutic alliance: A relational treatment guide.* New York: Guilford Press.

Safran, J. D., & Segal, Z. V. (1990). *Interpersonal process in cognitive therapy.* New York: Basic Books.

Sampson, E. (1989). The deconstruction of the self. In J. Shotter & K. Gergen (Eds.), *Texts of identity* (pp. 1–19). London: Sage.

Sandler, J., & Rosenblatt, B. (1962). The concept of the representational world. *The Psychoanalytic Study of the Child, 17,* 128–145.

Schafer, R. (1983). *The analytic attitude.* New York: Basic Books.

Schafer, R. (1992). *Retelling a life: Narration & dialogue in psychoanalysis.* New York: Basic Books.

Segal, Z. V. (1988). Appraisal of the self-schema construct in cognitive models of depression. *Psychological Bulletin, 103,* 147–162.

Segal, Z. V., & Blatt, S. J. (Eds.). (1993). *The self in emotional distress.* New York: Guilford Press.

Skinner, B. F. (1953). *Science and human behavior.* New York: Macmillan.

Skinner, B. F. (1957). *Verbal behavior.* New York: Appleton-Century-Crofts.

Smith, M. B. (1994). Selfhood at risk: Postmodern perils and the perils of postmodernism. *American Psychologist, 49,* 405–411.

Spence, D. P. (1982). *Narrative truth and historical truth: Meaning and interpretation in psychoanalysis.* New York: Norton.

Spence, D. P. (1987). *The Freudian metaphor: Toward paradigm change in psychoanalysis.* New York: Norton.

Stern, D. B. (1997). *Unformulated experience.* Hillsdale, NJ: Analytic Press.

Stern, D. N. (1985). *The interpersonal world of the infant.* New York: Basic Books.

Stolorow, R., & Atwood, G. (1992). *Contexts of being: The intersubjective foundations of psychological life.* Hillsdale, NJ: Analytic Press.

Stolorow, R., Brandchaft, B., & Atwood, G. (1987). *Psychoanalytic treatment: An intersubjective approach.* Hillsdale, NJ: Analytic Press.

Sullivan, H. S. (1953). *The interpersonal theory of psychiatry.* New York: Norton.

Sullivan, H. S. (1964). *The fusion of psychiatry and the social sciences.* New York: Norton.

Taylor, C. (1989). *Sources of the self: The making of the modern identity.* Cambridge, MA: Harvard University Press.

Teasdale, J. D., Segal, Z., & Williams, M. D. (1995). How does cognitive therapy prevent depressive relapse and why should attentional control (mindfulness) training help? *Behaviour Research and Therapy, 33,* 25–39.

Warnke, G. (1987). *Gadamer: Hermeneutics, tradition, and reason.* Stanford, CA: Stanford University Press.

White, D. R., & Hellerich, G. (1998). *Labyrinths of the mind: The self in the postmodern age.* Albany: State University of New York Press.

Winnicott, D. W. (1958). *Through paediatrics to psychoanalysis.* New York: Basic Books.

Winnicott, D. W. (1965). *The maturational process and the facilitating environment.* New York: International Universities Press.

Wittgenstein, L. (1953). *Philosophical investigations* (G. E. M. Anscombe, R. Rhees, &

G. H. von Wright, Eds.; G. E. M Anscombe, Trans.). London: Oxford University Press.

Wolstein, B. (1974). "I" processes and "me" patterns. *Contemporary Psychoanalysis, 10,* 347–357.

Wolstein, B. (1977). From mirror to participant observation to coparticipant inquiry and experience. *Contemporary Psychoanalysis, 13,* 381–386.

Yalom, I. D. (1981). *Existential psychotherapy.* New York: Basic Books.

Yontef, G. M. (1995). Gestalt therapy. In A. S. Gurman & S. B. Messer (Eds.), *Essential psychotherapies* (pp. 261–303). New York: Guilford Press.

Yontef, G. M. (1998). Dialogic gestalt therapy. In L. S. Greenberg, J. C. Watson, & G. Lietaer (Eds.), *Handbook of experiential psychotherapy* (pp. 82–102). New York: Guilford Press.

Young, J. (1990). *Cognitive therapy for personality disorders: A schema-focused approach.* Sarasota, FL: Practitioner's Resource Series.

CHAPTER 2

Toward a Theory of the Self

Sheldon Bach

It seems that the place of the self in psychoanalytic theory and practice has been, and continues to be, somewhat of a puzzle. For those of us who were trained almost 40 years ago, hardly anybody at all had a self. To be more exact, most patients had egos, which varied on a dimension from weak to strong, but hardly any of them had selves. Today, by contrast, if I can believe what my students and patients tell me, most people have selves, which vary on a dimension from true to false, but hardly any of them have egos. Are we simply witnessing a passing change in fashion, like short hemlines, tango dancing, or tulipomania, or is some substantive addition being made to our knowledge and understanding of human nature?

If one reviews the literature on the psychoanalytic self, as Meissner (1986) did in his very illuminating article, there seems to be little consensus about what the self is; where it belongs in theory; or even what difference, if any, it makes in practice. So it is with a certain temerity mixed with trepidation that I approach the subject in this chapter.

Freud, who at the time was just inventing psychoanalysis and had learned to live with ambiguity, deliberately used the term *das ich* to mean both *self*, an experience-near, subjective, and phenomenological construct, and *ego*, an experience-far, objective, and theoretical construct. In subsequent efforts to clarify Freud's usage of ego and self or at least to expose the ambiguities that exist, theoreticians such as Grossman (1982) and Spruiell (1981) have insisted that from the viewpoint of the structural theory, the self is quite simply a special set of fantasies about self-experience, important as these fantasies may be.

Perhaps one difference may be reflected in a story I have always enjoyed. Back in the days when people drank cocktails at bars, there was a popular cocktail called a Grasshopper. One day, a real grasshopper walked into the bar at the Ritz and sat down, waiting to be served. The bartender approached him with a smile and said, "We're very pleased to have you here! You know, we have a cocktail named after you." The grasshopper, equally pleased, replied, "You really do? You have a cocktail named Irving?"

From this story we can learn that whereas the viewer feels he may be observing a grasshopper, the subject knows that he is being an Irving—not that Irving could not learn to conceive of himself as a grasshopper, but I believe that it would be very difficult for him to simultaneously think of himself both as Irving and as a grasshopper. Thus there appears to exist a complementary relationship between self and ego: You can think of yourself subjectively as a self, or objectively as an ego, but perhaps not both at the same time. To view one's person as a self and as an ego seems to require two different kinds of thought processes, or two different perspectives or levels of mental operation. Yet for us to fully understand the grasshopper—to triangulate him, as it were —we must know him from at least two perspectives, both as a grasshopper and as Irving, just as the analyst must know his patient both as ego and as self. This viewpoint, of course, invokes Bohr's (1963) principle of complementarity.

Because the applicability of complementarity to psychology has been questioned (Edelheit, 1976), I was pleased to discover recently that Bohr's original insight into complementary relationships first occurred in the field of psychology and was only subsequently applied to physics. The incident is charming, and I relate it briefly, as recounted by Bruner (1986):

> Let me say now what Niels Bohr told *me*. The idea of complementarity in quantum theory, he said, came to him as he thought of the impossibility of considering his son simultaneously in the light of love and in the light of justice, the son having just voluntarily confessed that he had stolen a pipe from a local shop. His brooding set him to thinking about the vases and the faces in the trick figure–ground pictures: you can see only one at a time. And then the impossibility of thinking simultaneously about the position and the velocity of a particle occurred to him. (p. 51)

To consider his son in the light of love, of course, is to consider him from a subjective point of view, whereas to consider him in the light of justice is to consider him from an objective viewpoint.

I believe an analogous situation existed in psychology and that Freud was to a large extent aware of this when he deliberately used *das ich* to mean both ego and self. We tamper with genius at our own risk, and the unpacking of condensed meanings may sometimes open a Pandora's box and lead to confusion rather than to clarification.

The ego is a scientific fantasy of the psychoanalyst. It is a construct that integrates observations made of the subject's behavior from the viewpoint of psychic determinism, drive motivation, and conflict—that is, from the *intrapsychic* viewpoint of structural theory, isolated from the external relational context. It provides an impartial, objective, structurally equidistant and dispassionate view of the person as object of our scrutiny and investigation—a view, as it were, from the moon.

The self, in its common usage, is an experiential construct. It integrates observations about the subject's experience from a phenomenological and sub-jective point of view—that is, from the viewpoint of free will rather than of determinism because the person feels that his or her actions are free rather than determined—and from the viewpoints of spontaneity, activity, and intention-ality rather than of drive, conflict, and compromise formation. The self provides a partisan, subjective, and impassioned view of the person as the perceiver of his own experience. The self is one pole of an interpersonal or *interpsychic* rather than an *intrapsychic* theory, the other pole being the object.

Both these points of view or perspectives are necessary to fully understand a human being, just as position and velocity are necessary to specify an atomic particle or justice and love to deal with one's adolescent son. Neither one makes better theory, nor can one replace the other. I believe that people who use structural theory are also of necessity using a self theory or experiential theory without specifying it, just as Freud used *das ich* to sometimes mean the ego and sometimes the self, although personally he seemed more interested in the theoretical, or observational mode. But one could trace the tentative outlines of an experiential theory within psychoanalysis, beginning with the influence of Brentano's phenomenology on Freud (McIntosh, 1986) and continuing through the work of Schilder (1953), Federn (1953), Weiss (1942, 1957a, 1957b), Hoffer (1952), Erikson (1956), Schachtel (1959), Straus (1966), Win-nicott (1965) and Kohut (1971), into the more recent object-relational schools (Greenberg & Mitchell, 1983), but this would lead us far astray.

There can be no self without an other. We can, in a thought-experiment, conceive of a feral child raised without human contacts possessing some prim-itive body-ego or self-representation, but we cannot conceive of such a child possessing an identity or sense of self. For the ego, at least in Hartmann's (1964) sense, is primarily a maturational concept, that is, a group of functions that given the average expectable stimulation by the environment matures program-matically according to their genetic anlage. The self, however, is primarily a developmental concept; the self is constructed through the experience that re-sults from the interaction between a particular child and the caretaking envi-ronment. Consequently, theories centering on the developmental self tend to emphasize the object-relations viewpoint, whereas those centering on the ma-turational ego tend to emphasize the endogenous-drive viewpoint. Needless to say, we are dealing with interactions, and just as the environment has a major impact on how the ego matures, maturational factors have a major impact on how the self is constructed, but my point is precisely that these are comple-mentary perspectives on an ongoing holistic process.

The ego implies conflict: It is the mediator among the drives, the superego, and the world of objects, the integrator of multiple functions and of partial and conflicting drive and superego pressures. The role of the ego is that of a mod-erator and synthesizer between conflicting forces; as such, it may be strong or weak. It mediates between the urge to achieve some kind of gratification and the world's prohibitions internalized in the superego, on the basis of the reality principle. Although Hartmann (1964) delineated conflict-free spheres, the essential notion is that the ego is born in conflict.

The self is born in silence. It is born out of those relatively conflict-free moments of pure experience of sensations from within—of proprioception—and of sensations from without—of sensoriperception—including perceptions of being held, being touched, being smelled, being heard, being looked at, being recognized and their proprioceptive correlates. Out of these experiences of confirmation by the other comes a sense of *being*, of existing, what Federn (1953) called "ego feeling." The essence of the self lies in its relationship with itself and the world of objects; as such, these relationships may be either true or false. Infant researchers (e.g., Sanders, 1983) might perhaps say that the self first appears at moments of alert inactivity when the infant is not in a driven state and can afford the luxury of experiencing itself as just going-on-being. Although these moments are relatively brief, it is through this "window" of alert inactivity that the infant's capacities can be tested and reveal their highest potential. Thus, the self is a construct about the experience of relationships with oneself and with others and their developmental potential.

Reciprocally, the infant's self appears as a virtual image in the caretaker's eye, as a sort of hope that this bundle of needs and thrashings-about may one day become a whole person. This virtual image or faith is as essential to the baby as food because without this hope and the care that it engenders, we ultimately find hospitalism and marasmus (Spitz, 1965). We should note that the caretaker's function is crucial for the development of a sense of self—that there can be no self without an other. If we imagine a baby with such intense drive endowment that the usual periods of alert inactivity occur rarely or are washed away by the drives, we believe that this child will have uncommon difficulty in experiencing himself as a separate entity who possesses his drives, unless he is met by some very exceptional nurturance. But although high drive states may generally not seem conducive to a self-experience, the satisfactory outcome of such states may indeed strengthen the self-experience; for example, seeing that the object and the self are not destroyed after a high-drive experience of aggression. We could say that high-drive states, when contained in an adequate holding environment, may contribute to self-definition or, paraphrasing Winnicott (1965), that instinctual experiences strengthen the mature self but disrupt the immature self.

One can thus envision the possibility of a multiple or mixed model (Pine, 1990) that would accommodate both a subjective, phenomenological view of the person, interpersonal and interpsychic, built around the concept of self and using constructs such as free will, spontaneity, and creativity, as well as an objective and dispassionate view of the person, intrapersonal and intrapsychic, built around the concept of ego and using constructs such as psychic determinism, need motivation, and conflicts. The ego aspect would of necessity be maturational and epigenetic, incorporating elements such as Freud's psychosexual stages, Piaget's cognitive periods, Erikson's psychosocial stages, Mahler's developmental phases, Gedo's epigenetic stages, and so forth. The self aspect would focus on the phenomenological present and would emphasize its expression as a relational development. This view would incorporate elements of regulatory oscillations, such as between self and self-object (Kohut), between paranoid–schizoid and depressive positions (Klein), between illusion and disillusionment (Winnicott), between activity and passivity, between pleasure and pain (Freud), between symmetry and asymmetry (Matteo-Blanco), and so forth. Bucci (1985), in her multiple-processing model, noted the importance of incorporating not only a stage-to-stage model of processing but also a continuum model of processing. Although this kind of mixed model may present certain knotty or perhaps even unresolvable theoretical issues (Greenberg & Mitchell, 1983), I am nevertheless attempting to describe what a growing number of practitioners conceive of themselves as doing these days. Perhaps this involves an increasing flexibility in our definition of terms or a willingness to live with ambiguity and paradox, or perhaps it points to incorporating ambiguity and paradox into new theoretical approaches as foreshadowed by the development of fuzzy logic, complexity theory, or chaos theory.

I have elsewhere (Bach, 1977, 1985, 1994) suggested the view that we oscillate between two primary states of consciousness, which I call "subjective" and "objective" self-awareness. When the grasshopper thought of himself as Irving, he was in a state of subjective self-awareness; that is, he was completely and unreflectively immersed in his own subjective state of being, like the child of Mahler's practicing period (1972), whom we imagine to be totally "into himself" and perhaps somewhat hypomanic because of that. To enter a state of objective self-awareness, the grasshopper would have to reflect on himself and see himself from the outside as the bartender might see him, that is, as a grasshopper. In all probability, he would be less than enthusiastic to learn that the cocktail was not called "Irving" but was generically named "Grasshopper," and he might even be somewhat depressed at the thought. This is developmentally akin to the rapprochement child who is slowly and painfully learning to view himself as just one more object in his mother's world and is analogously somewhat depressed by that.

I believe that our normal states of consciousness usually oscillate between these two poles of subjective and objective awareness, although more complex versions of these basic states continue to evolve developmentally. In fact, it is when these complex integrations do not take place that we find pathological deficits in subjective awareness and in the ability to be spontaneous, creative, and unashamed, or deficits in objective self-awareness and in the ability to reflect on one's thoughts or actions and to achieve insight.

One could categorize psychopathology according to fixations in habitual states of consciousness. For example, in hysterical or dissociated types the pattern of lived experience is predominantly in subjective awareness, immersed in the self and with a greater emphasis on proximal, autonomic, and coenesthetic modalities such as touch, smell, equilibrium, and so forth. Conversely, in the schizoid or obsessional type the pattern of lived experience is predominantly in objective self-awareness, distanced from and observing the self, and with a greater emphasis on distal, cortical, and diacritic modalities, such as speech, vision, and so forth. Although healthier functioning would require a more fluid and appropriate transition between these two modes of awareness, it would also imply and require precisely that kind of intersubjective relatedness that is lacking in the pathologies and makes them appear so dichotomized.

I have elsewhere (Bach, 1998) suggested that these characterological preferences for subjective awareness or objective self-awareness seem to parallel the distinctions between the romantic and the classical attitudes toward life as well as between historical eras such as the Romantic period and the Enlightenment. I went on to suggest that we are currently living in a period in which subjective awareness is the culturally preferred modality so that feelings, actions, and the body are valued more highly than thought, self-reflection, and the mind. As a recent article in *New York* magazine proclaims, "nowadays people recommend their massage therapists to each other in the same way that in other decades they used to recommend their shrinks!"

It is consequently not surprising to find that in psychoanalysis there are also two general types of theory that broadly divide the subject into either ego or self and that they each describe an important aspect of the human situation. It seems that we often have great difficulty in grasping them both at the same time, but we may attempt to integrate them in oscillatory attention, that is, by moving back and forth as if we were to try to see each side of a reversing figure–ground to incorporate both of its dimensions. Just as it took a suicidal patient of mine many years before she could reliably attain a state of consciousness in which she could integrate both her subjectivity and her objectivity, it may indeed take a new generation of therapists unencumbered by past theories to be able to visualize a different way of integrating these disparate data.

I am suggesting that the basically complementary natures of our subjective and objective states of consciousness, which are the prime data of our existence, have been mirrored in our historical understanding of the proper nature of human beings and, consequently, in our views of psychopathology and even in the theories that we construct to understand ourselves. Although this view has many implications in a variety of directions, I shall here try to explore some of its relations to the therapeutic process.

From earliest times the injunction to "know thyself" has been seen as an important goal of any therapeutic endeavor. But whereas the Platonic dictum that "the unexamined life is not worth living" characterizes certain historical eras, other periods reverse this dictum and deem that "the unlived life is not worth examining." In truth, both living one's life or experiencing it, and thinking about that life or reflecting on it, seem equally indispensable. The real problem lies not in making this Hobson's choice but in having the mental capacity and flexibility to move freely and appropriately between subjectively experiencing and objectively reflecting on one's experience.

For example, one of my patients complained of her inability to have a mutual orgasm with her lover and said, "I can't make the smooth transition. . . . I'm either *me*, totally me and so excited that nothing else exists, or else I'm Tony's lover, and I can give him pleasure, but then I don't have any myself." In this instance, the patient was forced to choose between pleasing herself in subjective awareness or pleasing her lover in objective self-awareness; she seemed unable to make the smooth transition between these states and had either not developed or not been able to use a more complex state that might contain these polarities. One might say that she had difficulties integrating her narcissism with her object relatedness.

Another patient was frequently overwhelmed by totally subjective suicidal states in which the only contents of consciousness were her urgent needs and plans to immediately kill herself. After these suicidal states or attempts, I could talk with her about her children, whom she loved and did not wish to orphan; that is, after the attempt she could assume a state of objective self-awareness that was shut off to her when she was suicidal. After many frightening years, she eventually began to feel better but complained that the treatment had deprived her of her suicidal potential because she could no longer enter a state of subjective suicidality without also objectively remembering that she was the mother of little children. I understood this to mean that certain splits had been partially healed and that a more complex state of consciousness had developed in which varieties of subjective and objective self-awareness, or of narcissism and object-relatedness, had become better integrated. It was noteworthy that part of her found this depressing and experienced it as a loss, analogous to the way the rapprochement child feels slightly depressed at his loss of practicing omnipotence, or the way the grasshopper might presumably feel depressed when he realizes that he is being regarded not as a unique Irving but as a member of a larger class of insects.

Thus, one of our goals in therapy is to enlarge both subjective and objective self-awareness and to integrate these into increasingly complex states of consciousness. As regards objective self-awareness—or "reflective awareness," as it is often called—there has been a growing recognition in both the cognitive–developmental and the psychoanalytic literature of its importance, and there is some general agreement about the major landmarks in its development (Auerbach, 1998). One can find early prototypes of shame that may be viewed as precursors, but the first established landmark is the ability to recognize oneself in the mirror at age 18–24 months. This coincides with Mahler's rapprochement phase and with an increase in shame, embarrassment, and lowered self-esteem, as when the grasshopper realizes he is not being recognized as Irving. This situation may be somewhat redeemed by the child's increasing capability for transitional experiences and pretend play, which then allows him more room to reinflate his importance in fantasy. The grasshopper might, for example, replay the barroom incident with a more heroic outcome, or he might construct a transitional object from a cork, napkin, or other proto-symbol that would have the effect of both connecting with, yet distancing him from, the hurtful barman.

Auerbach (1998) noted that

> while children come to understand the separateness of their bodies sometime in the second year of life, they do not come to understand that their minds are distinct from those of others until sometime in the fifth or sixth year of life. (p. 677)

In this interval children may be slowly grasping various aspects of this concept: There is a difference between reality and appearance, someone can believe things that are false, one can successfully lie to another person, and so forth.

Still, although these cognitive stepping stones are indispensable, we must remember that they are acquired intersubjectively. The mortar that binds them together and indeed makes them possible is that from the very beginning, the infant's self appears as a virtual image in the caretaker's eyes, as a sort of hopeful vision that this bundle of needs may one day become a whole person with wishes and desires. In this way, the infant experiences the mother thinking and feeling about him, and then the mother experiences the infant experiencing her, which the infant in turn re-experiences. Through projection and introjection, subjectivity and objectivity become infiltrated and informed by each other; the inner world becomes penetrated and suffused by the outer world, and the outer world in its turn is permeated by the inner world. Opposing qualities become reconciled into a higher unity, and relatively simple states of consciousness are continually reorganized into increasingly more complex networks of interactive states that feed back into each other. In this way, the present is continuously interacting with the past, and the past is continually being retranscribed back onto the present and creating the future. This process has been extensively commented on in work on Freud's concept of *nachtraglichkeit* or *apres-coup* in temporality (cf. Green, 1998).

Thus, in an ideal situation the sense of an ongoing self, separate from and yet related to another separate and ongoing self, becomes established, and not only do subjective and objective awareness become firmly established, but they also become mutually interdependent and capable of generating and integrating more complex syntheses. But in the pathologies with which therapists deal, especially the borderline and narcissistic states, many things seem to have gone wrong with this rather complicated development, and it is to some of these that I now turn.

Just as objective or reflective awareness was formerly assumed as a given in the neurotic patient and its malfunctioning in the borderline and narcissistic patient often overlooked, so too, I believe, is subjective awareness assumed in most patients and its malfunctioning often overlooked, particularly in certain borderline, narcissistic, and hypochondriacal patients.

Now the pathological symptoms we find associated with a deficit in objective self-awareness are usually considered to be a lack of self-reflectiveness and insight, a deficit in symbolic functioning with consequent problems of self-control and the ability to delay, and various superego pathologies. We have seen that objective self-awareness develops in an intersubjective context as the child learns to see himself in the eyes of his caretaker and then of the world and that this is processed in the more specific diacritic modalities, especially verbally. Because of this verbal and intersubjective context, deficits in self-reflectivity and related symptomatology are often quite noticeable; that is, we can tell relatively easily when a person lacks insight into his or her actions.

The pathological symptoms we find associated with a deficit of subjective awareness, however, are a defective sense of aliveness, a lack of vitality, and a lack of a sense of self-cohesiveness, many of which are processed in the more generalized, nonverbal, proprioceptive and coenesthetic modalities and are consequently less noticeable to an outsider. Thus, it seems that they have been overlooked more often by therapists, especially before Balint, Winnicott, and Kohut drew our attention to them. Perhaps another reason for this historical inattention has also been the lack of a clear sense of the origins and treatment for these symptoms because they may well have been present in such classic diagnoses as neurasthenia but could not then have been translated into an intersubjective context.

In a general way, problems with objective or reflective self-awareness can be thought of as originating through the inadequate recognition of the child as a separate person by the caretaker, but problems with subjective awareness tend to originate through the inadequate libidinization of the child by the caretaker. I mean that in the total absence of early maternal bodily loving the child may die of marasmus (Spitz, 1965). It seems that a sufficient degree of body loving, hating, or both; of some bodily cathexis or energizing; of some kind of mother–infant sexuality is necessary to libidinize the body and enable the child to even have the potential to feel alive and whole, to love his own body and to love someone else sexually. In the absence of this, if the child manages to stay alive at all, we see the kind of pathology so accurately portrayed by Patrick Suskind in his novel *Perfume* (1991), in which the protagonist, who has no body scent of his own, first becomes a perfumer and eventually a murderer of women in an attempt to rob them of the scent of life that he feels so lacking in himself. Although the ordinary patient that we see has not been literally thrown away after birth, as was the protagonist of this novel, I have seen many patients whose problems with feeling vital, alive, and cohesive were traceable in part to some cumulative environmental deficiency such as not being sufficiently touched by their caretakers.

I should perhaps at this point clarify that I do not view psychological malfunctioning as traceable exclusively to environmental trauma, whether early or late, and that I am a firm believer in both endogenous and exogenous forces and the equal and interactive contribution, in most cases, of both biology and environment, of fantasy and trauma, and of psychic reality and external reality. So when I say that some patients have problems that are traceable in part to not being sufficiently touched by their caretakers, I am using shorthand for a series of propositions such as the following:

1. A caretaker who does not touch or sufficiently libidinize the child in infancy is characterologically likely to continue this behavior in other ways throughout the patient's lifetime, unless the behavior was due to some transient family difficulties, a temporary depression, and so forth.

2. The caretaker is from the beginning always reacting to the constitutional givens of the child, so that someone who may be an adequate caretaker for one child may be inadequate for another with high drive endowment, and so forth.

3. The child is from the beginning always reacting to the caretaker's reactions, and thus the child's inner life, whether in affect or fantasy, becomes a prime determiner of ensuing interactions.

In this connection, it may be worth underlining the seemingly obvious point that difficulties with, for example, reflective self-awareness, even when originating in the early dyad, almost always are picked up and used by the child and the adult patient for defensive purposes. It thus seems useless to debate whether a defect in self-reflectivity is the product of a deficit or an internal conflict because they seem to engender each other and are almost always mutually present. From a clinical point of view, it would seem important in every case to work with both the environmental trauma, so that the patient may come to understand his dependence on other people in his environment, and to work with the inner conflicts, so that the patient may come to understand his independence from the environment and experience his own agency.

Thus, in his own way, the therapist must also be able to move between subjectivity and objectivity, or between his empathy with the patient's subjectivity and his recognition of the patient's place in the objective world of reality. It is precisely this ability to oscillate flexibly and appropriately between subjective and objective awareness, between self and object, and between narcissism and object cathexes, that these patients lack. You may recall my example of the patient who said "I can't make the smooth transition. . . . I'm either *me*, totally me and so excited that nothing else exists, or else I'm Tony's lover, and I can give him pleasure, but then I don't have any myself." How do we go about working with such patients?

First, in most cases it is necessary to have the problem framed, so we direct our interest toward the vague complaints that are initially present in a way that enables the patient to begin to see the issues or to frame them, as the above-mentioned patient was in the process of doing. As this awareness develops, we are interested in both current examples as they occur, especially in the transference, and reconstructions about how this might have looked in childhood. If the patient's parents are still alive, then it is often useful to examine their interactions in close detail, for example, in telephone conversations. If the parent can be observed interacting with infants or children, then one can frequently make astonishingly convincing reconstructions of what the reality of the patient's childhood might have been and how he or she might have construed this. If, as often happens, this gets re-enacted in the transference and is susceptible to examination, then we are well on our way toward understanding the problem.

Unfortunately, when the problem is in the area of objective awareness or self-reflection, then the very tool on which we depend for therapeutic progress has been damaged, and although the issues may get repeatedly re-enacted, both in and out of the transference, we may not be able to examine them easily because the patient finds them too humiliating to look at, or is unable to take any distance from which to view them, or projects them onto the analyst or someone else to evacuate them, and so forth. Some patients may have scarcely developed any self-reflective capacity, whereas others go in and out of states in which they have some objective self-awareness, often depending on the particular state of the transference. When in states where self-reflection is unavailable, these patients typically consider transference occurrences as concrete manifestations of the one and only actual reality; they have little sense of playfulness and are generally unable to create or make use of transitional space. This has often been viewed as a defect or a defensive use of their symbolic capacities.

In treating such disturbances, I (Bach, 1985) suggested that our essential goal, as therapists, is to enter the patient's world or his psychic reality without attempting to impose our reality, our interpretations, or our view of the world on him. Often with these patients any attempt to assert one's own individuality is usually experienced as another traumatic environmental impingement and reacted to with attack or withdrawal. Thus, paradoxically, the critical step in developing the self-reflective capacity is precisely not to insist on it but rather to empathize with the patient's subjective world. Doing so enables the patient to use the analyst in a nonretaliatory way, to develop analytic trust (Ellman, 1991) and to depend on the analyst to contain and metabolize his mental and emotional states and return them with barely a just-noticeable difference. It is out of this just-noticeable difference or good-enough matching that the patient begins to tolerate the notion of an other with a separate and independent existence, develops a transitional space, and becomes able to deal not only with separate bodies but also with separate minds and separate and multiple realities. It is only when these preconditions exist or are coming into existence that the transference, with its implications of multiple minds and multiple realities, becomes interpretable.

As an example of this stage of treatment, let me offer this quote from a patient who was becoming aware of these issues and was trying to explain how I might best help him. He said,

> You can't be too much smarter than me or think of something I never could have thought of because then I'll become insanely envious, and of course you can't say anything stupid because then I'll be contemptuous. What you've got to do is to say something that I could have said myself if only I had bothered to think about it.

Although the above was said humorously, it was deeply meant and was already the result of a great deal of hard work by both patient and analyst. The humor itself was a fairly recent acquisition, for it implies some ability to look at oneself from an external perspective, whereas before the patient had been able to only subjectively express the envy, contempt, and rage that he was now able to reflect on and talk about symbolically. The poles of his dilemma were those typical of the sadomasochistic position that exists before the other is constructed as a whole, separate, and autonomous object (Bach, 1994). Either I as the analyst would be smarter than he and idealized, but then subject to envious destruction, or else I would be stupider, denigrated and ignored or destroyed with contempt. Only if I could stay within the narrow bounds of his ability to tolerate an other could I continue to exist alongside of him, within his subjective world. It is clinically very important to note that his ability to tolerate my otherness was absolutely dependent on my falling within the area of his own omnipotence—that is, what I had to do was to say something that he could have said himself if only he had bothered to think about it.

Thus, by slow degrees, the analyst establishes a foothold within the patient's subjectivity and begins to win his or her trust and form the empathic bond that is the basis for strengthening the patient's subjective sense of himself, his aliveness, and his own right to exist. As the patient's sense of his or her own self becomes secure, he is more and more able to tolerate the existence of another self and, ultimately, to recognize the analyst's right to a separate and autonomous life.

It is through this mutual recognition of and by the other, whether in the mirror of the mother's eyes or the virtual image in the analyst's mind, that the patient develops objective self-awareness and the capacity for symbolism and self-reflection. The good analyst has a sensitivity to growing symbolic functions, and although he never imposes his vision or virtual image on the patient, he nevertheless acts as a kind of container within which the patient's capacities may grow. This holding or containing function of the analyst, understood by Bion (1962) and Winnicott (1965) in somewhat different ways, is of crucial importance because it serves to repair the splits or discontinuities between states of consciousness and between multiple self-concepts that we find in most borderline and narcissistic patients. I offered the clinical example of the patient who complained that she could not make the smooth transition between being herself and being Tony's lover, between subjective awareness and objective self-awareness, or between her narcissistic states and her object-related states. This patient could be seen as lacking a transitional function or the ability to easily and appropriately negotiate between these two areas. It is interesting that I had the opportunity to observe this patient's mother playing with her infant grandchild and to note that the mother, who was so enthusiastically gazing at her grandchild, experienced great difficulty when the child sought to break off and avert his gaze. She repeatedly tried to force herself on him and eventually broke off all contact as if she had been personally offended. It seemed perfectly conceivable that something similar had also happened to the patient and that this was, in a sense, a paradigm for the mother's difficulty in holding, containing, and recognizing the patient's oscillating states and in affording her the transitional space in which a secure sense of self might grow.

Regardless of whether one conceptualizes this difficulty of the patient's mother as a problem of integrating multiple states of consciousness or as a problem with allowing the child to separate from her, if this behavior is typical, it makes it difficult for the patient herself to contain multiple states of self or multiple self-representations and to build up more complex states of consciousness. The ultimate examples of this kind of dissociative pathology are the multiple personality disorders, in which transitions between states are marked by a distinct "switching" behavior and are later integrated by a distinctive reorientation or "grounding" behavior (Putnam, 1989). Research studies have suggested that these switching and grounding markers can be found not only in patients but also in their therapists as they prepare to make interventions, that is, to change their state from an empathically listening, subjective state of awareness to an interpretatively reflective, objective state of awareness (Freedman & Berzofsky, 1995). In Freedman and Berzofsky's (1995) study, particular kinesic response sequences were noted, such as a foot kick, a postural rearrangement, or self-touching. But we can assume, in principle, that changes in states of consciousness are always accompanied by brain and body changes, whether they are grossly apparent, as in unintegrated multiple personalities, or subtle and scarcely noticeable, as in better integrated individuals.

In the course of normal caretaking, the parents facilitate the development of a variety of differentiated waking and sleeping states, encourage the self-regulation of these states so that they are stable and context appropriate, and encourage the integration of these states so that the transitions between them are relatively smooth and the sense of self remains relatively stable throughout. Although all these functions of differentiation, integration, and self- and mutual regulation proceed automatically and without much attention in the well-regulated dyad, in the dysregulated system they become issues that often eventuate in adult narcissistic and borderline pathology.

In Ellman et al. (1998), I discussed in some detail how such regulatory problems show themselves clinically and how they are handled. Here I would like only to re-emphasize how extreme discrepancies in states of consciousness between patient and therapist lead to crises in the transference relationship because the more disturbed patients have difficulty both in maintaining their own subjective awareness and in switching to or achieving states of reflective self-awareness. The attuned therapist, by his "free-floating attention" or "matching," helps to regulate the patient's states of consciousness and other mental and bodily functioning (Aron & Bushra, 1998).

We know that in addition to the particular dialectics of awareness I explore in this chapter, every state of consciousness also entails a particular body schema, a particular organization of thought and language, particular patterns of arousal and affect, particular thresholds, a particular sense of agency and spontaneity, and other such parameters (Bach, 1994; Rapaport, 1951a, 1951b). Indeed, Rapaport (1951a, 1951b) has suggested that one way of understanding the sense of self is to think of it as the pattern of relationships among all of these parameters, a concept that I find useful in grasping how the sense of self can seem both highly variable and yet enduringly constant. One corollary of this concept is that we communicate with each other in multiple modalities, sometimes out of awareness, and that our every experience involves cross-modal transfers and synesthesis of the kind that infant research is just now bringing to our attention. Yet another corollary is that differing states involve differing organizations of thought and language so that, for example, patients who lean predominantly toward a narcissistic state of consciousness show demonstrated idiosyncrasies of thought and language that can be characterized as their particular kind of "thought disorder" (Bach, 1977).

Thus, when we speak to a patient out of an extremely discrepant or non-matching state, we speak as if in another language, which the patient may sometimes be able to understand and sometimes not. Either the words do not have a shared emotional content and feel hollow, or their symbolic use may be momentarily or generally incomprehensible. For this reason, the transference, which is a metaphor, may be confusing to a patient who is unable to self-reflect or to accommodate the symbolism of metaphor, for he or she may become convinced that you are indeed the hated enemy that you subjectively feel like at the moment.

These patients are sometimes unable to understand that the same reality can be viewed in different ways by different people and that their point of view and the analyst's point of view can both have reality and legitimacy. This is because of their difficulty in shifting among levels of meaning, symbolism, and reality, but it is precisely at these shifts or transitions among levels, contexts, and states of consciousness that most therapeutic disruptions and transference crises occur and that the greatest potential for change emerges.

The disruptive potential lies in the possibility that the patient may feel misunderstood, tricked, betrayed, or otherwise mistreated and may ultimately break off the treatment. The constructive potential lies in the possibility that these same feelings may arise but will eventually be understood as a mutual re-enactment that clarifies the patient's difficulty integrating his past history into his current life and, more generally, his difficulty integrating different contexts, levels of meaning, and varying states of consciousness. In this way, through slow and patient efforts, the multiple aspects of the self can be brought to light, examined, linked together and reconnected and, finally, consolidated into a still variable but somewhat more cohesive system.

References

Aron, L., & Bushra, A. (1998). Mutual regression: Altered states in the psychoanalytic situation. *Journal of the American Psychoanalytic Association, 46,* 389–412.

Auerbach, J. (1998). Dualism, self-reflexivity, and intersubjectivity. *Psychoanalytic Dialogues, 8,* 675–683.

Bach, S. (1977). On the narcissistic state of consciousness. *Journal of the American Psychoanalytic Association, 58,* 209–232.

Bach, S. (1985). *Narcissistic states and the therapeutic process.* New York: Aronson.

Bach, S. (1994). *The language of perversion and the language of love.* Northvale, NJ: Aronson.

Bach, S. (1998). Two ways of being. *Psychoanalytic Dialogues, 8,* 657–673.

Bion, W. (1962). *Learning from experience.* London: Heinemann.

Bohr, N. (1963). *Essays 1958–1962 on atomic physics and human knowledge.* New York: Interscience.

Bruner, J. (1986). *Actual minds, possible worlds.* Cambridge, MA: Harvard University Press.

Bucci, W. (1985). Dual coding: A cognitive model for psychoanalytic research. *Journal of the American Psychoanalytic Association, 33,* 571–607.

Edelheit, H. (1976). Complementarity as a rule in psychological research. *International Journal of Psycho-Analysis, 57,* 23–30.

Ellman, C., Grand, S., Silvan, M., & Ellman, S. (Eds.). (1998). *The modern Freudians: Contemporary psychoanalytic technique.* Northvale, NJ: Aronson.

Ellman, S. (1991). *Freud's technique papers.* Northvale, NJ: Aronson.

Erikson, E. (1956). The problem of ego identity. *Journal of the American Psychoanalytic Association, 4,* 56–121.

Federn, E. (1953). *Ego psychology and the psychoses.* London: Imago.

Freedman, N., & Berzofsky, M. (1995). Shape of the communicated transference in difficult and not-so-difficult patients: Symbolized and de-symbolized transference. *Psychoanalytic Psychology, 12,* 363–374.

Green, A. (1998). The primordial mind and the work of the negative. *Journal of the American Psychoanalytic Association, 79,* 649–665.

Greenberg, J., & Mitchell, S. (1983). *Object relations in psychoanalytic theory.* Cambridge, MA: Harvard University Press.

Grossman, W. I. (1982). The self as fantasy: Fantasy as theory. *Journal of the American Psychoanalytic Association, 30,* 919–937.

Hartmann, H. (1964). *Essays on ego psychology.* New York: International Universities Press.

Hoffer, W. (1952). The mutual influences in the development of ego and id: Earliest stages. *Psychoanalytic Study of Children, 7,* 31–41.

Kohut, H. (1971). *The analysis of the self.* New York: International Universities Press.

Mahler, M. S. (1972). Rapprochement subphase of the separation–individuation process. *Psychoanalytic Quarterly, 41,* 487–506.

McIntosh, D. (1986). The ego and the self in the thought of S. Freud. *International Journal of Psychoanalysis, 67,* 429–448.

Meissner, W. W. (1986). Can psychoanalysis find its self? *Journal of the American Psychoanalytic Association, 34,* 379–400.

Pine, F. (1990). *Drive, ego, object and self.* New York: Basic Books.

Putnam, F. W. (1989). *Diagnosis and treatment of multiple personality disorder.* New York: Guilford Press.

Rapaport, D. (Ed. & Trans.; 1951a). *Organizational pathology of thought.* New York: Columbia University Press.

Rapaport, D. (1951b). States of consciousness: A psychopathological and psychodynamic view. In M. Gill (Ed.), *The collected papers of David Rapaport* (pp. 385–404). New York: Basic Books.

Sanders, L. W. (1983). Polarity, paradox, and the organizing process in development. In J. Call, E. Galenson, & R. Tyson (Eds.), *Frontiers of infant psychiatry* (pp. 333–346). New York: Basic Books.

Schachtel, E. (1959). *Metamorphosis.* New York: Basic Books.

Schilder, P. (1953). *Medical psychology.* New York: International Universities Press.

Spitz, R. (1965). *The first year of life.* New York: International Universities Press.

Spruiell, V. (1981). The self and the ego. *Psychoanalytic Quarterly, 50,* 319–344.

Straus, E. (1966). *Phenomenological psychology.* New York: Basic Books.

Suskind, P. (1991). *Perfume: The story of a murderer.* New York: Knopf.

Weiss, E. (1942). Emotional memories and acting out. *Psychoanalytic Quarterly, 11,* 477–492.

Weiss, E. (1957a). A comparative study of psychoanalytical ego concepts. *International Journal of Psycho-Analysis, 38,* 209–222.

Weiss, E. (1957b). The phenomenon of "ego passage." *Journal of the American Psychoanalytic Association, 5,* 267–281.

Winnicott, D. W. (1965). *The maturational processes and the facilitating environment.* New York: International Universities Press.

COMMENT:

Self-Observation and Subjective Self-Experiences

Mardi J. Horowitz

S heldon Bach begins his theory of self-organization from the perspective of the classical American ego psychologists and concludes it with a contemporary psychoanalytic view of intersubjectivity. I agree with his clinical observations. In what follows, I discuss his division of self-awareness into a polarity of subjective and abjective restate and then couch his theoretical perspective in a cognitive–psychodynamic language. I do so because I believe, such a language of theory offers some significant advantages (Horowitz, 1998).

Self-Observation and Character

Bach emphasizes the self-developmental importance of a capacity to oscillate between states of subjective and objective self-awareness. *Subjective experiences* are embedded in sensory impressions of the body and the external world. *Objective experiences* are distanced from this sensory bed. Both are important for evolving a complex and well-differentiated character structure. Character pathology can occur when subjective–objective oscillations are not fluid, when only one state is excessively maintained.

The person becomes limited in self-reflective contemplations when only subjective awareness occurs. Such a person may lack insight into his or her psychic dilemmas, interpersonal conundrums, and conflicts in roles. This type of individual would be likely to have (a) maladaptive interpersonal patterns, (b) impoverished self-observational capacity, (c) low conscious control over impulses, and (d) low recognition of motives. Rigid occupancy of only states of objective awareness can also lead to maladaptive character traits: low passion, absence of spontaneity, and impaired vitality.

Developing Adult Character

Advanced character development involves enhancement of self-observational skills. Eastern practices have emphasized mindfulness, and Western practices have emphasized insight. The split between experiencing and observing is useful in exploratory psychotherapy. How, then, can a mentor or therapist help a client develop self-observational skills?

Bach points out that for a therapist, "the critical step in developing the self-reflective capacity [of a patient] is precisely not to insist on it but rather to empathize with the patient's subjective world." Bach discusses the benefits that may then ensue using a contemporary psychoanalytic language of intersubjectivity: "As the patient's sense of his own self becomes secure, he is more and more able to tolerate the existence of another self and, ultimately, to recognize the analyst's right to a separate and autonomous life." I agree.

As a part of helping a patient to gain and use enhanced self-observational skills, I have found that it is valuable to teach him or her how to pay attention to, and deal with, multiple self-concepts. This corrects the view that one ought to have a unified, same, identity experience across diverse social contexts and different states of mind. These multiple patterns of self-concepts are derived from a repertoire of unconscious self-schematizations. Antithetical urges, contradictory self-beliefs, and clashing role values may result from conflicts within and between these self-schemas.

This multiplicity of self-concepts and schemas can lead to different states with different sensations of personal identity. The therapist can formulate this complexity of self-views as they are contained in role-relationship models. Role-relationship models are how schematic beliefs about traits of the self are associated with the characteristics of others and with expectations, intentions, and plans for transactions (Horowitz, 1998). Such formulations can be provided to a patient, allowing him or her to experience alternative self-concepts and role-relationship models as both—and rather than either—or.

Self-observation, which is an objective awareness of experiencing, allows a person to compare and contrast alternative views. The patient in the midst of a transference reaction can compare his or her distorted beliefs with a mental model stemming from a more realistic therapeutic alliance. The self-observing state can prime certain concepts and gate out other concepts. Such control processes can shift emotional balances. The patient may also forge new linkages between previously disparate concepts through improved self-observational skills. By work of this kind, a patient can learn to contain contradictions in aims and intentions. A larger, supraordinate structure of self-organization can be developed. Ambivalence may still exist, but beliefs of loving—trust and suspicion—hatred can be softened in the larger understanding.

A special duplication of ideas and feelings may occur during the split between self-experiencing and self-observing. Self-experiencing contains consciously represented ideas, feelings, and sensations. Some of these representations are duplicated in a mental model, during the process of self-observing.

The observing state allows an examination of these derivatives and, optimally, derivatives of other models as well. Some contradictions between mental models can be resolved by a reassessment. Other contradictions have to be understood, modified by choices, and the results accepted. Information processing then modifies previously enduring beliefs, cognitive maps, and schematizations of self. These changes can alter both current and future subjective self-experiences.

In other words, self-observing is a process that abstracts out and generalizes the package of elements involved in subjective conscious experiences. New kinds of information processing, revision of working models, and reschematization may result. This alters how future subjective experiences will occur. Many individual patients can learn this route to character growth, but this pathway is not for all comers.

Hazards

Self-observation and self-objectivity mean finding out more about the self. This has been hazardous for some people. Some people find that emergent meanings about the self lead to disorganized states, depersonalization, anxiety, confused thinking, or a chaotic sense of self-fragmentation.

A conceptual space for self-observation can be occupied with dreaded self-concepts that can diminish a sense of self-coherence. Although most people develop more self-sympathy, and although a better sense of a supraordinate self can contain contradictory motives, some people may become anxious and depressed, or vulnerable to exploitative mentors, such as in cults. That is why close therapeutic intersubjectivity, of the kind described by Bach, should be attempted only by well-trained and ethically solid clinicians.

Conclusion

Bach uses *ego* as a "scientific fantasy," an intrapsychic personification of a patient as observed by an analyst. He uses *self* as one pole of an interpsychic theory, the other pole being the object. I think a language that deals with person schemas, self-organization, and role-relationship models provides an improvement in theory (Horowitz, 1987, 1992, 1998; Horowitz, Eells, Singer, & Salovey 1995). Such language refers to *self* as a real entity (the whole of body, brain, and mind), to *self-concepts* as potentially conscious representations, and *self-schemas* as the stored and generalized models of self that can organize self-concepts and actual behaviors and that can be unconsciously communicated. Bach says his language is ambiguous and paradoxical, so I think he would agree.

References

Horowitz, M. J. (1987). *States of mind: Configurational analysis of individual psychology* (2nd ed.). New York: Plenum Press.

Horowitz, M. J. (1992). *Person schemas and maladaptive interpersonal patterns.* Chicago: University of Chicago Press.

Horowitz, M. J. (1998). *Cognitive psychodynamics: From conflict to character.* New York: Wiley.

Horowitz, M. J., Eels, T., Singer, J., & Salovey, P. (1995). Role-relationship models for case formulations. *Archives of General Psychiatry, 52,* 625–632.

CHAPTER 3

Configurational Analysis of the Self: A States-of-Mind Approach

Mardi J. Horowitz

A *state of mind* is a coherent pattern, a composite of observed experiences and expressions. The signs that combine into a pattern are verbal and nonverbal. Signs may include speech patterns (vocal inflection, pace, tone) and somatic patterns (facial expression, posture, gesture, action, style) as well as subjective experiences such as ideas, feelings, images, and bodily sensations. An important task in describing a state of mind involves noting the congruence or disparity of different signs. In some states of mind, the expressed verbal and nonverbal messages harmonize. The signs observed are comparable, compatible, and complementary. In other states of mind, discrepancy and contradiction between signs are noted. As discussed here, these may be *shimmering states*, which indicate conflicted motives. Shimmering states combine signs of two or more states. They are recognized by discords of emotion verbally and nonverbally.

Important factors to be observed include mood and apparent self-regulation. The latter factor involves the appearance of modulation of all forms of emotional communication. A state may be seen as undermodulated if leakage beyond what is intended occurs. Negative moods, even intense sad or angry ones, are not necessarily undermodulated. An expression of anger, sorrow, or fear can, for example, be quite frank and direct. In contrast to such *well-modulated* expressions, an *undermodulated* state would exhibit some sign of loss of control. Emotional expressions can also appear *overmodulated,* as in feigned nervousness, stony coldness, pouting, or simulated attention-seeking sadness. Thus, well-modulated states are those in which a person appears to be in self-command, appropriately spontaneous, openly expressive, and adequately controlled in terms of releasing and containing impulses. Overmodulated states are those in which the person appears unspontaneous, sealed off, and rigidly contained. In undermodulated states, expressions seem sudden, impulsive, and poorly controlled.

Giving states descriptive and customized names facilitates their recognition and explanation. For example, if the person has a throbbing pulse, weak knees, feelings of faintness, intense sweatiness, and thoughts of impending harm, with confusion about what to do next, a label of *distraught fear* or *flooded panic* might be used as a shorthand attempt to name the state. This individualized labeling is clearer, and more empathic, than using the word *anxiety* with all patients. A personal symbol may serve as a name, as in a patient who called a florid panic her "purple terror." Such a state name can then be used in the dialogue of psychotherapy and for independent self-observation as well.

Clarity and an early sense of control occur in psychotherapy when clinicians help patients to relate particular symptoms to the states that contain them. Transition into and out of these states then becomes a focus of self-observation, with an aim to find ways to avoid problematic and *dreaded states*. It is also helpful, when formulating a case, that the clinician be aware that the state of mind that contains symptoms may be the result of a defensive compromise. The defense is a problem, perhaps, but not as great as the one that might occur in a more dreaded state. Thus, formulation of states of mind introduces concepts about wishes for *desired states,* fear of dreaded states, and defenses.

There may be other *compromise states* that do not contain symptoms but simply omit desired experiences to avoid threats associated with wishes. These can be called *quasi-adaptive compromises* if they are too far removed from the qualities that would characterize desired adaptive states. Once again, in a states-of-mind approach, wishes are formulated as states of mind the person would like to enter. Fears are understood as states of mind that are dreaded—usually states colored by undermodulated, negative emotions of fear, shame, guilt, despair, or hate. Defenses are formulated as compromise states used to avoid the risk that dreaded states may occur. The dynamic interplay of wish, fear, and defensive motives is clarified as configurations of desired, dreaded, and compromise states.

The causes of state repetitions can be inferred to deepen a case formulation. This involves forming hypotheses about *person schemas,* the general cognitive maps of self–other relationships (Horowitz, 1988, 1992, 1998). Internal factors, such as memories, fantasies, motivations, and excitation levels, are also considered. Each state of mind tends to be organized by activation of particular person schemas from the person's repertoire of alternative views. These views are not conscious, yet they determine repetitive patterns, such as maladaptive state cycles. Different self-concepts may organize different states, evoking a variety of identity experiences and relationship expectations.

Patterned aggregations of meanings assemble to form each *self-schema*. These aggregations are complex networks of associational connections. The result is an unconscious cognitive map. Activation of the map or schema can influence information processing and conscious representations. An experience of a certain identity may result. In the absence of such influences, the person may feel depersonalized, chaotic, or fragmented.

Associated beliefs in a self-schema include body image, role of self vis-à-vis others, memories about self in the role, emotional response style, scripts of action, values, self-regulatory style, and future plans. Each self-schema is a complex package. To make matters more complex, overall self-organization includes multiple self-schemas. That complexity is essential, for each person has multiple possible identity experiences.

Such a theory tells clinicians that their patients may vary in level of supraordinate schematization. Some people have developed only relatively singular self-schemas, and these may be dissociated (e.g., narcissistically vulnerable and borderline characters). Other people have developed harmonizing supraordinate schemas (e.g., normal and neurotic characters). People with better supraordinate schemas can usually handle stress from their own contradictions without explosive changes in state. People with very limited hierarchical schematization may distort reality severely to account for explosive state changes or to protect themselves from chaos, shame, guilt, or despair.

As for the contents of repeated maladaptive interpersonal patterns, these are clarified by seeing how roles of the self pertain to internalized views of relationships with others, ones that include not only the roles of other people but also scripts of expected or intended transactions between the self and others. Such roles and scripts, including emotional expression sequences, are inferred as *role relationship models*. Like self-schemas, role relationship models are schemas. These cognitive maps about people influence information processing in ways that are not usually represented consciously. Derivatives, however, can be described, and the model can be interpreted from repeated patterns. What becomes conscious are the feeling or mood of the transaction, and memories and fantasies, as well as calculations, about the transactions that have been, are, and will be.

In each new relationship, the heart or soul may yearn for a new opportunity, but the unconscious mind tends to repeat past schemas and so past cycles. The mind forms a working model of a current interpersonal situation, and this working model is influenced by whatever past and enduring models become activated. The enduring schemas are generalizations from previous relationships. The actual social transaction contributes to the working model and to the activation of enduring role relationship models. The actual transactions are also influenced by the working model and the activated enduring models. A patient may operate from a working model that is quite irrational in regard to the actual ongoing situation and its opportunities; this is called a *transference reaction*. A great deal of the communication in psychotherapy is directed at modifying these interactions. The end result reschematizes enduring person schemas, and corrective relationship experiences are thus retained in a generalized form of memory.

Because people have varied self-schemas and varied role relationship models within their overall self-organization, they may behave differently at different times with the same significant other. They may shift schemas and so repeat a maladaptive cycle of states. Some of these shifts are from the ebb and flow of desire; others are from defensive reactions to threats, such as activation of a dreaded role relationship model that could lead to a dreaded state. To understand these cycles one can formulate configurations of role relationship models.

For any significant adult attachment a person may have several recurring role relationship models. These exist as a configuration for the internal bonding to the significant other. Cycles through the configuration may occur. An example is a state of loving another until a fear of rejection results in a shift to a state of tense hypervigilance and then to a sullen state on separation. A more complete example follows.

Configurational Analysis

States of mind are imbedded with other categories of explanation, such as person schemas, in a systematic approach to formulation called *configurational analysis* (Horowitz, 1979, 1987, 1992, 1997, 1998). A configurational analysis comprises five steps. The first, identified as *phenomena,* involves the selection and description of symptoms, the determination of what problems need to be explained, and the clarification of the events that precipitated the problems. This step leads to the description of the various *states of mind* in which the selected phenomena do and do not occur. This second step would include (if seen) a description of the recurrent and maladaptive cycles of states as well as the stressors that trigger the problematic states. The analysis of states then leads to the third step, which is a description of *topics of concern and defensive control processes* leading to problematic states. This step includes how expressions of ideas and emotions are obscured and how avoidant states may function to ward off dreaded, undermodulated states and defensive styles. The fourth step concerns *identity and relationships.* It includes descriptions of the organizing roles, beliefs, and scripts that organize important states, wish–fear dilemmas in relation to desired and dreaded role relationship models, how defensive-compromise role relationship models ward off dangers, and dysfunctional attitudes and beliefs. The final steps involve *integration into a configuration* and *therapy planning*—specifically, considerations of the interactions of phenomena, states, controls, and role relationship models and plans to stabilize working states, to prevent pathological actions, to alter dysfunctional beliefs and to advance biological, social, and psychological capacities. The following case illustrates this method of formulation (Horowitz, 1981, 1999).

Phenomena

Mr. Taylor presented mixed symptoms of anxiety and depression. These symptoms worsened when he became preoccupied that he might lose both his job and his recent marriage. Mr. Taylor had excessive rage attacks in which he was verbally abusive, arrogant, and insulting. Such episodes threatened his work and marriage.

States of Mind

Hostile verbal abuse occurred most frequently during Mr. Taylor's states of self-righteous indignation. A description of his behavior follows.

Mr. Taylor and his wife were constructing shelves in his office. He assigned her the task of screwing shelf brackets to the wall. She was cheerful and willing, but she nicked the wall when her screwdriver slipped off the head of the screw. He shouted, "You clumsy idiot!" and glared furiously at her. She was frightened and hurt. He then had a state transition. He felt shame and self-disgust as well as fear of her potential responses.

When Mr. Taylor described this experience in therapy, he relived the state of self-righteous indignation. His voice became an angry roar. Then, as more details emerged, he focused on the petty way he had responded, how he had hurt his wife's feelings. He was afraid she might divorce him. He entered a shimmering state, with a whiny, complaining, weak voice. He sought reassurance as he showed facial expressions that flitted from shame to anger and then to anxiety.

A state cycle from calm happiness; to self-righteous indignation; to shame, rage, and anxiety also had occurred at work. Mr. Taylor was in charge of supervising rigorous safety precautions. Much of the time, he observed these precautions, but there were times when he ignored them. After a period of noncompliance, he again would carry out the precautions. He was then vulnerable to a shift in state if he saw a coworker being noncompliant. When others committed an infraction of safety rules, he viciously censured them with curses and vindictiveness. He would eventually realize that he had been too loud and abusive. He would subsequently experience a confusing mood because of an emotional medley of shame, anger, and anxiety.

Topics of Concern and Defensive Control Processes

Mr. Taylor was preoccupied with whom to blame. To externalize blame, Mr. Taylor distorted the cause-and-effect sequences in his narrations. He slid meanings to minimize his own responsibilities for turbulent relationships. Before treatment, for example, he was unclear about the degree of his responsibility for the recurrent problem of abusiveness. His views of his own agency shifted from state to state. He was sometimes verbally abusive when the therapist focused on stories about his rage at others. "Obviously," he would say sarcastically, "you again think these things are only my fault, and not caused by the bad attributes of others." In some states of mind, he would tell a story as if the other person had caused the episode. If this view were challenged, he shifted to focusing on the topic of how the therapist was clumsy, negligent, and unnecessary.

Identity and Relationships

Mr. Taylor modified meanings in a slippery way to retell stories so as to exaggerate the faults of others. He did this to shift blame from self to other and so to prevent entry into a dreaded state of shame. Psychotherapy discussions clarified his alternative identity roles as a shamed person and as a righteous person. This also clarified an introject, a very harsh but unreliable critic who said whether self or other was at fault.

In the self-righteous rage state, Mr. Taylor felt the critic was on his side. He was in the role of an admired, heroic avenger, battling with another person in the role of a monstrous foe. Transition to the confusing mixed shame–rage–anxiety state occurred when Mr. Taylor felt his behavior was criticized. Then his role was less strong and grand, and he also felt in this transition of state as if the "critic" had betrayed him.

Such role relationship models applied to the instance when his wife nicked the wall with her screwdriver. His attachment to his wife was one in which her function was as an extension of himself. By his recent marriage, he had added his wife and her good attributes to himself. However, if his wife were bad, he would be contaminated. When she nicked his office wall, for example, his self-righteous rage stemmed from images of his wife as humiliating him before imagined others. He felt devalued personally, and he retaliated by calling her a clumsy idiot. He said she made him feel like an arthritic dog.

I have illustrated formulation, focusing on current intentions and expectations as well as ideas, emotions, and defenses. From here-and-now beliefs and fantasies, one may probe more deeply into the development of identity beliefs and relational schemas for affectional ties. For example, Mr. Taylor's mother and his father had historically, as he remembered it, conspicuously and rapidly shifted the nature of their alliances with each other and him when he was a child. The innocent became the guilty, and vice versa, in a treacherous sea of shifting affiliations. The roles that frequently shifted were (a) the hostile aggressor who would insult and injure a weak victim, (b) an innocent victim who could attack an aggressor, and (c) a critic who would rescue and soothe the innocent and evoke shame in the guilty party.

His mother was effusively warm, intrusive, and hypochondriacal. Some of the time she cared, but she easily missed the target of who needed that care. At other times, anxiety and depression made her seem remote and seemingly uncaring. The patient experienced this as a shift in her view of him from worthy of her attention to viewing him as unworthy of her compassion and love.

His father was a high-status, highly productive man who seemed unable to express interpersonal positive emotions. When Mr. Taylor stuttered, his father sneered. During episodes of "bad" behavior, his father disparagingly referred to him as "her son." When his father saw the family as deficient, he detached himself for weeks at a time, concentrating only on his work. The father modeled the role of a critic who would abandon relationships whenever displeased.

Each person in the mother–father–son triad alternately was admired and then blamed for problems by the other two. Mr. Taylor needed his mother, but he was repeatedly mortified by her incompetence. She had intense social anxiety and clung to him for support in social situations, as if to say, "Look at the mother with her son, not at just me." Just when she wooed his alliance most intensely, he wanted most earnestly to dissociate himself from her.

A similar pattern occurred between the mother and father. She could show off his high work status; he could show off her warmth. Each used a trait of the other to enhance self-esteem. But the father would suddenly shift from admiring attachment to remoteness and withdrawal when his wife erred in even a minor way. For example, he shifted to remoteness when she seemed self-preoccupied. She then retaliated with anger at being exposed to scorn, or she became glum. The father's shift from closeness to distance, and the mother's shift from admiration to shame, blame, anger, and despair provided Mr. Taylor with his expectations of betrayal. His father's shifts provided Mr. Taylor with the template for his own defensive maneuvers.

Mr. Taylor had learned from experience and identification various roles and defenses that had become maladaptive traits of character. His culture emphasized status through visible accomplishments and enhanced the importance of pride–shame polarities. It was unclear whether there were also traits of biologically determined temperament, such as easy arousal of shame and rage affects.

Integration Into a Configuration

Selected inferences about states, defenses, and person schemas can be patterned into configurations. Such configurations present information in a simultaneous format rather than the sequentially attended format formed in prose. The simultaneous format clarifies the possibilities for parallel processing of topics by multiple self- and other concepts. It shows defensive compromises used to avoid wish–fear dilemmas. Figures can illustrate how any memory or social event might be mentally processed, leading to various possible states.

What follows illustrates one such configuration for Mr. Taylor. It involves

FIGURE 3.1

A recurrent state cycle of Mr. Taylor.

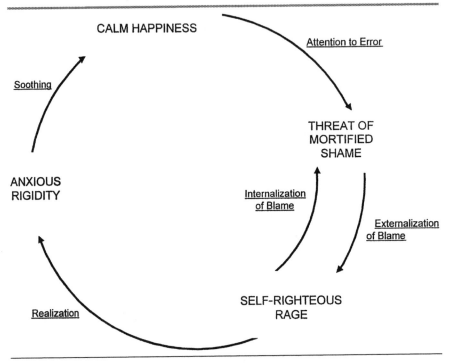

a repeated cycle of states that was noted in the stories he told. Mr. Taylor spoke of how he desired a mood of calm happiness but could not stabilize this state. He was hypervigilant to errors "in the air." Any threat of error in himself or a self-object might activate his potential for a state of mind organized emotionally by a very deflated set of self-concepts. He externalized blame to avoid this dreaded state of mortified shame—so much shame that it could kill him. This externalization triggered a shift into his most problematic state, that of an impulsive, self-impairing, but temporarily exhilarating anger. He felt, for a moment, strong and powerful in a state of self-righteous rage.

Mr. Taylor realized that his excessive hostility threatened to activate schemas that would lead him into the dreaded state of shame. To defend against either rage or shame, he rigidly monitored his every expression and tended to long remain in a state of anxious rigidity. He begged for reassurance from self-objects such as his wife. With enough soothing, he could experience calm happiness. Too readily, however, the cycle would turn again in motion, whenever error was once more in the spotlight of his vigilance for personal blemishes (see Figure 3.1).

Four states recur in the cycle shown in Figure 3.1: a dreaded state of shame instead of a desired state of calm, and two compromise (or defensive) states to ward off deflation of self-esteem. The most problematic of these compromise states was the rage that threatened to end Mr. Taylor's job and marriage. The more adaptive, but merely quasi-adaptive compromise was anxious rigidity. A role relationship model for each state in this configuration can be developed from his narratives. Such a configuration of desired, dreaded, and compromise role relationship models is shown in Figure 3.2.

Planning Psychotherapy

In any situation where blame was in the air, Mr. Taylor expected betrayal. This triggered him to enter into a self-righteous rage state because he externalized blame to others to avoid shame. The self-righteous rage was a defense against his most dreaded state; it predicted a negative response from Mr. Taylor if and when a therapist would clarify his problems and dynamics. Empathic support was considered an important initial technique to prevent an otherwise-likely disruption of treatment. Tact was important as a supportive measure. At first, criticism was carefully avoided in favor of remarks that heightened a sense of realistic rather than grandiose competence. Only gradually were the deeper beliefs about self and other, as related to rage and shame, interpreted.

At the level of phenomena, the therapist might offer to help Mr. Taylor avoid episodes of future abusiveness as a way of reducing the risk of losing his job and marriage; this would foster development of a therapeutic alliance. The next technique, at the level of states, would be to focus on his hypervigilance to error by helping him to use conscious attention to potential triggers before states of self-righteous rage occur. Clear labeling of each state would be an important activity; naming potential states often quickly increases a patient's sense of control. Clarifying a state cycle helps a patient anticipate what is coming, and conscious control of attention can sometimes prevent entry into a dangerous undermodulated state.

Next, the medley of emotions in his mixed anxiety, shame, and anger state could be "unpacked" because this was, for him, a very confusing and vexing combination. His anxious rigidity would be clarified by stating the beliefs involved in his expectations of embarrassment and his reactive hostility. As he gained awareness of his feelings, the beliefs that led to them could be compared and challenged. His wishes and intentions could be clarified. He could gain further control of his hostility. Then the beliefs, memories, and fantasies that led to his shame states could be explored. The level of interpretation could gradually deepen from a focus on phenomena to clarifications of his relationship motives, beliefs, values, intentions, and expectations.

The topic of concern—whom to blame—could be a focus at each level of depth. It is predicted to come up in transference phenomena and in stories

FIGURE 3.2

A configuration of role-relationship models for Mr. Taylor. For practical illustrations of "how to do it," see Horowitz (1997) and (1987); for theory, see Horowitz (1998); for research methods, see Horowitz (1992).

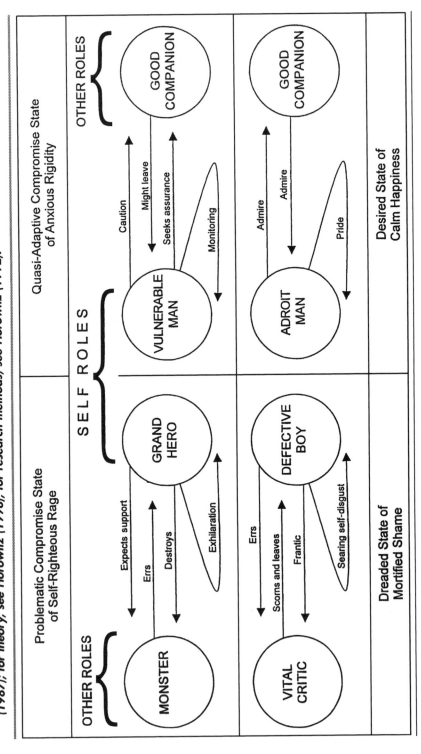

of outside relationships. The therapist could first establish an alliance on an agreed-on focus of joint attention. He could tactfully reduce cognitive and emotional distortions caused by sliding meanings. Then, as Mr. Taylor learned to use therapy and trust the therapist, core beliefs about self and others could be explored and dysfunctional attitudes challenged. A self-analytic process of awareness, insight, and new decisions could be encouraged. New models of how to deal with criticism, both his own and others, could be formed.

In process, one would look for the effects of such techniques. The therapist would hope that Mr. Taylor would gradually improve his state of anxiously rigid self-monitoring, that he would gradually be able to reduce his expectations of dire and harsh criticism or abrupt betrayal. His sense of self-competence would be expected to increase so that neither chaotic inferiority nor grandiose superiority would mar his ability to live well.

Establishing clear formulations help the patient and therapist specify goals in therapy. Such goals renew hope and encourage the struggle to form new self-regulatory abilities. Further formulations could then be made to correct the inevitable errors or shallowness in initial formulations.

Research

We psychotherapists are sometimes accused of "psychobabble." One reason is that we hatch new schools of thought rather than resolve arguments. Also leading clinical theorists are sometimes conquistadors rather than scientists. They seldom reach a consensus. One way to promote what we need—more integration and fewer brand names—is to tackle the problem of consensus. Even complex clinical constructs can be simplified so that some estimate of reliability of clinical judgments can be assessed. This effort has two fruits: One is that the results show whether or not reliable independent ratings were reached; the other is that stating what is to be judged gets very clear through a series of iterations—those steps required to reach any kind of reliable judgment between clinicians when they examine the same material.

The configurational-analysis method developed in that manner, a combined pathway of clinical practice, clinical teaching, and clinical research. The three major constructs—states of mind, cognitive defensive operations, and role relationship models—were tested for reliability and validity. On person schemas, I and my colleagues had (thanks to a major award from the MacArthur Foundation) multiple clinicians working on the same clinical materials from psychotherapy. From their diverse dispositions, some significant concordances were found, which are summarized in *Person Schemas and Maladaptive Interpersonal Patterns* (Horowitz, 1992) and *Cognitive Psychodynamics: From Conflict to Character* (Horowitz, 1998). The role relationship models format used in the figures evolved and proved reliable (Eells, Horowitz, et al., 1995; Horowitz & Eells, 1993; Horowitz, Eells, Singer, & Salovey, 1995). In addition, the defensive aspect contained categories (Horowitz, 1997) found to foster clinician agreement (Horowitz et al., 1992) and quantitative validity (Horowitz, Milbrath, & Stinson, 1995). That work succeeded in part because we departed from classical psychoanalytic lists of defensive mechanisms and used instead a cognitive science theory of how people could alter information processing to ward off dreaded states.

Perhaps the most user- (clinician-) friendly aspect of configurational analysis is the early step of formulation: states of mind. For that reason, I summarize research on the reliability and validity of state analysis in more detail. Empirical studies have shown that judges can reliably agree in rating categorically defined states (Horowitz, 1979, 1987; Horowitz, Milbrath, Ewert, et al., 1994; Horowitz, Milbrath, Jordan, et al., 1994; Horowitz, Milbrath, & Stinson, 1995; Marmar, Wilner, & Horowitz, 1984). Our clinical hypothesis is that certain topics will occur more frequently in certain states. Data from two patients with pathological grief reactions illustrate this link. General state definitions were used so patients could be compared. Common topics brought up by these patients in their psychotherapy sessions included the following: recent death; the relationship of self with the deceased; and identity, current intimacy, work, and other topics. In a series of individual case studies, we found we could reliably score topics and examine their correlations with process and form-of-expression variables (Horowitz et al., 1993; Horowitz, Milbrath, Jordan, et al., 1994; Milbrath, Bauknight, Horowitz, Amaro, & Sugahara, 1995; Stinson, Milbrath, & Horowitz, 1995).

Patient A

This patient met diagnostic criteria of posttraumatic stress disorder and major depressive disorder. She had lost her husband through a sudden, violent death and felt conflict over restoring intimacy by starting a new relationship. The topic of the death of her spouse, the conflictual focus of her psychotherapy, was more frequent in her discourse during undermodulated and shimmering states. The three most conflictual topics were (a) the death of her spouse, (b) her new intimacy, and (c) problems with self-development. This last one contained issues about her identity because she was no longer a wife. All three topics were disproportionately more present in the shimmering and undermodulated states. This patient initiated every topic, save one, at least 80% of the time. The one excepted topic involved the process of therapy, which included discussing her attitudes about the therapist, the dialogue, time, and the research context of the treatment. This topic was brought up half the time by the therapist, which occurred most often during periods of resistance and was disproportionately present during overmodulated states.

On a measure of the impact of her loss on everyday life, Patient A reported that she experienced more intrusion and avoidance episodes during the week preceding the therapy sessions in which she was judged to more frequently exhibit shimmering states of mind. That is, when she experienced more intrusive and avoidant experiences during the recent week outside therapy, she showed more emotion, with more stifling efforts in discordant states, during the discourse in her therapy sessions. When she reported less distress on the impact measure, she was more likely to manifest overmodulated states in therapy. She also evidenced significant correlational patterns between various states of mind experienced in session and various psychiatric symptomatology experienced in the week prior to her session; for example, there was a significant negative relationship between observed, well-modulated states and self-reports of anxiety and paranoid ideation.

Patient B

This patient had an adjustment disorder related to a loss event. He had had a long-term ambivalent relationship with his brother, who had been murdered a year earlier. He felt confused about the course of his career and his sexuality. The most conflictual topics were (a) sexuality, (b) the grieving process, and (c) expectations of criticism from the therapist. These topics were disproportionately more present during shimmering states, and two of them were more prominent during undermodulated states. Discourse on nonproblematic therapy process and nonproblematic self-evolution occurred predominantly during overmodulated states.

This patient also evidenced significant correlations between various observed state categories and fluctuating intrusions and avoidances on the self-report measure regarding the impact of the loss of his brother in his life outside of therapy for the prior week. Specifically, undermodulated states and shimmering states in session correlated negatively with more avoidant experiences outside of treatment. When Patient B reported more psychiatric symptoms, his therapy sessions had lower proportions of well-modulated states. When he reported more symptoms regarding somatization and hostility, he was more likely to exhibit undermodulated states in session. This correlation converged with the clinical observation of an association between angry feelings and his sense of feeling out of control. The proportion of overmodulated states was higher during periods in therapy when he reported more depression and psychoticism.

Summary

These results indicate interesting relationships between various states of mind experienced in psychotherapy and various topics of concern and defensive control processes, as well as between various in-session states and important clinical phenomena outside of therapy. For example, the presence of shimmering or undermodulated states identified conflictual topics. Furthermore, undermodulated states in therapy are likely to correlate with higher levels of intrusive thinking and unbidden affects in current life. Excessive defensive control, assessed by observation of overmodulated states in therapy, may be associated with consequences of avoiding vital but conflicted topics, leading to depression and somatization.

Conclusion

The key constructs of states, person schemas, and defensive control processes are combined in the steps of configurational analysis. This is a system of formulation that can lead to plans for helping patients change. It also leads to conceptualizations that can be communicated directly to patients. The configurational-analysis approach integrates cognitive and psychodynamic points of view. Although this integration could offend classicists of either position, there are gratifying aspects—and empirical support from clinical research.

Psychoanalysts may feel that the structural theory of id–ego–superego is missing, but the conflict model of interacting forces is still present, cast in close-to-observation and close-to-consciousness terms involving person schemas. Cognitive–behaviorists may feel that multiple selves and defensive layerings are too "unconscious" and complex, but these obscurities and knotted yarns are required for understanding why people may not change in response to simple suggestions. The advantage of integration outweighs, I believe, the advantage of retaining venerable theories.

References

Eells, T., Horowitz, M. J., Singer, J., Salovey, P., Dangle, D., & Turrey, C. (1995). The role relationship models method: A comparison of independently derived case formulations. *Psychotherapy Research, 5,* 161–178.

Horowitz, M. J. (1979). *States of mind: Analysis of change in psychotherapy.* New York: Plenum Press.

Horowitz, M. J. (1981). Self righteous rage and the attribution of blame. *Archives of General Psychiatry, 38,* 1233–1238.

Horowitz, M. J. (1987). *States of mind: Configurational analysis of individual personality* (2nd ed.). New York: Plenum Press.

Horowitz, M. J. (1988). *Introduction to psychodynamics.* New York: Basic Books.

Horowitz, M. J. (Ed.). (1992). *Person schemas and maladaptive interpersonal patterns.* Chicago: University of Chicago Press.

Horowitz, M. J. (1997). *Formulation as a basis for planning psychotherapy treatment.* Washington, DC: American Psychiatric Press.

Horowitz, M. J. (1998). *Cognitive psychodynamics: From conflict to character.* New York: Wiley.

Horowitz, M. J. (1999). Formulation to plan psychotherapy. In D. Spiegel (Ed.), *Psychotherapeutic frontiers.* Washington, DC: American Psychiatric Press.

Horowitz, M. J., Cooper, S., Fridhandler, B., Perry, J. C., Bond, M., & Valliant, C. (1992). Control processes and defense mechanisms. *Journal of Psychotherapy Research and Practice, 1,* 324–336.

Horowitz, M. J., & Eells, T. (1993). Case formulation using role-relationship configurations: Reliability. *Psychotherapy Research, 3,* 57–68.

Horowitz, M. J., Eells, T., Singer, J., & Salovey, P. (1995). Role relationship models for case formulations. *Archives of General Psychiatry, 53,* 627–654.

Horowitz, M. J., Milbrath, C., Ewert, M., Sonneborn, D., & Stinson, C. H. (1994). Cyclical patterns of states of mind in psychotherapy. *American Journal of Psychiatry, 151,* 1767–1770.

Horowitz, M. J., Milbrath, C., Jordan, D., Stinson, C. H., Ewert, M., Redington, D. J., Fridhandler, B., Reidbord, S. P., & Hartley, D. (1994). Expressive and defensive behavior during discourse on unresolved topics: A single case study. *Journal of Personality, 62,* 527–563.

Horowitz, M., Milbrath, C., & Stinson, C. (1995). Signs of defensive control locate conflicted topics in discourse. *Archives of General Psychiatry, 52,* 1040–1057.

Horowitz, M. J., Stinson, C., Curtis, D., Ewert, M., Redington, D., Singer, J., Bucci, W., Mergenthaler, E., & Milbrath, C. (1993). Topics and signs: Defensive control of emotional expression. *Journal of Consulting and Clinical Psychology, 61,* 421–430.

Marmar, C., Wilner, N., & Horowitz, M. (1984). Recurrent patient states in psychotherapy: Segmentation and quantification. In L. Rice & L. Greenberg (Eds.), *Patterns of change* (pp. 194–212). New York: Guilford Press.

Milbrath, C., Bauknight, R., Horowitz, M. J., Amaro, R., & Sugahara, C. (1995). Sequential analysis of topics in psychotherapy discourse: A single case study. *Psychotherapy Research, 5,* 199–217.

Stinson, C., Milbrath, C., & Horowitz, M. (1995). Dysfluency and topic orientation in bereaved individuals: Bridging individual and group studies. *Journal of Consulting and Clinical Psychology, 63,* 37–45.

Researchable States of Mind

Sheldon Bach

Although I do not really feel qualified to discuss many of the research aspects of Mardi J. Horowitz's chapter, I do know enough about this kind of research to appreciate the immensity and successfulness of this effort, which has been going for decades, and to admire the ingenuity, skill, and sheer persistence required to do creative research in this field. So I confine my remarks to those sections of the chapter that intersect with my own area of expertise.

I find the states-of-mind approach very congenial, as it fits well with my own approach, which is influenced largely by Rapaport's (1951a, 1951b) discussions of states of consciousness and Kohut's (1971) emphasis on self-states. Indeed, using a form of simple clinical observation that is a much less scientific enterprise than that of Horowitz, I tried early on to delineate the state of mind or state of consciousness of the typical narcissistic patient and show how it differed from the presumed normal state of consciousness (Bach, 1977). The parameters on which I made these distinctions were largely taken from Rapaport and included varieties of awareness, body schema, organization of thought and language, patterns of arousal and affect, individual thresholds, and senses of agency and spontaneity, among others. Many of these are implied in Horowitz's signs, but he has of course codified them in a way that makes them amenable to interrater reliability, statistical manipulation, and hard research. He has also emphasized the importance of congruency or disparity between signs and given the latter the evocative name of *shimmering states*.

More important, he has embedded the states-of-mind approach in a larger systematic program of research that he calls *configurational analysis* and has tested these constructs of states of mind, cognitive defensive operations, and role relationships models for reliability and validity. This leads to a reliable and validated system of formulations that can aid in planning and, I believe, in teaching psychotherapy and also helping the patient to change.

When I turn to the chapter's section on psychotherapy, I begin to feel more at home with the material. The case of Mr. Taylor appears, after all, to be similar to many cases that clinicians work with all the time. And certainly the recommendations for planning psychotherapy appear to make good clinical sense. Horowitz writes that "clear labeling of each state would be an important activity; naming potential states often quickly increases a patient's sense of control." I very much agree with this and with his contention that "clarifying a state cycle helps a patient anticipate what is coming, and conscious control of attention can sometimes prevent entry into a dangerous undermodulated state." The "unpacking" of emotions in states of mixed affects is also a useful clinical tool. These, and many other precepts that Horowitz condenses in a line or two, illustrate for me not only his hard-won clinical acumen but also the value of the states-of-mind approach for clinical work.

Mr. Taylor is a man whom psychoanalysts would see as having a narcissistic character disorder that affects his self-esteem and his ability to self-reflect and self-regulate and to make deep and enduring relationships with people. Patients like this are subject to extreme shame and rage reactions, and so it would certainly be important, as Horowitz suggests, to use tact, to avoid criticism, and to try to heighten the patient's sense of realistic rather than grandiose competence. But because the sense of competence and self-esteem is, in my experience, so intimately connected to partially unconscious issues of omnipotence, sadomasochism, envy, and shame, I would not really expect cognitive interventions to have a deep or lasting impact. I take it that this is what Horowitz means when he suggests that gradually deeper beliefs about self and other as related to rage and shame would be interpreted. This area has been much explored in the analytic literature by Balint (1968), Kohut (1971), and others.

As a minor quibble, I am not as certain as Horowitz is that offering to help the patient avoid episodes of abusiveness in the future would necessarily foster the development of a therapeutic alliance. This might work in short-term psychotherapy and achieve limited benefits if one were careful to terminate on the initial positive transference. But analytic experience with patients of this kind suggests that all of their relationships—whether with spouses, or coworkers, or therapist—are either idealized or devalued and based on a sadomasochistic paradigm (Bach, 1994). Consequently, one might expect that the same behavior Mr. Taylor demonstrated with his wife and coworkers would eventually come to permeate the transference or therapeutic alliance and would have to be dealt with not only through rational cognitive means—to which these patients are notoriously inaccessible—but also through what has come to be called "enactments" (Ellman & Moskowitz, 1998) between patient and therapist.

Here I come to the only substantial exception I take to this chapter, which is one primarily of omission. The psychoanalytic and therapeutic literature has been filled in recent years with articles emphasizing the interactional nature of the psychotherapeutic enterprise and the importance of the therapist's personality to the outcome of the therapy. Just as other fields, such as physics or psychosomatics, were in the 20th century obliged to come to terms with the influence of the observer on the observed, psychotherapists have also learned that in fact not all therapies are created equal. The personality of the therapist turns out to be a major factor in the responses elicited from the patient and is a subject of much current concern in investigations of enactments, or the playing out of unconscious role relationships by both patient and therapist.

Horowitz bypasses this knotty problem by seeming to implicitly assume that the pathology resides exclusively in the patient and that the personal equation of the therapist is not part of the total configurational analysis. Now, I am certain that Horowitz is well aware of this issue and has decided, for reasons of research strategy and perhaps other reasons as well, to not engage with it at the moment. Personally, I find it difficult even when writing a simple clinical description to give adequate recognition to the interpersonal and intersubjective complexities of the interactions. How much more difficult must it be to incorporate these interactions into research protocols that are designed to be tested by statistical analysis!

So I realize that this is asking a great deal, particularly because even the clinical literature has only recently come around to this position. But I think that research also must eventually tackle this problem of bringing the experimenter within the purview of the experiment, at least conceptually.

In the meantime, I have in this chapter a snapshot of a research program that is engaged in important conceptual and terminological clarifications that may or may not reduce the internecine warfare between "schools" of psychotherapy but will certainly be immensely informative for all those who are open enough to want to know what research actually shows. On the basis of this brief report, I cannot detect any gross incompatibilities with the clinical–anecdotal literature, which gives me a reassuring sense that at least we are all talking about the same thing. I know that this encourages me, and perhaps other clinicians as well, to want to read further in this literature, which gives us a complementary yet integratable perspective on the work we are all doing.

References

Bach, S. (1977). On the narcissistic state of consciousness. *International Journal of Psychoanalysis, 58,* 209–233.

Bach, S. (1994). *The language of perversion and the language of love.* Northvale, NJ: Aronson.

Balint, M. (1968). *The basic fault.* London: Tavistock.

Ellman, S., & Moskowitz, M. (1998). *Enactment.* Northvale, NJ: Aronson.

Kohut, H. (1971). *The analysis of the self.* New York: International Universities Press.

Rapaport, D. (1951a). *Organization and pathology of thought* (D. Rapaport, Trans. & Ed.). New York: Columbia University Press.

Rapaport, D. (1951b). States of consciousness: A psychopathological and psychodynamic view. In M. Gill (Ed.), *The collected papers of David Rapaport* (pp. 385–404). New York: Basic Books.

CHAPTER 4

The Self as a Singular Multiplicity: A Process–Experiential Perspective

William J. Whelton

Leslie S. Greenberg

*P*rocess–experiential therapy (Greenberg & Paivio, 1997; Greenberg, Rice, & Elliott, 1993) offers a conceptualization of the self based on a set of rudimentary tenets. In this emotion-focused approach, the self is constructed and is an ongoing, self-organizing process. The self is best understood as an emergent organization of more basic elements, in which emotion is the basic glue that binds the different elements at the most explicit level. Constructing the self involves an ongoing process of identifying with and symbolizing experience as one's own and, by so doing, disowning or not identifying with other aspects of experience. This process acts to separate one's experience from that of another and allows certain experiences to be seen as continuous within oneself. In this chapter, we develop this constructivist view of self-functioning, using dynamic-systems and dialectical–constructivist theories to show how the constantly evolving self operates as a synthesizing process, creating and being created anew in each moment and situation (Greenberg et al., 1993; Greenberg & Paivio, 1997; Greenberg & Van Balen, 1998; Perls, Hefferline, & Goodman, 1951; Rogers, 1959).

The Process–Experiential Concept of the Self

The theoretical framework that forms the basis for explaining the process–experiential view of self-functioning is provided by dynamic-systems theory (Thelen & Smith, 1994; Varela, Thompson, & Rosch, 1991) and by the theory of dialectical constructivism (Greenberg & Pascual-Leone, 1995; Pascual-Leone, 1987, 1991; Pascual-Leone & Johnson, 1991).

Dynamic-systems theory attempts to explain the process of change in certain complex systems. The elements that form a dynamic system are self-organizing, but within given parameters they assume a preferred or habitual state called an *attractor* state. These systems and their surroundings, however, are in flux, and a small shift in initial conditions can result in a different synthesis of elements or attractor states. Biological systems tend to be complex, dynamic systems of this type. Thelen and Smith (1994) pointed out that in living systems countless subsystems must be synthesized and coordinated if the organism is to survive. They stressed, though—and this insight is pivotal— that this labyrinthine task of coordination, on which survival is utterly dependent, is not the unfolding of an inborn blueprint or the work of a top-down master planner but the spontaneous emergence of novel and increasingly complex and differentiated states to adapt to shifts in the external and internal environments.

Dynamic-systems theory provides an excellent metaphorical framework for understanding the self (Mahoney, 1991). The self is the complex (in health), coherent organization of a variety of self-states, each one the coordination of innumerable bodily, emotional, and cognitive subsystems. This organization is fluid and dynamic and is not under the direction of a master self or homunculus; rather, a sense of identity emerges over time from the ownership of the experience of this dynamic organization and from how it is interpreted and explained to the self. The most habitual self-states are attractors that may lend the appearance of immutable structure, but this apparent structure is never absolute because it emerges from a dynamic organization (Thelen & Smith, 1994).

The second central theoretical framework for understanding the self is the theory of *dialectical constructivism* (Greenberg & Pascual-Leone, 1995; Pascual-Leone, 1987, 1991; Pascual-Leone & Johnson, 1991). This theory makes three fundamental assertions: (a) the self is constructed, as is all of reality as experienced by humans (Kelly, 1955); (b) reality and the self emerge from both personal and social sources, and meaning arises from the subjective organization and interpretation of sensory data and from socially acquired views; and (c) although our self-experience is singular and coherent when symbolized, producing a unified stream of consciousness, it is in fact a complex synthesis of many levels of processing produced by a variety of mental operations on many levels of information, most of which are outside of awareness (Pascual-Leone, 1987, 1991).

The essence of the dialectical constructivist approach to the self adopted here is that the self is constructed by organizing internal experience. The self is a multiprocess, multilevel organization built up at the highest level from the dialectical interaction between ongoing, moment-by-moment experience and higher level, conceptual processes of reflection that attempt to interpret, order, and explain these elementary experiential processes. In this view, affectively toned, preverbal, preconscious processing plays a central role and is seen as the major source of self-experience. According to this theory, the individual possesses both biologically based, "natural" wisdom and culturally acquired wisdom; and although occasionally these may conflict there is no inherent antagonism between them. Rather, they are both necessary streams of a dialectical synthesis. People live most viably by managing to integrate inner wisdom and social learning, reason, and emotion.

Experiential Processing

Although it makes good sense to separate the many processes that constitute the self into two major categories—conceptually based explaining and bodily based experiencing (cf. Guidano, 1991)—within each category there are numerous levels of processing and suborganizations. The experiential dimensions of the self involve an ongoing flow of contact with internal and external environments, and it is from this that the self emerges as a flowing, shifting field event. Experience is continuous from moment to moment, and the self organizes into emerging states at the leading edge of the experiencing process. These states emerge spontaneously from the processing of perceptual information and from the activation and synthesis of a number of tacit, bodily felt *emotion schemes*. These schemes are basic building blocks of experience and, in combination with mental operators that boost, interrupt, and organize them, are the agents of the self (Minsky, 1986; Pascual-Leone, 1987). Emotion schemes involve emotions and needs, sensorimotor experience and action tendencies, as well as learned perceptual cues and cognitive learning. The multitude of activated schemes dynamically synthesize to produce an immediate experiential state, which is a momentary self-organization. What the self is actually experiencing may or may not be in awareness, although parts of it may be brought into awareness by attention and expressed symbolically with words or actions.

Conceptual Processing

The conscious conceptual part of the dialectic performs several functions. The first of these is the function of consciously directing attention, of choosing to attend to things happening in the world or within the self. To express or explain aspects of experience, they must be brought into the light of awareness and made available for careful attention. Second, these higher functions reflect on, interpret, or symbolize the processes to which they attend. They assign meaning to events and processes which, as Varela et al. (1991) pointed out, in an embodied being can never adequately be understood as purely abstract or cognitive problem solving because numerous processes of different types are brought to bear on an act of interpretation. Information is assessed as to its meaning for the self. By means of emotion and its action tendencies, the self transforms information into goal-directed meaning that is relevant to personal well-being. This can then be symbolized and made available to consciousness.

Symbolization

The process of symbolization of experience is informed by a number of factors. One of these is culture, given that the language used to symbolize is the product of a society that has given it an established range of valid meanings and values. It is still used creatively, but it is a cultural given. Second, it is informed by all past personal and interpersonal learning by the self and how this past experience has been symbolized and represented to the self. It is clear that this learning, which is construed uniquely by each self, is somehow stored, but how this is done is a source of some controversy. Most models over the past few years have been strongly influenced by formal, logical systems of rule-governed symbolic representation, such as occur in computers, but constructivist and dynamic-systems models suggest far more sophisticated approaches. It is clear that the past strongly guides the perception and assimilation of new experience, through assumptions, beliefs, and expectations, but these are not clear, verbal, logical representations. These expectancies might seem to be verbally articulated beliefs, if symbolized at very high levels of abstraction, such as "I am unlovable" but, in fact, these "beliefs" are multilayered organizations of networks that intermingle physiological, emotional, and cognitive schemes and processes in a complex pattern that creates an experience of the self as unlovable.

Beliefs Versus Experiential Synthesis

Dynamic-systems theory posits that in complex systems there are certain attractors around which order and stability are created even in the apparently indecipherable confusion of multiple systems simultaneously interacting. An attractor is like a center of gravity in multidimensional "state space," pulling everything toward a certain configuration, a particular state. Thelen and Smith (1994) observed, though, that this assumes the possibility of other states, the real possibility of behavioral variability if some basic condition in the network were to change. The concept of systemic attractors applied to self-organizations suggests something similar to what is meant by personality structure, but the underlying building blocks are not cognitive, linguistic self-representations and beliefs. Beliefs about the self are high-level cognitive abstractions built up from an interpretation of numerous subsystems of physiological, emotional, and lower level schematic information processing.

In this sense, early behavioral approaches were partly right when they carefully operationalized trait terms. They unfortunately omitted internal experience and meaning from their analyses. They would ask someone who says "I guess I'm just a shy person" what precisely this means in behavioral terms. The person might describe meeting someone, feeling rubbery in the legs, butterflies in the stomach, trembling, sweating, the voice quavering, and the desperate desire to avoid the anxiety by withdrawing. This is already describing the incredible coordination in that moment of several physiological and perceptual systems. Most of it is automatic; none of it "pre-exists"; rather, it is the new emergent organization in that moment of countless subsystems within the self. This behavioral description misses a wealth of internal, experiential information, which is closely tied to the bodily information already presented. This information, these processes, are available to awareness if attention is focused on them, but for the most part they occur automatically, outside of awareness. They are emergent self-organizations that produce a certain state, given information from the field that is automatically construed in a certain way. In other words, several subsystems of the self synthesize at the point of contact with the environment.

These self-organizations, given fairly similar initial conditions, organize with a certain regularity into similar configurations, but this is not a program repeating itself but a dynamic system drawn into a particular pattern with a certain frequency. That order regularizes even further when higher order, abstract self-concepts get articulated and put into narrative form: "This is the sort of person I am." According to an experiential dialectical–constructivist framework, focused attention on the lower level, experiential processes that are being synthesized allows many of these processes to be brought into awareness and symbolized.

Several things become apparent when attention is paid to the process by which meaning is made from experience. At the most basic level, elements are synthesized into self-organizations, which are emotionally anchored in the body and which may be experienced. The self may, for example, be organized to feel vulnerable, or confident, or down in the dumps. These self-organizations may then be consciously attended to and symbolized. Through conscious awareness and language, experiential self-organizations become self-representations. There are many self-representations, and they are neither fixed nor static but are themselves synthesized into complex narrative structures. The human person is thus multivoiced, a "singular multiplicity," synthesizing self-representations to create coherence (Elliott & Greenberg, 1997; Greenberg, 1995). Through multilayered, complex processes bodily elements are synthesized into coherent experiential self-organizations, which are themselves synthesized into self-representations. These multiple self-representations, which express a variety of inner voices, are woven and blended into a coherent, singular self. What anchors the sense of self-coherence are the affectively based self-organizations because healthy emotion orients the self toward what is meaningful at levels available to, but more fundamental than, consciousness.

Anything related to the "self" involves all levels of the emotion system because by definition emotion results from appraisals of situations in relation to core concerns (Frijda, 1986). The well-being of the self is a core concern. Emotions thus express what is important to the self, and emotional meanings are not abstract conclusions from symbolic logic but processes of "embodied cognition," as Thelen and Smith (1994) articulated so well:

> The notion of an embodied cognition is this: humans can and do use prop-ositional logic to describe and think about their experiences. However, the stuff that our logic works on is nonpropositional and, indeed, is totally based on bodily experience. We deal with our perceptions and actions in terms of fluid, dynamic, contextual categories, patterns of organization, which form the very grist for our engagement of meaning. (p. 323)

Bodily experience is inherently emotional because emotion is the most fun-damental bodily system for processing what is of concern in a situation and for energizing and organizing the body for action. So as Thelen and Smith (1994) pointed out, implicit meanings, and any embodied cognitions that are part of these lower level, experiential processes, cannot be separated from action. At these basic levels of human, organismic processing, cognition, emotion, and action are fused into complex, dynamically synthesized states that prompt ac-tion.

So at a distance, our "shy" person might say "at that moment I was anxious because I thought the other person might think I'm stupid." This is an abstract, top-down, high-level picture of what was happening. A moment-by-moment analysis would prove messier, but more revealing. The self-organization in-volved would not be available without some type of approximate entry into the frightened, anxious state, which was the dynamic synthesis of that moment. This might include feelings of loneliness and a genuine desire for contact and support; a "coach" telling the person to not be shy; a "critic," internalized from a past significant other, telling the person that he or she is stupid and is rejected; fragments from a past, unfinished, painfully anchored encounter when the per-son was snubbed; and the consequent, self-organizing tendency to shy away from others. These organizations are knit together by means of emotion that provides the basis of an attractor, which then organizes a variety of emotions, cognitions, and motivations into a complex self-state. What emerges in dynamic synthesis, impelled by a powerful attractor, is an embarrassed, anxious person in a state approaching panic.

Boundaries

What is apparent from this example is the importance of a notion of boundaries, of establishing what is included and what is excluded, in any understanding of the self. Essentially, as William James (1890) understood so well, the self is a process of identification and alienation. To take an extreme example, whereas for one person a number of material possessions could come to be seen as a virtually indispensable part of the self, for another something as basic as the body could be cut off, barely kept alive, and completely alienated from the self.

This is the later Gestalt therapy idea of the self forming like a movable skin at the contact boundary, ready to shift its identifications and alienations as the field shifts. Higher order processes can consciously choose to direct attention to aspects of this boundary, establishing what is allowed or disallowed. Yet for the most part, in the flux of daily life this boundary formation is an automatic process slowly developed throughout childhood and strongly affectively based. Aspects of experience are carefully edited to fit deeply entrenched modes of being.

The Narrative and Embodied Self

A level of organization of self even higher than that of stable attractor-based organizations can be referred to as a *narrative identity*. This involves the unification of accumulated experience and of various self-representations into some sort of coherent story or narrative. Much current work has gone into showing that the self cannot be understood outside of these narratives.

Ricoeur (1984) and Kerby (1991) are two of a host of cross-disciplinary thinkers who have explored the necessary relationship among identity, meaning, and the structure of the stories that people tell. To assume coherence and meaning, human lives must be emplotted. *Emplotment* essentially means to fashion events into a symbolic representation in narrative discourse, to take up and configure the disparate actions and experiences of a human life so that it takes on the form of a coherent story. These stories are historically conditioned; that is, every culture has complex rules about the form meaningful narratives can take. These stories are not merely descriptive; they are also creative and interpretive. Rationality, imagination, myth, and metaphor all come into play in trying to discover and symbolize an intrinsic narrative structure in the temporal sequence of events that make up the flow of life. Kerby (1991) came very close to the dialectical view we propose by distinguishing in literary studies between "the experiencing self and the narrating self" (p. 38). He went on to assert, correctly, that these narratives, however creative, are not fashioned willy-nilly but must be grounded in experience. They are not preformed in experience but emerge in a dialectical interaction between the experiencing and the narrating selves. At its core, the self is embodied, but a body needs a story to act meaningfully, to relate past and future, to situate dreams, goals, regrets, plans, lost opportunities, hopes, and all the stuff of a truly human life:

> The physical body may well be the permanent locus of my insertion in the world, and it is indeed a fairly solid basis for continuity, but it is the events that unfold from this locus that generate the meaning of my existence. . . . Our lives are not experienced as random unconnected events. . . . Life is inherently of a narrative structure, a structure that we make explicit when we reflect upon our past and our possible future. (Kerby, 1991, pp. 38–39)

These stories constitute a discursive account of identity as it both changes and remains stable over time (Angus & Hardtke, 1994; Ricoeur, 1984). Narrative is part of a constructivist dialectic. It establishes a sense of the coherence and stability of the self by symbolizing patterns in experience across situations and by providing discursive explanations for the sometimes-inconsistent meanings and aspects of the self that predominate in different situations and relationships. Narrative, though, as Gregg (1995) showed, is as messy and complex as every other aspect of the self, consisting of a dialogical array of often-contradictory self-representations whose underlying coherence is as intricate as the point–counterpoint arrangements of layered musical scores. Given that the self experientially is a set of complex self-organizations in constant flux, narrative is crucial to the establishment of a stable identity (Hermans, 1996).

This view of the self has many similarities with other views that propose a complex multiplicity of identities, self-states, and self-modules as suborganizations within any human personality (Gregg, 1995; Guidano, 1991; Hermans, 1996; Minsky, 1986; Muran, 1997). Some researchers, such as Hermans (1996) or Gregg (1995), have shown how these modular self-organizations, which can even at times seem intrinsically bipolar or contradictory in nature, are woven together over time through stories or narratives that have the internal sophistication of counterpoint in complex musical arrangements. The structural and organizational links and couplings that allow such internal diversity to be integrated into a coherent, individual identity must be an aspect of the deficit suffered in multiple personality disorder.

What our view has developed and added to these engaging perspectives is a theory that grounds this "parliament of selves" (Minsky, 1986; Pascual-Leone, 1991), these many voices that compose the self, not just in the labyrinthine stories that people tell to account for themselves but also in the body, which irreducibly situates the self in the environment (Gendlin, 1996; Mahoney, 1991; Varela et al., 1991). Narrative is indeed one pole of the dialectic. The other pole is even more fundamental to embodied human experience. The other pole is the fabulously intricate network of bodily, sensorimotor, and affective subsystems whose information is organized and synthesized into experientially available self-states (see Figure 4.1). These, too, are multivocal. There are, in each of us, multiple self-organizations emotionally anchored in the body and orienting us toward or away from activity that would produce and sustain for us growth and well-being.

Pathology of the Self

The experiential tradition until recently has not emphasized the assessment and modeling of dysfunction. Because the concept of the self has always been central

FIGURE 4.1

Process–experiential view of the dialectical construction of the self.

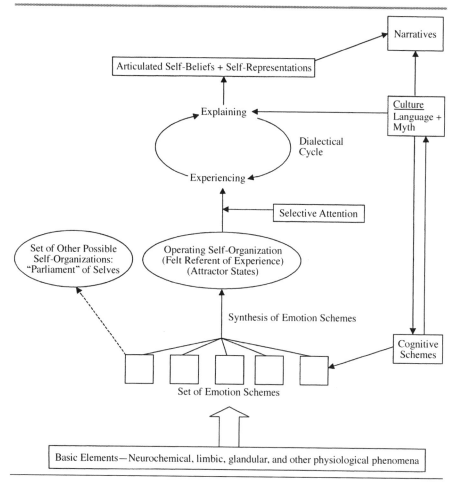

to these approaches, it has been implicated in views of dysfunction but never in a theoretically satisfactory way. Perhaps the simplest view is that of Perls (1969) in his later writing, when he said that the self emerges at the contact boundary with the environment, so dysfunction is a disturbance of contact functions, such as not establishing adaptive self-boundaries. In introjection, for example, something foreign is introduced into the self in such a way that it cannot be properly assimilated; in projection, a real process within the self is placed outside of the self into others.

In developing a dialectical–constructivist approach to dysfunction, three major processes involved in dysfunction have been specified (Greenberg et al.,

1993; Greenberg & Paivio, 1997). The first is the inability to symbolize affective experience, the second is the evocation and synthesis of maladaptive emotion schemes, and the third involves the loss of integration due to the conflict between parts of the self and the disowning of aspects of experience.

Thus, a person may be seen as depressed or anxious because of an inability to attend to and symbolize bodily felt experience, leaving the person confused and alienated from his or her own needs and wants. Awareness of feelings and associated motivations is curative in these cases. In addition, it is possible with very fragile clients that the self is very weak or fragmented and unable to form a clear articulation of its experience. Sometimes there is little sense at all of a coherent self. In such instances there is a need for long-term, empathic work that allows for the gradual development of a stronger sense of self. Second, a person may be stuck in a maladaptive fear- or shame-based sense of self as helpless and insecure, or bad, or worthless. Here, the maladaptive sense of self needs to be transformed by the activation of an alternate sense of self as valuable and strong (Greenberg & Paivio, 1997). This newly accessed, emotionally based sense of self serves to challenge the weak or bad sense of self by means of an internal dialectical process. In the third instance, two activated aspects of the self may be in conflict, and one part may be disowned in an effort to cope with the distress produced by this conflict. In this case, an integration of the two parts is required.

Emotion and Cognition in Dysfunction

In addition, in our view, negative self-interpretations or negative cognitions are generally second-order evaluations of experiential processes, and rather than producing dysfunction, they serve to maintain it. To return to the example of the "shy" man, he might increasingly interpret his social experiences and performances as evidence that he is a social incompetent and a klutz, and these thoughts, in turn, generate expectations that hamper his performances. But the original experience of shyness was centered not on conscious cognitions, which came later, but on rapid, complex, emotionally based responses rooted in emotion schemes. His shyness results from the synthesis of an emotionally based maladaptive self-organization. This is automatically triggered by patterns of perceptual cues that are out of awareness or by primary emotional responses (Greenberg & Paivio, 1997).

These maladaptive, modular self-organizations give rise to self-states that strongly influence both performance and self-perception of performance. Many of these maladaptive selves are rooted in traumatic memories from early development, memories that contain the schematic rudiments of the fused motoric, emotional, and physiological elements of the potential self-organization. These components are often present at earlier and more primitive stages of development than would even be accessible to clear, cognitive self-interpretation.

For example, Greenberg and his associates (Greenberg & Paivio, 1997; Greenberg, Elliott, & Foerster, 1990) have posited that the self-organizations that contribute to depression include the "weak" self-organization and the "bad" self-organization. They have hypothesized that an experience of loss or failure generates a primary adaptive emotional response of sadness but that in individuals who are vulnerable to depression this in turn evokes core, maladaptive, emotionally based schemes of weakness or badness that produce weak or bad self-organizations. The stable personality vulnerability to experiences of loss or failure is based in self-organizations that when evoked, are tacit, immediate experiences of the self as bad or weak, before they are interpretations of the self as such. They are affectively evoked. One might think of these maladaptive emotion schemes as residing at specific emotion-based addresses in memory. When an emotion is experienced in the present, it tends to activate all the materials and processes specific to that address, which is synthesized into that basic self-organization. For example, someone experiencing a failure in the present will probably experience a loss to self-esteem, sadness, and a decrement in mood. This is a temporary state. But someone vulnerable to self-critical depression activates a self-organization that encompasses past failures he or she has had and, with it, the affective sense of self often interpreted as "I am a failure; I am nothing but a loser." A hit at an emotion schematic address conjures up a core maladaptive scheme and all of the bad feelings associated with it. These potential self-organizations are maladaptive structures, given the dynamic-systems proviso that all structures are relative structures amenable to some degree of change.

To some degree, to speak of maladaptive schemes or syntheses is a change within the experiential approach. The classic experiential approach stressed that the self, unfettered by introjected beliefs that hamper its natural development and activity, is inherently healthy and adaptive. This attitude was rooted in the belief in a real self underneath or behind all learning, but in our view the self is itself constructed, and early experience can channel fundamentally healthy elements and processes into the construction of maladaptive self-organizations.

Psychotherapeutic Applications

In therapy, high-level, abstract, conceptual discourse between the therapist and an apparently unitary self, although indispensable at certain moments, is usually insufficient to produce deep and lasting change. Change at the conceptual level is necessary, but it is even more important to achieve change and reorganization within self-schemes. These are deeply emotionally anchored within the client and tacitly direct emergent self-states and responses within a variety of stimulus contexts.

What is focal in effective therapy is the therapist's empathic attunement to indications, which are sometimes no more than momentary glimpses, of various emerging self-organizations within the client. A collaborative judgment between client and therapist eventually is made about whether these are adaptive or dysfunctional and about how relevant they are to the symptomatic disturbances presented by the client. However, when these indications appear it is important to bring them into awareness, to give them a voice, to differentiate and possibly heighten them so that their role in the overall "parliament" of emergent selves can be understood.

One fundamental principle of process–experiential therapy—indeed, of all experiential therapies—is that it is not enough to talk about these self-organizations. They are embodied, intrinsically emotional, self-states, which are fully activated only when the requisite state is engaged experientially. To evoke and attain these states composes a good deal of the subtle art of therapy. Within a relevant state, the client is fully engaged in "being" a given self-organization, thus unifying and expressing the cognitive, emotional, physiological, and behavioral properties of that self-organization. Without such engagement, no reorganization touches the emotional core that glues together and stabilizes the central identity and meaning of that self-organization. These basic self-organizations occur at levels of the body–brain that are at the root of, and more fundamental than, consciousness and cognition. There is an indispensable immediacy to a client being subjectively engaged in the moment in a self-state. This allows for an experiential reprocessing of the beliefs, feelings, and meanings of a given self-organization.

Methods

These ideas underline a number of methods used in process–experiential therapy. Perhaps the best known are *enactment methods* developed from psychodrama and gestalt therapy involving dialogues between parts of the self or with a significant other. Other process–experiential techniques, such as exploration of a problematic reaction (Greenberg et al., 1993), or focusing (Gendlin, 1996), are also clearly consistent with this view of the self. In the former, for example, the high-level, cognitive, narrative self is puzzled by a disproportionate reaction that is rooted in an unexplored, experiential response to some dimension of a stimulus person or situation. The reaction has emerged from a self-organization that has erupted spontaneously in a given context but whose meaning has not been consciously established. In dialectical–constructivist terms, one part of the dialectic is missing. By returning to the scene and re-evoking the self-organization, working through what was rapid and automatic in a slow, deliberate way, a new dimension of self-experience can be articulated and assimilated.

Unfinished-business dialogues with significant others can also be understood in terms of this theory of the self. The other is represented within some modular self-organization as a living object invested with attributes and, often, with exceptional power. This internalized other is affectively represented within memory as it was originally experienced by the self, often nonverbally, such as in a bodily experience of shame in relation to a look of contempt on the face of the other. The self remains strongly tied to this representation of the significant other, and there are many lingering, unexpressed bad feelings toward him or her, which often include anger, resentment, guilt, sadness, and loss. The empty-chair dialogue allows for the expression of deep, unresolved emotions and for the mobilization of previously unmet needs resulting in both the reorganization of the activated modular self and of the representation of the other contained within this self-organization.

Perhaps the most studied of the process–experiential techniques is the *two-chair dialogue for splits*. This technique is used to facilitate the resolution of internal conflicts in which one aspect of the self is expressing a domineering, hostile, critical attitude toward another aspect of the self, resulting in discomfort. A relevant marker of such a split might be when the client says "I am so stupid and clumsy, and I feel so anxious about having to do anything that might show this." The full resolution model was described by Greenberg et al. (1993). The essential conceptualization is that involved in such a marker are two distinctly organized aspects of the self: a hostile, critical introject, whose message to the self is "you're clumsy and stupid," and an experiencing self, which is made self-conscious and anxious by the hostile critic. The essence of the two-chair technique is, within an empathic relationship, to differentiate and separate these two aspects of the self, to give them each a chair and a voice, to heighten their experience, develop their voices, and facilitate their engagement in an authentic dialogue. Such a dialogue, if it persists, results in significant experiential shifts, ultimately producing a softening of the critic, an assertion of the experiencing self, and an integrated resolution of the conflict (Greenberg et al., 1993).

This model is the result of a long-standing research program dedicated to understanding the experiential shifts that underlie the successful resolution of self-critical, internal conflicts (Clarke & Greenberg, 1986; Greenberg, 1984a, 1984b; Greenberg & Dompierre, 1981; Greenberg & Webster, 1982). This study of effective and ineffective therapeutic change processes for the resolution of internal conflict has used a task analytic methodology, one that cycles repeatedly among rational conjecture, model building, and empirical observations to map the various client self-states involved in conflict resolution.

Sample of Self-Process in Therapy

Some samples from an actual therapy session exemplifying this process are briefly presented here. These come from the 19th session of a 20-session, short-term, process–experiential therapy of a 44-year-old woman diagnosed with a major depressive disorder. The client was unhappily married and became very anxious and conflicted at the thought of taking any effective action on behalf of herself in interpersonal situations.

The two-chair split work occupied a large part of the session. The client had been unhappy for a long time in her marriage, and therapy had helped her clarify that she was in conflict about leaving. Part of her wanted to leave, but another part of her cautioned against this. The "critical" chair began the dialogue by telling her about her responsibilities to her husband and children and making her feel very guilty. It then moved to frightening her about the conflict and disrupted harmony that would result from her departure. What gradually happened, as shown below, is that an emotionally based, maladaptive, small, weak, and diminished self-organization was activated.

Client (C): You make me feel very tired, a feeling like going to sleep, and small.

Therapist (T): Uh-huh, stay with that feeling, of being small, what's it like —can you describe it?

C: Small and tired?

T: Mm.

C: How is it?

T: Yeah.

C: Um—it's like not having energy.

T: Mm-hm.

C: It's like giving up, instead of uh—

T: Yeah, a sense of just "what's the point"?

C: Mm-hm, helplessness.

T: Yeah, stay with that, I know it's sort of painful maybe, I don't know but, helplessness.

C: And uhm—no energy, I mean I am feeling now that I am exhausted, but uh, I feel that the energy level is zero.

T: Uh-huh. Stay there, it's sort of a hard place to be.

C: Mm-hm, mm-hm.

T: Just stay with that feeling. Just try to, and tell her what it is like for you when you're like this.

C: What is it like? Sad.

T: Uh-huh, it's sad. Tell her about the sadness (pointing to the other chair).

C: I feel sad because, I think that the way she puts it, all my life is going to be—there is no way out. . . . It's like there is no solution, there is no way out.

T: Yeah, it feels like you're stuck.

C: Yeah, mm-hm.

T: Can you tell her "I feel stuck"?

C: I feel stuck, I feel there is no way out, there is no, no—there is no light.

The client continues to enter more deeply into a sense of dark and hopeless desperation, being made to feel small, powerless, and hopeless by the critic. After she has entered into the pain of that hopeless state, a new self-organization emerges spontaneously within the client facilitated by the therapist helping her to focus on her organismic wants and needs. By attending to her needs, the client's more assertive self begins cautiously to emerge.

T: What do you need from her?

C: Mm-hm. Um, to let me—let me—um, let me make decisions, some decisions which may jeopardize my future but will make me more happy.

T: So "let me take a risk"?

C: Let me be riskier.

T: Mm-hm, so let me—okay, that's clear, so let me be risky, right?

C: Mm-hm.

T: Tell her again.

C: So let me be risky.

T: What do you feel when you say that?

C: How do I feel, scared.

She returns to the critic's chair and scares herself by saying things such as the following:

C: You don't even know what it is to be risky. I mean, if you are risky, think about the consequences, you're going to regret it. . . . You're going to get hurt, you are going to suffer, and you will regret it.

By attending to her emerging experience the reorganization happening within the more experientially based self gathers force, and the self-assertion is ever more strongly expressed:

C: Okay, so I mean what is it, why do you feel that we will not be able to make it? How about if everything goes right and turns around?

T: What are you saying to her, like "I don't think you know everything"?

C: Yeah, mm-hm, mm-hm, I don't think that you know what you say is going to be all right. You don't know everything.

T: So "you're not so smart." What do you want from her? What do you want her to do?

C: Go to sleep for awhile. Ha, ha.

T: So lay off me.

C: Yeah, mm-hm.

T: Just sort of, I don't know, ease up.

C: Yeah, mm-hm.

T: Tell her.

C: So could you please stop telling me all of those negative things, just stop it, just don't say anything, maybe things are not that um, that awful, so black.

T: Yeah, stop darkening things for me.

C: Mm-hm, mm-hm.

T: Can you say that to her?

C: Can you stop making things so negative for me.

The critic continues for some time to caution the self but then spontaneously softens into a stance of compassion and concern.

C: This being so critical is difficult.

T: Why?

C: This doesn't feel right.

T: It doesn't?

C: No.

T: What do you feel?

C: Uh—how can I do this?

T: That you don't want to do this to her?

C: Mm-hm.

T: Tell her that.

C: So, I, I would like to stop thinking so negatively every time you want to do something.

T: You'd like to stop.

C: Mm-hm.

T: And—

C: So every time, what you can do is, every time you have this negative me telling you something—put it aside, block it, don't think about it.

The emotionally based self-organization is now in a position to emerge from the cocoon of smallness, exhaustion, and fear. She decided to pursue the marital relationship issues without a paralyzing internal critic making her feel that all risk and conflict are unacceptable. The therapist asked her what it felt like to experience the power to block the critic:

T: Can you put words to it?

C: Yeah, oh, it feels really nice.

T: It feels nice over here?

C: Yeah.

T: What's it like?

C: Hmm, free.

T: Uh-huh. Can you tell her that?

C: I feel free.

T: Mm-hm.

C: A little bit more energetic.

T: Mm-hm, a little more energetic, a little brighter.

The therapy session ended with the now-softened critic's chair expressing continued care and concern for the self, reassuring it that it is there to offer support in difficult times, asking it to be careful but allowing it the scope to take risks and explore with a sense of power and self-respect and a new sense of attunement to its feelings and needs.

Conclusion

We have described a process–experiential theory of the nature of the self. Its main theoretical sources are dialectical–constructivism and dynamic-systems theory. Its practice is rooted in the importance of the integration of multiple self-aspects, each an authentic part of the self-identity and each grounded in an affective self-organization. Emotion theory has helped to elaborate and decipher a complex picture, by illuminating how emotion forms a distinct, physiological, information-processing system, one now universally conceded to have evolutionary precedence, which informs the self and prepares it for action in relation to issues of concern for its well-being. Dialectical–constructivism helps explain both the synthesis of multiple schemes into a complex whole and the interactive relation between this automatic, experiential system and higher conceptual processes. The self-states that emerge spontaneously in the organism–environment field from moment to moment are affectively organized. They are then explained through conceptual reflection and coherent narratives. We are thus consistently engaged in the process of making sense of our experience. The self is a process, not an object, and self-states are continually produced as part of an indescribably complex amalgam and synthesis of countless subsystems that self-organize in different contexts. Certain configurations emerge as attractors: These are recurring, frequent self-states for a given individual. Process–experiential therapy aims to activate dysfunctional and healthy self-states and to allow new experiential information to alter existing self-organizations in an internal dialectical process of self-challenge. This allows the self to reorganize along different lines. The self, supported and prized by another, can grow, and be recreated anew, by an enlargement of both experience and meaning. Its many voices are heard and freshly assimilated in a creative process directed at freeing the resources necessary to sustain itself indefinitely.

References

Angus, L., & Hardtke, K. (1994). Narrative processes in psychotherapy. *Canadian Psychology, 35,* 190–203.

Clarke, K., & Greenberg, L. S. (1986). Differential effects of the gestalt two-chair intervention and problem solving in resolving decisional conflict. *Journal of Counseling Psychology, 33,* 11–15.

Elliott, R., & Greenberg, L. S. (1997). Multiple voices in process–experiential therapy: Dialogues between aspects of the self. *Journal of Psychotherapy Integration, 7,* 225–239.

Frijda, N. H. (1986). *The emotions.* Cambridge, England: Cambridge University Press.

Gendlin, E. T. (1996). *A focusing approach to psychotherapy.* New York: Guilford Press.

Greenberg, L. S. (1984a). Task analysis: The general approach. In L. Rice & L. S. Greenberg (Eds.), *Patterns of change* (pp. 124–148). New York: Guilford Press.

Greenberg, L. S. (1984b). A task analysis of intrapersonal conflict resolution. In L. Rice & L. S. Greenberg (Eds.), *Patterns of change* (pp. 67–123). New York: Guilford Press.

Greenberg, L. S. (1995). The self is flexibly various and requires an integrative approach. *Journal of Psychotherapy Integration, 5,* 323–329.

Greenberg, L. S., & Dompierre, L. M. (1981). Specific effects of gestalt two-chair dialogue on intrapsychic conflict in counselling. *Journal of Counseling Psychology, 28,* 288–294.

Greenberg, L. S., Elliott, R. K., & Foerster, F. S. (1990). Experiential processes in the psychotherapeutic treatment of depression. In C. D. McCann & N. S. Endler (Eds.), *Depression: New directions in theory, research, and practice* (pp. 157–185). Toronto, Ontario, Canada: Wall & Emerson.

Greenberg, L. S., & Paivio, S. (1997). *Working with emotions in psychotherapy.* New York: Guilford Press.

Greenberg, L. S., & Pascual-Leone, J. (1995). A dialectical–constructivist approach to experiential change. In R. Neimeyer & M. Mahoney (Eds.), *Constructivism in psychotherapy* (pp. 169–191). Washington, DC: American Psychological Association.

Greenberg, L. S., Rice, L. N., & Elliott, R. (1993). *Facilitating emotional change: The moment by moment process.* New York: Guilford Press.

Greenberg, L. S., & Van Balen, R. (1998). A theory of experience-centered therapies. In L. Greenberg, J. Watson, & G. Lietaer (Eds.), *Handbook of experiential therapy* (pp. 28–57). New York: Guilford Press.

Greenberg, L. S., & Webster, M. (1982). Resolving decisional conflict by means of two-chair dialogue and empathic reflection at a split in counselling. *Journal of Counseling Psychology, 29,* 468–477.

Gregg, G. S. (1995). Multiple identities and the integration personality. *Journal of Personality, 63,* 617–641.

Guidano, V. F. (1991). *The self in process: Toward a post-rationalist cognitive therapy.* New York: Guilford Press.

Hermans, H. J. M. (1996). Opposites in a dialogical self: Constructs as characters. *Journal of Constructivist Psychology, 9,* 1–26.

James, W. (1890). *Principles of psychology* (2 vol.). New York: Holt.

Kelly, G. A. (1955). *The psychology of personal constructs* (Vol. 1 & 2). New York: Norton.

Kerby, A. P. (1991). *Narrative and the self.* Bloomington: Indiana University Press.

Mahoney, M. (1991). *Human change processes.* New York: Basic Books.

Minsky, M. L. (1986). *The society of mind.* New York: Simon & Schuster.

Muran, J. C. (1997). Multiple selves and depression. *In Session: Psychotherapy in Practice, 3,* 53–64.

Pascual-Leone, J. (1987). Organismic processes for neo-Piagetian theories: A dialectical causal account of cognitive development. *International Journal of Psychology, 22,* 531–570.

Pascual-Leone, J. (1991). Emotions, development and psychotherapy: A dialectical–constructivist perspective. In J. Safran & L. S. Greenberg (Eds.), *Emotion, psychotherapy and change* (pp. 302–335). New York: Guilford Press.

Pascual-Leone, J., & Johnson, J. (1991). The psychological unit and its role in task analysis: A reinterpretation of task analysis. In M. Chandler & M. Chapman (Eds.), *Criteria for competence: Controversies in the assessment of children's abilities* (pp. 153–187). Hillsdale, NJ: Erlbaum.

Perls, F. S. (1969). *Gestalt therapy verbatim.* LaFayette, CA: Real People Press.

Perls, F. S., Hefferline, R., & Goodman, P. (1951). *Gestalt therapy.* New York: Dell.

Ricoeur, P. (1984). *Time and narrative* (3 vol.). Chicago: University of Chicago Press.

Rogers, C. R. (1959). A theory of therapy, personality, and interpersonal relationships as developed in the client-centered framework. In S. Koch (Ed.), *Psychology: The study of a science* (Vol. 3, pp. 185–256). New York: McGraw-Hill.

Thelen, E., & Smith, L. B. (1994). *A dynamic systems approach to the development of cognition and action.* Cambridge, MA: MIT Press.

Varela, F. J., Thompson, E., & Rosch, E. (1991). *The embodied mind: Cognitive science and human experience.* Cambridge, MA: MIT Press.

COMMENT:

E Pluribus Unum

Stuart A. Pizer

William Whelton and Leslie Greenberg offer a fascinating view of their process–experiential model for understanding the dynamic nature of the self and the therapeutic action of their clinical approach. I was struck, on first reading their chapter, by the similarities in our arguments. We each regard the self in terms of a dynamic bridging of multiplicity. At the same time, particularly as I read their clinical illustration, I was struck by our differences. With markedly similar goals—the gathering of a multiplicity of disowned, disenfranchised, devalued, or dysfunctional self-states into a vitally experienced and coherent internal dialogue—our clinical techniques are, interestingly, quite different. Rather than review here their many points with which I agree, regarding the significance of affect, the complex dynamic system of nonlinear state shifts, the contradictory voices of the inner "parliament," the relationship between the continuities and discontinuities of self-experience—I focus my comments on the ways in which our technical frameworks lead us to approach the same clinical phenomena and the same therapeutic goals with distinctly different modes of working in the treatment hour. I hope that by contrasting their process–experiential therapeutic framework with my own version of a relational psychoanalytic framework, I may generate some useful questions about these alternative routes toward therapeutic benefit.

Now, having announced my intention to contrast our clinical approaches, I first affirm some important similarities. Perhaps I could broadly summarize our similarities and differences by suggesting that while using quite compatible approaches to facilitating internal dialogue *within* the patient's internal parliament, I believe we most dramatically, and significantly, differ in the handling of dialogue *between* patient and therapist in terms of the use of transference and countertransference.

Whelton and Greenberg, in their use of the empty-chair technique, stage a direct (and directed) dialogue between subselves, modular selves, or self-states within the patient. They sponsor weaker voices within the patient to become present and accounted for and promote a modification of rigid perceptual or affective positions entrenched in the multiple stations within the self. In effect, they seek to engage internal parliamentary debate, dialogue, and ultimate negotiation within the patient. Although I do not tend to use an empty-chair exercise in concrete terms, I do frequently find it helpful to conjure, in metaphorical terms, the patient's awareness of what I call an *internal board of directors* or *executive committee*. I may ask the patient to visualize such an intrapsychic committee sitting around a table, and I emphasize that each party needs to be heard. My patients consistently have found this metaphor to be a useful way to describe their self-experience and to register and accept internal multiplicity and contradiction. As one patient told me, "my table inside is more like the dinner table of a large Italian family, of all ages—and they're all talking at once, and no one is listening very well!"

Whereas I make use of such metaphorical means to access the complex dimensionality of a patient's self-experience and to encourage each inner voice to speak, vote, and negotiate, I tend not to recommend techniques that concretely dramatize this internal dialogue in the immediate clinical moment. Whelton and Greenberg, when they use the empty-chair technique, enter the role of dramatic coach. My own position, from a relational psychoanalytic framework, may be described as participant–observer (see Sullivan, 1953); that is, I engage in conversation with the patient about his or her own experience, or our experience together, and I make inquiries or observations about moments or patterns of perception, affect, state, state shift, or potential meaning. While offering a welcoming atmosphere and my attentiveness, acceptance, and containment, I may range in my responses to a patient from empathic resonance, or support, to interpretive conjecture or affective challenge. Part of my own technical range in analytic therapy is determined by the matrix of transference–countertransference, in which I am not a dramatic coach but a fellow actor on the analytic stage (to borrow a metaphor from McDougall, 1985).

Whelton and Greenberg's process–experiential technique and my relational psychoanalytic technique each ask the patient to engage in a clinical process and an experience that are concrete, abstract, and paradoxical. Whelton and Greenberg, in their use of the empty chair, ask the patient to concretize aspects of self-experience in a dramatization of reciprocal subself positions. I ask my patients, psychoanalytically, to accept the concrete affective exchange between us as a line of access to their internal worlds of relational representations, affects, needs, memories, and fantasies. Whelton and Greenberg rely, in their technique, on the abstractions of "internal critic" and "weak self" as organizing personas that may validly crystallize meaningful clusters of disparate self-experiences. I rely, in my technique, on the abstraction that the immediate relational moment enacted between the patient and myself symbolically renders recurrent affective truths about the patient's intrapsychic and interpersonal life. Also Whelton and Greenberg rely on the acceptance and use of a paradox: The patient engaged in an empty-chair dialogical dramatization is experiencing a simultaneous multiplicity and unity of self that is both differentiating and integrating at the same time. I rely on the paradox that in the transference, my presence represents an absent relationship that may now be addressed, or I represent (or our coconstructed interaction represents) a projected aspect of the patient's self-experience that the patient may encounter and engage through our dialogue.

Each technique has its advantages, costs, and risks. Whelton and Greenberg seem able to engage a patient quickly in a vital interchange between parts of the self that ordinarily ignore, dismiss, defeat, or humiliate each other. Their coaching makes possible access to multiple dimensions of self-experience within a relatively short-term clinical framework. In contrast, as we all know, psychoanalysis may take a long time. Is this because, in analysis, we wait for the patient's subselves to emerge spontaneously and precipitate into the transference–countertransference potential space? How can the analyst be player and prompter, coconstructor and coach? On the other hand, does deep, complex, and thoroughgoing change within the self require the experience of interactive engagement and reflective functioning in a dialogue, over time, between two whole persons (each of whom is rendering the amalgam of mutually evocative, multiple subselves in the therapeutic relationship)? Russell (1994) referred to this psychoanalytic form of therapeutic action as "process with involvement." In chapter 5 of this volume, I elaborate on this process.

Turning now to Whelton and Greenberg's clinical example, I would like to suggest how, rather than serving as a coach promoting dialogue between the patient's self-states, I would engage in the exploration and negotiation of the reciprocal self-states elicited in patient and therapist within the present transference–countertransference relationship. Their clinical vignette begins with the client saying, "You make me feel very tired, a feeling like going to sleep, and small." The therapist replies, "Uh-huh, stay with that feeling, of being small, what's it like—can you describe it?" It is not entirely clear whether this expression is a direct or indirect allusion to the transference or what implication it has for the patient–therapist relationship. Here, the therapist immediately becomes a coach. The therapist in the vignette guides the patient to stay with a description of the feeling. She feels helpless. Indeed, she is enacting helplessness and dependence in relation to the benignly powerful therapist. Do they examine this coconstructed relationship? Do they need to, for therapeutic benefit? As I recall Gendlin saying, "we don't feel our feelings; we feel our situations" (personal communication, February 20, 1967). So, paradoxically, in asking the patient to focus concretely on the description of her feelings in a weak, small, diminished self-state, is the therapist inviting in the patient an abstraction from the immediacy of feeling as it is delivered spontaneously into the interplay of the therapeutic relationship?

Eventually, as the empty-chair exercise develops, the client's "more experientially based self" is helped to speak more assertively to her internal critic-self. At one point, the therapist prompts the experientially based self to confront her critic by asking her "What do you want from her? What do you want her to do?" The client replies, "Go to sleep for awhile. Ha ha." It is clear that the client is enjoying a more emboldened state and is beginning to have fun with it. We might ask her whether "go to sleep for awhile" is related to her earlier statement ("You are making me feel very tired, a feeling like going to sleep, and small"). We might ask, would it be useful to explore whether these two statements are linked? Is the patient now addressing the powerful therapist-figure displaced onto her own critic-self, and reversing the direction of influence? Is the patient expressing a feeling she might wish to express toward her therapist but of which she remains unconscious and is not yet ready to venture interpersonally? Is this line of exploration and potential learning unnecessary to accomplish the patient's therapeutic goals? For me, what is missing in this vignette is the heart and soul, blood and guts, messiness of an intimate therapeutic relationship. I would ask, does there need to be a person sitting in the empty chair? If the nature and configurations of the complex, multiply distributed self have been determined through the formative dynamics of child–caregiver relationships, can a substantial reconfiguring of the self conceivably be accomplished without the dynamics of an intimately engaged patient–therapist relationship? I believe that for the patient to develop her capacity for reflective functioning and internal dialogue, she needs to know more of what goes on in the mind of her therapist in their intersubjective dialogue (see Fonagy & Target, 1998).

By the end of the session, the patient's critical self-organization has assumed a softer attitude, more of a protective shepherd than a humiliating debunker of the experiential self. The internal critic now seems more like the benign therapist–coach. I wonder, is this a transference identification that is not worked through, not yet an authentically emergent and integrated property of the patient's self? Does this matter? Have guidance, coaching, and empathic modeling expeditiously served a clinical necessity without the protracted negotiations of multiple transference–countertransference constructions over time? Are there multiple roads to Rome? Or when we get there by these different routes, do we find ourselves in a different state?

References

Fonagy, P., & Target, M. (1998). Mentalization and the changing aims of child psychoanalysis. *Psychoanalytic Dialogues, 8,* 87–114.

McDougall, J. (1985). *Theaters of the mind.* New York: Basic Books.

Russell, P. (1994). *Process with involvement: The interpretation of affect.* Unpublished manuscript, Harvard Medical School.

Sullivan, H. S. (1953). *The interpersonal theory of psychiatry.* New York: Norton.

CHAPTER 5

The Capacity to Tolerate Paradox: Bridging Multiplicity Within the Self

Stuart A. Pizer

Minutes before her scheduled appointment with me, Joyce telephoned my answering service to say she could not come because the babysitter for her 3-year-old daughter never showed up. Joyce had been in twice-weekly therapy for 4 years. A European émigré in her early 30s, the only surviving child of a depressed and narcissistically self-absorbed mother, Joyce had been working determinedly to extricate herself from her mother's psychologically abandoning, controlling, and emotionally demanding orbit of influence. But Joyce did not want to abandon her mother altogether. Across great geographic (and empathic) distance, Joyce had dedicated herself to negotiating a mutually viable relationship with her mother that would maintain their active kinship, and she had used her treatment to buttress her own ability to receive her mother's "poison messages" without succumbing yet again to despair and depressive collapse. In the course of our work together, Joyce had established a positive and trusting relationship with me and was able to link her recurrent feelings of hopelessness to the pervasive affective tone of her lonely childhood. She had brought us vividly back to those interminable afternoons at home, her mother in the next room not to be disturbed at her desk, and her father, out of economic necessity and marital alienation, spending long hours at work. We sat together as Joyce remembered her young self sitting alone on the floor of the vestibule surrounded by the disarray of objects she had pulled out of drawers. She had recalled the night she had been spanked for going to her parents' bedroom seeking comfort after waking from a nightmare (in which she had found her mother all in pieces). Thus, using her therapy to help moderate her desperate, suicidal sinking spells, Joyce had been able to make affirmative life choices to improve her work situation, to marry, and to become a mother.

This chapter is from *Building Bridges: The Negotiation of Paradox in Psychoanalysis*, by S. A. Pizer, 1998, chapter 4, Hillsdale, NJ: Analytic Press. Copyright 1998 by Analytic Press. Adapted with permission.

On this particular day, when I received Joyce's message that she would have to miss her session, I telephoned her to check in. Joyce answered the telephone with a tense voice. She was distraught. She said she felt angry at her thwarted session and trapped by her daughter's dependence on her, and she took all of this as a sign of the impossibility of her life. Hoping that we might find a way to help Joyce transition out of her tumbling mood, I asked her if she would like to have our session now, over the telephone. She questioned how she could do this with her daughter present, so insistent and interruptive, and requiring her attention. I suggested we give it a try.

As we proceeded to talk, it became clear indeed that Joyce's wonderfully assertive 3-year-old was indifferent to the therapeutic frame. As Joyce repeatedly broke off from her dialogue with me to address her daughter, she would report to me, "Now she's got my lipstick and wants to draw on our faces," or "Now she's found the chocolates and is taking them all out of the box—No, Emily! You can have only one now!" Joyce paused to gather crayons and paper for Emily, and we were allowed a few minutes of conversation, until Emily came to sit on Joyce's lap. "See," exclaimed Joyce, "this is hopeless." But then, taking a breath, she asked me to hold on while she selected a videotape to play for Emily. I heard Joyce as she started the video and invited her daughter to sit next to Mommy on the couch. "Maybe this will work," said Joyce, "it's one of her favorites."

Now, with jingles and laughter in the background, Joyce attempted to pursue her therapy session with her arm around Emily. "This seems to be okay for now," said Joyce. "But I don't know what we can do. I don't know. I don't see how we're ever gonna fix me. What can we do? I'm never gonna be okay!" I said to Joyce, "I'm not sure what we may yet do. But I picture something that you need, and I don't know how you might find it. You need something like what you just did for Emily, helping her with her own state of need and disarray. You found a way to include her and managed to settle her and provide for both of you at the same time. Picturing you at Emily's age, it seems to me like that's just what you were missing, and it's what you're missing even now: someone to just be with you when you're in a mood, so you can make your way to a new feeling." Joyce was silent. I added, "And, I think you're right; we don't yet know when or how you may find something like that for you, or within you." With that, Joyce reported feeling better. For this day, this moment, we had managed to negotiate for Joyce a bridge that conducted her from the island of despair to the island of hope.

The Tolerance of Paradox

The caregiver function of affect regulation (or "ego coverage," in Winnicott's words [1965]), in its agency of organizing the intensity, totality, timing, flow, and concertedness of affect, would be aptly described by another metaphor to replace Mother as "mirror": the mother as conductor, or transitional mirror. Mother-the-conductor does not coerce, or coax, a false-self yielding, or shielding, of an authentic state in her child. Rather, she engages a subtle and delicate negotiation of affect and intention, allowing her child the time and space to hesitate, to subjectivize, and potentially to own her transformational gesture, and she and her child both find their way to tolerating the moments in which a negotiated harmony or transition is beyond their mutual reach. The conducting, or bridging, function of the caregiver is a version of mirroring that meets the child's affect, mood, or intensity state and sponsors a transition toward intensification, relaxation, resolution, or shifting of state. Thus, the mirroring must be both empathic (attuned) and inexact (different). Transitional mirroring is a negotiation of state regulation. Mother-the-conductor is serving as a transitional mirror.

So, mother, or other caregiver, helps us to tolerate surprise and startle, helps us to bear sudden state shifts, helps us to manage transitions of state and affect, helps us to accept discrepancies, to feel that what may be beyond our comprehension or our competence may still be okay to live with. I mean to suggest by this metaphor the ordinary, everyday experiential basis for each child's developmental attainment of an affective tolerance for disjunctive, discrepant, paradoxical juxtapositions of state. The key to feeling okay amid the disconcerting multitude of internal and relational states is to be found in lived moments of affective exchange that constitutes, and establishes in the mind, an experience of bridging. By means of such negotiations of state and state transitions, sponsored in the parent–child relational dialogue, each person develops the competence to bridge a multiplicity of contradictory and paradoxical experiences of self and self-with-other and to contain them within.

Here, I elaborate on the particularly compelling nature of paradox and attempt to discriminate what sets paradox apart from conflict. I explore, in particular, how the tolerance of paradox becomes a developmental achievement that provides for the ability to straddle the multiplicity of private and relational experiences while preserving a sense of personal integrity over time. I consider the specific contributions of the caregiver toward the infant's mastery of paradoxical experience and the establishment of the affect accompanying the acceptance of paradox: the feeling that the existence of the impossible is okay, even as it strains the accommodating embrace of mind.

Negotiation of paradox and negotiation of conflict can be discriminated as subjective experiences. Conflict connotes dichotomous (trichotomous, etc.) interests or tugs between people or groups or, in individuals, between divergent tendencies within a bounded nucleus of the self. On the other hand, paradox resides in the multiplicity of bounded nuclei within the self, where simultaneously coexisting nuclei (self-states, affects, self–other representations, etc.)

reciprocally contradict or negate each other. Conflict can be resolved through interpersonal negotiation or mediation. Intrapsychic conflict may be resolved through choice or renunciation or repression. On the other hand, paradox cannot be resolved (Winnicott, 1971); mutually negating elements continue to coexist, and the negotiation of paradox yields not resolution but a straddling, or bridging, of contradictory perspectives.

We can understand the compelling power of paradox by virtue of its violation of the law of the excluded middle—that a proposition cannot be both true and false at the same time (P. Russell, personal communication, June 10, 1995). As Sainsbury (1988) wrote, paradoxes "immediately provoke one into trying to 'solve' them" (p. 1). Indeed, philosophers and logicians, as well as jokesters, have devised solvable paradoxes along with unsolvable paradoxes. Life hands us the unsolvable paradoxes. According to Sainsbury, paradoxes are "fun," and they are "serious." He classified paradoxes on a continuum from "weak or shallow" to "cataclysmic" and offered his own definition of paradox: "an apparently unacceptable conclusion derived by apparently acceptable reasoning from apparently acceptable premises" (p. 1). He then argued that

> appearances have to deceive, since the acceptable cannot lead by acceptable steps to the unacceptable. So, generally, we have a choice: Either the conclusion is not really unacceptable, or else the starting point, or the reasoning, has some nonobvious flaw. (p. 1)

Sainsbury's argument honors the constraints of logic, the domains of philosophy and mathematics. However, in psychoanalysis, when Winnicott (1971) wrote of the essential acceptance of paradox, he was arguing not a matter of logic but a matter of subjectivity, intersubjectivity, noninvasive human relating, transitional phenomena, and affect. A paradox that is logically unacceptable may seem acceptable to us while remaining cognitively unsolved. As Tagore observed, a mind all logic is like a knife all blade: It cuts the hand that uses it. In this chapter, I consider how a person attains, in the course of development, a tolerance for paradox, a feeling that paradox is okay even as it violates the accustomed laws of sequential thought.

Let us examine the paradoxes of everyday life in the matrix of familiar object relationships, wherein the multitude of self-experiences, and the spaces between them, are being registered, distributed and, with varying success, bridged. What about the following paradox?

> Mother is the person I run to when someone hurts my feelings. Mother is the person who hurt my feelings.

I believe that no developing child escapes experiences of such paradoxical relational truths. Each good-enough mother of the average-expectable family environment presents each child with her array of self-states, ranging in relative attunement, complementarity, harmony, or dissonance. The parent–offspring conflict paradigm in modern evolutionary biology (Slavin & Kriegman, 1992) predicts the inevitability of multiple vectors in every parent–child relationship. Then there is always the inadvertent or the circumstantial cause of disjunctive relational experience (i.e., accidents and setbacks befall even the best of parents). Each child, barring extremes of interaction, learns to straddle the multiplicity of mutually negating experiences of self-with-other. Perhaps the child senses that his mother's state changes when she registers her child's hurt feelings and her tenderness re-emerges. Perhaps the child tacitly recognizes that his mother did not seek sadistically to hurt his feelings. Perhaps eventually there is a poignant reunion in sharing a soothing moment after an emotional storm (the foundation for refinding later in life all object experiences of "kiss and make up"). However, possibly the discordant representations of Mother as soother of hurt feelings and Mother as provoker of hurt feelings have begun to distribute in the child's mind into a Fairbairnian (1944/1952) endopsychic structure: the frustrating mother, the overexciting and rejecting mother, or the mother of attachment aligned with the central ego. When developing the capacity to tolerate paradox in vital human relationships, the child is handling such discrepant selfobject moments or representations of interactions that have been generalized (RIGs, in Stern's, 1985, theory) by storing them under different "affect categories" (Edelman, 1992) in the mind, and the multiple and contradictory quality of self- and object representations, the distribution of segregated aggregates, or islands, of self-experiences clustering around memories of affect, state, percepts, fantasies, somatic intensities, and intentions, has been laid down for life.

If multiplicity of relational experience is the rule and not the exception, and the unitary self-in-relation is a necessary illusion, how does the child become able to straddle this multiplicity of intimate object relationships and internal object representations? If the infant is capable, early on, of "perceiving both self-invariance and invariance in others" (Mitchell, 1993, p. 116), how is the mind's inherent faculty for negotiation of paradox cultivated in development? We have considered the caregiver as transformational object, mirror, or conductor, but we need to look more closely at how the polyphony of affect and the cacophony of parental voices are orchestrated within the musicality of the child's mind, and we must focus more closely on the consequences for self-experience when the "shadow of the object" that falls on the ego is more accurately a shadow show of shifting silhouettes, leaving lasting traces of discrepant shades of meaning and affect that cluster around separate islands within each person's internal universe. When we tolerate the "Mother hurts my feelings" paradox, we exercise the self's competence at bridging from the island of "Mother soothes" to the island of "Mother hurts" while maintaining the feeling of unruptured unity of self and relationship. Most such paradoxical gaps between selfobject relational nuclei are bridgeable but, just before considering further models for understanding the capacity to tolerate paradox, and the paradoxically multiple-yet-bridgeable structure of the self, I want to introduce a different level of paradox (closer to the cataclysmic end of Sainsbury's spectrum)—one that overwhelms the mind's capacity to bridge. We could name this the paradox of "Father's lap," one version of which would be "Father's comfy, protective lap presents an erect penis."

Paradoxes of this severity may not be tolerated within the mind. The effort to bridge intolerable paradox places a demand on the mind to work on overload. Indeed, we shall see how the child's mind, defending against psychic meltdown, resorts to dissociative defenses that are tantamount to the death of the self as constituted up until that traumatic moment. (I do not mean to suggest that intolerable paradox is exclusively a function of the severity of environmental, or relational, contradictions. The strain entailed in an internal multiplicity of intentions, desires, needs, identifications, purposes, and self-states may render an "identity diffusion" [Erikson, 1968], a difficulty bridging inherent multiplicity within the self.)

Again we reflect on the universal structure of the human psyche: a virtually infinite multiplicity of nuclei, or islands, of self-state gathering, and variously organizing, elements of percept, memory, personifications, fantasies, physiological adjustments, mood, metaphor, and lexicon clustered around intentions, impingements, and affects that arise during relational experiences that inherently pull for distribution into such mental categorizations (see Bollas, 1995; Bromberg, 1994; Edelman, 1987; Mitchell, 1993; Modell, 1993). These islands each contain conflict consistent with Freud's (1923) structural model of the mind as well as levels of consciousness consistent with his (1915) topographical metaphor. But the primordial structure of the mind is constituted of multitudinous islands, and an "aerial map" of each person's mind would indicate these islands and the bridges between them. Some of the bridges connect closely allied islands, and their solid, multilane construction allows a steady commute in both directions. Other bridges are paradoxical, with their stanchions on either end rising from islands that mutually negate the reality of the other; and yet the capacity to negotiate paradox permits the self to tolerate this straddling and sustain constructive or creative commerce along the span. One can set out from the island of "Mother hurts feelings" toward the island of "Mother soothes feelings" and, despite the warnings of some inhabitants that from the perspective of this island the other one could not exist, the bridge is crossed with the trust that it holds and extends to a tenable location—and so the paradoxes of everyday life are tolerated with an okay feeling.

Then there are those islands—more rare and, fortunately, showing up on fewer maps—that have no bridge between them. Like the two islands of the "father's lap" paradox, all bridges have been destroyed, and commerce is forbidden, a proscription strictly enforced by vigilant dissociation. An aerial view may show stanchions and incomplete ramps left suddenly abandoned during construction, with the skeletons of some workers crushed by collapsing structures and buried forever under debris. An occasional catamaran from one island strays inadvertently near the other island, senses the pull of a cataclysmic "black hole," and flees.

In the extreme case, we see severely discrepant relational experience not only violating the usual laws of thought but also violating the mind's capacity to tolerate and bridge a range of paradox, forcing recourse to a dissociative damage control that leaves islands of relational experience epistemically expunged from each other's register. Bromberg (1995), presenting the implications of such defensive dissociation for the analytic process, quoted Laub and Auerhahn's statement that "trauma overwhelms and defeats our capacity to organize it" (p. 183). Bromberg asserted that

> it is the more primary nature of trauma to "elude" our knowledge because of what [Laub and Auerhahn] call a deficit—a gap that has to do with the formation of psychic structure into "me" and "not me"—a dissociative gap, by virtue of which the experience of original trauma is relegated to a part of the self that is unlinked to that part of the self preserved as a relatively intact "me." It is not the "contents" of the mind that are primarily at issue; it is the dissociative structure of the mind itself ("me" and "not me") that resistance is most fundamentally addressing, at least during much of the ongoing treatment. (p. 183)

Elsewhere, Bromberg (1994) maintained that

> dissociation is not inherently pathological, but it can become so. The process of dissociation is basic to human mental functioning and is central to the stability and growth of personality. It is intrinsically an adaptational talent that represents the very nature of what we call "consciousness." (p. 520)

I wish to emphasize here the distinction between dissociation as an "adaptational talent" and dissociation as a defensive recourse and the implications for the origins of mental structure in development. I also wish to emphasize a distinction between the distributed self and the dissociated self.

I believe that the more universal nature of "consciousness" is its multiplicity, not necessarily brought about formatively by dissociations. That is, as I understand it, such experiences as "Mother soothes" and "Mother hurts" occur originally as disparate events (or RIGs, schemas, or narratives) that become gathered into relative orchestration only as the developing mind's synthetic capacities establish the bridges between these intrinsically distinct islands and produce what Bromberg (1994) called the "necessary illusion of being one self." Hence, the more universal nature of consciousness is its inherent distribution into an archipelago of multiple meaning-and-affect centers that come to be more bridgeable than not as the mind develops in health. I suggest, then, that when traumatic overload forces the mind to deploy a defensive dissociation, the network of connections that have been formed to span multiple meaning-and-affect centers suffers catastrophic breaches in communication, the demolition of bridges between the mind's islands of associated self–object relational representations. It is under these conditions that the distributed multiplicity of self yields to a dissociated multiplicity of self. Hence, I would agree that the "dissociative" process by which consciousness is selectively focused, and attention is adaptively concentrated, reflects the operation of basic "human mental functioning." I would stress, however, the distinction between dissociation as a process of selectively focusing attention and dissociation as an organization of unlinked mental structure persisting over time.

I believe Winnicott's (1965) articulation of unintegration and disintegration, even in its Kleinian, object-relational antiquity, presaged more current infant observational reports (e.g., Beebe, Jaffe, & Lachmann, 1992; Beebe & Lachmann, 1992; Stern, 1985; Trevarthen, 1979) and the contemporary literature on the self and on trauma and dissociation. I read in (perhaps *into*) Winnicott's language the distinction between an *unintegration*—in which the natural welter of self-states experienced in a relational holding context are not forced into a conglomerate psychic unity but rather are tolerated in their multiplicity, with unresolved paradoxes accepted under the supplemental sponsorship of the caregiver's ego coverage (transformational object function)—and, however, a *disintegration*, which reacts to stimulus overload, object impingement, or cataclysmic-level paradox by a defensive dissociation that seeks to establish internal mastery over external assault. Winnicott's observations provide the origins of the infant's spontaneous gesture, the creative bridging of internal islands, and negotiations of paradox that extend the individual's stamp of personal agency into interpersonal existence.

Edelman's Theory of Neuronal Group Selection

Edelman's (1987, 1989, 1992) theory recognizes the adaptive advantage enjoyed by creatures that can discriminate self from nonself, coordinate homeostatic and environmental regularities and novelties, and selectively attend to impingements to deploy efficacious motor responses. He defined a complex dynamic-systems model of neurobiology that he called the "matter of the mind" and described the complex reciprocal pathways whereby the genetic, molecular, synaptic, and structural realms, as well as the developmental and experiential, affective and appetitive, intersubjective and socially constructed, conceptual, semantic, and linguistic realms all converge and interact to produce human mental activity.

A thorough presentation of Edelman's complicated and detailed neuronal group selection theory is beyond the scope of this chapter. However, one critical element in Edelman's dynamic-systems model of consciousness is germane here: the process of re-entry. Edelman's term *re-entry* refers to the large-scale criss-crossing of multiple neuronal activations along selectively energized linkages between salient neuronal groups (or local "station" maps). Re-entrant signaling conveys raw perceptual features to neuronal clusters specific to processing each perceptual property (e.g., linear edges, color, movement, etc.) and local neuronal maps linked to the hedonic centers and the limbic system and, in higher order consciousness, to global maps of conceptual, symbolic, and linguistic meaning. Edelman's model, without positing the existence of a supervisory homunculus within the mind, thus accounts for the shuttling of synaptic currents in a recursive system of perceptual category and value centers—islands of remembered experience and instinctual or affective charge—aggregated and coordinated through adaptive selection. By myriad reciprocally modifying correlations signaled along re-entrant loops, the mind transforms the objects of immediate perception into personally meaningful experiences and simultaneously adds further shades of meaning to its memorial mapping system. Each person develops a unique topographical and functional mapping system whereby the self's perceptual categories, instincts and affects, and socially constructed meanings converge on the moment of present perception. This neural system seems to be capable of a dizzying number of couplings or correlations passed reciprocally across re-entrant loops linking localized areas of brain–mind activity. In this sense, the dynamic process of re-entry that recategorizes immediate perceptions and renders them meaningful, thereby shaping the basis for responsive behaviors, constitutes in itself a kind of neurobiological negotiation among inputs from the environment and from internal value–category clusters. In this negotiation, the impinging environmental event may claim salience (as in looking up from a reverie to notice the curtains on fire), or the internal value, or meaning, may be relatively more predominant (as when a saint accepts death at the stake rather than betray his faith).

Edelman applied his model of re-entry to explain neurological and psychological disorders in terms of interrupted re-entrant loops. For example, he suggested that *blindsight*, a condition in which a person has no awareness of vision yet can locate objects in space when tested, is caused by a disruption of re-entrant loops necessary for primary consciousness regarding visual input. Similarly, Edelman considered schizophrenia "a generalized disease of re-entry," in which communications between re-entrant maps may be disabled in areas responsible for synchrony between maps, coordination between perceptual modalities, assignment of predominance to image versus percept, or in linkages between conceptual or semantic centers. We might then conjecture that Edelman's model of pathology as breached re-entrant loops provides a distinct neurological basis for the more metaphorical notion of the demolition of bridges between islands of inner experience—dissociation in the mind must correspond to a neurophysiological event. We may also conjecture that the human affect tolerance for paradoxical experience confers an evolutionarily adaptive advantage, sustaining a continuity of self amid contradictory, or mutually negating, mappings of concept, affect, and meaning and, thus, that higher order consciousness has evolved a capacity to handle paradox, up to a point, during the negotiated re-entrant signaling of disjunctive value–category matches.

We could look at Edelman's (1989) statement that "current perceptual events are recategorized in terms of past value–category matches" (p. 102) and ask what happens when trauma "unhooks" certain relevant islands of "value-laden memories" and relegates them to exile by defensive dissociation (interrupted re-entrant loops). We can see why Russell (2000) invoked Freud's observation that "consciousness arises instead of a memory trace" as the posttraumatic residue governing the repetition compulsion: The impossibility of completing the bridging between dissociated islands of "value-laden memories" maintains the perseveration of "meanings" hostage to "real time," because access to full "recategorization" has been cut off by the unbearable affect signals associated with the approach to those black hole islands where intolerable paradox made its violent appearance. Hence, cut off from the mind's full potential for metaphoric recategorization consonant with a coherently continuous self, what "arises" instead is a split-off, and therefore concretized, enactment of an unmodifiably dissociated self–other percept telescopically encoded for "survival reaction" only. In James's (1890) terms, the mind is disenfranchised of its spontaneous "vote."

Now we can revisit Bromberg's (1994) model of the person dispersed into multiple self-states through dissociations forced by, as he described, "drastically incompatible emotions or perceptions" (p. 520). I, however, suggest an emendation of Edelman's (1989) model to account for the universal multiplicity of self, within the integrity of "value-laden memory" systems, under nontraumatic environmental conditions of development. I propose that what Modell (1993) described as the language-equipped self's "ability to create a coherent internal model of past, present and future" (p. 158) is an ability to bridge separate islands of self-state and self-relating memory categories. Thus, the coherent self is paradoxical not only in bridging the continuity of memory and the discontinuity of consciousness but also in bridging the multiplicity of self and self-other experiences, even reciprocally negating juxtapositions of experience, while preserving the "coherence" of a singular identity over time. As I suggested earlier, perhaps the bridges I describe in my portrait of the internal world are themselves translatable into the relatively selected and deselected neural pathways of Edelman's model, constituting the self's potential for straddling intrasubjective systems of systems.

Bromberg (1994) also emphasized a model of the psyche that "does not start as an integrated whole, but is nonunitary in nature" (p. 521)—and, as I see it, such an original mental structure would not be the result of dissociation; that is, a process of unlinking or unhooking. We need to consider organizing factors other than dissociation to account for what Bromberg termed "a mental structure that begins and continues as a multiplicity of self-states that maturationally attain a feeling of coherence which overrides the awareness of discontinuity" and preserves "the necessary illusion of being 'one self'" (p. 521). I believe that these basic organizing influences on the structure of the self, other than dissociation, can be conceptualized as general features of complex dynamic systems, or deterministic chaos. Bromberg implied this conceptual framework as well when he invoked Putnam (1988) to support his "nonunitary" model of the psyche. Bromberg noted Putnam's assertion that "states appear to be the fundamental unit of organization of consciousness and are detectable from the first moments following birth" (p. 522)—hence, prior to the mind's deployment of dissociation. Putnam's model of psychological states, and state shifts, is essentially a complex dynamic system of "self-organizing and self-stabilizing structures" that manifest discrete and discontinuous properties yet allow for nonlinear state changes. Putnam depicted states as cohesive clusterings of multiple variables; specifically, affect, state-dependent memory, attention and cognition, regulatory physiology, and a sense of self. Each state "acts to impose a quantitatively and qualitatively different structure on the variables that define the state of consciousness" (p. 522). Yet transitions in states of consciousness do occur, most often heralded by changes in affect and mood, and each new state structure "acts to reorganize behavior and resist changes to other states" (p. 522).

Chaos Theory and State Shifts

Chaos theory—or the theory of complex dynamic systems—supports, with notably close correspondence, the paradigm of nonlinear, discontinuous self-states that exercise a conservative inertial drag on change yet allow for shifts and access to intersystemic bridging. In the terms of deterministic chaos theory, each state would be depicted geometrically as a swirl of multiple variables forming a stabilizing orbital pattern, or basin, around a hypothetical attractor core. Each attractor basin tends to hold its organizational pattern, preserving the integrity of that cohesive state. Yet true to the complex reciprocal influences intrinsic to multivariable dynamic systems, small changes in the quantitative or qualitative properties of any element in the system may set in motion bifurcating, ramifying, recursive feedback and, ultimately, profound effects, prompting the transition in dynamic organization from one attractor cluster, across a separatrix, to another attractor. Such transitions may be subtle or gradual shifts, or relatively abrupt switches. Nonlinear state shifts, as in Putnam's (1988) psychological model, vary in their smoothness or abruptness of transition, in the degree to which they are reversible or absolute and, hence, bridgeable or un-bridgeable. The distributed multiple self represents a model of relatively bridge-able nonlinear state shifts between contradictory attractors—perhaps along a gradient of interpenetration, overlap, and reversibility—whereas the dissociated multiple self represents a model of virtually unbridgeable gaps between attrac-tors.

To further develop this discussion of distributed and dissociated multiplic-ity, and the bridging of paradoxical states, I introduce, from dynamic systems theory, the distinction between chaos and dischaos, and the notion of fractals. Fractal geometry presents us with the dilemma of "the sandy beach," in the form of this question: "How long is the coast of Britain?" Imagine flying over the coast of Britain with a camera. Now zoom in with your camera lens, and you begin to see very small islands, even pebbles, in a densely packed structure (Abraham, 1995). Now get off the plane and stand on the beach along the coast of Britain. Take a good wide stance at the water's edge and look down between your feet. Now how long is that part of the coastline between your feet? And what about the froth, the swirls of surf foam, the grains of wet sand frothing up, the sucking in of holes, the pebbles interspersed in the water, and the water penetrating the land? Now do we measure in a straight line? How long, then, is the coast of Britain? As Abraham (1995) wrote,

> all this is the coast: It has a fractal dimension. . . . Not only is the coast a fractal, with a dimension more than one but less than two, but it is a fractal region: the coastal zone. The ocean and land are not divided by the coast in a binary fashion; they interpenetrate in a fractal geometry. The fractals of chaos theory—attractors, separatrices . . .—are all of the sandy beach variety. (p. 163)

Abraham, a mathematician, used the sandy beach model to consider psy-chological systems. Within the person, he argued, "the sandy beach concept applies to the boundary between two different behavioral regions" (1995, p. 163). Now bear in mind Putnam's (1988) model of "nonlinear state changes" applied to the relatively healthy person as well as to the person, described by Bromberg (1994), who has deployed intrasubjective dissociation in the face of "drastically incompatible emotions or perceptions," as I quote Abraham's (1995) description of the "dischaotic personality":

> We now assume a . . . dynamical model for self or life space of an individual. Different aspects of the personality, depending critically on the individual, are represented in this model by groups of basins of attraction. These may be slowly changing in time under the effects of learning, adaptation, stimuli, and so on. Now that chaos theory and fractal geometry have emerged, we expect that fractal boundaries of these psychological regions are the rule, rather than the exception. Following the lead of chaos theoretical models in medical phys-iology, we may expect that chaotic attractors and fractal separatrices are im-portant for health. Specifically, we may suggest that thick fractal separatrices

in the psyche have an integrating effect. For under the effect of random or chaotic stimuli, the trajectory of the . . . model jumps about in small discontinuities, landing in different basins because of the fractal boundaries. This has the effect of integrating the different behaviors of the different attractors into a strongly associated . . . personality. On the other hand, when the boundaries have become (perhaps in a pathological situation) too ordered, or dischaotic, or if the fractal dimension is too small, there would be a tendency to manifest one attractor for some time, until an exceptional stimulus pushes the trajectory over the edge into the basin of another aspect of the self and there is a dramatic change in behavior. (p. 164)

Thus, the shifts in self-state in Putnam's paradigm become more absolute, and less bridgeable, as the boundaries between nonlinear states become less fractal. Dissociations, or other "splitting" mechanisms that reduce communication between subsystem attractor basins, establish "dischaotic" dynamic systems in which the separatrices (the potential spaces) between attractor basins become categorical divider lines and the trajectories of self-experience (affect, image, memory, cognition, physiological adjustment, and self-representation) tend not to cross over, or bridge, into other basins. Consistent with Putnam's model, discrete self-states exercising their structuralizing influence on the trajectories of variables resist changes to other states with a varying range of inertial force correlated with the "thickness" of fractal boundaries. Here we can picture again, in metaphoric terms, a basic model of the self distributed into multiple islands (basins) of states, each clustering around affect-laden meanings ascribed to memory, thought, fantasy, percept, and body sense and variously interconnected by bridges; those particular basins that are formed traumatically remain islands cut off, their fractal bridges sabotaged by defensive dissociation (repelling the approach of trajectories that might strengthen connections).

Perhaps it is a matter of the degree of paradox, wherein tolerable paradox is bridged and cataclysmically discrepant paradoxical experience that strains the elasticity of mind beyond its capacity to span a fractal separatrix coerces a dischaotic splitting to sustain basic survival. We might further picture the chaotic metamodel of self, with its relatively more or less fractal boundaries between states allowing for varying facility for integration, state shift, or the "interstate" sharing of resources, according to Edelman's (1992) neurophysiological model of the self. Perhaps the bridges between states represent neuronal pathways preferentially selected, or deselected, for salience according to their advantageous efficacy at linking clusters of memorial systems with currently arriving percepts in the interest of preserving the continuity of the self. Boundaries between discrete self-states that are more bridgeable, more fractal, are neuronal networks that are selectively more available, or more utilized, during ongoing *re-entrant signaling*—Edelman's term (1992) for the neuronal process that correlates stored memory and current perception—and the adaptive and creative processes by which we negotiate meaning. Trauma kills the unity and continuity of the self by necessitating a defensive "dischaos" that interrupts the neurophysiological, and psychic, integrity of freely associative recategorization.

In the life of each of us, our particular internal template of meaning and affect categories, or "value-laden memories" in Edelman's model, that dynamically determine retranscriptions may be regarded as the legacy of all object-relational experiences. Indeed, "the shadow of the object fell upon the ego" (Freud, 1917, p. 249), and the resultant imprints within the psyche, whatever might be the neurophysiological interface, define those "shades of meaning" available to the person for each moment of recategorization. As Sullivan (1953) observed, the person has the sign. Herein lies the individual's unique potential for creativity, the negotiation of fresh acts of meaning (Bruner, 1990). Because all object experiences are not only conflictual but also variously paradoxical, the internal memorial structure that defines the identity and coherence of the self must consist of multiple nuclei of relational affect categories—multiple attractor basins—whose thick fractal boundaries (or lack thereof) describe the self's internal universe of potential recategorizations. The capacity to tolerate and bridge paradoxical relational experiences and their associated self-states, stored memorially within the psyche as value-laden attractor basins, is thus a vital evolutionary and ontogenetic achievement. Without the bridging of paradox, re-entrant signaling of new perceptions may find only curtailed pathways toward a stunted recategorization. Without freely associated recategorization, the links between the unconscious (value-laden memory) and the conscious (current perceptual awareness) are diminished. Consciousness arising with diminished memory trace reduces retranscription (*Nachtraglichkeit*) and thereby dwarfs the self as an agent of meaning. The person feels "empty," unanchored in personal subjectivity, poorly equipped to negotiate with the tidal surge of environmental impingements or to select response options other than those repetitive patterns governed by a posttraumatically gerrymandered re-entrant signaling network. The tolerance for paradox that makes possible the bridging of multiplicity within the self is essential for the intactness of consciousness. Whereas the process of dissociation may be central to the stability of personality, I believe that it is the inherent capacity to tolerate and bridge paradox that is central to the development and growth of personality.

Our conception of the mind's capacity to tolerate paradox gains a useful dimension when viewed in the terms of chaos theory. Take the mother paradox: "I run to Mother when someone hurts my feelings. Mother is the person who hurt my feelings." We could picture the child's internal mapping of this paradoxical relational configuration as two attractor basins, roughly labeled "Mother soothes feelings" and "Mother hurts feelings." The affect trajectories at the theoretical center of these attractor basins do indeed mutually negate each other —and strain the child's logic to maintain their coexistence in mental representation. Numerous (countless?) trajectories of percept, affect, memory, sensation, and identity, however, do continuously arc across the fractal boundaries separating these value-laden islands of potential meaning. Hence, the thick fractal thoroughfares between these discrepantly valent experiences with the mother indeed cross over as bridging tendencies (e.g., the sense-memory of her embrace), belonging on both islands of experience, both self-states, while the attractor cores of these states remain an unreconciled paradox. The psyche's tolerance for paradox relies on the free passage of variables that congregate naturally together and thereby maintain relatively fractal boundaries between mutually negating cores of meaning, around each of which these variables yet remain complexly orbited. In this way, bridges extend between islands that could not exist from the perspective of each other's core. I propose that this model describes the human mind in health, to the degree that intolerably paradoxical attractor cores have not been traumatically introduced, necessitating a dischaotic prohibition on the free interplay of evocative trajectories between the distinct islands of internal space.

Now let us consider the mother as the conductor who facilitates passage for her child from one state to another. I suggest that the caregiver's transformational-object function makes a necessary contribution to the child's development of the capacity to tolerate paradox. The mother, whose affect "matching" and tactfully adroit conducting conveys her child from one state to another, is communicating to the child a message that can be internalized: "The discrepancy that divides these two states is okay." Also it is significant not only that the caregiver facilitates the shift from one state to another but also that the child experiences in these moments the very process of bridging itself. The transition, or transformational process, between discrete, nonlinear, affect-laden states is, in and of itself, a critical experience in development.

The development of our capacity to bear, hold simultaneously, and feel the unforced reconciliation of paradoxical, multiple states is facilitated by our integration of—and practice with our mother's (and others') convoying us across—countless nonlinear switches. For example, the transition from "mastery of walking" to "tumbling downward," and onward to "up and at it," has been accompanied by parental ego-coverage that helped to hold the moment together and negotiated a tolerable mediation of unthinkable anxiety at the brink of "going into pieces" or "falling forever." The mother whose anger startled her child, and who then aided the child's return to an affective relaxation, provided more than the experience of a trustworthily repeated sequence of relational and internal states because the child has experienced not only the daily repetitions of sequence but also the repetitions of the transitions between sequences. Thus, paradoxical relational states come to be tolerated not only through the repetition of their juxtaposition, or sequence, but also through the affectively meaningful experience of transitions sponsored within a relational context: the experience of bridging. We construct value-laden memories of the negotiation of affective bridges that serve as the affective experience and regulatory mechanism accomplishing shifts in state. We come to trust the experience of getting from here to there without yet knowing how. Hence, by internalizing the affective experience of state transitions we form the basis for our ability to bridge—straddle—paradox without a disruption of our sense of self, although we may be cognitively or affectively strained. The feeling that unsolved paradox is okay is tantamount to what Bollas (1995) described as a sense of humor, a spirit of enjoyment in the sense of self amidst its multiplicity.

It is also obvious, then, that when a state shift is instigated (rather than facilitated or mutually regulated) by a mother (other) who is herself in a relatively dissociated state, we find the context for traumatic impingement and the likelihood of intolerable paradox. When the personality interacting with a child is not relatively integrated, with fractally separated subsystems at play, then state shifts tend to be abrupt cleavages, interruptions of going-on-being. The child who has experienced state switches induced by nonnegotiated, or dischaotic, impingement faces life proportionately less equipped with the competence to tolerate and bridge paradoxical realities.

The Analyst's Role in the Building of Bridges

Eventually, this child, now grown up, may enter psychoanalysis. I have elsewhere (Pizer, 1992, 1998) described the psychoanalytic process as an ongoing negotiation of paradox, in which the patient's capacity to participate in the intersubjective creation of meaning is cultivated within the analytic duet. I have also considered elsewhere (Pizer, 1996, 1998) specific elements of technique—play, metaphor, and the subjunctive—that enhance available analytic potential space for the uses of negotiation. Here, I focus on a particular dimension of therapeutic action and the role of the analyst, in the light of this examination of multiple self-states, dischaotic and fractal boundaries, switches and transitions, and the building and repair of bridges between paradoxically associated, or dissociated, islands within the self's value-laden memorial system.

I outline my ideas through a dialogue with selected statements of Bromberg's (1994).

> It is in the process of "knowing" one's patient through direct relatedness, as distinguished from frustrating, gratifying, containing, empathizing, or even understanding him, that those aspects of self which cannot "speak" will ever find a voice and exist as a felt presence owned by the patient rather than as a "not-me" state that possesses him. (p. 537)

Here, Bromberg is advocating the analyst's awareness of moments when the analytic technique itself may impose too dischaotic a hold on the intersubjective attunement of the analyst to the relationally enacted multiplicities of the patient. Thus, Bromberg cautioned the analyst to remain open to shifting his or her own responsive posture as an act of recognition that might meet the spontaneous gesture from a remote trajectory within the patient. Celebrating the wonder of parapraxes, Bromberg affirmed their value thus

> not because they provide a window into what a patient "really" believes but because they allow opposing realities held by different self-states to coexist, and mutuality can increase simultaneous access to a fuller range of self through the analytic relationship. (p. 531)

Here, Bromberg emphasizes the value of moments of surprise heralded by parapraxes, wherein "opposing realities" in the patient's mind may be juxtaposed and given a recognition in the analytic dialogue that sponsors their acceptable coexistence. Thus, we might regard a parapraxis not only as a "slip" but also as a "bridge." When we stumble on a parapraxis, we discover a potentially meaning-laden trajectory across a gap within the patient's internal world, separating the attractor basins of "different self-states." I fully agree with Bromberg but would add that such moments deliver access not only to a "fuller range of self" but also to the conscious experience and potentially augmented use of bridges that may connect states. Perhaps, in Edelman's (1992) terms, the neuronal mappings of bridges themselves may become more salient re-entrant loops as "opposing realities" find linkages cultivated within the analytic relationship.

Bromberg encouraged the analyst to join in duet with those affective notes issued from multiple self-states within the patient. As participant–observer, the analyst offers the structuralizing efficacy of linguistic symbolization (interpretation) along with the transformational influence of his authentic-yet-disciplined presence. The analyst's responsively adjusting self goes out to meet the multiplicity within the patient's self and, like the good-enough mother, holds the moment together by the grace of "ego-relatedness." As Bromberg (1995) wrote,

> it is this "room for relatedness" that turns static, frozen space into "potential space" and allows the creative encounter between a patient's multiple realities and those of his analyst to form something new—a negotiated enhancement of the patient's perceptual capacity and an increased surrender of the dissociative structure of his personality organization. (p. 185)

Perhaps Bromberg used the word *surrender* because he offers this statement in an article on resistance. Nonetheless, I want to emphasize that we can recognize in the "surrender of the dissociative structure" a dialogical practice of bridge building that potentiates ego development within the patient (and analyst); the enhanced "perceptual capacity" that may result is, in essence, the capacity for recategorization, retranscription, freely associative state shifts during re-entrant signaling, and the working through of transferences. We might playfully describe the therapeutic action of the psychoanalytic relationship in these terms: Where dischaotic boundaries were, there shall fractal boundaries be.

How does the analyst straddle the paradox between maintaining the necessary analytic frame and maintaining the necessary "room for relatedness"? As Bromberg (1994) acknowledged,

> over the years I've come to believe that it may be the limitation in my flexibility —the fact that I do implicitly draw a line in the sand—that has the most impact because it emanates from relational authenticity. If I do ultimately move the line, *the process through which that happens is at least as important as the accommodation itself*. It carries the fact that what I'm doing is not a technique but a personal effort I am willing to make as long as it does not exceed the limits of what I establish as my personal boundaries and is thus part of a genuine relational negotiation. (p. 544, emphasis in original)

Bromberg, grappling internally with the conservatism inherent in his own value-laden memories as analyst, negotiates fresh meanings with his patient in the immediacy of the analytic encounter. Here, we have the sandy beach: What begins as the analyst's line in the sand becomes a fractal zone, an area of overlap, during the intersubjective dialogue. Thus, a negotiated shift may occur reciprocally (see Aron, 1996). As I conceptualize such moments, the analyst joins the ranks of mothers, comics, and conductors who offer their own precariously maintained comfort with the discomforts of paradox as an intersubjective bridge for the linking of discontinuous worlds and the regulation of harmonies, through a process of reciprocal influences.

When analysts are receptive to the multiplicity within their patients, they serve as transformational objects sponsoring their patients' tolerance for paradoxical self-states by holding them within the unity of a single negotiated relationship. In this way, patients may bear "the spaces between realities" and maintain an enriched unity of self-experience. When "the spaces between realities" are named by interpretations, or straddled by transitions, arrived at together by therapist and patient, realities are not lost because the person now stands "in the spaces" on a bridge that spans paradoxical realities.

Winnicott (1967/1971) began his article "The Location of Cultural Experience" with an epigram from Tagore: "On the seashore of endless worlds, children play." Of course, Winnicott had not encountered the as-yet-uninvented chaos theory, but he implicitly understood the sandy beach dilemma. He recognized that potential space, the area of overlap and transition, is a fractal region. As he commented, "The quotation from Tagore has always intrigued me. In my adolescence I had no idea what it could mean, but it found a place in me, and its imprint has not faded" (p. 95). With Winnicott's gift for creative recategorization, he knew the seashore to be a thick fractal boundary, an endlessly paradoxical potential space in which children, playing, construct their bridges among a multitude of internal and external worlds.

References

Abraham, R. H. (1995). Erodynamics and the dischaotic personality. In F. D. Abraham & A. Gilgen (Eds.), *Chaos theory in psychology* (pp. 157–167). Westport, CT: Praeger.

Aron, L. (1996). *A meeting of minds: Mutuality in psychoanalysis*. Hillsdale, NJ: Analytic Press.

Beebe, B., Jaffe, J., & Lachmann, F. (1992). A dyadic systems view of communication. In N. J. Skolnick & S. C. Warshaw (Eds.), *Relational perspectives in psychoanalysis* (pp. 61–81). Hillsdale, NJ: Analytic Press.

Beebe, B., & Lachmann, F. (1992). The contribution of mother–infant mutual influence to the origin of self- and object representations. In N. J. Skolnick & S. C. Warshaw (Eds.), *Relational perspectives in psychoanalysis* (pp. 83–117). Hillsdale, NJ: Analytic Press.

Bollas, C. (1995). *Cracking up*. New York: Hill & Wang.

Bromberg, P. M. (1994). "Speak! That I may see you": Some reflections on dissociation, reality and psychoanalytic listening. *Psychoanalytic Dialogues, 4,* 517–547.

Bromberg, P. M. (1995). Resistance, object-image, and human relatedness. *Contemporary Psychoanalysis, 31,* 173–191.

Bruner, J. (1990). *Acts of meaning*. Cambridge, MA: Harvard University Press.

Edelman, G. M. (1987). *Neural Darwinism*. New York: Basic Books.

Edelman, G. M. (1989). *The remembered present*. New York: Basic Books.

Edelman, G. M. (1992). *Bright air, brilliant fire*. New York: Basic Books.

Erikson, E. H. (1968). *Identity: Youth and crisis*. New York: Norton.

Fairbairn, W. R. D. (1952). Endopsychic structure considered in terms of object-relationships. In W. R. D. Fairbairn, *An object-relations theory of the personality* (pp. 82–132). New York: Basic Books. (Original work published 1944)

Freud, S. (1915). The unconscious. In J. Strachey (Ed. & Trans.), *Standard edition of the complete psychological works of Sigmund Freud* (Vol. 12, pp. 99–108). London: Hogarth.

Freud, S. (1917). Mourning and melancholia. In J. Strachey (Ed. & Trans.), *Standard edition of the complete psychological works of Sigmund Freud* (Vol. 14, pp. 237–258). London: Hogarth.

Freud, S. (1923). The ego and the id. In J. Strachey (Ed. & Trans.), *Standard edition of the complete psychological works of Sigmund Freud* (Vol. 19, pp. 1–66). London: Hogarth.

James, W. (1890). *The principles of psychology* (Vol. 1). New York: Holt.

Mitchell, S. (1993). *Hope and dread in psychoanalysis*. New York: Basic Books.

Modell, A. (1993). *The private self*. Cambridge, MA: Harvard University Press.

Pizer, S. A. (1992). The negotiation of paradox in the analytic process. *Psychoanalytic Dialogues, 2,* 215–240.

Pizer, S. A. (1996). Negotiating potential space: Illusion, play, metaphor, and the subjunctive. *Psychoanalytic Dialogues, 6,* 689–712.

Pizer, S. A. (1998). *Building bridges: The negotiation of paradox in psychoanalysis.* Hillsdale, NJ: Analytic Press.

Putnam, F. (1988). The switch process in multiple personality disorder and other state-change disorders. *Dissociation, 1,* 24–32.

Russell, P. (2000). *The crises of emotional growth.* Unpublished manuscript, Harvard Medical School, Cambridge, MA.

Sainsbury, R. M. (1988). *Paradoxes.* Cambridge, England: Cambridge University Press.

Slavin, M., & Kriegman, D. (1992). *The adaptive design of the human psyche.* New York: Guilford Press.

Stern, D. (1985). *The interpersonal world of the infant.* New York: Basic Books.

Sullivan, H. S. (1953). *The interpersonal theory of psychiatry.* New York: Norton.

Trevarthen, C. (1979). Communication and cooperation in early infancy. In M. Bullowa (Ed.), *Before speech* (pp. 321–347). Cambridge, England: Cambridge University Press.

Winnicott, D. W. (1965). *The maturational processes and the facilitating environment.* New York: International Universities Press.

Winnicott, D. W. (1971). The location of cultural experience. In D. W. Winnicott (Ed.), *Playing and reality* (pp. 95–103). New York: Basic Books. (Original work published 1967)

COMMENT:

A Dialectical Synthesis Rather Than a Paradox

Leslie S. Greenberg
William J. Whelton

We are in basic agreement with Stuart A. Pizer's view that the healthy self is constituted of multiple voices and that in health these voices are tolerated in their multiplicity. Following Winnicott, Pizer suggests that this healthy state of "unintegration" allows for a natural welter to coexist in a singular multiplicity of self-states rather than be forced into a false unity. Pizer contrasts this healthy state of unintegration with a state of "disintegration" that he proposes is a defense against the lack of support required to help tolerate unintegration.

His most appealing idea, in our view, is that of seeing the other as a "transitional mirror" or conductor who helps the self tolerate and contain disjunctive states by helping the developing self affectively bridge these states. By acting as a gentle conductor who guides the person from one state to another, one promotes the self's ability to accept its own multiplicity. Pizer offers a useful description of the other's role in promoting affect regulation within the self. It seems that the caretaker's ability to tolerate affective disjunctions—say, from anger to sadness, or fear to rage—does make these states more coherent for the self who is experiencing them. If these disjunctions were met with horror or disapproval or with concern for their irrationality or contradictoriness, it would become difficult for the individual to integrate these opposing states into a coherent sense of self.

This view of the self leads Pizer to recommend a dialogical form of therapeutic practice in which the therapist is seen as bridge builder, linking clients' discontinuous internal worlds and helping them regulate different inner harmonies. A therapist thus facilitates the transformational process of bridging different affective states, much as a mother who adroitly conducts her child from one affective state to another by her affective attunement. It is the empathic attunement to and acceptance of the child's emotions that provides the reas-

131

surance that these two states and their difference are all okay. In this view, a facilitator of development at any stage of life, be it a caretaker or a therapist, needs to communicate to the developing self that the discrepancy between two seemingly contradictory states is tolerable. The most important aspect of this communication is an attitude that conveys "you can surely make the transition." Thus it is the actual living through of the experience of the process of bridging discrepant affect-laden states that is critical in promoting the development of self-coherence.

In addition to discussing the development of coherence through mirroring, Pizer offers a model of the self as a dynamic system. He uses chaos theory and fractal geometry as metaphors to give us an image or picture theory of how the self in its complexity might work. He suggests that the self, rather than being a structure, is a discontinuous process by which shifting states can emerge in a nonlinear but coherent way. This appeal to chaos theory and specifically to the notion of fractal boundaries, although interesting, is highly abstract, and until it can be applied in a more detailed and rigorous fashion to self-function it remains a metaphor—an analogue that expresses the hope for explanation without offering an actual explanation.

An important aspect of Pizer's argument concerns paradox. Paradox, as he uses the concept, involves the coexistence within the self of multiple, contradictory, simultaneously coexisting self-states. He argues, citing Winnicott, that psychological paradoxes must remain unresolved and that any attempt to resolve them is liable to be injurious to psychic health. Paradox should be accepted and bridged, and the contradictions at its core must be allowed to continue to exist even after this bridging. Pizer maintains that for this reason paradox is essentially different from conflict, in which it is possible to attain resolution. A difficulty with this argument is definitional. The word *paradox* has different meanings in different domains. Pizer often speaks from a metaphorical stance, but ultimately he seems to want to rest his argument on the strict logical definition of the word: a proposition that is technically absurd by being self-contradictory. He invokes Sainsbury's book, which is about formal deductive reasoning and the resolution of logical paradoxes. As an example, he proposes as paradoxical the experience of discovering that "Mother is the person I run to when someone hurts my feelings. Mother is the person who hurt my feelings." This, however, in our view is not a logical paradox. Behavioral inconsistency of this type, however painful and disillusioning, does not constitute a logical paradox because the strict rules that govern formal deductive reasoning are not applicable to the extraordinary potential for inconsistency in human experience and behavior. Obviously, this inconsistency is logically possible. One could not be dead and alive at the same time (except metaphorically), nor could one be in two places at the same time, but the rules of formal logic do not preclude one from being both a nice guy and a bastard, as indeed many people are.

Pizer's use of paradox is closer to a loose, more "psychological" definition of paradox as offered by the *Oxford English Dictionary*: "A phenomenon that exhibits some contradiction or conflict with preconceived notions of what is reasonable or possible" (Burchfield, 1978, p. 450). The key word here is *preconceived*. Human beings form expectations, beliefs, and assumptions so they can impose some order on the variability and diversity of human experience. Confusing new experiences can challenge these assumptions and create serious internal conflict. Children need a certain amount of consistency and, with a need to explain things to themselves, but with limited cognitive capacities, they find inconsistency very difficult to assimilate. This can lead to intolerable conflict and confusion, and Pizer is exactly right in saying that the affective accompaniment and stability of a caretaker makes it possible to tolerate what is as yet not understood. Most of what Pizer calls paradox, however, is best interpreted as a form of dialectical conflict—a product of the complexity, multiplicity, and contradictoriness that constitute both the world and the self.

Let us expand on the example that Pizer introduces, of a little girl sexually molested by her trusted and apparently loving father. For the child, there is engendered an intense and painful conflict. She needs safety and comfort from her father, and previously she would have expected these. Now, though, she begins to experience anxiety, fear, and confusion in relation to her father. However paradoxical the form that it takes, this is clearly a conflict, and one that needs resolution of some kind. The most disastrous form of resolution, one usually precipitated by prolonged and intense abuse, is some element of disintegration of the self. But it is clear that when sexual abuse is discovered early and safety is offered, along with good psychotherapy, some form of resolution can be attained, although it may include the containment of complex and contradictory feelings. Paradox, as Pizer uses the term, is a class of conflict produced by the difficulty of assimilating the inconsistencies and contradictions of the self and of others, contradictions that so often confound the human desire for experience and behavior to be logical and consistent. Humans, however, work not by logic but by a dialectical process of the synthesis of elements— often, opposing elements—into a coherent whole.

This young girl's conflictual experience is better viewed in ways that create less semantic confusion than the use of the concept of paradox. Pizer himself used a number of images and metaphors that are very effective, such as the self as an archipelago with dozens of islands. These descriptions as such are not those of logical paradox but of singular multiplicity. We are in complete agreement with Pizer that the self is a dynamic system in which material is stored in memory at certain affect addresses, and we agree that the self is constituted of a multiplicity of self-states, each with state-dependent memory, affect, intention, perception, bodily adjustment, judgment, fantasy, and conflict. These states are diverse, and even contradictory, but not paradoxical or logically inconsistent; rather, they are the complex elements of an ongoing dialectical process of synthesis.

The process of organizing and integrating opposing states into a coherent identity does seem in part bound up with an emotionally attuned caretaker who can provide emotional regulation by proxy until this can be internalized. This view is important because it suggests a hypothesis that researchers can investigate: that empathic attunement leads to greater self-coherence and that it opens the door for a study of the process by which coherent identities organize, or fail to organize, out of a diverse welter of emotional states.

Finally, although it agrees with Pizer's interpersonal view of self development, our dialectical–constructivist view (Greenberg & Pascual-Leone, 1995; Greenberg & Van Balen, 1998) sees the self as forming from a synthesis of both inside and outside forces, thereby integrating intrapsychic and interpersonal perspectives. Thus, in our view development is not dependent on interpersonal experience alone. As important as the caretaker is in providing transitional conducting, it is also important to recognize that there exists a natural organismic tendency in people to integrate their own functioning into higher, and higher order, levels of organization. Thus, at some critical point in development walking emerges out of a synthesis of standing and falling, integrating the two internal organizations that govern standing and falling into a higher order organization, an organization that combines elements of both into the emergent order of walking.

In this way, the brain is constantly forming higher level schemes that integrate the repeated co-occurrence of lower order schemes, thereby forming higher level skills and abilities. There is an internal organizing tendency to integrate schemes that are coactivated and cofunctional. Thus, changing gears and moving one's foot on the clutch in a standard car automatically becomes integrated into a single driving scheme. Here, it is true that there is no direct opposition between the necessary hand and foot movements. If, however, opposing tendencies, such as an approach scheme and an avoidance scheme, are coactivated, it is not as easy to coapply the two sets of actions. They are in conflict. People and their brains, however, still operate by attempting, by means of a dialectical synthesis, to build a higher order model to integrate lower level models that are coactivated and cofunctional (Greenberg & Pascual-Leone, 1995). Thus, a child might both cling and hit as a resolution to this conflict, or freeze. There is always some organismic organizing principle operating and attempting to integrate disparate tendencies into a whole, however it is done. Thus, the ability to tolerate multiplicity does not come from the facilitation of a soothing caretaker alone; there is also an internal tendency to integrate all our disparate parts into a higher level sense of coherence. This is what it means to view the self as a dynamic, dialectical system.

Therefore, it is not contradictory for one to recognize that although a singular self, one both loves and hates one's spouse. One may wish for the closeness of one's children and also long for their separation. Many of us are, as individuals, both unsure and confident, tense and loose, sometimes happy and optimistic, sometimes sad and pessimistic. None of this seems hard to integrate into a single self that is a dialectical system in a dynamic process. The self is thus highly context and state dependent, often feeling one thing and then another, and at times feeling many more than one thing at a time. Thus, we are all highly complex, multileveled, multicomponent systems that operate as dynamic systems organizing into different states at different times (Greenberg & Van Balen, 1998). In a healthy developing self, there is a natural form of internal bridging that allows easy flow from one state to another and allows one to recognize that a variety of contradictory states coexist within one's self. Both internal tendencies and external influences thus help to create a tolerance for this complexity. When the responses to me from outside match and reflect my spontaneous internal processes, I form the strongest sense of self possible. Thus, it is very helpful to have an empathically attuned caretaker or therapist who confirms transitions as psychologically valid and understandable, but people also naturally achieve some bridging on their own.

References

Burchfield, R. W. (Ed.). (1978). *The Oxford English dictionary* (Vol. 7). Oxford, England: Oxford University Press.

Greenberg, L., & Pascual-Leone, J. (1995). A dialectical-constructivist approach to experiential change. In R. Neimeyer & M. Mahoney (Eds.), *Constructivism in psychotherapy* (pp. 169–191). Washington, DC: American Psychological Association.

Greenberg, L., & Van Balen, R. (1998). A theory of experience-centered therapies. In L. Greenberg, J. Watson, & G. Lietaer (Eds.), *Handbook of experiential therapy* (pp. 28–57). New York: Guilford Press.

CHAPTER 6

Intersubjectivity in the Analytic Situation

Lewis Aron

Although many cultural, social, and scientific developments have contributed to a relational view of the psychoanalytic process, I believe that the shift to an intersubjective perspective has emerged predominantly out of our accumulated clinical experience in psychoanalytic work with patients. In this chapter, I highlight the clinical centrality of examining the patient's experience of the analyst's subjectivity in the psychoanalytic situation. I also examine the notion of self-reflexivity, which I believe is the basis on which participation in the psychoanalytic process rests for both the patient and the analyst.

Intersubjectivity

Only with the recent development of feminist psychoanalytic criticism has it become apparent that psychology and psychoanalysis have contributed to and perpetuated a distorted view of motherhood (Balbus, 1982; Benjamin, 1988; Chodorow, 1978; Dinnerstein, 1976). In all our theories of development, the mother has been portrayed as the object of the infant's drives and as the fulfiller of the baby's needs. We have been slow to recognize or acknowledge the mother as a subject in her own right.

Jessica Benjamin (1988) argued that the child must come to recognize the mother as a separate other with her own inner world and her own experiences and as being her own center of initiative, an agent of her own desire. According to to Benjamin, this expanding capacity on the part of the child represents an important, and previously unrecognized, developmental achievement. Benjamin has proposed that the capacity for recognition and intersubjective relatedness is an achievement that is best conceptualized as a separate developmental line,

This chapter is an adaptation of the chapter published as "The Patient's Experience of the Analyst's Subjectivity," in *A Meeting of Minds: Mutuality in Psychoanalysis* (Lewis Aron, Analytic Press, 1996).

and she has begun to articulate the complex vicissitudes involved in this advance. The developmental achievement she describes is radically different from that previously described in the literature. The traditional notion of "object constancy" is limited to the recognition of the mother as a separate "object." The focus of the intersubjective perspective is the child's need to recognize the mother as a separate subject, which is a developmental advance beyond viewing the mother only as a separate object.

The term *intersubjectivity* has been used in a variety of ways by philosophers and by psychoanalysts. Benjamin's (1988) work on intersubjectivity emphasizes mutual recognition as an intrinsic aspect of the development of the self. Regarding the clinical psychoanalytic situation, Benjamin (1990) wrote that "an inquiry into the intersubjective dimension of the analytic encounter would aim to change our theory and practice so that 'where objects were, subjects must be'" (p. 34). Benjamin, drawing on her background in critical theory, adopted the term from Habermas and other philosophers who deliberately formulated the concept of a subject–subject relation in contrast to the subject–object relation. For Benjamin (1992), *intersubjectivity* "refers to that zone of experience or theory in which the other is not merely the object of the ego's need/drive or cognition/perception, but has a separate and equivalent center of self" (p. 45). How it is that a person may come to recognize the other as an equivalent subject is the central problem that she, following Winnicott, attempts to address. She argued that we need to maintain a tension in our theory between relating to others as objects and relating to others as separate subjects. She used the terms *intrapsychic* and *intersubjective*, respectively, to indicate these two realms, and she insisted on maintaining both intrapsychic and intersubjective theory.

Robert Stolorow, Atwood, and Ross (1978) introduced intersubjectivity into American psychoanalysis; for them, "intersubjectivity theory is a field theory or systems theory in that it seeks to comprehend psychological phenomena not as products of isolated intrapsychic mechanisms, but as forming at the interface of reciprocally interacting subjectivities" (Stolorow & Atwood, 1992, p. 1). They noted that their use of the term has never presupposed the attainment of symbolic thought, of a concept of oneself as subject, or of intersubjective relatedness in the sense used by Daniel Stern (1985). "Unlike the developmentalists," they wrote, "we use 'intersubjective' to refer to *any* psychological field formed by interacting worlds of experience, at whatever developmental level these worlds may be organized" (p. 3).

There are important differences in the ways the term is used by Benjamin, Stolorow, and Stern. For Benjamin (1988), intersubjectivity is a developmental trajectory, in which recognition is inconsistently maintained. Intersubjectivity refers to a dialectic process in which subjects recognize each other as separate centers of subjective experience but also continually negate the other as a separate subject. For Stern, intersubjectivity refers to the developmentally achieved capacity to recognize another person as a separate center of subjective experience with whom subjective states can be shared. By contrast, for Stolorow and his colleagues, the term is applied whenever two subjectivities constitute the field, even if one does not recognize the other as a separate subjectivity (Stolorow & Atwood, 1992). The difference between Benjamin and Stern, on one hand, and Stolorow and colleagues, on the other hand, in their use of the term is that Benjamin uses the term to describe a developmental achievement in which there is mutual recognition of each other's subjectivity. Her thinking includes the idea that intersubjectivity is a category that refers to a whole dialectical continuum that includes movement toward and negation of mutual recognition, whereas Stolorow and colleagues use the term to indicate the principle of mutual regulation and unconscious influence.

Natterson (1991) presented a detailed comparison of a variety of uses of intersubjectivity in contemporary psychoanalytic theory. His own work moves in the direction of a radical and relentless intersubjective analysis. Critical of Stolorow and his colleagues, he argued that in their reported case studies, they conflate intersubjectivity and countertransference. According to Natterson, Stolorow and his followers limit their focus on intersubjectivity to the pathological aspects of the analyst's interaction with the patient. From Natterson's perspective, Stolorow's brand of intersubjectivity does not pay consistent enough attention to the therapist's continual influence on the treatment. For Natterson, "nothing short of a complete inclusion of all psychological input and reactions of both participants will permit optimal understanding of the issue" (p. 99). Intersubjectivity must be carefully distinguished from the more traditional view of transference–countertransference, in which the direction of influence remains largely from the patient to the analyst. The more traditional view pathologizes countertransference. For Natterson, intersubjectivity implies the "essential, initial, coequal role of the analyst in the analytic process" (p. 109).

Although I am in general agreement with Natterson's argument, I would emphasize too the analyst's essential, continual, bidirectional, or mutual influence in the analysis; my own view is that Natterson is mistaken in referring to the mutual influence as "coequal" because mutual influence need not imply equal influence. It does seem to me that speaking of the organization of the analyst's subjectivity or subjective experience has advantages over referring to the analyst's countertransference, and speaking of intersubjectivity has advantages over referring to transference–countertransference because (a) subjectivity and intersubjectivity do not imply the pathological; (b) they do imply bidirectional, if not necessarily equal, influence; and (c) they do imply a continuous, ongoing flow of influence, in contrast to countertransference, which implies an occasional or intermittent event.

More than any other psychoanalytic theorist writing today, Thomas Ogden (1986, 1989, 1994) has systematically formulated a theory of the interplay of subjectivity and intersubjectivity in development, psychopathology, and psychoanalytic treatment. Ogden traced the establishment of subjectivity to the distinction between the symbol and the symbolized. Subjectivity is seen as emerging in the space between the thought and the object of thought. Built on the contributions of Freud, Klein, and Winnicott, his elaboration of the dialectical nature of subjectivity culminates in the development of his original concept, the "analytic third"—neither subject nor object but jointly created, intersubjectively, by the analytic pair. "The intersubjective and the individually subjective each create, negate, and preserve the other," and created out of the dialectical interplay of these forces is "the intersubjective analytic third" (Ogden, 1994, p. 64).

In spite of the boldness of Ogden's theoretical innovations, a reading of his work suggests that he is quite conservative technically, particularly in his advocacy of using the analyst's subjectivity primarily to understand the patient's experience. Ogden emphasized the asymmetrical nature of psychoanalysis, has written forcefully against attempts at "mutual analysis," and does not advocate any active use of self-disclosure. But, more fundamentally, my reading of Ogden leaves me with the impression that he views his own subjectivity largely as reactive to the patient rather than as initiating particular forms of interaction; neither does he view the analytic participation as mutually influenced from the beginning. The relational–perspectivist view that I am propounding here assumes the mutual, even if unequal, participation of patient and analyst from beginning to end. For Ogden, subjectivity is paradoxically both always already present and a developmental achievement.

Elsewhere, I (Aron, 1993, 1995) have argued for the Oedipal stage and the internalized primal scene as a fundamental structure in the establishment of one's sense of self and of internal object relations, and I have referred to its role in the establishment of intersubjectivity. Prior to the Oedipal stage, the child lives in a two-person world. The child relates to both the mother and the father, but to each of them differently; that is, the child has a separate and unique relationship with each parent. The child relates to only one parent at a time, however, even if alternating from one to the other in momentary glances. It is only in the Oedipal stage of triadic object relations that the child perceives that he or she is part of a system that includes a separate relation between the parents from which the child is excluded. Britton (1989) used the term *triangular space* (p. 86) to describe the internalization of this relation.

The Oedipus complex entails not just the child's viewing of the parental relationship as an excluded outsider but also the myriad fantasies of the child in which the entire system of family relations is experimented with and internalized. The little boy or girl is at one moment the small, excluded child barred from the gratifications of adult sexuality; at another moment is the fantasized rival of the father for the mother's love; and at the next moment loves the father and is seeking a separate, private, and exclusive relationship with him. The child alternates between seeing him- or herself as outside of a two-person relationship, as the observer, or as inside a two-person relationship being observed by a third. Thus, it is in the Oedipal stage that the child first alternates between observation and participation. This oscillating function, the moving back and forth smoothly between experiencing and observing, can come about only with the attainment of Piaget's period of concrete operations because it requires maintaining two perspectives in mind at once (Flavell, 1963). The oscillating function is clinically important because the oscillating function becomes the basis on which a person can participate in an analysis.

From the standpoint of the development of intersubjectivity, it is critical that in reversing the configurations of the Oedipal triangle, the child comes to identify the self-as-subject with the self-as-object and the other-as-subject with the other-as-object. The child internalizes the image of the parent as an object and the image of the parent as a separate subject; but just as important because this involves the dialectical relations of subjectivity and objectivity, the child internalizes and identifies with the parent's image of the child (*reflected appraisals*; Sullivan, 1953, p. 17). Thus, the child's identification with the parent's subjectivity includes, as one component, an identification with the parent's subjective image of the child as both a subject and an object. In effect, these ideas are consistent with Benjamin's (1988) view of intersubjective and intrapsychic complementarity.

Pre-Oedipal and Oedipal development are always interconnected. The development of intersubjectivity should not be seen as an early or exclusively pre-Oedipal development—for example, one tied to the anal–rapprochement subphase—to be studied in isolation from later Oedipal issues. Rather, I am suggesting that the establishment of subjectivity and of intersubjectivity continues to evolve with Oedipal development.

Children are confronted with a multitude of tasks surrounding the establishment of self- and object constancy. They need to establish a sense of self as a center for action and thought, and they need to view this self in the context of other selves as an object among other objects (Bach, 1985). Similarly, they need to establish a sense of the other as a separate center of subjectivity as well as a view of the other as the object of their own subjectivity (Benjamin, 1988). These developments are of central importance to psychoanalysts because the analytic process consists of introspection and reflective self-awareness as well as of awareness of the self's interpersonal relations. Thus, one needs to develop a cohesive sense of self as a subjective self, a separate center of subjectivity, a sense of self-as-agent, an experiencing ego, and one needs to be aware of and able to reflect on oneself as an object of one's own investigation as well as of oneself as an object of the wishes and intentions of others. Each of these two dimensions of the self needs to be attained, and one needs to be able to recognize each of them as one's own self.

What I have been describing thus far can be significantly elaborated by mention of self-reflexivity, the capacity to move easily between subjective and objective perspectives on the self—or, to put this in the terms that I prefer, the capacity to maintain the dynamic tension between experiencing oneself as a subject and as an object (Auerbach & Blatt, 1996). My use of the term needs to be carefully distinguished from the more usual understanding of self-reflection. Self-reflection ordinarily connotes a cognitive process in which one thinks about one's self as if from the outside, that is, as if examining oneself as an object of thought. The way I am using the term here, by way of contrast, includes the dialectical process of experiencing oneself as a subject as well as of reflecting on oneself as an object. It is not, therefore, exclusively an intellectual observational function but an experiential and affective function as well.

My understanding of this notion has been influenced by a number of sources (see Aron, 1998, for a more elaborate discussion). For example, it has been decisively shaped by Sheldon Bach's (1985, 1994, chapter 2, this volume) contributions, particularly his distinction between subjective awareness and objective self-awareness, as well as by Peter Fonagy and Mary Target's (Fonagy & Target, 1995, 1996; Target & Fonagy, 1996) fascinating studies of "reflective functioning," or what they call the person's capacity for "mentalization." Reflective functioning implies the ability to understand another's state of mind as a state of mind. It entails the ability to understand mental states as essentially propositional and intentional, that is, as entailing beliefs and wishes. The development of this ability to understand another's mental states in turn facilitates one's own sense of mental agency or an intentional stance.

The Postmodern Challenge

Postmodernist or poststructuralist thought has questioned the very existence of a unitary, cohesive, nonmultiple, essentially unique identity. Poststructuralism deconstructs and decenters the human subject and insists that the notion of a unique, bounded individual is socially and historically constituted. It is from this postmodernist perspective that Dimen (1991) and Goldner (1991) have challenged the idea of a unitary gender identity as anything other than a simplified version of a self from which opposing tendencies have been split off and repressed: "a universal, false-self system generated in compliance with the rule of the two-gender system" (Goldner, 1991, p. 259). The postmodernists insist on each of our "multiplicities" and view our "identities" with suspicion. Consequently, intersubjectivity should not be taken to mean relations between two cohesive subjects; rather, intersubjective and interpersonal refer to relations among multiple personifications (Barratt, 1994; Bromberg, 1994, 1995; Mitchell, 1993).

Sympathetic critics (e.g., Flax, 1990; Rivera, 1989), however, have argued that postmodernists have erred by not distinguishing between a core self and a unitary self. Flax (1990), for example, proposed that "those who celebrate or call for a 'decentered' self seem self-deceptively naive and unaware of the basic cohesion within themselves that makes the fragmentation of experiences something other than a terrifying slide into psychosis" (pp. 218–219). Similarly, I suggest that instead of abandoning the notion of identity, as the postmodernists would have us do, our understanding of subjectivity must include both identity and multiplicity. Identity emphasizes a person's sense of continuity, sameness, unity, constancy, consistency, synthesis, and integration. Postmodernism is correctly concerned with the way in which the idea of identity obscures differences within and between human beings. Although people certainly need a cohesive and integrated sense of self, they also need to be able to accept a lack of integration and to tolerate—perhaps enjoy—confusion, contradiction, flux, and even chaos in their sense of who they are. They need to accept their own internal differences, their lack of continuity, their multiplicity, their capacity to be different people at different times, in different social and interpersonal contexts. Thus, I suggest that rather than abandon identity and subjectivity, we maintain both identity and multiplicity as aspects of human subjectivity.

Intersubjectivity and Clinical Practice

The theory of intersubjectivity has profound implications for psychoanalytic practice and technique as well as for theory. Just as psychoanalytic theory has focused on the mother exclusively as the object of the infant's needs while ignoring the subjectivity of the mother, so too psychoanalysis, neglecting the subjectivity of the analyst as he or she is experienced by the patient, has considered the analyst only as an object.

The traditional model of the analytic situation has retained the notion of a neurotic patient who brings his or her irrational childhood wishes, defenses, and conflicts into the analysis to be analyzed by a relatively mature, healthy, and well-analyzed analyst who studies the patient with scientific objectivity and technical neutrality. The health, rationality, maturity, neutrality, and objectivity of the analyst have been idealized, and thus countertransference has been viewed as an unfortunate, but (it was hoped) infrequent, lapse. Within the psychoanalytic situation, this bias, which regarded the patient as sick and the analyst as possessing the cure (Racker, 1968), has led to the assumption that only the patient had transferences. It was as if only the patient possessed a "psychic reality" (see McLaughlin, 1981), the analyst being left as the representative of objective reality. If the analyst were to be a rational, relatively distant, neutral, anonymous, scientist–observer, an "analytic instrument" (Isakower, 1963), then there was little room in the model for the analyst's psychic reality or subjectivity, except as pathological, intrusive countertransference.

As well known, only in the most recent decades has countertransference been viewed as a topic worthy of study and as potentially valuable in the clinical situation. For Freud (1910/1957), countertransference reflected a specific disturbance in the analyst elicited in response to the patient's transference, necessitating further analysis of the analyst. Contemporary theorists are more inclined to take a "totalistic" (Kernberg, 1965) approach to countertransference. They view it as reflecting all the analyst's emotional responses to the patient and therefore useful as a clinical tool. Rather than viewing countertransference as a hindrance to the analytic work that should be kept in check or overcome and that should in any event be kept to a minimum, most analysts today recognize the ubiquity of analysts' feelings and fantasies regarding patients and hope to utilize their reactions to understand their patients better. Psychoanalysis has thus broadened its database to include the subjectivity of the analyst. It has not yet, however, sufficiently considered the patient's experience of the analyst's subjectivity.

In my view, referring to the analyst's total responsiveness as countertransference is a serious mistake because doing so perpetuates the defining of the analyst's experience in terms of the subjectivity of the patient. Thinking of the analyst's experience as "counter" or responsive to the patient's transference encourages the belief that the analyst's experience is reactive rather than subjective, emanating from the center of the analyst's psychic self (McLaughlin, 1981; Wolstein, 1983). It is not that the analyst is never responsive to the pressures that the patient puts on him or her. Of course, the analyst responds to the impact of the patient's behavior—but countertransference obscures the recognition that the analyst is often the initiator of the interactional sequences, and therefore the term minimizes the impact of the analyst's behavior on the transference.

The relational–perspectivist approach I am advocating views the patient–analyst relationship as continually being established and re-established through ongoing mutual influence in which both patient and analyst systematically affect, and are affected by, each other. A communication process is established between patient and analyst in which influence flows in both directions. This implies a "two-person psychology" or a regulatory-systems conceptualization of the analytic process. Transference and countertransference too easily lend themselves to a model that implies a one-way influence in which the analyst reacts to the patient. That the influence between patient and analyst is not equal does not mean that it is not mutual; the analytic relationship may be mutual without being symmetrical. This model of the therapeutic relationship has been strongly influenced by the recent conceptualizations of mother–infant mutual influence proposed by Lachmann and Beebe (1995).

I believe that patients, even very disturbed, withdrawn, or narcissistic ones, always accommodate the interpersonal realities of the analyst's character and of the analytic relationship. Patients tune in, consciously and unconsciously, to the analyst's attitudes and feelings toward them, but insofar as they believe that these observations touch on sensitive aspects of the analyst's character, patients are likely to communicate these observations only indirectly, through allusions to others, as displacements, or by describing these characteristics as aspects of themselves, as identifications (Gill, 1982; Hoffman, 1983; Lipton, 1977). An important aspect of making the unconscious conscious is to bring into awareness and articulate the patient's denied observations, repressed fantasies, and unformulated experiences of the analyst (Hoffman, 1983; Levenson, 1972, 1983; Racker, 1968).

All children observe and study their parents' personalities. They attempt to make contact with their parents by reaching into their parents' inner worlds. The Kleinians have vividly emphasized this tendency of children through concrete metaphors of the infant's seeking literally to climb inside and explore the mother's body and to discover all the objects contained inside. Children imagine with what and with whom their mothers are preoccupied. They have some sense of how their mothers related to their own mothers, the children's grandmothers. A mother's internal working model of her relationship with her own mother affects her child's attachment to her (Main, Kaplan, & Cassidy, 1985). Children acquire some sense of the characters who inhabit their parent's inner worlds and of the nature of the relations among these inner objects. Most important, children formulate plausible interpretations of their parents' attitudes and feelings toward the children themselves. Children are powerfully motivated to penetrate to the center of their parents' selves. Pick (1985) stated this thought in Kleinian language: "If there is a mouth that seeks a breast as an inborn potential, there is, I believe, a psychological equivalent, i.e. a state of mind which seeks another state of mind" (p. 157). There is a pre-experiential motivational push, a drive, for a meeting of minds, although there is also a drive to remain hidden, an isolate, unfound and untouched by others. These conflicting desires operate in both patient and analyst. Hence, intersubjectivity is always intensely conflictual.

As McDougall (1980) asserted, if "a baby's earliest reality is his mother's unconscious" (p. 251), then a patient's psychic reality may be said to implicate the analyst's unconscious. Patients have conscious and unconscious beliefs about the analyst's inner world. Patients use their observations of their analysts —which are plentiful no matter how anonymous an analyst may attempt to be —to construct a picture of their analyst's character structure. Patients probe, more or less subtly, in an attempt to penetrate the analyst's professional calm and reserve. They do this probing not only to turn the tables on their analysts defensively or angrily but also because people need to connect with others. They want to connect with others where they live emotionally, where they are authentic and fully present. So they search for information about the other's inner world. (They do this conflictedly, however, because they also wish not to know or be known by the other.)

An analytic focus on the patient's experience of the analyst's subjectivity opens the door to further explorations of the patient's childhood experiences of the parent's inner world and character structure. Similarly, patients begin to attend to their observations about the character of others in their lives. This is an inevitable and essential part of how patients begin to think more psychologically in their analyses. The analytic stance being described considers fantasies and memories not just as carriers of infantile wishes and defenses against these but as plausible interpretations and representations of patients' experiences with significant others (Hoffman, 1983). This point was anticipated by Loewald (1970/1980), who wrote that

> the analysand in this respect can be compared to the child, who if he can allow himself that freedom, scrutinizes with his unconscious antennae the parent's motivations and moods and in this way may contribute, if the parent or analyst allows himself that freedom, to the latter's self awareness. (p. 280)

In the clinical situation, I often ask patients to describe anything that they have observed or noticed about me that may shed light on aspects of our relationship. When, for example, patients say that they think that I am angry at them, or jealous of them, or acting seductively toward them, I ask them to describe whatever it is that they have noticed that led them to this belief. I find that it is critical for me to ask the question with the genuine belief that I may find out something about myself that I did not previously recognize. Otherwise, it is too easy to dismiss the patient's observation as a distortion. Patients are often all too willing to believe that they have projected or displaced these feelings onto their analyst, and they can then go back to viewing their analyst as objective, neutral, or benignly empathic. Insisting that there must have been some basis in my behavior for their conclusions, I encourage patients to tell me anything that they have observed. I often ask patients to speculate or fantasize about what is going on inside of me, and in particular I focus on what patients have noticed about my internal conflicts.

For instance, a patient said that when he heard my chair move slightly, he thought for a moment that I was going to strike him. I asked him to elaborate on what he thought I was feeling: What did he think were the quality and nature of my anger? What had he noticed about me that led him to believe that I was angry in this particular way? How did he imagine that I typically dealt with my anger and frustration? I asked the patient what he thought it was like for me to be so enraged at him and to not be able to express that anger directly, according to his understanding of the "rules" of psychoanalysis and professional decorum. I asked him how he thought I felt about his noticing and confronting me with my disguised anger.

Rather than examining either the patient's own projected anger or the displaced anger of others in the patient's current or past life, I choose to first explore the patient's most subtle observations of me, which reflect my attitudes toward him or her as well as my character and personal conflicts. All of this ultimately needs to be explored but, following Gill's (1983) recommendations, I begin with an analysis of the transference in the here and now, focusing on the plausible basis for the patient's reactions. I proceed in this way regardless of whether I am aware of feeling angry at that point. I assume that the patient may very well have noticed my anger, jealousy, excitement, or whatever, before I recognize it in myself.

Inquiry into the patient's experience of the analyst's subjectivity represents one underemphasized aspect of a complex psychoanalytic approach to the analysis of transference. A balance needs to be maintained between focusing on the interpersonal and focusing on the intrapsychic, between internal and external object relations. Although at times exploring patients' perceptions of the analyst deepens the work, at other times this path is used defensively, by both patient and analyst, to avoid the patient's painful inner experience (see Jacobs, 1986, p. 304, for a clinical illustration of this problem). For each time that I ask patients about their experience of me, there are other times when I interpret their concentration on the interaction with me as an avoidance of their inner feelings and of looking into themselves. Of course, I need to remain open to the possibility that my interpretation is itself an expression of my own resistance to being probed. Ultimately, patient and analyst need to maintain a dialogue in which these meanings are negotiated between them. Agreement may or may not be reached, but the dialogue is essential. Intersubjective negotiation is the essence of relational practice.

Although asking direct questions about the patient's observations of the analyst is often necessary and productive, the most useful way to elicit the patient's thoughts and feelings about the analyst's attitudes is to analyze the defenses and resistances that make these feelings so difficult to verbalize. Asking patients direct questions about their experience of the therapeutic relationship has the disadvantage that it may appeal to more surface and conscious levels of discourse. The analyst needs to listen to all of the patient's associations for clues to the patient's experience. Often patients fear offending their analysts and provoking the analysts' anger by confronting them with aspects of the analysts' character that have been avoided. Patients fear that they are being too personal, crossing the boundary of what the analyst is willing to let them explore. Patients are especially likely to fear that if they expose the analyst's weaknesses and character flaws, the analyst will retaliate, become depressed or withdrawn, or crumble (Gill, 1982). Implicit in this fear is not only the patient's hostility, the patient's own projected fears, or simply the need to idealize the analyst but also the patient's perception that the analyst's grandiosity would be shattered by the revelation of a flaw.

All of this is related to the ways in which the patient's parents actually responded to the child's observations and perceptions of them. How did the parents feel about the child's really getting to know who they were, where they truly lived emotionally? How far were the parents able to let the child penetrate into their inner worlds? Was the grandiosity of the parents such that they could not let the child uncover their weaknesses and vulnerabilities? To return to the rich Kleinian imagery of the infant's attempts in unconscious "phantasy" to enter into the mother's body, we may wonder whether the violent, destructive fantasies encountered are due only to innate greed and envy or whether they are not also the result of the frustration of being denied access to the core of the parent. Could these fantasies be an accurate reflection of the child's perceptions of the parents' fears of being intimately penetrated and known?

What enable patients to describe their fantasies and perceptions of the analyst are the analyst's openness and intense curiosity about the patients' experience of the analyst's subjectivity. Patients benefit from this probing only if the analyst is truly open to the possibility that they will communicate something new to the analyst about themselves, something they have picked up about the analyst of which the analyst was unaware before. If, on the other hand, the analyst listens to a patient with the expectation of hearing a transference distortion and is not open to the likelihood and necessity of learning something new about him- or herself, then the analysis is more likely to get derailed or to continue on the basis of compliance and submission to authority. There is a tradition within psychoanalysis, although it has always remained on the periphery of the analytic mainstream, that has emphasized this mutual aspect of psychoanalysis. It began in the writings of Groddeck (1923/1950) and Ferenczi (1932/1988) and proceeded especially through the work of Harold Searles (1975, 1979).

When patients are encouraged to verbalize their experiences of the analyst's subjectivity, it is likely that they will put increased pressure on the analyst to verify or refute their perceptions. It is extremely difficult and frustrating for patients to be encouraged to examine their perceptions of their analysts' subjectivity and then to have their analysts remain relatively "anonymous." Once an analyst expresses interest in a patient's perceptions of the analyst's subjectivity, the analyst has tantalized the patient (Little, 1951) and surely is pressured to disclose more of what is going on inside of him- or herself. Furthermore, how the analyst pursues the inquiry into a patient's perceptions of him- or herself is inevitably self-revealing. I assume that one reason analysts have historically avoided direct inquiry into their patients' experience of analytic subjectivity is that they recognized that pursuing this line of inquiry would unavoidably result in self-disclosure.

But self-revelation is not an option: It is an inevitability. Patients accurately and intuitively read into their analysts' interpretations the analysts' hidden communications (Jacobs, 1986). In unmasking the myth of analytic anonymity, Singer (1977) pointed out that the analyst's interpretations were first and foremost self-revealing remarks. It cannot be otherwise because the only way we can truly gain insight into another is through our own self-knowledge; our patients know that.

Hoffman (1983) emphasized that the psychology of the analyst is no less complex than that of the patient, as our patients know. He challenged what he termed the *naive patient fallacy,* the notion that the patient accepts at face value the analyst's words and behavior. For analysts simply and directly to say what they are experiencing and feeling may encourage the assumption that they are fully aware of their own motivations and meanings. An analyst's revelations and confessions may tend to close off further exploration of a patient's observations and perceptions. Furthermore, we can never be aware in advance of just what it is that we are revealing about ourselves and, when we think we are deliberately revealing something about ourselves, we may very well be communicating something else altogether. Is it not possible that our patients' perceptions of us are as plausible an interpretation of our behavior as the interpretations we give ourselves? If so, then it is presumptuous for us to expect patients to take at face value our self-revelations. Pontalis (1975, cited in Limentani, 1989) asked, "What is more paradoxical than the presupposition that: I see my blind spots, I hear what I am deaf to, . . . and (furthermore) I am fully conscious of my unconscious?" (p. 258).

Analysts, it is hoped, have had the benefit of an intensive analysis of their own, but this training in no way ensures that they have easy access to their unconscious or that they are immune from subtly enacting all sorts of pathological interactions with their patients. It is this recognition that has led to the contemporary acceptance of the inevitability of countertransference. Whereas in the past the idealized, well-analyzed analyst was thought to have no countertransference problem, today's idealized analysts are thought to be so well analyzed that they have immediate and direct access to their unconscious. But it is well to keep in mind that the trouble with self-analysis is in the countertransference. When analysis is viewed as a coparticipation (Wolstein, 1983) between two people who are both subjects and objects to each other, then the analyst can read the patient's associations for references to the patient's perceptions of the analyst's attitudes toward the patient. This approach provides additional data with which the analyst can supplement his or her own self-analysis. In this way, the analyst and patient coparticipate in elucidating the nature of the relationship that the two of them have mutually integrated.

Christopher Bollas is among the most creative analytic writers in the field today. Although often referred to as Winnicottian, Bollas's approach is unique, expressed in his own idiom, and he is not to be pigeonholed. Blending elements of many analytic approaches, including British object relations, classical, Kleinian, Lacanian, and interpersonal theories, his writings have been very influential on relational authors in America. Bollas (1989) advocated that the analyst establish him- or herself as a subject in the bipersonal analytic field. He encouraged analysts to reveal more of their internal analytic process to their patients; for example, describing to a patient how a particular interpretation was arrived at or sharing with the patient one's associations to a patient's dream. He argued that if the analyst's self-disclosure is congruent with who the analyst really is as a person, then the disclosure is unlikely to be taken as a seduction. In establishing themselves as subjects in the analytic situation, analysts make available to their patients some of their own associations and inner processes for the patient to use and analyze. It is important to note that Bollas's revelations have a playful and tentative quality. He does not take his associations or "musings" as containing absolute truth but rather puts them into the analytic field to have them used or even destroyed by the patient. Furthermore, Bollas is reserved and cautious in his approach because he is aware that an incessant flow of the analyst's associations could be intrusive, resulting in "a subtle takeover of the analysand's psychic life with the analyst's" (1989, p. 69).

When arguing that the analyst should be available to the patient as a separate subject, Bollas would certainly agree that we must be cautious in advocating an approach that focuses on the analyst's subjectivity because of the danger that analysts may insist on asserting their own subjectivity. Analysts may impose on patients their own need to establish themselves as separate subjects, thus forcing patients to assume the role of objects. This is not intersubjectivity; it is simply an instrumental relationship in which the subject–object polarities have been reversed. I find Bollas's work particularly useful because in his emphasis on ordinary moments of therapeutic regression and on traditional analytic reserve, he balanced his own focus, and that of most other relational theorists, on the therapeutic value of the analyst's expressiveness. Nevertheless, in spite of the high value that Bollas placed on analysts' use of their subjectivities, and in spite of his cautious endorsement of self-disclosure, from my perspective Bollas paid too little attention to the analyst's personal contributions to the analytic process. For Bollas, the analyst's subjectivity is a means to search for the patient's subjectivity, and his work does not do justice to the impact of the analyst's subjectivities on a patient or on the patient's subjectivity as a reflection of the impact of the analyst.

In my view, self-revelations are often useful, particularly those closely tied to the analytic process rather than those relating to details of the analyst's private life outside the analysis. Personal revelations are, in any event, inevitable; they are simply enormously complicated and require analysis of how they are experienced by the patient. We benefit enormously from the analytic efforts of our patients, but we can help our patients only if we can discipline ourselves enough to put their analytic interests ahead of our own.

The major problem for analysts in establishing themselves as subjects in the analytic situation is that because of their own conflicts, they may abandon traditional anonymity only to impose their subjectivity on patients. They thus deprive patients of the opportunity to search out, uncover, and find the analyst as a separate subject, in their own way and at their own rate. Although the patient's experience of the analyst needs to be central at certain phases of an analysis, there are other times, and perhaps long intervals, when to focus on the perceptions of the analyst is intrusive and disruptive; such a focus does not permit the patient, even temporarily, to put the analyst into the background and indulge in the experience of being left alone in the presence of the analyst. Analysts' continuous interpretations of all material in terms of the patient–analyst relationship, as well as their deliberate efforts to establish themselves as separate subjects, may be correctly experienced as an impingement stemming from their own narcissistic needs. To some degree this outcome is inevitable, and it can be beneficial for patients to articulate it when it happens (Aron, 1990a, 1990b, 1991, 1992).

Winnicott (1971) suggested that psychoanalysis occurs in an intermediate state, a transitional space between the patient's narcissistic withdrawal and full interaction with reality; between self-absorption and object usage; between introspection and attunement to the other; between relations to a subjective object and to an object, objectively perceived; between fantasy and reality. In my own clinical work, I attempt to maintain an optimal balance between the necessary recognition and confirmation of the patient's experience and the necessary distance to preserve an analytic space that allows the patient to play with interpersonal ambiguity and to struggle with the ongoing lack of closure and resolution. A dynamic tension needs to be preserved between responsiveness and participation on the one hand, and nonintrusiveness and space on the other hand, intermediate between the analyst's presence and absence.

My manner of maintaining this tension is different with each patient and varies even in the analysis of a single analysand. I believe that each analyst–patient pair needs to work out a unique way of managing this precarious balance. The analysis itself must come to include the self-reflexive examination of the ways in which this procedure becomes established and modified. Analysis, from this perspective, is mutual but asymmetrical, with both patient and analyst functioning as subject and object, as coparticipants, and both working on the very edge of intimacy (Ehrenberg, 1992). The degree and nature of the analyst's deliberate self-revelation are left open to be resolved within the context of each unique psychoanalytic situation.

In my frequent attempts to present these thoughts to groups of colleagues and students, I have been struck by the overwhelming tendency on the part of my listeners to focus the discussion on the issue of the analyst's self-revelations. In my view, what is most important is not the analyst's deliberate self-disclosure but rather the analysis of the patient's experience of the analyst's subjectivity. The very expression by the patient of his or her perceptions of the analyst leads to the acknowledgment of the analyst as a separate subject in the mind of the patient. So why do analytic audiences focus on self-revelation?

Of course, one reason that analysts are interested in these issues is that until recently self-disclosure had never been considered acceptable as part of psychoanalytic technique, which has drive theory as its underlying foundation. As analysts have abandoned drive theory, they have had to rethink the basic principles of analytic technique. Because analysts who are beginning with a new set of principles and assumptions must reconsider how they work, they have become interested in the therapeutic value, as well as in the dangers, of self-disclosure.

There are other reasons for the intense interest in self-disclosure as well. I believe that people who are drawn to analysis as a profession have particularly strong conflicts regarding their desire to be known by another; that is, they have conflicts concerning intimacy. In more traditional terms, these are narcissistic conflicts over voyeurism and exhibitionism. Why else would anyone choose a profession in which one spends one's life listening and looking into the lives of others while one remains relatively silent and hidden? The recognition that analysts, even those who attempt to be anonymous, are never invisible and that patients seek to "know" their analysts raises profound anxieties for analysts who are struggling with their own longings to be known and defensive temptations to hide. This recognition leads to the question of to what extent and in what ways it might be useful for the analyst purposefully to disclose aspects of the countertransference to the patient. If we admit that our patients do indeed observe a great deal about us no matter how anonymous we may try to be, then is it clinically indicated for analysts purposefully to reveal aspects of themselves to their patients as part of the analytic work? This question has stimulated a heated controversy among analysts of all schools of thought.

Establishing one's own subjectivity in the analytic situation is essential and yet problematic. Deliberate self-revelations are always highly ambiguous and are enormously complicated. Our own psychologies are as complicated as our patients', and our unconsciouses are no less deep. We need to recognize that our own self-awareness is limited and that we are not in a position to judge the accuracy of our patients' perceptions of us. Thus, the idea that we might "validate" or "confirm" our patients' perceptions of us is presumptuous. Further-more, direct self-revelation cannot provide a shortcut to, and may even interfere with, the development of a patient's capacity to recognize the analyst's subjec-tivity. Nevertheless, I believe that there are clinical circumstances in which self-disclosure is analytically useful, at least for some analysts (because technique is highly personal). In this chapter, my goal is to highlight the importance of analyzing a patient's conflicts about knowing the analyst. Elsewhere, I explored the question of self-disclosure in more detail and have argued for a good deal of personal flexibility in deciding when, what, how much, and why to self-disclose (Aron, 1996).

A Clinical Illustration

The following is an example of the impact of an analyst's inquiry into the patient's experience of the analyst's subjectivity. I was consulted by a young analyst trained in the classical tradition who was treating a patient who was himself a psychology graduate student. The analyst came to me for supervision specifically because he wanted to be exposed to a relational approach. He was about to deliver a scholarly paper, and the patient had seen a brochure adver-tising the conference presentation. For the last 5 weeks, this had been the dominant topic of the patient's associations. The patient was conflicted about whether to attend the meeting and see and hear his analyst present the paper. He spent a good part of his sessions associating about his ambivalence con-cerning this decision.

The patient's considerations included that he thought he would be envious of the analyst, that he would sit in the audience feeling resentful that it was his analyst giving a paper and not himself getting this admiration and recognition from the audience. He was concerned about seeing his analyst with other peo-ple. He wondered to whom he would see his analyst talking. Would the analyst be there with a woman—his wife, perhaps? He was concerned that he would then feel jealous of the analyst's sexual relationship with a woman. At the same time, he thought that he would be filled with admiration for the analyst. He might sit in the audience feeling so impressed with the analyst that he would have a sexual fantasy about him; he would fantasize performing fellatio on his analyst so as to absorb the analyst's strength and potency. However, he was sure that he would be tempted to find a fatal flaw in his analyst's presentation. He would be the one in the audience who would stand up at the end of the presentation and ask the most penetrating and devastating question, humiliating his analyst in front of everyone. He was thrilled that it seemed as though his analyst might become famous. He always wanted to be analyzed by a famous analyst so that he could tell people and they would all recognize the name and be impressed. He, though, was afraid to present papers even in class; he was afraid of the humiliation he would suffer if he were criticized.

I listened to the analyst as he presented the process notes of many of these sessions. I was indeed impressed that the analysis seemed in many ways to be going well. The patient, after all, was telling the analyst all sorts of personal fantasies directly concerning his relationship with the analyst. The analyst had created an environment safe enough that the patient could expose all these thoughts—including sexual, particularly homosexual ones—aggressive, competitive, rivalrous, jealous, admiring, loving, and hateful thoughts. Yet listening to the session notes, I was struck by the level of intellectualization about the material. In fact, the patient seemed to be excited about producing this material, perhaps to please the analyst and even give him something to write a paper about. The analyst, I should say, had been helpful to the patient in asking him about his feelings as he associated and helping him to articulate these thoughts and fantasies, as well as his feelings.

I asked the analyst what he would in fact feel if the patient showed up to see him present the paper. The analyst deflected my question by answering that he really did not expect that the patient would come. I asked again: "If he did come, what would it be like for you?" He said that he was not sure; he felt rather indifferent. He did not think that he would feel anything much one way or the other.

I suggested that in the next session, when the patient discussed his thoughts and feelings about this topic once again, he might find a suitable moment to ask the patient the following question, or something like it, in his own words and style:

> What do you imagine that it will be like for me to have you come hear the paper? Picture me up at the podium about to read the paper, I look out into the audience, and I notice you are there. What do you imagine I feel at that moment?

The analyst laughed when I made this suggestion. He wondered why it had never occurred to him to ask anything like that. It was not his style, he said. He thought it might direct too much attention to his feelings and detract from the patient's experience. But, he said, he would think about it. I told him that I certainly would not pressure him to make any intervention that felt uncomfortable to him. After all, he knew the patient better than I and, more important, his interventions and his style of working would have to fit his own character and personal style.

The next few consultations proved interesting. Indeed, the analyst had asked the question as I recommended. He was not prepared for what happened next—not to the patient, but to himself. For the first time, the patient stopped finding it so easy to free associate. All of a sudden, instead of being able to think of one idea after another about what it would be like to go to the presentation, now the patient felt blocked, uncomfortable, and intensely anxious. The analyst, too, began to feel anxious, but now his thoughts were racing concerning the upcoming talk. He began to imagine what it would be like to meet the patient at the talk, and he realized that, indeed, he would have feelings about it, many of them not at all unlike those of his patient.

He was able to work with the patient and show him that his difficulty associating now had to do with his fears of making the analyst more anxious by talking about him in a way that was much more personal. The analyst had gone from being the patient's object to being a separate subject, and this change had happened not because of a developmental step on the patient's part but because the analyst had shifted his stance and opened himself up to his own subjectivity. Although the analyst may have conveyed something of his own anxiety and conflict in pursuing this work, it was all done with relatively little direct self-disclosure of the content of his own reactions. Nevertheless, this intervention significantly shifted the analysis. This example illustrates the importance of exploring the patient's experience of the analyst's subjectivity; it also demonstrates the power of an intervention to have a mutual impact on both the patient and the analyst as it expands the self-reflexive functioning of both of them.

The exploration of the patient's experience of the analyst's subjectivity represents only one aspect of the analysis of transference. It needs to be seen as but one underemphasized component of a detailed and thorough explication and articulation of the therapeutic relationship in all of its aspects. The psychoanalytic encounter constitutes an intersubjective exchange that leads not simply to agreement or acquiescence but rather to dialogue and connection, to a meeting of minds.

References

Aron, L. (1990a). Free association and changing models of mind. *Journal of the American Academy of Psychoanalysis, 18,* 439–459.

Aron, L. (1990b). One-person and two-person psychologies and the method of psychoanalysis. *Psychoanalytic Psychology, 7,* 475–485.

Aron, L. (1991). The patient's experience of the analyst's subjectivity. *Psychoanalytic Dialogues, 1,* 29–51.

Aron, L. (1992). Interpretation as expression of the analyst's subjectivity. *Psychoanalytic Dialogues, 2,* 475–507.

Aron, L. (1993). Working toward operational thought: Piagetian theory and psychoanalytic method. *Contemporary Psychoanalysis, 29,* 289–313.

Aron, L. (1995). The internalized primal scene. *Psychoanalytic Dialogues, 5,* 195–238.

Aron, L. (1996). The patient's experience of the analyst's subjectivity. In *A meeting of minds: Mutuality in psychoanalysis* (pp. 65–92). Hillsdale, NJ: Analytic Press.

Aron, L. (1998). The clinical body and the reflexive mind. In L. Aron & F. S. Anderson (Eds.), *Relational perspectives on the body* (pp. 3–37). Hillsdale, NJ: Analytic Press.

Auerbach, J. S., & Blatt, S. J. (1996). Self-representation in severe psychopathology: The role of reflexive self-awareness. *Psychoanalytic Psychology, 13,* 297–341.

Bach, S. (1985). *Narcissistic states and the therapeutic process.* New York: Aronson.

Bach, S. (1994). *The language of perversion and the language of love.* Northvale, NJ: Aronson.

Balbus, I. D. (1982). *Marxism and domination.* Princeton, NJ: Princeton University Press.

Barratt, B. B. (1994). Review essay: *The Intimate Edge* by D. Bregman Ehrenberg. *Psychoanalytic Dialogues, 4,* 275–282.

Benjamin, J. (1988). *The bonds of love.* New York: Pantheon.

Benjamin, J. (1990). An outline of intersubjectivity: The development of recognition. *Psychoanalytic Psychology, 7,* 33–46.

Benjamin, J. (1992). Recognition and destruction: An outline of intersubjectivity. In N. J. Skolnick & S. C. Warshaw (Eds.), *Relational perspectives in psychoanalysis* (pp. 43–60). Hillsdale, NJ: Analytic Press.

Bollas, C. (1989). *Forces of destiny.* London: Free Association Books.

Britton, R. (1989). The missing link: Parental sexuality in the Oedipus complex. In J. Steiner (Ed.), *The Oedipus complex today* (pp. 83–102). London: Karnac Books.

Bromberg, P. M. (1994). "Speak! That I may see you": Some reflections on dissociation, reality, and psychoanalytic listening. *Psychoanalytic Dialogues, 4,* 517–548.

Bromberg, P. M. (1995). Resistance, object-usage, and human relatedness. *Contemporary Psychoanalysis, 31,* 173–191.

Chodorow, N. (1978). *The reproduction of mothering.* Berkeley: University of California Press.

Dimen, M. (1991). Deconstructing difference: Gender, splitting, and transitional space. *Psychoanalytic Dialogues, 1,* 335–352.

Dinnerstein, D. (1976). *The mermaid and the minotaur.* New York: Harper & Row.

Ehrenberg, D. B. (1992). *The intimate edge.* New York: Norton.

Ferenczi, S. (1988). *The clinical diary of Sándor Ferenczi* (J. Dupont, Ed., M. Balint & N. Z. Jackson, Trans.). Cambridge, MA: Harvard University Press. (Original work published 1932)

Flavell, J. H. (1963). *The developmental psychology of Jean Piaget.* Princeton, NJ: Van Nostrand.

Flax, J. (1990). *Thinking fragments.* Berkeley: University of California Press.

Fonagy, P., & Target, M. (1995). Understanding the violent patient: The use of the body and the role of the father. *International Journal of Psycho-Analysis, 76,* 487–501.

Fonagy, P., & Target, M. (1996). Playing with reality: I. Theory of mind and the normal development of psychic reality. *International Journal of Psycho-Analysis, 77,* 217–233.

Freud, S. (1957). The future prospects of psychoanalytic therapy. In J. Strachey (Ed. & Trans.), *Standard edition of the complete psychological works of Sigmund Freud* (Vol. 11, pp. 141–151). London: Hogarth. (Original work published 1910)

Gill, M. M. (1982). *The analysis of transference* (Vol. 1). New York: International Universities Press.

Gill, M. M. (1983). The interpersonal paradigm and the degree of the therapist's involvement. *Contemporary Psychoanalysis, 1,* 200–237.

Goldner, V. (1991). Toward a critical relational theory of gender. *Psychoanalytic Dialogues, 1,* 249–272.

Groddeck, G. (1950). *The book of the it.* London: Vision Press. (Original work published 1923)

Hoffman, I. Z. (1983). The patient as interpreter of the analyst's experience. *Contemporary Psychoanalysis, 19,* 389–422.

Isakower, O. (November 20, 1963). Minutes of the faculty meeting of the New York Psychoanalytic Institute.

Jacobs, T. J. (1986). On countertransference enactments. *Journal of the American Psychoanalytic Association, 34,* 289–307.

Kernberg, O. F. (1965). Notes on countertransference. *Journal of the American Psychoanalytic Association, 13,* 38–56.

Lachmann, F. M., & Beebe, B. (1995). Self psychology: Today. *Psychoanalytic Dialogues, 5,* 375–384.

Levenson, E. A. (1972). *The fallacy of understanding.* New York: Basic Books.

Levenson, E. A. (1983). *The ambiguity of change.* New York: Basic Books.

Limentani, A. (1989). *Between Freud and Klein.* London: Free Association Books.

Lipton, S. D. (1977). Clinical observations on resistance to the transference. *International Journal of Psycho-Analysis, 58,* 463–472.

Little, M. (1951). Countertransference and the patient's response to it. *International Journal of Psycho-Analysis, 33,* 32–40.

Loewald, H. W. (1980). Psychoanalytic theory and the psychoanalytic process. In *Papers on psychoanalysis* (pp. 277–301). New Haven, CT: Yale University Press. (Original work published 1970)

Main, M., Kaplan, N., & Cassidy, J. (1985). Security in infancy, childhood and adulthood: A move to the level of representation. In I. Bretherton & E. Waters (Eds.), *Growing points in attachment: Theory and research* (Monographs of the Society for

Research in Child Development, Serial No. 209, pp. 66–104). Chicago: University of Chicago Press.

McDougall, J. (1980). *Plea for a measure of abnormality*. New York: International Universities Press.

McLaughlin, J. T. (1981). Transference, psychic reality and countertransference. *Psychoanalytic Quarterly, 50*, 639–664.

Mitchell, S. (1993). *Hope and dread in psychoanalysis*. New York: Basic Books.

Natterson, J. (1991). *Beyond countertransference*. Northvale, NJ: Aronson.

Ogden, T. (1986). *The matrix of the mind*. Northvale, NJ: Aronson.

Ogden, T. (1989). *The primitive edge of experience*. Northvale, NJ: Aronson.

Ogden, T. (1994). *Subjects of analysis*. Northvale, NJ: Aronson.

Pick, I. B. (1985). Working through in the countertransference. *International Journal of Psycho-Analysis, 66*, 157–166.

Racker, H. (1968). *Transference and counter-transference*. New York: International Universities Press.

Rivera, M. (1989). Linking the psychological and the social: Feminism, poststructuralism, and multiple personality. *Dissociation, 2*, 24–31.

Searles, H. (1975). The patient as therapist to his analyst. In P. Giovacchini (Ed.), *Tactics and techniques in psychoanalytic therapy* (Vol. 2, pp. 95–151). New York: Aronson.

Searles, H. (1979). *Countertransference and related subjects*. New York: International Universities Press.

Singer, I. (1977). The fiction of analytic anonymity. In K. Frank (Ed.), *The human dimension in psychoanalytic practice* (pp. 181–192). New York: Grune & Stratton.

Stern, D. (1985). *The interpersonal world of the infant*. New York: Basic Books.

Stolorow, R., & Atwood, G. E. (1992). *Contexts of being*. Hillsdale, NJ: Analytic Press.

Stolorow, R., Atwood, G. E., & Ross, J. (1978). The representational world in psychoanalytic therapy. *International Review of Psycho-Analysis, 5*, 247–256.

Sullivan, H. S. (1953). *The interpersonal theory of psychiatry*. New York: Norton.

Target, M., & Fonagy, P. (1996). Playing with reality: II. The development of psychic reality from a theoretical perspective. *International Journal of Psycho-Analysis, 77*, 459–479.

Winnicott, D. W. (1971). *Playing and reality*. Middlesex, England: Penguin.

Wolstein, B. (1983). The pluralism of perspectives on countertransference. *Contemporary Psychoanalysis, 19*, 506–521.

Subjects and Objects

Jeremy D. Safran

In this valuable chapter, Lewis Aron has done a superb job of synthesizing and refining some of the most important contemporary psychoanalytic thinking about the topic of intersubjectivity. This type of synthesis is both timely and important, given the tremendous interest in intersubjectivity in the clinical literature, the different ways in which the concept is used, and the lack of conceptual clarity that characterizes many discussions. Aron's treatment of the topic is both scholarly and complex, and in my attempts to bring into focus and dialogue with some aspects of it I inevitably neglect others. I hope, however, that the benefits of this type of selective strategy will outweigh the costs.

As Aron points out, there are a number of different perspectives on intersubjectivity in the literature. A first is the view that any two members of a dyad (including therapist and patient) influence one another in a bidirectional fashion at both conscious and unconscious levels in an ongoing fashion. A second is the view that human beings have an innate (developmentally sequenced) ability to recognize that others have their own internal mental states as well as a capacity for and motivation to share these states with others. A third is the view that the process of coming to recognize that the other is an independent subject rather than an object of one's own desire is a developmental achievement, and that coming to experience the therapist as a subject, can be an important part of the change process for patients. A fourth is that intersubjectivity is linked to the process of interpersonal negotiation. A final theme is the notion that the capacity for intersubjectivity has something to do with acquiring the ability to oscillate between experiencing oneself as a subject and as an object.

What I want to do in this discussion is focus on Aron's examination of clinical implications, raise certain questions in an attempt to clarify his understanding of the role of intersubjectivity in the particular clinical phenomenon he focuses on, and attempt to flesh out certain aspects of his thinking on the topic that are less explicit than others. My sense is that he focuses most explicitly on the first two perspectives on intersubjectivity listed above, and that it may be useful to try to make the link among some of the other perspectives on intersubjectivity and his clinical thinking more explicit.

In terms of the first perspective (i.e., "mutual regulation"), Aron emphasizes the importance of recognizing the fashion in which the therapist is always contributing to the relational field in both conscious and unconscious ways. He suggests that patients are always registering aspects of the therapist's contribution to the matrix both consciously and unconsciously, and that the exploration of their perceptions of and fantasies about the therapist can be an important part of the change process. What distinguishes this type of exploration from being simply an analysis of the transference in the classical sense, is the therapist's recognition that the patient may see things about him or her that the therapist is not aware of, and the therapist's openness to learning something about his or her own internal conflicts.

In terms of the second perspective (the capacity and desire to share subjective states), Aron emphasizes the importance of recognizing that for patients, the process of attempting to get beyond the therapist's professional demeanor can be an expression of a natural (albeit conflicted) desire "to connect with others where they live emotionally, where they are authentic and fully present." In the same way that children observe and study their parents' personalities and make inferences about their attitudes and feelings toward them, patients (at least at one level) have a desire to know their therapists as people. This, according to Aron, is a reflection of a "pre-experiential motivational push, a drive, for a meeting of minds."

What remains somewhat unclear to me is Aron's understanding of the processes through which providing an atmosphere in which patients experience the freedom to make observations about their therapists' personal characteristics and to speculate about their inner conflicts promotes the experience of intersubjectivity. At times he seems to suggest that the capacity for intersubjectivity is a type of psychologically minded thinking, that is, a general capacity to think about the subjectivity of others. For example, he indicates that an analytic focus on the patient's experience of the analyst's subjectivity helps "patients begin to attend to their observations about the character of others in their lives. This is an inevitable and essential part of how patients begin to think more psychologically in their analyses." Or "the very expression by the patient of his or her perceptions of the analyst leads to the acknowledgment of the analyst as a separate subject in the mind of the patient." One could interpret statements of this type to mean that there is something about simply encouraging patients to begin thinking about their analysts as real, three-dimensional people that promotes a more generalized capacity for intersubjectivity. This type of interpretation, however, would be out of character with many of the important points that Aron has made about the nature of intersubjectivity throughout his chapter. What I would like to do in the rest of my discussion is to comment on a number of these points in an attempt to explicate more fully the way in which exploring the patient's experience of the therapist's subjectivity may promote the experience of intersubjectivity.

To begin, I believe that a critical question to consider in this context is what it really means to acknowledge the other as a separate subject. Although it may seem obvious, it is worth making it explicit that we are talking about something beyond a trivial conceptual recognition that the other is an independent center of subjectivity. For an adult to come to recognize the independent subjectivity of the other is something more than what goes on developmentally for the child as he or she becomes less egocentric. The struggle to truly experience the independent subjectivity of the other is an ongoing dilemma of human existence. It is here that another perspective on intersubjectivity, which Aron mentions—the capacity to recognize the other as a person rather than as an object of one's desire—warrants further elaboration. Theorists such as Benjamin and Winnicott and philosophers such as Buber and Hegel have important things to say in this context. Although Aron incorporates Benjamin's, Winnicott's, and Buber's perspectives on this issue, as evidenced in his chapter and other writings (Aron, 1996), my sense is that his discussion of clinical implications does not capitalize on their thinking as much as it might.

Buber's take on intersubjectivity can be understood to be both ontological and ethical. He was concerned with articulating both the fundamental nature of human existence and the nature of authentic human existence. According to him, the nature of an individual's experience of self is always shaped by the nature of his or her relationship to the other. There are two fundamental modes of relating to the other: the I–thou mode (in which the other is related to as a subject) and the I–it mode (in which the other is related to as an object). Both modes are necessary to human existence, but it is only the I–thou mode that allows one to experience things fully as an authentic human being. The I–thou mode is desirable psychologically, ethically, and spiritually because it involves an experience of wholeness, realness, connection, and mutuality. Buber described the characteristics of this mode of being (e.g., directness, presentness, mutuality, openness, absence of contrivance), but he has not described the process through which one achieves this experience.

Hegel's description of the master–slave dialectic provides a starting point for understanding the way in which the struggle between two consciousnesses can lead to either I–it or I–thou modes of relating. The dilemma is that we cannot experience ourselves as truly existing without the recognition of the other, but this dependency makes our existence a tenuous matter. We can try to master or control the other to achieve our independence and reduce this tenuousness. The problem, however, is that if we succeed, it deprives the other of the power necessary to confirm our existence and leaves us alone, without the companionship of another subjectivity. Alternatively, we assume the slave's position and give the other the power necessary to confirm our existence. Our existence is tenuous in this position as well, however, because we are now dependent on the recognition of the other.

The dimensions of power and intersubjectivity are thus intricately connected. There is something about the ongoing struggle to determine who defines the other and who accommodates whom that plays a central role in allowing the individual to experience him- or herself as a vitally alive subject in a relationship with another three-dimensional subject. Settling into the position of either the master or the slave makes this impossible. As Benjamin (1988) suggested, Winnicott's thinking on the use of an object can be understood as a version of Hegel's master–slave dilemma. The point that Winnicott makes is that it is only through seeing that the other can survive one's destructiveness that one can come to experience him or her as a subject, that is, as a real being who exists outside of oneself.

An important theme on which Aron touches, one that warrants further elaboration, is the role of the power imbalance in the therapeutic relationship. One of the reasons that patients are conflicted about really knowing their therapists, just as children are conflicted about really knowing their parents, is because they have an investment in keeping them in the position of the authority, the one who has the knowledge and power to help and protect. At the same time, patients are conflicted about relating to their therapists in their role as authorities because this can place them into a denigrated one-down position vis-à-vis their therapists. This is particularly problematic when patients are full of self-loathing and experience themselves as alienated from the human community. Under such circumstances, the therapist who emphasizes the asymmetrical and nonmutual aspects of the therapeutic relationship through his or her attitudes and actions can exacerbate this experience of alienation.

As Irwin Hoffman (1994) pointed out, although it is true that the therapist's spontaneity and personal responsivity can be therapeutically valuable, it is important to recognize that this is so in the context of his or her assigned role as the authority. In other words, it is not the exploration of the therapist's subjectivity in itself that is important, but rather what it means to the patient in the context of a relationship in which the therapist has the power and in which this power is traditionally maintained, in part, by minimizing the extent to which the therapist acknowledges his or her subjectivity.

The patient who speculates aloud about his or her therapist's motives is making a bid (no matter how tentative) to define the reality in a certain way. The therapist's genuine willingness to consider the patient's perceptions can be understood as a willingness to negotiate about the nature of reality. It is here that the perspective on "intersubjectivity as negotiation" comes into play. Stuart Pizer (1992, chapter 5, this volume) builds on Winnicott's thinking about object usage (with clear shades of Hegel as well) in placing the process of intersubjective negotiation at the heart of therapeutic change. According to Pizer, it is critical for therapists to, on the one hand, be able to adapt to the needs and desires of their patients and, on the other hand, at times hold fast and refuse to accommodate. The therapist's accommodation helps the patient come to see the world as a negotiable place and to experience him- or herself as alive and vital. The therapist's lack of complete accommodation allows the patient to experience the therapist as a separate subject.

There is something about the ongoing negotiations between patients and therapists that are always part of the therapeutic process, that plays a role in helping patients to experience themselves as vitally alive subjects in relationships with other subjects. This type of negotiation inevitably involves an element of disappointment and mourning as patients come up against the limits of the therapist's accommodations and to some extent let go of their cherished hopes of how things would be if their fantasies were actualized (I say "to some extent" because we never give up these fantasies completely). This in turn helps them to develop the capacity to relate to the other as a Thou rather than exclusively as an object of their fantasies (Safran, 1993, 1999). I think that this relates to the perspective on intersubjectivity as oscillation between experiencing oneself as a person and as an object. There is something about paradoxically being able to experience oneself both as the center of the world and as the object of others that is linked to maintaining the necessary tension in the master–slave dialectic.

To summarize, as I see it, the process of encouraging patients to speculate about the therapist's subjectivity is a complex one. It is probably most useful to understand it as one turn in a dialectic, in which patient and therapist negotiate over what reality is and who defines it. From one perspective, it is self-evident that speculating about the therapist's subjectivity involves relating to him or her as a subject. From another perspective, however, it can involve relating to the therapist as an object, insofar as the patient is encouraged to take a stab at defining the therapist. In fact, the therapist's willingness to be open to the patient's speculations can be understood, in Winnicott's terms, as a type of survival in the face of his or her aggression. Paradoxically, then, encouraging the patient to speculate about the therapist's subjectivity can be a way of allowing him or her to use the therapist as an object, which can in turn help him to ultimately experience the therapist as a subject.

References

Aron, L. (1996). *A meeting of minds: Mutuality in psychoanalysis*. Hillsdale, NJ: Analytic Press.

Benjamin, J. (1988). *The bonds of love*. New York: Pantheon.

Hoffman, I. (1994). Dialectical thinking and therapeutic action in the psychoanalytic process. *Psychoanalytic Quarterly, 63,* 187–218.

Pizer, S. A. (1992). The negotiation of paradox in the analytic process. *Psychoanalytic Dialogues, 2,* 215–240.

Safran, J. D. (1993). Breaches in the therapeutic alliance: An arena for negotiating authentic relatedness. *Psychotherapy, 30,* 11–24.

Safran, J. D. (1999). Faith, despair, will and the paradox of acceptance. *Contemporary Psychoanalysis 35,* 5–24.

CHAPTER 7

The Therapeutic Alliance as a Process of Intersubjective Negotiation

Jeremy D. Safran

J. Christopher Muran

In this chapter, we suggest that the therapeutic alliance is best conceptualized as an important dimension of the therapeutic relationship that involves an ongoing process of intersubjective negotiation, that is, the negotiation of the respective needs of two independent subjects. We also suggest that strains in the therapeutic alliance tap into a fundamental dilemma of human existence— the tension between the need for agency and the need for relatedness—and that the process of working through these strains can provide patients with a valuable opportunity to learn to constructively negotiate these two needs.

The concept of the therapeutic alliance has historically played an important role in the evolution of the classical psychoanalytic tradition, insofar as it has provided a theoretical justification for greater technical flexibility (see Safran & Muran, 1998, 2000). By highlighting the critical importance of the real, human aspects of the therapeutic relationship, the therapeutic alliance has provided grounds for departing from the idealized therapist stance of abstinence and neutrality. With the growing ascendance of relational thinking (e.g., Aron, 1996; Mitchell, 1988, 1993), the question arises as to whether the concept of the alliance is still valuable. Interpersonal and relational perspectives do not adhere to classical notions of therapist abstinence and neutrality and therefore provide considerably more scope for technical flexibility. Moreover, from these perspectives, the experience of a constructive relational experience with the therapist is viewed as a critical component of change. In fact, one might say that the processes of developing and resolving problems in alliance are not a prerequisite to change but rather the essence of the change process. Nevertheless, we believe that a broadened conceptualization of the therapeutic alliance along the lines that Bordin (1979, 1994) has suggested is still useful, for several reasons.

This chapter includes material from *Negotiating the Therapeutic Alliance: A Relational Treatment Guide*, by Jeremy D. Safran and J. Christopher Muran, 2000. Copyright 2000 by Guilford Press. Adapted with permission.

Bordin conceptualized the therapeutic alliance as consisting of three inter-dependent components: tasks, goals, and the bond. According to him, the strength of the alliance is dependent on the degree of agreement between patient and therapist about the tasks and goals of therapy and on the quality of the relational bond between them. The tasks of therapy consist of the specific ac-tivities (either overt or covert) in which the patient must engage to benefit from the treatment. The goals of therapy are the general objectives toward which the treatment is directed. The bond component of the alliance consists of the af-fective quality of the relationship between patient and therapist (e.g., the extent to which the patient feels understood, respected, valued, etc.). The bond, task, and goal dimensions of the alliance influence one another in an ongoing fash-ion. The quality of the bond mediates the extent to which the patient and therapist are able to negotiate an agreement about the tasks and goals of therapy, and the ability to negotiate an agreement about the tasks and goals in therapy in turn mediates the quality of the bond.

Bordin's conceptualization emphasizes the complex, dynamic, and multi-dimensional nature of the therapeutic alliance. It suggests a number of impor-tant implications. First, it highlights that at a fundamental level the patient's ability to trust, hope, and have faith in the therapist's ability to help always plays a central role in the change process. Second, it suggests that different types of alliance are necessary depending on the relevant therapeutic tasks and goals. Third, it highlights the interdependence of relational and technical factors in psychotherapy. It suggests that the meaning of any technical factor can be understood only in the relational context in which it is applied. Fourth, it provides a framework for guiding the therapist's interventions in a flexible fash-ion. Rather than basing one's approach on some inflexible and idealized crite-rion, such as therapeutic neutrality, one can be guided by an understanding of what a particular therapeutic task means to a particular patient in a given moment. Fifth, it suggests that ruptures in the therapeutic alliance are the royal road to understanding the patient's core organizing principles. Accordingly, the therapist should attend, on an ongoing basis, to the ways in which patients respond to their interventions. The exploration of the factors underlying the patient's construal of an intervention as hindering can provide a rich under-standing of the patient's idiosyncratic construal processes and internal object relations. Finally, it highlights (a) the importance of the negotiation between therapist and patient at both conscious and unconscious levels about the tasks and goals of therapy and (b) that this process of negotiation both establishes the necessary conditions for change to take place and is an intrinsic part of the change process. This is consistent with an increasingly influential way of con-ceptualizing the therapeutic process in contemporary relational thinking (e.g., Benjamin, 1988; Mitchell, 1993; Pizer, 1992).

This line of thought deepens our understanding of the significance of the negotiation between therapists and patients about therapeutic tasks and goals. It suggests that this process is not only about a superficial negotiation toward consensus. At a deeper level, it taps into fundamental dilemmas of human existence, such as the negotiation of one's desires with those of another, the struggle to experience oneself as a subject while at the same time recognizing the subjectivity of the other, and the dialectical tension between the need for agency or self-definition versus the need for relatedness or communion (see Safran & Muran, 2000, for an extended discussion).

Stage-Process Models of Alliance Rupture Resolution

We define *ruptures* in the therapeutic alliance as deteriorations in the relationship between therapist and patient (Safran & Muran, 1996). They are patient behaviors or communications that are interpersonal markers indicating critical points in therapy for exploration. Ruptures often emerge when therapists unwittingly participate in vicious cycles that in some respects parallel a patient's characteristic relational matrix (Mitchell, 1988), thereby confirming his or her dysfunctional relational schema (Safran & Muran, 2000). For example, a therapist who responds to a hostile patient with counterhostility confirms the patient's view of others as hostile and obstructs the development of a good therapeutic alliance. The therapist who responds to a withdrawn patient by distancing confirms the patient's view of others as emotionally unavailable, thereby perpetuating a vicious cycle. Ruptures vary in intensity, duration, and frequency depending on the particular therapist–patient dyad. In some cases, they may go undetected by the therapist or remain out of conscious awareness for the patient and may not significantly obstruct therapeutic progress. In more extreme cases, they can lead to patient dropout or treatment failure. If properly dealt with, however, alliance ruptures can provide an important opportunity for therapeutic change. By systematically exploring, understanding, and resolving alliance ruptures the therapist can provide patients with a new constructive interpersonal experience that will modify their maladaptive relational schemas.

We have found it useful to organize ruptures into two subtypes: withdrawal and confrontation (see Harper, 1989a, 1989b). In *withdrawal* ruptures, the patient withdraws or partially disengages from the therapist, his or her own emotions, or some aspect of the therapeutic process. Withdrawal ruptures can manifest in many different forms. In some cases, it is fairly obvious that the patient is having difficulty expressing his or her concerns or needs in the relationship. For example, a patient expresses her concerns in an indirect or qualified way. In other cases the patient complies or accommodates the perceived desires of the therapist in a subtle fashion of which it may be difficult for the therapist to become aware. It is not uncommon for therapists and patients to form a type of pseudo-alliance that corresponds to the type of false self organization described by Winnicott (1960). In such cases, therapeutic progress may take place at one level but nevertheless perpetuate a self-defeating aspect of the patient's style. In *confrontation*, ruptures the patient directly expresses anger, resentment, or dissatisfaction with the therapist or some aspect of the therapy.

Withdrawal and confrontation ruptures reflect different ways of coping with the tension between the dialectically opposed needs for agency and relatedness. In withdrawal ruptures, patients strive for relatedness at the cost of the need for agency or self-definition. In confrontation ruptures, patients negotiate the conflict by favoring the need for agency or self-definition over the need for relatedness. Different patients are likely to present a predominance of one type of rupture over another, and this reflects different characteristic styles of coping or adaptation. Over the course of treatment, however, both types of ruptures may emerge with a specific patient, or a specific impasse may involve both withdrawal and confrontation features. Thus, it is critical for therapists to be sensitive to the specific qualities of the rupture that are emerging in the moment, rather than becoming locked into viewing patients as exclusively confrontation or withdrawal types.

We outline two stage-process models that can be useful for understanding some of the characteristic ways in which ruptures in the therapeutic alliance are resolved in psychotherapy. The development of these models is the product of more than 10 years of research (see Safran & Muran, 1996, 2000). Stage-process models are schemas that have been empirically developed to distill recurring patterns of change that take place across cases. Psychotherapy process researchers have found the development of such schemas to provide a useful way of modeling important mechanisms of change in psychotherapy (e.g., Rice & Greenberg, 1984). Psychotherapy process can be seen as a sequence of recurring stages that take place in identifiable patterns. By identifying these stages and modeling patterns of transition between them, it is possible to develop maps that can sensitize clinicians to sequential patterns that are likely to occur. The idea is not to develop rigidly prescriptive models but to help clinicians develop pattern recognition abilities that can facilitate the intervention process. It is important to emphasize that although these models can have heuristic value, they are inevitably oversimplifications of the complex processes that they attempt to capture. In the rest of this chapter, we elucidate the differences in resolving withdrawal and confrontation ruptures. The various stages of the models can be conceptualized as different tasks that are critical for the patient to engage in at different points in the resolution process, as well as therapist interventions that can be facilitative. The patient tasks are tasks not in the sense of intentional actions but rather in the sense of complex intrapsychic operations and interpersonal negotiations.

FIGURE 7.1

Rupture resolution model for withdrawal ruptures.

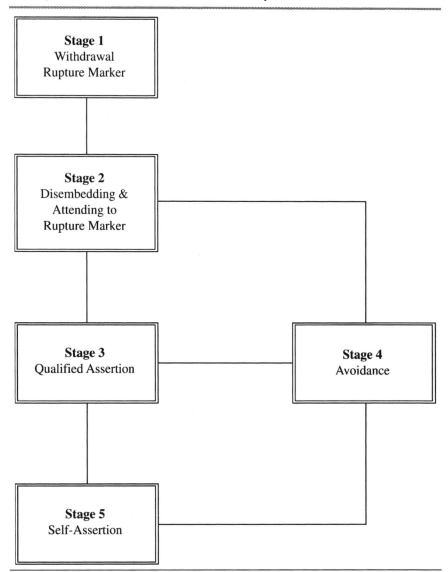

A Resolution Model for Withdrawal Ruptures

The resolution model for withdrawal ruptures consists of five stages (see Figure 7.1). Each stage consists of a particular patient task and specific therapist interventions that we have observed to be facilitative. The specific interventions we describe in this chapter do not constitute an exhaustive list but should be taken as examples of facilitative interventions.

Stage 1: Withdrawal Marker

The first stage is signaled by a patient withdrawal marker. For example, the patient complies with or defers to the therapist by agreeing with an interpretation in an acquiescent fashion. This type of withdrawal is often part of an ongoing enactment in which the therapist becomes embedded in the patient's relational matrix and responds to the patient's passive or submissive behavior by brushing over any subtle indications of concern or by acting in an overly directive or domineering fashion. For example, the patient responds to an interpretation in an acquiescent fashion, and the therapist continues to elaborate on his interpretation.

Stage 2: Disembedding and Attending to the Rupture Marker

In this stage, therapists begin drawing attention to the rupture and establishing a focus on the here and now of the therapeutic relationship. To the extent that they are embedded in the patient's relational matrix at this point, they need to begin to develop some awareness of the nature of their contribution to it. Although for heuristic purposes we are discussing this disembedding process as if it is one discrete step in a linear direction, it is important to bear in mind that the process of disembedding is never complete. Over the course of the resolution process, the therapist and the patient cycle back and forth between greater and lesser degrees of embeddedness.

In situations in which the withdrawal marker is particularly subtle, the therapist's awareness of his or her own feelings or action tendencies may be the best indicator that something is taking place that warrants exploration. For example, therapists may find themselves working harder than usual to give advice to a patient, or being less attentive to a patient's concerns than they typically would be with other patients; they may find themselves ignoring a patient's concerns or pushing a patient to accept an interpretation or to look at things in a certain way. In situations where the patient withdraws by dissociating threatening feelings about the therapist, therapists may find themselves suddenly losing interest in the patient or becoming aware that their attention has been drifting.

Once the therapist begins to become aware of the configuration being enacted, the tasks are to both disembed from it and begin to explore the feelings that are being avoided by the patient. These two processes are interdependent. For example, a therapist who becomes aware of her attention drifting begins to metacommunicate (i.e., dialogue about what is being enacted in the relationship) by disclosing this experience to her patient and probing for his experience: e.g., "I'm aware of my attention wandering. I'm not sure what's going on, but I think it may have something to do with a kind of distant sound in your voice. Any sense of what's going on for you right now?" In response, the patient is able to acknowledge that he is withdrawing from the therapist because he feels hurt by something she said.

During this stage it is important to direct the patient's attention to the here and now of the therapeutic relationship. Useful interventions consist of statements such as "What are you experiencing?" or "I have a sense of you withdrawing from me" or "How are you feeling about what's going on between us right now?"

It is critical for the therapist to maintain a curious, empathic stance toward the patient and to be open to and receptive to any negative feelings that begin to emerge. It is common at this point for patients to speak about negative feelings in general terms rather than directly confronting the therapist. For example, the patient may complain about the mental health profession in general. In response, it is useful for the therapist to explore the relevance of these feelings to the present situation: e.g., "If you're willing, I'd like to ask you to experiment with personalizing what you're saying. Do these concerns apply to me as well?"

This exploration should be conducted in noncontrolling fashion, which respects any decision on the patient's part not to discuss negative feelings toward the therapist in the present context. This is particularly important with patients who tend to be compliant because to push for something the patient is not ready to explore may invite more compliance. It is important for therapists to be mindful of the possibility of contributing to a new variation of an enactment through their attempts to re-establish contact with patients who are withdrawing. Any intervention can be made in the service of perpetuating an ongoing enactment.

Although we have highlighted the role of the therapist in the process of disembedding, we by no means intend to portray this process as a one-sided enterprise; rather, it is collaborative. It invariably includes the patient's willingness to participate in a process of collaborative inquiry about the nature of the interactions. In some way, the patient must also be willing and able to step out of the enactment to some extent to begin an exploration of what is going on in the therapeutic relationship.

The disembedding stage is followed by two parallel pathways of exploration. The first is termed the *experiencing pathway* and involves the exploration of thoughts and feelings associated with the rupture (Stages 3 and 5). The second, referred to as the *avoidance pathway*, involves the exploration of internal processes and defensive operations that interfere with or interrupt feelings and thoughts associated with the rupture experience (Stage 4). The experiencing pathway can be subdivided into two successive stages: Stage 3 (qualified assertion) and Stage 5 (assertion).

Stage 3: Qualified Assertion

In the qualified-assertion stage, the patient begins to express thoughts and feelings associated with the rupture experience. These, however, are mixed with features of the initial rupture marker. For example, the patient begins to express negative sentiments and then qualifies the statement or takes it back (e.g., "I'm feeling a little irritated, but it's not a big deal"). In this stage, the patient comes closer to contacting and expressing underlying wishes that are typically self-assertive in nature and are often associated with angry feelings. It becomes too anxiety provoking, however, and the patient ultimately withdraws from full acknowledgment and experience.

There are a number of therapist interventions that can be helpful in the context of this type of qualified assertion. These are grouped together under the general rubric of facilitating assertion. The most important principle here is to empathize with and display a genuine interest in and curiosity about the negative sentiments that are expressed. One intervention involves differentiating and exploring different self-states (see Bach, 1985; and Bromberg, 1996). When the patient qualifies his statements or indicates that he is uncertain or conflicted about his negative feelings, the therapist can acknowledge both sides and then focus selectively on the concerns that the patient is having difficulty acknowledging or articulating. For example, "I understand that you're uncertain about how important your concerns are. If you're willing to go into it, however, I'd be interested in hearing more." Or "It sounds like you have two perspectives on this issue. One part of you feels that it's no big deal, but the other part has some concerns. If you're willing to pursue this a little further, I'm going to suggest that you try putting the part that feels 'It's no big deal' aside for a moment, and let me hear more from the part that's concerned."

Another useful intervention consists of providing the patient with feedback about the way in which she qualifies or softens her statement to heighten her awareness of this process. For example, "My sense is that you start to express some negative feelings, but then you end up pulling your punch. Do you have any awareness of this?" If the patient is able to become more aware of this defensive operation, the therapist can begin to explore the internal processes associated with this avoidance. For example, "Any sense of what the risk would be of putting things in an unqualified way?"

A third intervention consists of suggesting an awareness experiment. This involves encouraging the patient to experiment with directly expressing feelings that the therapist hypothesizes are being avoided and then to attend to whatever feelings are evoked by the experiment. In some cases, the experiment evokes anxiety, which can then lead to an exploration of the internal processes associated with the avoidance. For example, a patient says, "I'm feeling a little frustrated with the pace at which things are moving, but I know that there's no magic pill," and the therapist responds, "I'm wondering if you're willing to try saying something as an experiment. Try saying, 'I want more from you' and see how it feels." The patient responds, "I can't say that," to which the therapist responds with "Why not? What happens for you when you think of saying it?" The patient then responds, "I start to feel childish." This subsequently leads to an exploration of the patient's harsh and condemning attitude toward his own needs. In other cases, the experiment helps to deepen the patient's awareness and acknowledgment of the avoided experience. In the above illustration, the patient might, for example, repeat the phrase, "I want more from you" or some variant of it; and when the therapist asks, "What do you experience as you say that?" the patient contacts some of his disowned yearning.

Stage 4: Avoidance

In a typical resolution process, the exploration of the rupture experience pathway proceeds to a certain point and then becomes blocked. This is indicated by the patient engaging in coping strategies, defensive verbalizations, and actions that function to avoid or manage the emotions associated with the rupture experience. Examples are changing the topic, speaking in a deadened voice tone, and speaking in general terms rather than the here-and-now specifics of the therapeutic relationship. The avoidance pathway involves the exploration of beliefs, expectations, and other internal processes that inhibit the acknowledgment and expression of feelings and needs associated with the rupture experience.

There are two major subtypes here. The first consists of beliefs and expectations about the other's response that interfere with the exploration of the experiencing pathway. For example, the patient who expects expressions of anger to evoke retaliation will have difficulty acknowledging and expressing angry feelings. The patient who believes that expressions of vulnerability and need will result in abandonment will have difficulty expressing such feelings. The therapist responses that are most facilitative in this context are exploration and sustained empathy. For example, the patient speaks critically about therapists in general but has difficulty being directly critical of the therapist. For example, the therapist responds, "I'm aware of you speaking about therapists in general, but not specifically about me. Any sense of what the risk would be of speaking specifically about me?" In another example, the patient begins to ask the therapist to be more helpful and then qualifies his request (e.g., "It's not a big deal"). The therapist responds, "I'm aware of you qualifying or softening your request. Any sense of what makes it difficult to ask without qualifying?"

Explorations of this type are best conducted as close as possible to the moment in which the avoidance has taken place. Moreover, they should be phrased in a way that encourages patients to discover their experience in the moment (e.g., "I'm afraid of offending you") rather than to engage in intellectual speculation (e.g., "It relates to my fear of authority figures"). A sustained empathic stance is critical at this point. It is important for the therapist not to challenge the patient's fears in any way because this makes it difficult for the patient to articulate them more fully, which then allows the patient the opportunity to evaluate them in light of the therapist's actual actions.

The second subtype of avoidance consists of self-doubt or self-criticism, which function to block the exploration of the rupture experience pathway. For example, a patient who believes she is childish for wanting help will not be able to express her needs to the therapist. The patient who believes that she is immature for being angry will have difficulty expressing those angry feelings to the therapist. This type of self-criticism can be understood developmentally as an introject, that is, as a negative response of a significant other that has been internalized. A common mistake therapists make at this point is to view the self-doubt or -criticism in this context as a mark of progress rather than an avoidance. This is particularly likely to happen when therapists are feeling threatened by the negative feelings or the wishes that patients are avoiding.

In general, it is useful for the therapist to help the patient to differentiate and explore different self-states in this context. The therapist can draw the patient's attention to the way in which he shifts into a state of self-criticism when he begins to contact self-assertive feelings and can help the patient to frame his experience as a conflict between two different parts of the self. He can then ask the patient to speak directly from each aspect of the self, alternating between the part of the self that wishes to assert and the part of the self that criticizes that wish. In this way, a dialogue can be established between the two aspects of the self, which allows the patient to ultimately come to have a tangible experience of the way in which he interferes with his own desire to assert.

As patients explore their avoidance and gain awareness of the processes interfering with their experience and develop more of a sense of ownership of these processes, feelings associated with the rupture experience naturally begin to emerge more fully. Patients may spontaneously move back to the experiencing pathway, or therapists may redirect attention to it once again. Typically, a resolution process involves an ongoing alternation between experiencing and avoidance pathways with the exploration of each pathway functioning to facilitate a deepening of the exploration of the other.

Stage 5: Self-Assertion

In Stage 5, the patient accesses and expresses underlying needs to the therapist. It can sometimes be difficult for therapists to distinguish between this type of self-assertion and the preliminary assertion that takes place in Stage 3. Self-assertion in this context entails an acceptance of responsibility for one's needs and desires rather than an expectation that the other will automatically know what one needs or that he or she is obligated to fulfill them. It thus implies a certain degree of individuation with respect to the therapist. In contrast, the expression of wishes and needs in Stage 3 often has a pleading, apologetic, or demanding tone. It is mediated by the patient's self-criticism or expectation that his or her needs will not be met.

Once the patient has begun to assert herself and express an underlying wish, it is important for the therapist to respond in an empathic and nonjudgmental way. This plays an important role in challenging the expectations (both conscious and unconscious) that have made it difficult for the patient to assert herself in the first place. A common pattern is for patients to initially assert themselves in a way that is structured by their characteristic relational schema. For example, a patient whose father was tyrannical and critical asks the therapist to be more confrontational. When this takes place, it can be important for the therapist to empathize with the patient's desire rather than to interpret it as a reflection of an old relational schema. The latter response risks discouraging patients from asserting themselves further and can lead to further submerging of their underlying wishes. In contrast, when therapists empathize with patients' desires it helps them to assert themselves in a fashion that is less structured by their old schema. Thus, the patient in the above example may ultimately be able to ask the therapist to be more supportive.

A Resolution Model for Confrontation Ruptures

Confrontation ruptures are likely to arouse intense and disturbing feelings of anger, impotence, self-indictment, and despair in therapists. Although such feelings are a common response to withdrawal ruptures as well, there is something about being the object of intense aggression for a prolonged period of time that is particularly difficult to deal with for most therapists. In the face of such intense and disturbing feelings, it is critical to remember that in many ways what is most important is not the specific therapeutic interventions used but rather the process of surviving (Winnicott, 1958). To tolerate patients' critical and angry feelings is a difficult task, and it is inevitable that therapists will respond as human beings, with their own anger and defensiveness. What is most important is for therapists to stay mindful and aware of the difficult feelings that are emerging in them as they experience themselves as objects of the patients' aggression and to be willing to acknowledge their contributions to the

FIGURE 7.2

Rupture resolution model for confrontation ruptures.

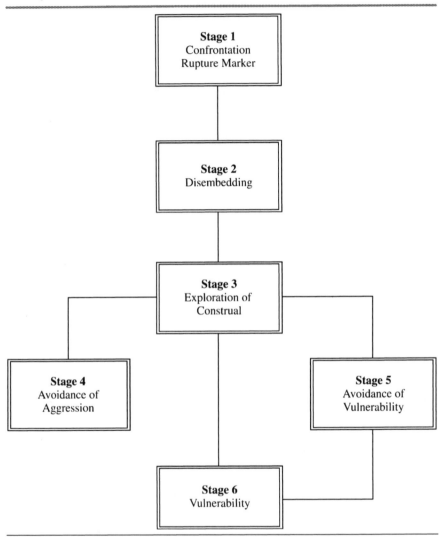

interaction on an ongoing basis. Their task in this context is not to avoid or transcend angry or defensive feelings but to demonstrate a consistent willingness to stick with the patient and to work toward understanding what is going on between them in the face of whatever difficult feelings emerge for both of them.

The resolution model for confrontation ruptures in many ways resembles the resolution model for withdrawal markers (see Figure 7.2). It begins with the rupture marker in Stage 1 and continues with the disembedding process in Stage 2. It also includes the two parallel pathways of exploration: the experiencing pathway and the avoidance pathway. It differs, however, in a number of respects. First, to the extent that patients present with intense aggression, the processes of disembedding and of surviving the patient's aggression over an extended period of time become more central. Second, the emphasis in Stage 3 is on elucidating patients' construal of the situation rather than on helping them begin to assert themselves and individuate. For example, the patient may begin to put into words the way in which he feels let down and disappointed by the therapist. Third, the wishes and needs emerging in the final stage typically entail a desire for contact or nurturance rather than individuation. Fourth, we make a distinction between patients' avoidance of aggression (Stage 4) and their avoidance of vulnerable feelings (Stage 5).

A confrontation marker can be conceptualized as an aggressive action characteristic of the patient's relational matrix that is perpetuated by a vicious cycle in which the patient believes her wish for nurturance will continue to go unmet; that others will respond with abandonment, impingement, or retaliation; and that the only hope for survival and possible remediation of the situation consists of self-protection and attempts to coerce the other into meeting her needs. There is thus, in Ghent's (1992) terms, an expression of neediness that covers an underlying need. The common progression in the resolution of confrontation ruptures consists of moving through feelings of anger (Stage 1); to underlying feelings of injury, disappointment, or hurt (Stage 3); to contacting vulnerability and underlying wishes for nurturance (Stage 6).

Stage 1: Confrontation Marker

Confrontation ruptures typically begin with an aggressive response that reflects the patient's expectations that direct expressions of need and vulnerability will be responded to in a traumatizing fashion. For example, a patient has a long-thwarted desire to be nurtured or taken care of and a readiness to perceive the therapist as one more in a long line of people who will fail him. He thus enters into the therapeutic relationship with a reservoir of rage and disappointment waiting to be triggered by the therapist's inevitable failings and shortcomings. When confrontation ruptures take place, it can be difficult, if not impossible, for therapists not to respond to the patient's demands or criticisms defensively, thereby providing the expected response of the other characteristic of the relational matrix. As Henry, Schacht, and Strupp (1986) showed, it is all too common for therapist interpretations to subtly convey blaming and belittling messages to their patients or to consist of complex communications that simultaneously convey helping and critical messages.

Stage 2: Disembedding

A critical step in working through a confrontation rupture involves disembedding from the relational matrix of hostility and counterhostility that is being enacted by metacommunicating about the current struggle. As discussed in the context of withdrawal ruptures, although we are representing disembedding as a distinct stage the entire resolution process involves an ongoing cycling back and forth between greater and lesser degrees of embeddedness. During the disembedding process, it is often critical for therapists to acknowledge responsibility for their contribution to the interaction. For example, "I think that what's been going on is that I've been feeling criticized by you and have responded by trying to blame you for what's going on in our interaction." It can also be extremely useful in this context for therapists to comment on the experience of a mutual struggle; for example, "It feels to me like you and I are in a power struggle right now, with me trying to hold you responsible for your frustrations with therapy, and you trying to pin the blame on me."

Therapists who feel pressured to prove to the patient that therapy will be helpful can comment on their dilemma rather than responding to this pressure with ineffectual attempts at persuasion or with angry defensiveness. For example, "I'm feeling pressured to convince you that I can help you, but I have a feeling that nothing I say will seem compelling to you." Therapists who feel criticized or attacked can comment on this experience rather than counterattacking or defending themselves. For example, "I feel wary of saying anything because I feel criticized when I try to respond to your questions or concerns." This type of metacommunication can serve a number of functions. The first consists of helping the therapist to re-establish internal space (i.e., the type of double consciousness necessary to be a participant–observer) that has collapsed. The process of articulating aspects of their experience that may feel threatening in this context, thereby saying the unspeakable, can begin the process of freeing therapists and restoring internal space. The second involves providing the patient with feedback that can help him to acknowledge negative feelings toward the therapist that are disowned. This can also help the patient to begin to experience the therapist as a subject rather than as an object. The third involves helping patients to stand behind their actions.

Confrontation ruptures occur on a continuum in terms of how directly or indirectly the initial confrontation is expressed. When the initial confrontation takes place in a more direct fashion the therapist does not need to begin by facilitating a more direct expression of the underlying demand or negative sentiments. In many cases, however, the initial confrontation is mixed with features of a withdrawal marker. When this takes place, therapists may become embedded in an enactment that is particularly difficult to see because patients are communicating in a complex and incongruent fashion. When this happens, the therapist's first task, as part of the process of disembedding, is to attempt to clarify the nature of the incongruent communication that is taking place. This involves helping patients to express their underlying negative feelings more directly, thereby standing behind their actions. A useful intervention to facilitate this process is for therapists to disclose the impact the patient is having on them. For example, "I feel attacked and protected at the same time." As with the withdrawal model, interventions of this type can lead either to an exploration of the experience associated with the rupture or the avoidance of that experience, and as with the withdrawal model, this phase of the resolution process typically involves an oscillation between the experiencing and avoidance pathways.

The transition toward the exploration of construal (Stage 3) is facilitated through a number of processes that take place in the disembedding stage. For example,

1. By metacommunicating about the interaction rather than simply retaliating or withdrawing, therapists can begin the process of articulating what is going on in the interaction and exploring patients' construal of it. For example, the therapist says, "I have a sense that anything I say strikes you the wrong way right now. Does that fit with your experience?" The patient tentatively acknowledges that it does, and the therapist then asks her to elaborate on the experience of having everything the therapist says strike her the wrong way.

2. By acknowledging patients' impact on them, including whatever vulnerable or impotent feelings they may have, therapists can deescalate the attack and pave the way for exploring the construal underlying it.

3. When patients confront therapists in an indirect fashion, the process of helping them to confront more directly can help them to develop a greater awareness of the feelings motivating the confrontation, thereby facilitating access to the underlying construal processes.

4. Sometimes therapists' ability to express their own feelings of anger in a reflective fashion or to acknowledge their conflicts around their feelings can help to establish them as real subjects, rather than as objects, to patients. Moreover, in contrast to therapists' attempts to interpret patients' anger or to hide their disturbing feelings, this type of acknowledgement can help patients to experience their own potency, thereby giving them the necessary security to begin exploring their underlying construal. In addition, expressing their own negative and aggressive feelings in a modu-

lated fashion can play an important role in detoxifying patients' own aggression for them by providing a model of the way in which aggression can be processed without being catastrophic (Carpy, 1989; Gabbard, 1996; Slochower, 1997).

5. When therapists can acknowledge their own contribution to the interaction, it can decrease the experience that patients may have of feeling persecuted or assaulted. As a result, patients may feel less of a need to protect themselves by attacking, thereby allowing them to begin exploring their construal of the situation in a more differentiated way.

Stage 3: Exploration of Construal

The therapist's task in Stage 3 is to help patients begin to unpack their construal of the interaction. For example, a patient experiences the therapist as patronizing him or as blaming him for the fact that treatment is not progressing more quickly, or a patient experiences the therapist as withholding and as not providing needed direction. The task here is to elucidate nuances of the patient's perceptions (often associated with feelings of anger, injury, or disappointment). This process of unpacking involves a phenomenological exploration of patients' conscious experience and an articulation of that which is on the edge of awareness but not fully explicit. It does not involve interpretations that require inferences about unconscious dynamics.

Interpretations of patients' anger in terms of disowned aggression or envy are usually not helpful at this stage. Similarly, attempts to bypass patients' anger by interpreting it as a response to underlying need or vulnerability are often not helpful. As contemporary ego analysts such as Gray (1994) and Busch (1994) suggest, attempting to bypass the patient's conscious experience in this fashion can be experienced as unempathic and disempowering. Moreover, such an attempt may be motivated in part by therapists' attempts to take themselves out of the line of fire and to put them back in control. It is often important for patients to experience any feelings of anger, hurt, or disappointment that exist as valid, acceptable, and tolerable before they can begin to explore primary yearnings that are more vulnerable in nature. The acknowledgment of underlying needs of a more vulnerable type must emerge in an organic fashion out of the therapeutic relationship as the patient and therapist struggle together to work through whatever cycle is being enacted.

When therapists are able to become aware of their own contribution to the relational matrix, it is important to acknowledge this. When they cannot initially see their contribution to the situation, it can be useful to encourage patients to articulate their perception of how the therapist has contributed. In this process, it is critical for therapists to be open to learning something new about themselves and their contributions to the interaction rather than to think of this exclusively as a way of exploring patients' underlying construal processes (Aron, 1996). This openness can transform the situation by reducing patients' need to be defensive and by making it easier for them to verbalize subtle perceptions, which may be difficult to fully articulate in the absence of a receptive audience.

For example, in one case, where the patient felt his therapist was insensitive and callous in rearranging an appointment time, it was critical for the therapist to be open to acknowledging this possibility to facilitate the exploration of the patient's concern that the therapist did not care for him. This led into the exploration of his general mistrust of people's caring. In another case, where the therapist had recently had a child, it was critical for her to listen and learn about the ways in which she had changed in her manner toward the patient before the patient could contact and explore fears regarding the emotional availability of others. As patients articulate the nuances of their perceptions, therapists begin to understand them from an internal point of reference. When this happens, they are less likely to take things personally and respond defensively. At the same time, patients begin to feel understood and validated, and some of the pent-up fury and rage begins to dissipate.

In some cases, the therapist's ability to help the patient unpack her construal and to empathize with her experience constitutes the end of the resolution process. In other cases, things proceed to a deeper exploration of underlying wishes of a more vulnerable nature (Stage 6), a process we discuss subsequently.

Stage 4: Avoidance of Aggression

During Stages 2 (disembedding) and 3 (exploration of construal), it is important for therapists to monitor subtle shifts in the patient's self-states on an ongoing basis. Even patients who are most overtly aggressive or hostile toward their therapists experience moments of anxiety or guilt about the expression of aggressive feelings and attempt to undo the harm they feel they have done by justifying their actions or attempting to depersonalize the situation to defuse the danger.

If therapists are feeling too overwhelmed by their own emotional response to the patients' aggression, they may have difficulty tracking these shifts and will miss an important opportunity to explore a habitual mode of functioning for them. For example, patients may express feelings of rage toward their therapist, feel guilty for expressing these feelings, and then shift into a defensive rage because they experience their feelings of guilt as intolerable. In this situation, it can be very helpful for the therapist to track these subtle shifts in self-states and to help the patient to become aware of the internal processes that lead to these shifts. For example, patients may cycle back and forth between a state of anger at their therapist and guilt over their expression of aggression, followed by a state of anger triggered by the feelings of guilt that are experienced as intolerable (Horowitz, 1987).

Stage 5: Avoidance of Vulnerability

A second type of avoidance that sometimes emerges during the resolution of confrontation ruptures consists of the defensive withdrawal from vulnerable feelings. In some situations, patients begin to contact vulnerable feelings and then shift back into a more familiar and secure state of aggression. When this happens, it can be useful for the therapist to track the shift and attempt to draw the patient's attention to it. For example, "My sense is that you began to contact some sadness there and then suddenly shifted into a harder or more aggressive stance. Did you have any awareness of this?" If the patient is able to become aware of the shift, the therapist can then explore his or her internal processes. For example, "Any sense of what went on inside just before the shift took place?" Patients often have difficulty becoming aware of this type of shift at first and, even when they can, have difficulty identifying relevant internal triggers. Over time, however, they can develop some facility at tracking their own shifts in self-state and can begin to explore internal processes triggering the shift (e.g., fears of abandonment or self-criticism for being vulnerable).

Stage 6: Vulnerability

Primary needs and wishes underlying the patient's aggression may take a long time (months or years) to emerge and in some more extreme cases may never do so. When the therapist has demonstrated consistently, over an extended period of time, a willingness to take the concerns underlying the patient's aggression seriously, an attempt to understand them from the patient's internal point of reference, a willingness to explore and acknowledge his or her own contribution to the interaction, and an ability to survive the patient's aggression, it paves the way for vulnerable feelings and wishes that have been defended against to emerge. When they do emerge, it is often initially in the form of an acknowledgement of despair.

In contrast to earlier stages of the resolution process, however, in which despair may emerge in a cynical, angry fashion that pushes others away, the relationship has evolved to the point that there is something different about both patient and therapist. Over time, the patient has come to trust the therapist to the point where she can begin to let him in on the pain and sadness associated with her despair, and the therapist has evolved to the point where he has a deeper appreciation of the patient as a whole person and is better able to empathize with her despair.

The experience of having the therapist care for her in her pain and despair can be an important new experience for the patient—one that allows her for the first time to escape her feeling of isolation and to begin to have more compassion for herself. This in turn facilitates the emergence of underlying needs for nurturance that have been disowned. It is critical for therapists to respond to any primary and more vulnerable feeling states that emerge in this context in an empathic and validating way. They should try to understand these feelings not as archaic infantile needs that need to be understood and re-nounced, or even as remobilized developmental yearnings, but rather as normal human yearnings for nurturance and support. In some cases, it can be important for therapists to gratify the wish. For example, a patient who had traditionally had a tremendous amount of difficulty acknowledging and expressing under-lying needs eventually came to a point in his therapy where he began to contact some of these needs. In one session, he directly asked his therapist for some advice about how to handle a conflict with a friend—something he had never done before. The therapist responded by giving him advice and then asked him how it felt. He responded with tears, as he contacted the relief and gratitude toward the therapist for being willing to act on his behalf in this context and the underlying yearning for nurturance that had motivated his question.

In situations where therapists are unable or choose not to gratify the un-derlying wish, it is important for them to be empathic and understanding while at the same time making it clear what their limits or boundaries are. It may, for example, be important for a patient to acknowledge her desire for the ther-apist to magically transform her and for the therapist to empathize with this desire rather than invalidate it. Or a therapist may not grant a patient's request to extend the session time but nevertheless empathize with the desire. Or a therapist may empathize with the desire for personal contact between sessions without accommodating it and without denigrating it as merely transferential. In such cases, it is important to empathize with the underlying yearning and the pain and frustration that inevitably result from having the wish go unful-filled.

The disappointment that patients experience when their therapist fails them plays a critical role in helping them come to terms with the reality of the therapist's limitations. Coming to accept the limitations of the other's ability or willingness to meet all of one's needs is a critical part of the maturational pro-cess. In the absence of working through this disappointment in an empathic fashion, however, the risk is that patients will retreat into a type of pseudo-maturity or pseudoindependence, which recognizes the therapist's limitations but masks an underlying despair about the possibility of things ever being different. This results in a shutting down of their spontaneous vitality, yearning, and hope (Safran, 1993, 1999).

When the therapist is able to empathize with this disappointment, however, patients are able to experience it as meaningful and the underlying yearning and desire as valid. This is critical because it promotes a growing acceptance of the patients' own feelings and needs. At the same time, they are able to experience the therapist as being there for them in a certain way (Winnicott's "good-enough therapist," 1965), despite the fact that he or she is not able to fulfill their fantasies of the ideal therapist.

As patients come to accept the therapist's limitations and to appreciate what he or she has to offer, without stifling their own vitality and bodily felt need, they are able to begin to let go of their attempts to manipulate both self and other in pursuit of perfection. As their acceptance of their own pain and irrevocable aloneness—as well as their faith that moments of comfort and real contact are possible—increases, they become less desperate in pursuit of nurturance and less relentless in pursuit of some idealized state. This permits them to be more receptive to those things that the therapist (and others) can provide (Safran, 1999).

Conclusion

After approximately 50 years of psychotherapy research, one of the most consistent findings is that the quality of the therapeutic alliance is the most robust predictor of treatment success. This holds true across a wide range of treatment modalities (see Horvath & Symonds, 1991). A consensus is emerging that ruptures in the therapeutic alliance are an inevitability and that one of the most important therapeutic skills consists of negotiating them in a constructive fashion (Binder & Strupp, 1997; Bordin, 1994; Foreman & Marmar, 1985; Henry & Strupp, 1994; Horvath, 1995; Rhodes, Hill, Thompson, & Elliott, 1994). In this chapter, we outline two different prototypical change processes through which ruptures in the alliance can be resolved. These two different change processes correspond to two broadly different types of alliance ruptures—withdrawal and confrontation—and these in turn correspond to two broadly different dysfunctional ways of reconciling the conflicting needs for relatedness and agency. At the immediate level, the process of resolving therapeutic-alliance ruptures establishes the necessary preconditions for successful treatment. At a deeper level, it provides an important new relational experience through which patients can learn to negotiate their needs for agency and relatedness in a constructive fashion. This takes place by means of a process of intersubjective negotiation through which patients learn that they can express their needs for agency without destroying the relationship and that the expression of vulnerable and dependent needs will not have traumatic consequences.

References

Aron, L. (1996). *A meeting of minds: Mutuality in psychoanalysis.* Hillsdale, NJ: Analytic Press.

Bach, S. (1985). *Narcissistic states and the therapeutic process.* New York: Aronson.

Benjamin, J. (1988). *The bonds of love.* New York: Pantheon Books.

Binder, J. L., & Strupp, H. H. (1997). "Negative process": A recurrently discovered and underestimated facet of therapeutic process and outcome in the individual psychotherapy of adults. *Clinical Psychology: Science and Practice, 4,* 121–139.

Bordin, E. (1979). The generalizability of the psychoanalytic concept of the working alliance. *Psychotherapy: Theory, Research, and Practice, 16,* 252–260.

Bordin, E. (1994). Theory and research in the therapeutic working alliance: New directions. In A. O. Horvath & L. S. Greenberg (Eds.), *The working alliance: Theory, research, and practice* (pp. 13–37). New York: Wiley.

Bromberg, P. (1996). Standing in the spaces: The multiplicity of self in the psychoanalytic relationship. *Contemporary Psychoanalysis, 32,* 506–535.

Busch, F. (1994). Some ambiguities in the method of free association and their implications for technique. *Journal of the American Psychoanalytic Association, 42,* 363–384.

Carpy, D. V. (1989). Tolerating the countertransference: A mutative process. *International Journal of Psycho-Analysis, 70,* 287–294.

Foreman, S. A., & Marmar, C. R. (1985). The therapist actions that address initially poor therapeutic alliances in psychotherapy. *American Journal of Psychiatry, 142,* 922–926.

Gabbard, G. C. (1996). *Love and hate in the analytic setting.* Northvale, NJ: Aronson.

Ghent, E. (1992). Paradox and process. *Psychoanalytic Dialogues, 2,* 135–160.

Gray, P. (1994). *The ego and analysis of defense.* Northvale, NJ: Aronson.

Harper, H. (1989a). *Coding guide I: Identification of confrontation challenges in exploratory therapy.* Sheffield, England: University of Sheffield.

Harper, H. (1989b). *Coding guide II: Identification of withdrawal challenges in exploratory therapy.* Sheffield, England: University of Sheffield.

Henry, W. P., Schacht, T. E., & Strupp, H. H. (1986). Structural analysis of social behavior: Application to a study of interpersonal process in differential psychotherapeutic outcome. *Journal of Consulting and Clinical Psychology, 54,* 27–31.

Henry, W. P., & Strupp, H. H. (1994). The therapeutic alliance as interpersonal process. In A. O. Horvath & L. S. Greenberg (Eds.), *The working alliance: Theory, research and practice* (pp. 51–84). New York: Wiley.

Horowitz, M. J. (1987). *States of mind* (2nd ed.). New York: Plenum Press.

Horvath, A. O. (1995). The therapeutic relationship: From transference to alliance. *In Session: Psychotherapy in Practice, 1,* 7–18.

Horvath, A. O., & Symonds, B. D. (1991). Relation between working alliance and outcome in psychotherapy: A meta-analysis. *Journal of Counseling Psychology, 38,* 139–149.

Mitchell, S. A. (1988). *Relational concepts in psychoanalysis.* Cambridge, MA: Harvard University Press.

Mitchell, S. A. (1993). *Hope and dread in psychoanalysis.* New York: Basic Books.

Pizer, S. A. (1992). The negotiation of paradox in the analytic process. *Psychoanalytic Dialogues, 2,* 215–240.

Rhodes, R., Hill, C., Thompson, B., & Elliott, R. (1994). Client retrospective recall of resolved and unresolved misunderstanding events. *Counseling Psychology, 41,* 473–483.

Rice, L., & Greenberg, L. S. (Eds.). (1984). *Patterns of change.* New York: Guilford Press.

Safran, J. D. (1993). Breaches in the therapeutic alliance: An arena for negotiating authentic relatedness. *Psychotherapy: Theory, Research, and Practice, 30,* 11–24.

Safran, J. D. (1999). Faith, despair, will, and the paradox of acceptance. *Contemporary Psychoanalysis, 35,* 5–23.

Safran, J. D., & Muran, J. C. (1996). The resolution of ruptures in the therapeutic alliance. *Journal of Consulting and Clinical Psychology, 64,* 447–458.

Safran, J. D., & Muran, J. C. (Eds.). (1998). *The therapeutic alliance in brief psychotherapy.* Washington, DC: American Psychological Association.

Safran, J. D., & Muran, J. C. (2000). *Negotiating the therapeutic alliance: A relational treatment guide.* New York: Guilford Press.

Slochower, J. (1997). *Holding and psychoanalysis.* Hillsdale, NJ: Analytic Press.

Winnicott, D. W. (1958). *Through paediatrics to psychoanalysis.* New York: Basic Books.

Winnicott, D. W. (1960). Ego distortion in terms of true and false self. In *The maturational process and the facilitating environment* (pp. 140–152). New York: International Universities Press.

Winnicott, D. W. (1965). *The maturational process and the facilitating environment.* New York: International Universities Press.

COMMENT:

The Therapeutic Alliance, the Dyad, and the Relational Triad

Lewis Aron

In his magisterial overview and synthesis of his life work, philosopher John Searle (1998) wrote that

> Freudian psychology, whatever its ultimate contribution to human culture, is no longer taken seriously as a scientific theory. It continues to exist as a cultural phenomena [sic], but few serious scientists suppose it gives a scientifically well-substantiated account of human psychological development and pathology. (p. 5)

Searle thus invalidates psychoanalytic psychology even as he goes on to make strong claims for the importance of unconscious self-deception as a powerful motivation in human behavior: "We simply deceive ourselves about our own mental states because it is too painful to confront our jealousies, hostilities, weaknesses, and so on. We refuse to admit, even to ourselves, our most shameful feelings and attitudes" (p. 70).

Nor is Searle a solitary sniper. As authoritative a scholar of medical historiography as Edward Shorter recently wrote that "Freud's ideas, which dominated the history of psychiatry for the past half century, are now vanishing like the snows of winter" (1996, p. vii). These criticisms are mild compared to the views of Frederick Crews (1998), who has systematically attacked the intellectual foundations of "psychoanalytic knowledge." This very phrase is dismissed by Crews as an "oxymoron." What is the besieged psychoanalytic psychologist to do? Is the *New York Times* (Goode, 1999) correct with "the threat of extinction has inspired a new vigor" among psychoanalysts?

The research and scholarship of Jeremy Safran and Christopher Muran need to be examined and assessed in light of the contemporary intellectual context, in which psychoanalytic psychology is on the ropes, if not down and out. Psychoanalysis must first acknowledge its own mistakes and its complicity in its intellectual downfall. Psychoanalysis remained isolated from its intellectual neighbors for too long, developing outside of academia where it did not have to consistently participate in dialogue with other disciplines, and it fostered an elitist attitude that trivialized the contributions of other areas of psychology and psychotherapy. Perhaps most problematic was the self-satisfaction and narcissistic overconfidence that contributed to the attitude that supportive research was unnecessary because everything that psychoanalysis needed to learn could be learned in the consulting room and only in the consulting room.

Safran and Muran's chapter is a model of the kind of work needed by psychoanalysis. Safran and Muran draw on a comprehensive understanding of both the psychoanalytic literature and the psychotherapy research literature, but more important, they articulate a model of the therapeutic action of psychoanalytic therapy that is both teachable and empirically testable. This is a significant achievement because articulating and teaching any therapeutic technique always runs the risk of degenerating into a mechanistic, formulaic exercise, as it does in so many treatment manuals. Safran and Muran, however, have managed to specify precise principles, each one subject to rigorous empirical investigation, so that the therapeutic process can be broken down into steps and taught systematically, without neglecting the subjectivity of patient and therapist and the unique emergent character of the therapeutic dyad.

In this brief commentary, I take up only two themes that touch on important aspects of my own recent work (Aron, 1996; see especially Aron, 1999). I begin by taking up the theme of the interdependence of relational and technical factors in the therapeutic alliance and then move on to a discussion of the dyad and the relational triad in contemporary psychoanalytic thinking.

I first want to elaborate on a point that Safran and Muran identify as among their fundamental assumptions. For Safran and Muran, "the meaning of any technical factor can be understood only in the relational context in which it is applied," and so they highlight the "interdependence of relational and technical factors" in psychotherapy. Although I very much agree with this proposition, I would like to place some emphasis on another dimension of this observation. Safran and Muran, like most who theorize about the therapeutic relationship, tend to emphasize the meaning that technical interventions have to the *patient*. This may be seen in their observation, regarding the tasks of therapy, that "each of these tasks places different demands on *patients* and tend to be experienced by *them* as more or less helpful depending on *their* capacities and characteristic ways of relating to themselves and others" (emphasis added). They also state that any intervention may have a positive or negative effect "depending on *its idiosyncratic meaning to the patient*" (emphasis added).

I believe that what have been seriously neglected in the psychotherapy literature, and in the psychoanalytic literature more specifically, are the meanings of technical interventions and styles of intervening to the therapist. Each of the various tasks that may be conceptualized as components of psychoanalytic treatment undoubtedly has a different meaning for different therapists as well as for patients. Consider a few simple examples: Some analytic schools and approaches place great emphasis on confronting pathological defenses, some place greater emphasis on maintaining an empathic responsiveness, some on conducting an active detailed inquiry, some on formulating articulate interpretations, some on identifying subtle resistances. Some analytic approaches require relative anonymity on the analyst's part, some sanction a fair degree of self-disclosure, some encourage long periods of silent listening, whereas others invite more active participation. My point is that not only do patients experience these differences in therapeutic role and functioning differently but also, just as important, therapists–analysts come to this work with very different sensibilities, and they too react very differently to the quality of therapeutic interventions.

Elsewhere (Aron, 1999), I elaborated on this point in greater detail. One specific example may help clarify my argument. Consider the various suggestions that have been made in regard to handling an idealizing transference. Some analytic approaches encourage the analyst to confront such idealization swiftly and directly because it is understood that behind such idealization lie resistance and aggression. The thinking here is that the idealization needs to be confronted before this negativity surfaces and destroys the treatment. However, there are analytic approaches that argue that such idealization may represent the leading edge of the patient's previously unmet developmental need to idealize a parent or parent figure. Following this approach would lead the analyst to leave the idealization alone or allow it to flourish, with the expectation that it will serve an important developmental need and ultimately lead to a deepening and enhancement of the analytic process.

Now, it is one thing to consider what the idealization means to the patient. Certainly, it has a different meaning and significance to different patients, and the analyst must determine its meaning to the specific patient and follow a course individually tailored for this patient. This is along the lines of the recommendations Safran and Muran make in their chapter, and I think that this is valuable as far as it goes. But I want to push the point further.

It is not only patients for whom idealization and its confrontation have a variety of meanings; it has a variety of meanings for the analyst as well. Does the best technical approach in the face of a patient's idealization depend at least somewhat on how comfortable the individual analyst is with being idealized? Does it not also depend a great deal on how comfortable an analyst feels being confrontational? Some of us love being idealized and work well in mutually admiring relationships. Some of us become uncomfortable being idealized and avoid these situations. Some of us are quite confrontational in our daily lives, whereas some of us go to great lengths to avoid confrontation. (And, I should quickly add, just as those who are confrontational assume that those who avoid confrontation need more analysis, so too do those who avoid dispute assume that those who are drawn to it need more analysis.) Therapists vary in many other ways as well. Some of us are more comfortable with quiet, others are more active or inquisitive, some are more argumentative, and some more comfortable than others with personal self-disclosure. We each have different personal proclivities, and we each struggle with different conflicts. Different interventions and styles of intervention inevitably have different meanings for each of us and suit some of us better than others. I (Aron, 1999) elaborated on the implications for training of these considerations. To reiterate my point, in discussing the therapeutic alliance and negotiating differences within the dyad we need to consider not only the meanings of technical interventions to the patient but also the individuality and idiosyncrasies of the therapist. There are two subjectivities constituting the interactive matrix, and an examination of the therapeutic alliance must consider contributions from both members of the dyad.

At the heart of the relational and intersubjective sensibility in contemporary psychoanalysis is the importance placed on the "interactive matrix" (Greenberg, 1995). Not only does this conceptualization of the interactive or relational matrix (Mitchell, 1988) make room for what Freud called the "subjective factor" (cited in Grubrich-Simitis, 1986, p. 271)—that is, the analyst's individuality—but, even more, it places this unique singularity of the analytic dyad at the very center of its concerns.

In my view, this contemporary psychoanalytic emphasis on the unique features of the analytic dyad brings psychoanalytic thinking very much into the mainstream of conceptualizations of the therapeutic process more generally. As Safran and Muran point out, one of the most consistent findings of the psychotherapy research endeavor has been the importance of the therapeutic alliance and the negotiation of gaps and ruptures by the dyad. With its specific focus on relational factors and intersubjective negotiation, and especially with its unique focus on the unconscious aspects of this process, psychoanalysis has a great deal to contribute to articulating the nuances of this dimension of all treatments that operate in an interpersonal context.

In their exploration of the therapeutic alliance as a process of intersubjective negotiation, Safran and Muran focus on the analytic dyad. I want to broaden this investigation by adding triadic considerations to the more obvious dyadic ones. Recent psychoanalytic writings have begun to focus on triadic considerations that remind us that the dyad always exists as part of a broader context. There is a trend among contemporary psychoanalysts to take increasing account of the context within which the analytic dyad operates—to think of the contextual third in addition to the Oedipal third. Altman (1995) and Cushman (1995) each independently referred to the larger social, cultural, and institutional contexts in which the dyadic interaction takes place.

Our identities as psychoanalysts are established through our relationships to psychoanalytic theory and to the psychoanalytic community, and to the values and ideals established by this society and embedded in its theories and practices. (Therapists associated with other schools of thought and other technical approaches must derive their professional identities in similar ways.) Thus, our theories and loyalties to any school of thought function as the Third to therapists' one-on-one relationship with their patients. This Lacanian concept of the Third points beyond the psychoanalytic dyad to the larger context, background, or container within which the dyad exists. Because the dyad is framed by the Third, the partners are able to relate without merging. For Muller (1996), it is the semiotic code (the cultural limits and borders) that frames and holds the dyad. Theory functions as an expression of the Third, as psychoanalytic theory, and the psychoanalytic community within which it is always embedded, exists as one aspect of our common cultural context. (For a comparison of current views on the third, see Aron, 1999; Crastnopol, 1999; Greenberg, 1997; Ogden, 1994; and Spezzano, 1998.)

For my purposes here, in discussing the therapeutic alliance and intersubjective negotiation, what I want to emphasize about the Third is that this concept points beyond the patient and the analyst as two individuals meeting in isolation, which might lead to an overly romanticized view of the psychoanalytic process as purely a personal encounter. Instead, conceptualizing the Third pushes us to consider the psychoanalytic relationship as always existing within the context of both the psychoanalytic community and the broader culture and, therefore, although contemporary psychoanalysis emphasizes the subjective, the intersubjective, and the unique relational matrix, there are some (relatively objective) constraints placed on what we mean by psychoanalysis, and these restrictions are imposed not only by the individuals directly involved (subjectively) but also by a wider set of forces, including not only contemporary influences but the voices of history and tradition as well.

The theoretical and the technical form a complex system of mutual influence with the personal, the subjective, and the intersubjective, and these factors need to be considered as functioning in intricate and often elusive ways. Among the strengths of Safran and Muran's approach is that in considering the personal and the technical dimensions of the therapeutic alliance, they articulate a systematic point of view that is both teachable and researchable without reducing this complexity.

References

Altman, N. (1995). *The analyst in the inner city*. Hillsdale, NJ: Analytic Press.

Aron, L. (1996). *A meeting of minds: Mutuality in psychoanalysis*. Hillsdale, NJ: Analytic Press.

Aron, L. (1999). Clinical choices and the relational matrix. *Psychoanalytic Dialogues, 9,* 1–29.

Crastnopol, M. (1999). The analyst's professional self as a "third" influence on the dyad: When the analyst writes about the treatment. *Psychoanalytic Dialogues, 9,* 445–470.

Crews, F. C. (Ed.). (1998). *Unauthorized Freud.* New York: Viking.

Cushman, P. (1995). *Constructing the self, constructing America.* Reading, MA: Addison-Wesley.

Goode, E. (1999, January 12). Return to the couch: A revival for analysis. *New York Times,* p. F1.

Greenberg, J. (1995). Psychoanalytic technique and the interactive matrix. *Psychoanalytic Quarterly, 64,* 1–22.

Greenberg, J. (1997, April). *Analytic authority and analytic restraint.* Invited address presented at the meeting of the Division of Psychoanalysis of the American Psychological Association, Denver, CO.

Grubrich-Simitis, I. (1986). Six letters of Sigmund Freud and Sandor Ferenczi on the interrelationship of psychoanalytic theory and technique. *International Review of Psychoanalysis, 13,* 259–277.

Mitchell, S. (1988). *Relational concepts in psychoanalysis.* Cambridge, MA: Harvard University Press.

Muller, J. P. (1996). *Beyond the psychoanalytic dyad.* New York: Routledge.

Ogden, T. (1994). *Subjects of analysis.* Northvale, NJ: Aronson.

Searle, J. R. (1998). *Mind, language and society.* New York: Basic Books.

Shorter, E. (1996). *A history of psychiatry.* New York: Wiley.

Spezzano, C. (1998). The triangle of clinical judgement. *Journal of the American Psychoanalytic Association, 46,* 365–388.

CHAPTER 8

Understanding and Treating the Postmodern Self

Stanley B. Messer

C. Seth Warren

In the Middle Ages, the configuration of the self was rather modest; individuals were defined largely by their social rank, family ties, and religion. There is little evidence that people engaged in the kind of introspection and inner struggles that we currently view as normative. At the time, the self had a negative connotation, implying greed, sin, weakness, and debasement, in contrast to the higher values of God, church, and community, all of which lay outside the self (Baumeister, 1986).

In this chapter, we focus on the greatly expanded concept of the modern self as well as on the postmodern self that is now said to be superseding it. Although some authors emphasize the virtues of the postmodern self, our view is that it frequently represents psychopathology insofar as it posits a lack of unity or even the existence of an inner core. We present a case that illustrates the developmental origins and pathological characteristics of the postmodern self as viewed within a clinical context rather than the purely sociological or social psychological perspective emphasized in the literature. Our contribution stands in contrast to that of the other chapters in this volume, which for the most part endorse postmodern renderings of the self.

The Modern Self

With the advent of modernity, the self took on new proportions. "To put it crudely, society stopped telling people who they were, and instead it was left up to the individual to construct his or her identity" (Baumeister, 1991, p. 95). This had the advantage for the individual of greater freedom of movement, thought, and self-expression, but it brought with it all the stresses and strains of having to establish one's place in the world, a task that falls particularly heavily on adolescents. It may be that such demands on the self have led to

194 MESSER AND WARREN

the vast increase in depression in our age because the self is ill suited to provide meaning and value to human life (Seligman, 1988).

Contributing to the expansion and valorization of self was the Industrial Revolution and the rational pursuit of self-interest. Increased mobility meant a weakening of dependence on one's farm and village and the necessity for self-initiated decisions and economic actions. Power shifted from local government, with its close ties to family and community, to central government, which expanded the rights and obligations of individuals. In fact, current laws continue to weaken the social forces that hold families together in favor of individual rights. New divorce laws, for example, encourage people to pursue their own self-interest during marriage rather than sacrificing themselves for the good of the family, as would once have been the case (Weitzman, 1985).

In earlier periods, both occupation and marriage were determined by the family. As people moved to the cities for jobs and, later, as education became more widespread, the importance of family receded, and the role of individual choice ascended. All of this came about because people were no longer dependent on parental financing for jobs or dowries or on family contacts for potential spouses. Moral issues, too, were now more likely to be resolved on the basis of individual inclinations rather than community standards (Bellah, Madsen, Sullivan, Swidler, & Tipton, 1985). Values came to be regarded as an expression of one's inner self (Baumeister, 1991) rather than a reflection of external norms.

Along with the expansion of the self came its *interiorization,* that is, the sharp separation of what was "inside" the mind from what was "outside" it, and an increased value placed on that which was inside it. In Cushman's (1995) words, "Augustine looked inward and found absence, which eventually led to and was filled by God; Rousseau looked inward and found the sole source of unity and goodness, the individual, radically autonomous self" (pp. 579–580).

Most scholars attribute the modern concept of mind and its consequences for the self to Descartes and Kant (e.g., Solomon, 1988). The modern standard of autonomous man derives from the Cartesian view of a self-defining, self-enclosed subject, radically separated from a lifeless, mechanistic world. Consciousness, Descartes posited, has direct access not to the external world but only to inner ideas that represent the world. Thus, the modern self is disengaged, private, and inward turning.

Kant was even more radical than Descartes in encouraging the sense of separation from the world and withdrawal to the interior. He asserted that the categories of mind—time, space, causality, and materiality—are what constitute our world of experience (Sass, 1992b). The notion of self-sufficiency took on a prescriptive or ethical cast that human beings had a moral obligation to exercise—a precursor of the rugged individualism so prized in America. Kant also argued for the necessity of assuming the existence of a unified self, which contributed to the radical individualism of the modern self.

It is not surprising, then, that our concept of self in Western society has been that of the "bounded, masterful self" with "specific boundaries, an internal locus of control, and a wish to manipulate the world for its own personal ends" (Cushman, 1990, p. 600). That is, we exercise agency and willpower and feel we can even alter our own psychological attributes. "A number of expressions, in fact, focus on the powers of the self with respect to itself, e.g., 'self-determination,' 'self-possession,' 'self-respect,' and 'self-assurance'" (Heelas, 1981, p. 4). Even our theories of human development have come to reflect this concept of self, probably because the self is historically and culturally situated, both maintaining and reflecting the current sociocultural milieu. Theories such as that proposed by Mahler, emphasizing separation and individuation, and by Stern (1985), emphasizing the "core self" of infants, which is characterized by "an integrated sense of themselves as distinct and coherent bodies, with control over their own actions, ownership of their own affectivity, and a sense of continuity" (p. 69) can be seen as reflections of the current conception of self rather than as encompassing universal, scientific truths regarding human development (Cushman, 1991).

There is a second historical thread in the development of the concept of self known as *expressivist* (Taylor, 1975) that rejects Cartesian dualism and Newtonian mechanism. It is "an attempt to overcome all forms of separation, both those within man and those that separate man from the social or natural world, for these are seen as leading to a sterile, devitalized, and alienated sense of human existence" (Sass, 1988, p. 561). The root metaphor (Pepper, 1942) based on the biological organism applies, stressing unity, wholeness, and purposiveness. It allows for an overcoming of the polarization between man and the external world and between body and soul. Achieving understanding in this mode is not the objectifying vision of Descartes but the empathic entering into the inner and emotional life of the other person. Self-exploration and self-expression, rather than the self-control of the autonomous conception of self, are valorized. Whereas the concept of "autonomous man" is expressed in ego psychology, especially Schafer's action language, that of "expressivist man" is cultivated in Kohut's self psychology (Sass, 1988).

The Postmodern Self

Although major elements of the modern Western self are still very much in evidence, postmodernist writers claim that the nature of the self is changing. Instead of a bounded, disciplined, autonomous self what we now possess is variously described as an "empty self" (Cushman, 1995), a "saturated self" (Gergen, 1991), a "protean self" (Lifton, 1993), or "multiple selves" (Linville & Carlston, 1994; Markus & Kitayama, 1991). Related to the concept of multiple selves is the position that there is no single, unifying self at all—no inner core, no true self, no essentialist self, and no deep, hidden self—and, for some, this is a fact to be celebrated. Why is this? Because according to Foucault (1979) and other poststructuralist writers, such as Derrida and Lyotard, the self is formed on the basis of social practices and loci of power that are not necessarily benign. Thus, to be self-less is to be politically and socially emancipated. They "reject any notion of a self which implies that deeper structures may be necessary for the self's orientation and capacity in the world" (Glass, 1993, p. 5). For these postmodernists, life is a work of art that we create; it is to be lived freely, playfully, and fluidly—which requires a multiple or fragmented self.

The Saturated and Multiple Self

Kenneth Gergen (1991) attributed the advent of the postmodern self to our being socially overstimulated with roles, relationships, and a constantly changing culture:

> Social saturation furnishes us with a multiplicity of incoherent and unrelated languages of the self. For everything we "know to be true" about ourselves, other voices within respond with doubt and derision. This fragmentation of self-conceptions corresponds to a multiplicity of incoherent and disconnected relationships. These relationships pull us in myriad directions, inviting us to play such a variety of roles that the very concept of an "authentic self" with knowable characteristics recedes from view. The fully saturated self becomes no self at all. Under postmodern conditions, persons exist in a state of continuous construction and reconstruction; it is a world where anything goes that can be negotiated. Each reality of self gives way to reflexive questioning, irony, and ultimately the playful probing of yet another reality. The center fails to hold. (pp. 6–7)

Gergen (1991) went on to say that as humans we absorb the views, values, and visions of others; we lose any secure sense of self, or even a notion of being a bounded entity. We develop a condition that he calls *multiphrenia*—"a splitting of the individual into multiple self-investments" (p. 74). Each truth about ourselves is merely a construction that is good only for a certain time, place, and relationship.

Gergen (1991) posited that a new and improved postmodern self can arise from the ashes of the modern self. Instead of individual autonomy, we achieve immersed interdependence in which it is the relationship that constructs the self. Similarly, Markus and Kitayama (1991) put forward the interdependent view of the self, which is more characteristic of non-Western societies, as an alternative, stressing the connectedness of human beings to each other: "One's behavior is determined, contingent on, and, to a large extent, organized by what the actor perceives to be the thoughts, feelings and actions of others in the relationship" (p. 227). Thus, there seems to be some overlap between examples of the non-Western self and some of the more optimistic conclusions of postmodern writers on the self.

The Protean Self

Robert Jay Lifton (1993) referred to the current configuration of self as *protean*: Like the Greek god Proteus, the self takes on the form required by each current life situation. That is, we assume a variety of personas—husband, father, friend, academic, athlete, and so forth.

> The protean self represents, therefore, an adaptation to cultural trauma wherein modern people find it impossible to make meaningful and long-term commitments to each other, to their institutions, or to the more enduring aspects of selfhood that may reside beneath the surface of everyday role-playing. (McAdams, 1997, p. 48)

Like Gergen, however, Lifton saw positive aspects to such an adaptation to postmodern life that allows for "explorations and new combinations, for life-enhancing" response (p. 24). Similarly, McAdams pointed out that multiplicity in selfhood need not be seen only as evidence of personal distress and cultural unrest but as flexibility of self-presentation, as adaptation by means of a "close confederacy of multiple self-conceptions" (p. 51).

Of course, another way of referring to the multiple self is less benign, namely, as fragmented and alienated (what Lifton called "negative proteanism"). To not be held accountable, to be chameleonlike, with no sense of a firm, centered identity, is tantamount to remaining uncommitted to a set of values or beliefs. Even William James (1892/1963), who declared that "man has as many social selves as there are distinct groups of persons about whose opinion he cares" (p. 169), made a case for the necessity of a central self:

> But to make any one of them actual, the rest must more or less be suppressed. So the seeker of his truest, strongest deepest self must review the list carefully, and pick out the one on which to stake his salvation. All other selves thereupon become unreal, but the fortunes of his self are real. Its failures are real failures, its triumphs, real triumphs, carrying shame and gladness with them. (p. 174)

The clinical case we offer in this chapter attests to James's view. From our perspective, a fragmented self that lacks a central core, or a sense of cohesion, is like the spokes of a wheel without an anchoring point at its center to hold them in place to create a stable structure. There are pathologies, such as schizophrenia, multiple personality disorder, and schizoid and borderline conditions, in which a sense of a stable identity is frequently lacking. Without it, the personality becomes overwhelmed and confused. To handle such diversity of experience, James Glass (1993) argued, requires "an inner resiliency capable of psychologically withstanding the onslaught of a fragmented, existential field ... to sustain that kind of plurality necessitates a self ready to organize the chaos, to assimilate forces attempting to pull or tear the self apart" (p. 11). In our view, there is a great deal of human suffering that accompanies the self-less or identity-less state, even if there is the possibility for flexibility and variety.

Stephen Mitchell (1993) attempted—successfully, we believe—to steer between the views of self as unitary, possessing depth and continuity, and the self as multiple and discontinuous from role to role and situation to situation. The former, *spatial* metaphor, said Mitchell, leads us to locate a core of the self, to peel back the layers and differentiate the authentic parts from its false covering. The latter, *temporal* metaphor refers to a self that people experience over time and the meanings one creates as one moves and does things through time. According to this view, one's object relations, for example, derive from the multiple organization of the self as expressed in different relational contexts, which Mitchell saw as enriching life insofar as it avoids a bland blending of different versions of the self.

Self psychology, on the other hand, stresses that one can connect with others in a vital way only if one is first centered in, and deeply connected with, one's core subjectivity. It also allows for the sense of continuity in action and for agency. "The experience of the self as singular and constant serves an important adaptive, psychological purpose" (Mitchell, 1993, p. 110). The sense of a core self may be illusory, but it is a central one in organizing our experience and guiding our behavior. Mitchell contended that the apparent contradiction between the spatial and temporal views creates a tension that leads to a more useful concept of self. The process of psychoanalytic therapy should give people a view of self not only more varied, more complex, and layered but also as having more fluidity and texture within multiple situations than might be first apparent to them.

The Empty Self

Finally, we describe a variation of the postmodern self referred to by Philip Cushman (1990, 1995) as "empty." He argued

> that our terrain has shaped a self that experiences a significant absence of community, tradition and shared meaning. It experiences these social absences and their consequences "interiorly" as a lack of personal conviction and worth, and it embodies the absences as a chronic, undifferentiated emotional hunger. It is a self that seeks the experience of being continually filled up ... in an attempt to combat the growing alienation and fragmentation of its era. (1990, p. 600)

Cushman saw evidence of the empty self in the currently fashionable diagnoses of narcissism and borderline states. Lasch's (1978) narcissist, for example, hungers for the feeling of personal well-being, health, and psychic security. The borderline patient shifts from identity to identity, with no stable self-image or sense of self. Goals, values, and vocational aspirations keep shifting, as do sexual identity and friendships. Cushman attributed the empty self in part to the loss of family, community, and tradition. There is a never-ending search for self-actualization and growth, along with a sense of meaninglessness and emptiness that consumerism, advertising, and psychotherapy have stepped in to fill. Patients with disorders of the self in particular, said Cushman, are empty and hungry for idealizing and merging experiences.

Thus, Cushman, like others, such as Taylor (1989), Bellah et al. (1985), and Sass (1992b), are critical of the features associated with the postmodern self, emphasizing its estrangement, hyper self-awareness, loss of sense of unity, alienation, fragmentation, anomie, and solitude. Along with Glass (1993), we see many of these descriptors as indicative of pathology of the self, deriving not from postmodern culture alone but also from developmental disturbances. That is, the postmodern self is not just an alternate lifestyle but is dysfunctional as well. We believe that there is value in the concept of a "true self" from which one can be alienated, and that the work of therapy is to help the person get to that sense of authenticity, even if there is also the possibility for some fluidity. Sass (1992a) pointed out that for therapists to adopt a strong relativistic or pluralistic stance regarding the existence of a true or inner self is to jeopardize the benefit to be derived from therapy for people who suffer from problems of emptiness, meaninglessness, unrelatedness, and hyper self-awareness, with a lack of continuing goals, values, and ideals.

To reiterate, we view the self neither as an essential given, as would a positivist, nor as socially or interpersonally constructed, as would those who advocate the concepts of a "multiphrenic," protean, empty, or saturated self. Rather, we think of it as akin to Winnicott's (1951/1975) notion of the "transitional object," which refers neither to the external object as a given nor to the object as pure fantasy. We suggest that the self, like Winnicott's transitional object, exists in a region between what is real, biologically given, anchored, and coherent and what is created by means of cultural, historical, and interpersonal categories. Karl Marx (1852/1969) described the concept of praxis in a similar way; he asserted that although humans create history, they cannot do so in any way they choose. History is determined by human actions in the context of a material reality that already has come before. Thus, we seek to place the self in a region that is not totally relativistic but partakes of a sense of inner authenticity and "truth." Winnicott indicated that it is difficult to point precisely to what the true self is, but this does not mean that it does not exist. Despite the self being indeterminate and known only through inference, it is, for all that, no less real. (For further expansion of this view, see our comment on chapter 9 of this volume.)

Henry: A Case of Postmodern Pathology

The case that follows is intended to illustrate some of the points we have made thus far. Specifically, we highlight the psychopathological implications of a more extreme self-awareness, with a concomitant experience of inauthenticity, alienation, and purposelessness. Furthermore, we wish to buttress our argument by examining, as one would in a clinical situation, the etiology in this particular case of the sense of falseness. The developmental context provides a grounding framework in which the hyperreflexive self can be understood as a defensive deviation from a possible sense of self as relatively free, spontaneous, and authentic. Although we do not wish to return to the reified, essentialist, and idealized self of modernist theorizing, we note that the clinical situation is relevant to the evaluation of claims made regarding the evolution of the self from modern to postmodern. In addition, it is our view that the therapeutic dimension inevitably provides what we consider to be a necessary grounding framework in which to examine such claims.

Formulating the Postmodern Self

Henry was in his mid-40s when he came for therapy. He complained of chronic depression; a sense of futility; frustration in his career and, to a lesser extent, in his marriage; and the feeling that there must be something more to life than he had been able to find. He had previously been in psychotherapy of about 5 years' duration with a pastoral counselor, a "nice enough person" with whom he felt he had chatted but not gone into real depth. He had been married for about 15 years to a woman who he felt was good for him and with whom he got along well in a companionable way, but he also felt that there was no real spark of intimacy. He complained that she didn't really know him. In the early sessions, he spoke of feeling "invisible."

Henry's main complaint was the sense that life did not matter to him as much as he thought it should. He described feeling hidden and unseen. Where he was visible to others, he felt shame and inadequacy. His experience was accompanied by a constant self-consciousness, a kind of internal editor or critic that never let up. Henry felt himself to be completely false, with the appearance of being a human being but in reality being a sham, an imposter. He felt a deep sense of shame that was crushing to him in all areas of his life.

A dream he had during the middle of the treatment illuminates this sense of inadequacy and acute self-consciousness:

I was leaving from somewhere, not sure where. Maybe I was at work, I don't know, like a workplace, yeah, the people on this bus were somehow connected to each other, I came out of this place, and there were like employee buses taking people home. I was feeling confused, not knowing which bus to get on. I was too embarrassed to ask, this sense of shame, so I wind up getting on a bus at random, hoping. It was a sunny day, still light, it was real clear it wasn't going to take me home. We passed through some town I recognized, was it S_____? I saw all these things that were familiar, a movie house, stores, etc., I thought to get off, but I couldn't ask, everyone would know what I was doing, this sense of shame, so I stayed on the bus. It went out into the countryside, nowhere, some rural area, this complete sense of being completely lost. It never got resolved.

The dream highlights the sense of anonymity, rootlessness, falseness, and arbitrariness that constitutes so much of Henry's usual conscious experience of himself. He feels that he does not belong anywhere. One might say that shame is at the heart of this experience of alienation, but it also seems true that what Henry is ashamed of is how alienated he feels. His passivity is extreme; he chooses a bus at random and watches helplessly and hopelessly as he is taken to nowhere (an apt expression of his feelings about the therapy as well).

When the treatment began, Henry was working in a mid-level position in a large commercial bank. Consistent with his sense of self, his department was a kind of corporate backwater, off the main paths of advancement and power, so there was not much possibility of further career development. Although the atmosphere of the office was deadening to Henry, it was a great improvement over a previous job. He had worked for the U.S. Postal Service in a vast and featureless sorting facility, an experience that stood in the treatment as emblematic of the alienated and estranged existence Henry felt he had led all his life. Losing the bank job in a large-scale layoff was the trigger to a more relaxed and creative period during which Henry wrote for a number of periodicals, got involved in community cultural organizations, and in general felt more engaged with others. During this time, a deep involvement developed with a woman he met at the bank, a relationship that was never overtly sexual but was intensely erotic in spite of the fact that she was a lesbian.

Even in this more lively and open time, there was always the gravitational pull back into states of futility and despair. Under the influence of that force, all his accomplishments—professional, emotional, and relational—would flatten out and seem to Henry to be part of a false self (Winnicott, 1965), a self of compliance and social accommodation. It was as though these activities did not truly belong to him. But the problem was that the sands of self-experience were always shifting: What seemed real enough in one moment would be undone, as though Henry were always asking, "How could I have been so naïve as to believe that was real?" To have been taken in, duped, was the worst disaster of all.

202 MESSER AND WARREN

Related to this sense of falseness was a profound and pervasive sense of futility, much as described in Fairbairn's (1941/1952) discussions of schizoid problems: "for *the characteristic affect of the schizoid state is undoubtedly a sense of futility*" (p. 51, emphasis in original). Although not always in such a frame of mind, Henry often feels that life is without any purpose or meaning, that is, it is empty. This experience ebbs and flows, without apparent clear causes or precipitants. Like many people with schizophrenia, Henry has no tolerance for the slightest degree of inauthenticity, in others or himself. In the treatment, Henry and his therapist liken this capacity to a kind of overactive "bullshit detector," which in some ways makes Henry a more complicated and developed observer but in other ways completely paralyzes him. In the dichotomy of observing ego and experiencing ego, Henry slides into an almost completely observational stance, often unable to actually do anything. As Fairbairn (1941/1952) wrote,

> amongst other schizoid phenomena which may be mentioned here are a sense of being wasted, a sense of unreality, intense self-consciousness and a sense of looking on at oneself. Taken together, these various phenomena clearly indicate that an actual splitting of the ego has occurred. (p. 51)

Although Henry has made fairly successful forays into writing, photography, and other creative pursuits, he feels so much a sham in these roles that he eventually gives up the activity. When he is not writing, he claims, "I'm not a writer, a writer is someone who writes." When he has written things, the pleasure of creating is heavily burdened by a constantly self-critical attitude. At certain moments, he is able to break through and do something he values. Although these breakthroughs can take place in a variety of situations—such as at work, in travel, in moments of connection to other people including sex with his wife—they do not last. Like an automobile with a faulty alternator, Henry is always leaking the charge he can generate. The next start is as difficult as the first. The sense of futility returns, sometimes with a vengeance, as though in part fueled by the momentary expansion of hopefulness or ambition, a force of psychic annihilation that needs to smash any increase in meaningfulness. It is as though accomplishments cannot stick to him, he cannot take in the goodness of his own efforts, and no sense of self accrues through experience that he can bear into the next situation to shore him up.

Instead, it is as though Henry starts from scratch every day, a kind of clean or empty slate of self-esteem that may or may not evolve into a workable sense of self for that day. Fairbairn (1940/1952) wrote of the schizoid dilemma in terms of the inability to give: "When such individuals give, they tend to feel impoverished, because when they give, they give at the expense of their inner world" (p. 18). He went on to say, "to mitigate a sense of impoverishment following giving and creating, the individual with a schizoid component often employs an interesting defense. He adopts the attitude that what he has just given or created is worthless" (p. 19).

It is interesting to consider the way such a sense of futility plays itself out in the therapy situation. It would be a mistake to assume that such experience does not have an interactional life within the ongoing therapeutic dyad. One cannot be in the presence of such annihilating futility and remain "neutral." Certainly, the therapist's reassurance has made no difference, except perhaps to convey a feeling of concern for Henry of which he could make some slight use. Most of the people in his life, including a number of good friends, many acquaintances, and his wife, are often in the position of reassuring him. This usually has the effect of making him feel more despairing, as he feels that others cannot understand the experience of depression and pointlessness within which he dwells. It makes him feel even more alien and "other." But this does speak directly to a countertransference pressure that Henry induces. No one could stand to be as ineffectual as Henry would render him. Thus, the therapy has been an evolving situation aimed at containing the experiences of futility, without denying or minimizing them, and yet paradoxically offering something that may be of use. This possible usefulness has been the target of substantial attack, especially when too overt, although Henry rarely has gotten angry at the therapist in any direct way. Instead, the negative transference–countertransference has been more a corrosive undermining of the therapist's sense of self, with Henry putting the therapist in the position of being an advocate for life and meaning and then attacking that position with extreme cynicism.

This ultra-ironic stance, an externalizing version of Henry's brutal self-criticism noted earlier, becomes the central defense mechanism in the form of an acute knowingness (Eigen, 1996; Phillips, 1995; Warren, 1997). Winnicott (1951/1975) described this mental state of extreme self-consciousness as a "hypertrophied ego," the result of traumatic impingements in the early stages of ego integration. Such a development protects the self, making it impossible to be surprised, disappointed, or duped into a naïve dependency. Such cynicism must also be related to aggressiveness, according to the Kleinian tradition; it has been described as a variety of sadism that is directed at internal objects (Joseph, 1982) and at the very capacity to make experience meaningful and valuable (Bion, 1957).

It may be noted at this point that this is precisely where we would locate some notions of a postmodern self. In this light, the postmodern self can be viewed as a pathological formation resulting from an imbalance between moments of "being-ness" and those of "knowing-ness," resulting in an overly reflexive mode of being. This "hyper-reflexivity" (Sass, 1992b), which is a hallmark of postmodern experience, may point less to progress, as advocates of a deconstructionist view of the self such as the protean or multiple self would claim, and more to a collapse of a grounding sense of self that might serve as the origin of purpose and desire.

There is an aggressiveness with which Henry points out specifically to the therapist the futility of everything—thus alerting us to an interpersonal dimension to his complaining. But we wish to emphasize the defensive aspect of this transference–countertransference arrangement. What he needs to conceal (although admittedly rather baldly) in this way is the undeniable fact that he does return for his sessions, week after week and year after year, reflecting a most hapless optimism. It would appear that Henry needs to place the therapist transferentially in the "untenable" position (from the point of view of the extreme cynic) of defending life, so that he can attack any sign of hope or optimism as foolish, naive, and gullible. Perhaps this makes it safe for him to experience his own naive and vulnerable self in a fuller way than ever previously possible. Such a formulation points directly to Winnicott's (1965) "true self," a center of emotional experience that is the source of personal meaning and purpose. This also aligns with Winnicott's notion that cynicism, or the "hypertrophied ego" mentioned earlier, can be understood as a defense against the destruction of the personal sense of self that he described as "unthinkable" (Winnicott, 1965). One retreats into the mind in a need-denying arrangement that precludes the possibility for spontaneous expression (Corrigan & Gordon, 1995; Phillips, 1995).

This brings us back to Henry's rather postmodern dilemma, which now can be framed in terms of a defensive strategy in the service of guarding an extremely threatened body-rooted sense of self, resulting in the paralyzing inability to "be." At the core of this dilemma is a terrible vulnerability and deep, crushing feelings of shame linked to the inevitable emotional needs that arise in the course of development and which for Henry were largely unmet. What we are suggesting, then, following Fairbairn (1941/1952), Winnicott (1965), Balint (1968), Ferenczi (1980), Kohut (1984), and others, is that a self of authenticity and groundedness has its origins in developmental experience. Rather than being an evolutionary accomplishment in transition from its modern to postmodern guise, as some authors have suggested, it seems to us that the failure to develop a sense of authenticity can be the result of certain forms of psychic trauma arising in the context of early experience. It seems to be extremely important to differentiate the fluid, open, and democratic self celebrated by some postmodern theorists from the alienated, rootless, and arbitrary self that we are suggesting arises from such trauma.

Treating the Postmodern Self

Here, we can turn to the question of treatment and the notion of what may be reparative for an individual such as Henry. Articulating the relationships between his early life and his present states, affects, moods, and reactions has been useful. Even in his most defeated frame of mind, Henry is able to hear connections made between that sense of futility and his early emotional life.

His mother, an extremely anxious, phobic, and self-centered woman, could tolerate no expression of anxiety on Henry's part. Henry and his therapist have discussed how any expression of distress by him to his mother would result in something like "metal pellets ricocheting around the inside of a steel can," with the sense that the anxiety would escalate to an unmanageable level. In addition to this environmental failure, Henry reported that because of a serious kidney illness in early childhood, he was thought to be vulnerable to infection and was therefore kept home in total isolation from other children. He has articulated how this time was like an endless desert of emotional barrenness, where he had to choose between the nothingness of no contact at all and the intrusiveness of his mother's anxious helplessness. His father was a very distant and demanding man, apparently struggling with his own sense of masculinity and efficacy. He pushed Henry into athletics although Henry had no such inclinations (neither had his father). He insisted on calling his son "Butch," although the name seemed to Henry to be absurdly inappropriate. It seemed to reflect absolutely no sense of who he felt himself to be. Thus, what has become apparent to both therapist and patient in the course of his treatment is a rather extreme disjunction between Henry's evolving sense of self and the perceptions of these caretakers. In this unusually large gap in recognition, despair blossomed, and the "true self" hid.

Links made between these developmental contexts and his current emotional experiences have often led to rare moments of meaningful and engaged contact, usually colored by a mood of grief and loss. At such moments, Henry has seemed at last able to take in something, often listening silently and weeping as the therapist spoke quietly to him of his sense of desolation and loneliness in his early life.

We would also like to note another aspect of the therapeutic process, pertaining to the transference and countertransference. Here, we would suggest that what has been therapeutically useful has been the internal processing of countertransference feelings in the therapist parallel to those described by the patient. Feelings of inadequacy, hopelessness, and schizoid cynicism were activated in the therapist. One tactic Henry has used is to joke lightly about the therapist's cynicism. "I guess this therapy will end when your children graduate from college," he has said on more than one occasion. "It seems like the same session, over and over and over again," he has noted. "Why do I keep coming?" he asks rhetorically.

These sorts of comments, made in an offhand and casual manner, are peppered throughout the sessions. Individually, they are hard to make much of, yet they reflect an undercurrent of dissatisfaction, disillusionment, and criticism that Henry does not articulate directly. Here, the therapeutic task has been to hold and tolerate these projections and, beyond this, for the therapist to work through the internal states generated in him. Henry's cynicism inevitably stimulated that of the therapist—perhaps less crushingly so, but present and with a life of its own. After all, the therapist does not want to be the dupe, either. One wants to join with the cynic, who seems so smart and invulnerable. Then the earnest and innocent self is left behind, ridiculed and humiliated. The innocent self becomes a kind of "hot potato" to be passed back and forth, no one wishing to be the final receptacle of such vulnerability. Working with Henry has meant working with one's own schizoid self, the distant, intellectualizing, reflexive self that judges self and others, criticizes, and deconstructs. In many respects, it has seemed that Henry has been helped by continual contact with the therapist's willingness to be the more vulnerable one, with his owning both hopefulness and possibility without falling into a masochistic position that the patient would have to reject as overly naïve. The therapist's shifting between being knowing enough to make contact with the patient's cynical self, yet being open and vulnerable enough to speak for the patient's protected innocent self has mitigated Henry's cynicism, making it less all encompassing and destructive. Henry has learned, to a degree, to play with his cynicism, and with his shame and vulnerability.

The Postmodern Self

Henry brings to mind John Barth's (1972) short story *The Bellerephoniad,* in which the protagonist sets out consciously to be a mythic hero by trying to emulate the mythic pattern of the life of the great hero Perseus. Naturally Bellerephon, a minor hero of Greek mythology, discovers that mythic greatness resides in more than just the external correspondence to a mythic pattern. The story highlights the postmodern dilemma of the hyperreflexive subject burdened by the awareness of narrative patterns and mythic structures that preexist one, as it were. Henry felt he might look like a banker, he might act like a banker, and he might even do all the things a banker does, but nevertheless, he was not really a banker.

Henry feels himself to be a sham in all facets of his life. Thus, he lives with a periodic oscillation between moments of participation and engagement in which the awareness of self disappears, and prolonged periods in which the activities undertaken in those moments are felt to be false and self-deluding. In a retrospective act of destructiveness, the meaningfulness of those engaged times are unraveled as foolishly naive, as though he had only fooled himself for a short time. It would seem that Henry idealizes the modernist sense of realness and assumes that reality is "more real" for others, or that others have a felt sense of realness that he can never truly possess.

One could say that Henry suffers fundamentally from the tendency to objectify himself. This hypertrophied ego—or "mind object," as Corrigan and Gordon (1995) described it—reflects an extreme version of the Western tendency to abstract the self from the matrix of experience. One becomes a knowing subject at the expense of the subject of being. This knowing subject, with its hyperinteriority, is always in a position of alienation from the self as the center of being. It would not do to overly pathologize this state of affairs because it appears to be a universal condition of human life, especially today. Lacan (1949/1977) placed this fundamental split subject at the center of his theorizing about the self, and Buddhism as a psychology can be viewed as a centuries-old method for addressing this very same split in the self.

An implication of these discourses on alienation is that the self-as-object, or the alienated subject, results from trauma that while being inevitable in the course of human life, nonetheless can be thought of as existing on a continuum of health to pathology. Each individual has a unique capacity for tolerating experience; each individual faces a particular set of environmental factors, and the resultant outcome determines the capacity for immersion in the ongoing flow of experience, including the experience of oneself as agent. The relationship to play, or playfulness, is here brought into view. One might say that Henry lacks just such a capacity for transitional experiencing, a place between the fixedness of self as "really this" or "really that." What Henry has not fully appreciated is that no one is "really" a banker in some transcendent sense, nor is anyone really not a banker; if one looks closely enough, one finds that there is really no such a thing as a banker in a Platonic or essentialist sense.

It is possible to move into and out of the roles created by others, and ourselves, taking none with excessive seriousness while giving each its due. If we idealize reality—that is, inadvertently utilize notions of transcendental categories, as Henry does—then we simultaneously create the sense of alienation from this unattainable realm. But a relativist rejection of any grounding context, as is the case with some postmodern critiques of positivist notions about the self, has led to a diminishment of the value of psychological theorizing about the self, the etiology of psychopathology, and the uses of psychotherapy. Although we would not wish to anchor health and sickness, authenticity and alienation, in an objectivist, transhistorical framework, it appears to us that the constructivist critique leads to a theoretical position akin to the schizoid dilemma of alienation and emptiness that Henry illustrates. The error that Gadamer (1975) described as the "prejudice against prejudices" results in a kind of paralyzing self-consciousness in which no configuration of elements of the self can be celebrated over any other and no sense of self can be spoken of as real.

References

Balint, M. (1968). *The basic fault*. London: Tavistock.

Barth, J. (1972). *Chimera*. New York: Basic Books.

Baumeister, R. F. (1986). *Cultural change and the struggle for self*. New York: Guilford Press.

Baumeister, R. F. (1991). *Meanings of life*. New York: Guilford Press.

Bellah, R. N., Madsen, R., Sullivan, W. M., Swidler, A., & Tipton, S. M. (1985). *Habits of the heart: Individualism and commitment in American life*. Berkeley: University of California Press.

Bion, W. R. (1957). Attacks on linking. *International Journal of Psycho-Analysis, 40*, 308–315.

Corrigan, E. G., & Gordon, P. (1995). *The mind object: Precocity and pathology of self-sufficiency*. Northvale, NJ: Aronson.

Cushman, P. (1990). Why the self is empty. *American Psychologist, 45*, 599–611.

Cushman, P. (1991). Ideology obscured: Political uses of the self in Daniel Stern's infant. *American Psychologist, 46*, 206–219.

Cushman, P. (1995). *Constructing the self, constructing America*. New York: Addison-Wesley.

Eigen, M. (1996). *Psychic deadness*. Northvale, NJ: Aronson.

Fairbairn, W. R. D. (1952). A revised psychopathology of the psychoses and psycho-neuroses. In *Psychoanalytic studies of the personality* (pp. 28–58). London: Routledge & Kegan Paul. (Original work published 1941)

Fairbairn, W. R. D. (1952). Schizoid factors in the personality. In *Psychoanalytic studies of the personality* (pp. 3–27). London: Routledge & Kegan Paul. (Original work published 1940)

Ferenczi, S. (1980). *Further contributions to the theory and technique of psycho-analysis* (J. Rickman, Ed., & J. I. Suttie, Trans.). New York: Brunner/Mazel.

Foucault, M. (1979). *Discipline and punish: The birth of the prison*. Townsend, WA: Bay Press.

Gadamer, H. G. (1975). *Truth and method*. New York: Continuum Press.

Gergen, K. J. (1991). *The saturated self*. New York: Basic Books.

Glass, J. M. (1993). *Shattered selves*. Ithaca, NY: Cornell University Press.

Heelas, P. (1981). Introduction: Indigenous psychologies. In P. Heelas & A. Lock (Eds.), *Indigenous psychologies: The anthropology of the self* (pp. 3–17). New York: Academic Press.

James, W. (1963). *Psychology*. Greenwich, CT: Fawcett. (Original work published 1892)

Joseph, B. (1982). Addiction to near-death. *International Journal of Psycho-Analysis, 63*, 449–456.

Kohut, H. (1984). *How does analysis cure?* Chicago: University of Chicago Press.

Lacan, J. (1977). The mirror-stage as formative of the function of the "I." In *Ecrits: A selection*. New York: Norton. (Original work published 1949)

Lasch, C. (1978). *The culture of narcissism*. New York: Norton.

Lifton, R. J. (1993). *The protean self*. New York: Basic Books.

Linville, P. W., & Carlston, D. E. (1994). Social cognition of the self. In P. G. Devine, D. L. Hamilton, & T. M. Ostrom (Eds.), *Social cognition: Impact on social psychology* (pp. 143–193). San Diego, CA: Academic Press.

Markus, H., & Kitayama, S. (1991). Culture and the self: Implications for cognition, emotion, and motivation. *Psychological Review, 98,* 224–253.

Marx, K. (1969). *The 18th Brumaire of Louis Bonaparte.* New York: International Universities Press. (Original work published 1852)

McAdams, D. P. (1997). The case for unity in the (post)modern self. In R. D. Ashmore & L. Jussim (Eds.), *Self and identity: Fundamental issues* (pp. 46–78). New York: Oxford University Press.

Mitchell, S. A. (1993). *Hope and dread in psychoanalysis.* New York: Basic Books.

Pepper, S. C. (1942). *World hypotheses: A study in evidence.* Berkeley: University of California Press.

Phillips, A. (1995). The story of the mind. In E. G. Corrigan & P. Gordon (Eds.), *The mind object: Precocity and pathology of self-sufficiency* (pp. 229–240). Northvale, NJ: Aronson.

Sass, L. A. (1988). The self and its vicissitudes: An "archaeological" study of the psychoanalytic avant-garde. *Social Research, 55,* 551–607.

Sass, L. A. (1992a). The epic of disbelief. In S. Kvale (Ed.), *Psychology and postmodernism* (pp. 166–182). London: Sage.

Sass, L. A. (1992b). *Madness and modernism.* New York: Basic Books.

Seligman, M. E. P. (1988, April). Boomer blues. *Psychology Today, 22*(10), 50–55.

Solomon, R. C. (1988). *Continental philosophy since 1950: The rise and fall of the self.* New York: Oxford University Press.

Stern, D. (1985). *The interpersonal world of the infant.* New York: Basic Books.

Taylor, C. (1975). *Hegel.* Cambridge, England: Cambridge University Press.

Taylor, C. (1989). *Sources of the self.* Cambridge, MA: Harvard University Press.

Warren, C. S. (1997). The disavowal of desire: A relational view of sadomasochism. *Psychotherapy and Psychoanalysis, 14,* 107–124.

Weitzman, L. J. (1985). *The divorce revolution: The unexpected social and economic consequences for women and children in America.* New York: Free Press.

Winnicott, D. W. (1965). Ego distortion in terms of true and false self. In *The maturational and the facilitating environment* (pp. 140–152). New York: International Universities Press.

Winnicott, D. W. (1975). Transitional objects and transitional phenomena. In *Collected papers: Through paediatrics to psycho-analysis* (pp. 229–242). London: Hogarth. (Original published 1951)

COMMENT:
A Tale of the Three Selves

Muriel Dimen

The exchange in which Stanley Messer and Seth Warren and I are participating is a rare opportunity to evaluate postmodernism in clinical context. Messer and Warren go about this project with verve and moral passion. While acknowledging postmodernism's contribution to recent intellectual life, they worry that it promotes a self that hinders treatment and damages patients. This concern is not inappropriate. Psychoanalysis is a profoundly moral profession, and the clinical vignette is one place where that passionate morality manifests itself: If ideas do not help patients, if they do not speed clinical process, then their value is suspect. Oddly enough, however, postmodernism turns out, in the particular case Messer and Warren present, to be just what the doctor ordered. Although they dispute postmodern ideas and values, their clinical work evinces so much ambiguity, multiplicity, and paradox that one can scarcely help thinking that maybe there is more to postmodernism than they thought and more of postmodernism in their thought than they think.

It seems right, then, to address a misapprehension, under which Messer and Warren appear to be operating, about exactly what postmodernism is and does and values. On the one hand, they regret that the "postmodern self" is celebrated by a great variety of psychologists, psychoanalysts and, especially, philosophers. Yet they are not alone in diagnosing the postmodern self's dysfunctionality, a condition to which they suggest clinical approaches. They are joined by many social theorists (e.g., Bordo, 1990), including poststructuralists, few of whom believe that "to be selfless is to be politically and socially emancipated." More striking, perhaps, is the attack on poststructuralism by progressive theorists and activists, who indict postmodernism for an ultimate conservatism (e.g., Jameson, 1991).

On the other hand, Messer and Warren evince ambivalence about deconstructive approaches to this postmodern self. I can think of no other explanation for their equation of self and lifestyle: "The postmodern self is not just an alternate lifestyle but is dysfunctional." With one blow, they equate a self with a lifestyle (a conceptual choice they do not explain) and diagnose both as

211

dysfunctional (an assessment with which, as I note below, they in fact disagree later on). But surely a self and a lifestyle are quite different creatures. The self is a sedimented product of unconscious process, history, experience, and desire, whereas a lifestyle is a culturally constructed way of being toward which one may be inclined—for unconscious as well as conscious reasons and for reasons of personal, intersubjective, and social history—but which one may also actively cultivate and choose to adopt. What is at stake in postmodern theory, however, is not a matter of choice; to think so is to underestimate the scope of its challenge to the Enlightenment heritage (Flax, 1990), including Michel Foucault's (1976) implicit disagreement with psychoanalysis.

Most deeply, I suspect that Messer and Warren are distressed by poststructuralists' inattentiveness to psychic suffering. In their brief history of the postmodern self, they deplore not only its fragmentation but also its emptiness and anguish, a concern they find noticeably absent in the postmodernist literature. They are correct. Theorists who approach life problems as though interpreting a text can betray a callousness to the need, vulnerability, and helplessness that compel clinicians every day. One academic, I remember, was going to join a seminar on psychoanalysis and feminism but said, with some ironic revulsion, and anxiety, too, "I don't want to have to help people." Still, therapeutic zeal was not in her job description, as it is in ours. It is quite clear, moreover, that academics know one psychoanalysis and that practicing analysts know another. Literary critics, art historians, and culture theorists read a different Freud than analysts do. A fine essay on the *décalage* between psychoanalytic academia and clinical psychoanalysis is yet to be written.

Different practices make for different psychoanalyses. Ideas cultivated in the rationalist preserves of the academy need revision before they can be applied to the passionate rough-and-tumble of the clinic. In fact, some postmodern theories are now being critiqued for the lacunae that void them of clinical utility and, paradoxically, strip psychoanalysis of its proper subject matter. Within poststructuralist philosophy, specifically the Lacanian tradition, Tim Dean (1994; see also Layton, 1998) recently pointed out that Judith Butler's immensely influential theory of gendered desire (e.g., 1990) leaves no room for either the unconscious or agency, two critical clinical concepts. Butler's use of the Imaginary and the Symbolic, Dean contends, deprives the psyche of its proper domain and the person of volition. In contrast, the real, as that which, resisting symbolization, escapes linguistic determination, reintroduces postmodern discourse to the difficulty of the psychic interior first postulated by psychoanalysis. Reciprocally, the real, signifying a deep and broad indeterminacy, restores to subjectivity its mystery and reinstates, as psychoanalysis's special province, the inner life with its weirdness and indecipherability.

At the same time, concepts developed by poststructuralist theorists writing outside clinical practice can usefully defamiliarize ideas developed by those inside it. Take, for example, the idea of "the self." Even within the present volume, the self begets widely ranging interpretations. As a signifier with a multiplicity of referents, it bears a brief deconstruction. Are there as many sorts of self as there are practices of the self? What work does self do in our clinical and theoretical practices? In psyche? In culture? As Messer and Warren's chapter begins, we are treated to a tale of three selves: the premodern self, the modern self, and the postmodern self, each linked to a different historical or cultural period. Yet as the story progresses, the dividing lines among them appear to blur, while still other distinctions arise. Let us see how a contradiction in Messer and Warren's historical narrative of the self can tell us something more about how we think it and treat it, and maybe even about the thing itself.

Messer and Warren create two divides: between the premodern self and the modern self and between the modern self and the postmodern self. The premodern self and the modern self seem polarized, the former embedded in family, farm, and village, the latter set loose in an industrial, urban world of cutthroat rationality and personal freedom. On closer inspection, however, these putatively mutually exclusive ways of being turn out to be interimplicated and coeval. When Messer and Warren look at modern marriage and unmarriage, for example, the premodern and modern selves do not seem to be so distinct after all: "[Contemporary] divorce laws ... encourage people to pursue their own self-interest during marriage rather than sacrificing [sic] themselves for the good of the family, as would once have been the case." To exemplify their point that today people pursue their own personal needs and not those of others, Messer and Warren cite divorce laws, which, they say, once disposed people to forfeit selfhood on behalf of the family but now prompt people to act on behalf of themselves. The premodern embedded self was, as they argue, not an individual self. Rather, it was a self-in-relation, which defines the good of the self in relation to the good of others. In my view, however, if in the past the self was for others (as opposed to the present, when the self is for the self), then in the past there could not have been a self that could deny—"sacrifice"—itself in favor of something other, or larger, than it. How, in other words, could there have been self-sacrifice if there were no self to sacrifice itself, that is, no (modern, individual) self that would regard such renunciation a forfeit rather than, say, a pleasure, or a joyously or piously discharged obligation of love?

I want to hold off answering this question until I look at the second instance of this same sort of contradiction. As premodern and modern selves are said to be radically other to one another, so modern and postmodern selves confront each other. According to Messer and Warren, from "a bounded, disciplined, autonomous self" has emerged an "empty," "saturated," "protean," "multiple" self lacking an "essential," "inner," "deep," "hidden," "true" core. Although the modern self came with the early capitalist package, the postmodern variety, with its splits and fragmentations and hollow ache, seems to be produced by, and compatible with, late capitalism. Yet by the chapter's end we find that the split self is not very new after all: "Buddhism as a psychology can be viewed as a centuries-old method for addressing this very same split in the self." This datum scrambles Messer and Warren's orderly historical line from premodern to modern to postmodern selves. The raveled postmodern self is not a late-capitalist phenomenon. The split self, out and about since at least the 5th century BC, when Buddhism was birthed, actually predates the embedded medieval self. It is interesting that Messer and Warren even find some value in this divided self, warning that "it would not do to overly pathologize this state of affairs because it appears to be a universal condition of human life."

A shift in perspective may be in order. Perhaps what is going on here is not that selves succeed each other in neat historical sequence. Neither do Messer and Warren get the selves they see all wrong. The problem lies in the positivist idea of the self as a stable, coherent entity that although it changes over time, is always self-identical. Jacques Lacan's contribution, noted by Messer and Warren, has been explicitly to challenge this idea. Lacan proposes instead a decentered self, at once fictional and substantial, a self of parts and instances that comforts and structures itself with the illusion of coherence (Bowie, 1990; J. Mitchell & Rose, 1982). If the self is always already not one thing but potentially many, then perhaps these three selves that Messer and Warren list have all been around all the time.

The apparent contradiction in their theory, then, signals a different truth: Not one self, but many selves, coexist, only a few of which are perceptible at any given cultural moment. Maybe the remaining possibilities can be sensed only from outside, by people from other cultures or times. From their millennial vantage point, Messer and Warren look back to the Middle Ages and see there both self—the individual self, for whom serving the other's interest is a sacrifice —and other—and the embedded self for whom the distinction between the interests of self and other is nigh unintelligible. Possibly they are correct in ascribing to the (European) Middle Ages what we know from contemporary EuroAmerica: The seed of that modern self may have been but dormant in the premodern self, just waiting for the right conditions to burst into flower.

From an entirely different perspective, that of the "second sex," that very premodern, embedded self turns out to have been hanging around the modern, autonomous self for quite some time. I refer here to what Messer and Warren term the *expressivist self*, which attempts to bridge separateness within and between individuals, between human beings and nature, "between body and soul." In trying to connect self and self (as one might put it), the expressivist self engages in and valorizes not self-control but self-exploration. Because it treasures the practices of attachment, interpersonal connection, and intimacy, it attempts to span the divide between self and other. In its effort to reach out to nature, it emphasizes not instrumentalism and exploitation but identification and care.

Gender, in short, marks the dialectical tension in which the expressivist (self-sacrificing) self and the modern (self-interested) self co-arise. Put differently, the embedded self has changed discursive places in (post)modernity. Once distinguishing rural and urban—or, perhaps more accurately, local and global —it now signifies the gendered division of emotional labor in which masculinity is wed to subjectivity and individuality, and femininity is wed to connectivity and the oceanic feeling (rejected by Freud, 1930/1961). At the same time, the gendered division of practical labor creates a doubled reality. It locates men, as "self-defining, self-enclosed" subjects embarked on the pursuit of happiness, in the public domain of sharp individuality and clear-cut self-interest—the modern self. It situates women in the private, domestic interior that cultivates "intimacy, relatedness, and warmth, as well as complexity, confusion, and the half-lights of bodies and minds growing into and out of each other" (Dimen, 1999, p. 430)—the premodern, embedded self of connection, attachment, and (what the modern self sees as) self-sacrifice. In the historic "convergence between psychoanalysis and feminism" (Benjamin, 1984, p. 37), feminism began to claim legitimacy and recognition for this Second Self at the same time as what came to be relational psychoanalysis (think Fairbairn, Kohut, Sullivan, and Winnicott) was starting to salute the self of connection and attachment as the center of clinical process, development, and sanity.

Are Messer and Warren postmodernists despite themselves? Their tale of three coexisting selves certainly registers of multiplicity. To situate the self in transitional space, as they do, is to teeter between modern and postmodern: "The self . . . exists in a region between what is real, biologically given, anchored and coherent, and what is created by means of cultural, historical, and interpersonal categories." On the one hand, this characterization cleaves to modernist, binary thinking. It equates the "real" with biology, which it opposes to culture, which is in turn implicitly likened to the "artificial." The resultant nature–culture dualism harmonizes with another implicit binary that emerges when the three selves of history collapse into two: The postmodern self, being schizoid and ill, loses out, diagnostically, to the integrated modern self, leaving us with a recurring opposition between two standards of mental health, a once-normative, somewhat romanticized premodern self of embeddedness and a socially necessary, if hard-edged modern self of autonomy and self-interest.

On the other hand, this attachment to dualism smoothes a more textured, but less resolvable complexity inherent in Messer and Warren's chapter. Their acknowledgment of a necessary fluidity in a self-at-odds-with-itself hints at the de facto, even if resisted, impact of postmodernism on their thought and work. Here, they are in the good company of contemporaries drawing on what might be called psychoanalysis's "proto-postmodernism." Chief deconstructionist

Jacques Derrida, whom Messer and Warren cite, took inspiration from Freud who, in interpreting dreams, found absence—that is, the latent, as potent as presence—that is, the manifest. Freud's own acceptance of paradox is often breathtakingly pithy; for example, "What are commonly called the sexual instincts are looked upon by us as the part of Eros which is directed toward objects" (1920/1955, p. 60, footnote 1). Implicit, if not foreshadowed, in this footnote are the bridges psychoanalysts are now building between many binaries—biology and psychology; psychology and culture; self and other; sex and attachment; subject and object; masculine and feminine; premodern, modern, and postmodern selves. The avid elaborations of Winnicott's notion of paradox are almost too numerous to cite (e.g., Aron, 1995; Barratt, 1993; Benjamin, 1988; Bromberg, 1998; Ghent, 1992; Hoffman, 1991; S. Mitchell, 1993; Pizer, 1998; Stern, 1997).

This embrace of paradox pervades Messer and Warren's clinical discussion, in which they use the idea of the split, postmodern self both to evaluate Henry's psychic state and to make technical recommendations. On the one hand, this postmodern state of mind signifies and causes illness. Without a core, Henry lacks a

> sense of self [that] accrues through experience that he can bear into the next situation to shore him up. . . . Instead, it is as though Henry starts from scratch every day, a kind of clean or empty slate of self-esteem that may or may not evolve into a workable sense of self for that day.

On the other hand, reality matters too much to him: "Like many people with schizophrenia, Henry has no tolerance for the slightest degree of inauthenticity, in others or himself"; his "bullshit detector" is too sensitive, paralyzing his experiencing ego in favor of his observing ego. The healthy solution, they propose, is the postmodern one that Bromberg (1998) termed "standing in the spaces." They want Henry to be able to occupy "a place between the fixedness of self as 'really this' or 'really that.' What Henry has not fully appreciated is that no one is 'really' a banker in some transcendent sense, nor is anyone really not a banker." Documenting Henry's progress, they mention that "Henry has learned . . . to play with his cynicism, and with his shame and vulnerability."

For their part, Messer and Warren deploy their own postmodern selves to manage their countertransference. They make clear the overwhelming frustration of the long journey with Henry. "One cannot be in the presence of such annihilating futility and remain neutral." They, too, walk that fine line between authenticity and alienation: "Working with Henry has meant working with one's own schizoid self, the distant, intellectualizing, reflexive self that judges self and others, criticizes, and deconstructs." The analyst has more than one self, it would appear, or at least more than one self-state, a multiplicity that is useful, even necessary, for this work. It is, furthermore, interesting that a chapter so manifestly critical of postmodernism has in fact been written by two selves. Could some of this essay's ambiguity, its simultaneous rejection and embrace of postmodernism, stem from its intersubjective conception and execution?

The chapter's doubleness of voice suits the postmodern condition. Messer and Warren advocate that we playfully get in touch with the very inauthenticity they diagnose and deplore. In this, they are true to the classical psychoanalytic tradition: Irony, so much the mark of postmodern sensibility, is vital to mental health, a modern truth embodied if not inaugurated by Oscar Wilde. At the same time, postmodernism need not deprive us of the earnest, modernist task of making life better for our patients and others (e.g., Rivera, 1989). In their polemic against postmodernism, Messer and Warren reverse a paradox articulated by Adrienne Harris (1994). We may think postmodern, she says, but we practice in the Enlightenment. That Messer and Warren think Enlightenment while practicing in the postmodern manifests the powerful cross-currents enriching psychoanalytic thought and practice today.

Recall their assertion that "the [modern, self-creating, individual] self is ill suited to provide meaning and value to human life." On the contrary, the self that can lose itself is the self that can find itself and, in the process, create meaning. Is not this loss-and-recovery, this *fort/da*, in fact the psychoanalytic credo? Consider Marshall Berman's (1982) remarkable appreciation of the modern spirit: "a desire to live openly with the split and unreconciled character of our lives, and to draw energy from our inner struggles, where ever they may lead us in the end" (p. 171). If it is possible to think that postmodernism is simply a late stage of both capitalism and modernism (Jameson, 1991), then perhaps premodern, modern, and postmodern selves cohabit. Like Henry, each of us lives close to the postmodern fragmentation that is right next door to modern integration and not too far away from premodern expressivism. How fortunate to be able to know that it is both true and false that we start "from scratch every day," that each day is a new day even as memory grounds us in the past and foresight pulls us toward the future. The capacity to inhabit this bittersweet and uncertain multiplicity marks contemporary selfhood. Paradox and irony, serving as both values and practices (see Benjamin, 1998), sum up the spirit of psychoanalysis at the new millennium.

References

Aron, L. (1995). The internalized primal scene. *Psychoanalytic Dialogues, 5,* 195–238.

Barratt, B. (1993). *The postmodern impulse in psychoanalysis.* Baltimore: Johns Hopkins University Press.

Benjamin, J. (1984). The convergence of psychoanalysis and feminism: Gender identity and autonomy. In C. M. Brody (Ed.), *Women therapists working with women* (pp. 37–45). New York: Springer.

Benjamin, J. (1988). *The bonds of love.* New York: Pantheon.

Benjamin, J. (1998). *The shadows of the other.* New York: Routledge.

Berman, M. (1982). *All that is solid melts into air.* New York: Penguin.

Bordo, S. (1990). Feminism, postmodernism, and gender-skepticism. In L. Nicholson (Ed.), *Feminism and postmodernism* (pp. 133–156). New York: Routledge.

Bowie, M. (1990). *Lacan.* Oxford, England: Oxford University Press.

Bromberg, P. (1998). *Standing in the spaces.* Hillsdale, NJ: Analytic Press.

Butler, J. (1990). *Gender trouble.* New York: Routledge.

Dean, T. (1994). Bodies that mutter: Rhetoric and sexuality. *Pre/Text, 15,* 1–2.

Dimen, M. (1999). Between lust and libido. *Psychoanalytic Dialogues, 9,* 415–440.

Flax, J. (1990). *Thinking fragments.* Berkeley: University of California Press.

Foucault, M. (1976). *The history of sexuality* (Vol. 1). New York: Vintage Press.

Freud, S. (1955). Beyond the pleasure principle. *Standard edition* (Vol. 18, pp. 7–64). London: Hogarth Press. (Original work published 1920)

Freud, S. (1961). Civilization and its discontents. *Standard edition* (Vol. 21, pp. 64–146). London: Hogarth Press. (Original work published 1930)

Ghent, E. (1992). Process and paradox. *Psychoanalytic Dialogues, 2,* 135–160.

Harris, A. (1994, August). *Gender practices, speech practices.* Paper presented at the annual meeting of Division 39 of the American Psychological Association, Washington, DC.

Hoffman, I. (1991). Some practical implications of a social constructivist view of the psychoanalytic situation. *Psychoanalytic Dialogues, 2,* 287–304.

Jameson, F. (1991). *Postmodernism, or the cultural logic of late capitalism.* Durham, NC: Duke University Press.

Layton, L. (1998). *Who's that girl? Who's that boy?* Northville, NJ: Aronson.

Mitchell, J., & Rose, J. (Eds.). (1982). *Feminine sexuality: Jacques Lacan and lécole freudienne.* New York: Pantheon.

Mitchell, S. (1993). *Hope and dread in psychoanalysis.* New York: Basic Books.

Pizer, S. (1998). *Building bridges.* Hillsdale, NJ: Analytic Press.

Rivera, M. (1989). Linking the psychological and the social: Feminism, poststructuralism, and multiple personality. *Dissociation, 2,* 24–31.

Stern, D. (1997). *Unformulated experience.* Hillsdale, NJ: Analytic Press.

CHAPTER 9

Deconstructing Difference: Gender, Splitting, and Transitional Space

Muriel Dimen

I n an early session, Elizabeth, then 43 years old, held back her tears because, she said, "I don't want to cry on your shoulder." When I questioned her reluctance, she replied that the danger lay in the shoulder, not in the crying: She would cry only on a man's shoulder; she was not interested in women.

I want to understand Elizabeth's reply by thinking about gender not as an essence but as a set of relations (May, 1986) and to propose that at the heart of gender is not "masculinity" or "feminity" but the difference between them. My thinking is located in two interesting contexts: feminist and psychoanalytic. The first may be described as *the critique of gender*, a phrase whose ambiguity is deliberate. I mean to suggest, simultaneously, gender as critiqued and gender as critique, gender as a concept that not only requires scrutiny but also can itself illuminate other matters. Reciprocally, understanding gender depends on the second, psychoanalytic context of this chapter, framed here in terms of splitting and transitional space, concepts themselves capable of furthering the clinical relevance of the critique of gender. I am using the concept of "splitting" loosely, signifying in its psychoanalytic sense both splitting of the ego and split-ting of the object (Laplanche & Pontalis, 1973, pp. 427, 430) and in its cultural sense the many dichotomies and dualism paradigmatic in Western thinking since Descartes and of critical relevance to feminist discourse. The doubled-critique of gender I am proposing can, by defamiliarizing the emotion- and value-laden notions of femininity and masculinity, help to peel away what we think gender is (and believe it to be) from what it might be. When I speak thus of gender's possibility, I refer to the present, not the future. Deconstructing gender in our minds can help us stretch our clinical imagination about what our patients' inner worlds are like and, indeed, could be like.

This chapter is an updated version of the article with the same title and author in *Psychoanalytic Dialogues, 1,* 1991, 335–352. Copyright 1991 by Analytic Press. Adapted with permission.

Gender and Self

Because the category of sex seems plain enough, the concept of gender likewise appears unproblematic, even though, in fact, it requires clarification—or, better, deconstruction. Conventionally, *gender* denotes the psychological and social dimensions of the biological category of sex. This characterization sounds like a clear enough division of epistemological labor. But it is not. What gender seems to denote is one thing; what it actually connotes is another. Indeed, the connotations of gender are so complex as to generate an enormous indeterminacy, which Scott (1988), a feminist historian, phrased as the following:

> Often in patriarchal discourse, sexual difference (the contrast masculine/feminine) serves to encode or establish meanings that are literally unrelated to gender or the body. In that way, the meanings of gender become ties to many kinds of cultural representations, and these in turn establish terms by which relations between women and men are organized and understood. (p. 37)

In other words, the category of sex is not transparent but is itself a dense weave of cultural significance, and the "contrast masculine/feminine," as the representation of what psychoanalysts commonly refer to as the "anatomical difference," addresses a variety of matters, not all of which are germane to sex, gender, or the genitals. This slippage from sex to culture not only provides us with our understandings of gender as personally experienced but also informs gender as a social institution.

Another elision, equivalent in power to that from sex to culture, informs what we might term the *mutual definition* of selfhood and gender identity, such that problems of self may come to be coded in terms of gender, and those of gender, in terms of the self. Self and gender identity inhabit one another so intimately that questions such as these become familiar: If I feel "womanly," am I at my most "feminine"? Or am I feeling most fully "myself"? When I do feel "like myself," does that feeling have anything to do with my female identity? If I feel, by contrast and, perhaps more pertinently, "unwomanly," am I feeling somehow "not myself"? If I am "not myself," is gender identity somehow also, and more secretly, involved? And so on.

The overriding question is, Would these puzzles even arise if selfhood and gender identity were not already in problematic relation? In other words, although selfhood and gender identity are structurally different, their contemporaneous crystallization in development makes them seem—indeed, feel—joined at the heart and leaves their relationship simultaneously unquestioned and questionable. The intrapsychic proximity of sense of self to sense of gender identity often obscures and deepens the complexities of gender representation generated. At the same time, the contrast masculine–feminine, by collapsing many representations of selfhood that are unrelated to gender, can disguise, and even create, dilemmas of self as well.

Sometimes the mutual coding of gender and self is directly translatable. For example, the conventional split between masculine and feminine in psychology and culture—that is, the contrast masculine–feminine—speaks also to pleasure, activity, and passivity. Pleasure in activity is wont to carry the valence of masculinity, whereas pleasure in passivity is charged with femininity, a split aligned with the traditional dichotomy in sex roles. As this splitting has been challenged socially, it is more often questioned in the clinical situation, where one may suspect, for example, that women's sense of activity may be gender dystonic and therefore anxiety inducing, just as men's fantasies of passivity may express a fear of being homosexual, itself often code for the fear of being feminine.

This example seems straightforward enough. But the plot thickens. For example, gender identity, normatively defined as watertight, may normally be porous. We do not always feel in gender; when we do not, we feel anxiety, which makes us less likely to remember that sometimes one's gender resembles an ill-fitting garment. When I asked a friend who had lost a tennis match how he felt during the game, he replied, "like a girl"; he had trouble wielding the racket. Clearly feeling like a girl was not a pleasant experience for him. Still, was he anxious because he felt out of gender? Or did he feel out of gender because he was anxious about something else? Or both? Why was losing incompatible with masculinity? Is losing the same as castration? Does not losing also make us feel small? Could this man have been feeling like a child as well as like a girl? Does feeling like a girl represent a narcissistic wound (S. Shapiro, personal communication, August 15, 1988)? By way of comparison and contrast, another friend, who has always seen herself as nonathletic, represented her successful attempt to play squash by drawing a yapping, rushing Pekingese, which she reluctantly identified as male. One might say that in her activity, she first and consciously experienced herself as not herself but as an other and, only second, unconsciously, and more painfully, as out of gender, as a junior, ridiculous male person. If my female friend experienced the narcissistic wound ultimately as gender loss, could my male friend have represented it finally by loss of self, by an encounter with the second-sex otherness that femininity represents?

Gender as a Set of Relations

Let me review what I have discussed thus far, so as to make my main conceptual point. I began by critiquing the alignment of femininity with passivity and of masculinity with activity. In doing so, I came on a whirl of dualisms orbiting in relation to the contrast masculine–feminine and to each other as well: self–other, pre-Oedipal–Oedipal, infancy–adulthood, autonomy–dependency, superiority–inferiority, and heterosexuality–homosexuality. In this process, gender appears to be less a determinate category than something resembling a force field. Much like the atom, once thought of as a substance but now construed as a set of interacting forces, so gender looks to consist not of essences but of complex and shifting relations among multiple contrasts or differences. Sometimes these contrasts remain distinct, at other times they intersect, and at still other times they fuse and exchange identities.

As a way of turning to how problems of self and gender may encode one another, let us focus for a moment more on activity and passivity and their relation to sexual difference. Recognizing the force field that marries the inherently unrelated contrasts masculine–feminine, self–other, and active–passive to one another permits us to understand, for example, that women's anxiety in activity may be a problem equally of gender as of self. On the other hand, this recognition also lets us understand that gender-neutral qualities of self, such as activity and passivity, can reciprocally organize and thereby evoke sexual and gender splits. I have alluded, for example, to the fact that, for at least heterosexual, if not at all men, passivity may represent both homosexuality and femininity.

An analogous, although not identical, slippage among activity state, object choice, and gender identity shows up in the experience of Elizabeth, whose refusal to cry on a woman's shoulder now emerges as a negotiation among dangerous polarities. Her response to my inquiry implied that she was neither a dependent child nor a lesbian but an autonomous, heterosexual woman and, as such, her need for comfort was not a danger. To have admitted being a woman who wanted a woman's shoulder to cry on would have revealed what crying on a man's shoulder concealed: that sometimes she still felt like a child. The idea of leaning on a man defended against dependency longings because, in culture and psyche alike, heterosexuality lines up with, and symbolizes, adulthood and autonomy.

Sex, Gender, and Splitting

Heterosexuality, even though it is classically (although not always, according to Freud) the object choice of choice, can and does serve to conceal and express splits in the self. Nominally heterosexual, Elizabeth had not, in 15 years, had sex with anyone but herself (she acknowledged masturbation but refused to discuss it). Having had one homosexual encounter in junior college, she later married a mainly impotent man 20 years her senior with whom she had intercourse perhaps half a dozen times before a heart attack killed him 3 months after the wedding. Later, she had three major but short-lived love affairs; the last breakup had so bereaved her that she resolved never to let anyone get close again.

These facts of Elizabeth's life, and those to be recounted, emerged slowly and painfully over the course of our work together. Contemplating our shared history now, I feel as I did then—dismayed, conscious of both reluctance and helplessness to grasp the full damage. Not untouched, I still was sensible of her wish that I not touch her uninvited, that I respect the cocoon of privacy protecting her most secret self. Shielding her was her obesity which, she believed, distanced men in particular. In her fat, she was like a great big baby, reminding me of no one so much as Ralph Kramden. The gender ambiguity in my association reflects Elizabeth's sexual ambiguity. Elizabeth's attachment to a suspended heterosexuality masking childhood longings was a powerful means to dismember the sexual abuse that, from ages 3 to 5, she experienced with her adored brother Johnnie, 9 years older than she. Almost daily, Johnnie would masturbate before her in the parlor at quarter to five in the afternoon, while they listened to a favorite radio program and their mother prepared dinner in the kitchen, which happened to be in the next room. Torn between feelings of specialness and betrayal, Elizabeth never revealed these encounters; she always believed that if she told her mother, she, not Johnnie, would be punished; when she was older and thought about taking the story to confession (the family was Catholic), she would somehow forget.

Not only her flesh but also her words protected her. I was both moved and often made to feel helpless by the verbal fence Elizabeth planted around her private self. When one time she said, by way of explanation, "Johnnie set me up too early," she sounded like a forlorn child prostitute turned out by her lover, a child now homeless but denying the despair of her psychic bondage to him. Yet even as Elizabeth's speech (e.g., she often used cliches) deftly dispatched emotion to some unreachable part of the galaxy, it served to consolidate her personal universe. Shattered, she wrapped the wounds of her amputated feeling in tried-and-true language that normalized her tragedy. At the same time, Johnnie's betrayal of her trust disrupted not only the consolidation of her selfhood but also the emergence of her sexuality and gender identity and left her caught between identification with and desire for men. Was she female or male? While watching Johnnie's performance, was she watching and desiring her idol or identifying with him, or both? It was not clear. The only way she found relief was not to choose, not to be either gender (a dilemma identified by Harris, 1991).

Here, in summary fashion, is the sequence as it appears, in retrospect, to me, for it was not one Elizabeth could have constructed herself. The cessation of the incest coincided with the birth of her younger sister (the last of five children) and the start of school, a traumatic concatenation of events that resulted in the tantrums for which she was punished after she started school. At age 5, she wanted to drown her newborn younger sister "because she wasn't a boy." She remembered playing with her clitoris when she was 8. Between the ages of 9 and 10, she frequently wore one of her father's cast-off ties, which she hoped would transform her into a boy. During her 11th year (when, after Johnnie's return from the Army, the incest recurred briefly, until she put a stop to it), she began her avid consumption of novels and was at the time equally drawn to stories of swashbuckling pirates and tales of lascivious sultans.

She was disappointed that menstruation was not a one-time-only event yet was humiliated that her first brassiere was her oldest sister's yellowed cast-off (delivered, to her embarrassment, by Johnnie as a present at a holiday dinner). By adolescence, she had come to feel that boys were dangerous. As an adult, she had arrived at what she regarded as the prejudiced opinion that boys should not be allowed to baby-sit. Finally, she feared sexually assertive men and preferred those who were shy and a bit unsure.

Frozen between femininity and masculinity, on guard against painful affect, and just out of others' reach, she was, in her adult life, cleft between body and mind, a cleavage that was apparently odd but, down deep, a source and sign of shame. Trained in physical therapy (by which she was supporting herself), she was finishing a scholarly doctorate, was already becoming known in her field, and had friends who like her therapist were liberal, intellectual, and sophisticated. Yet she resided alone, next door to a sister's household, in a lower middle-class conservative suburb. Her work life was also polarized. Her specialty within her field relied more on concrete data than on speculation, and the theoretical abstraction found in other sectors of her discipline made her very anxious. She preferred Gothic and horror genres for extracurricular reading but generally found the news media too distressing to witness.

Her major symptoms were consistent with splitting—not only obesity but myriad physical ailments and a dependence on an oral hypnotic; dissociation in sessions and amnesia between them; a sometimes dogged, sometimes mischievous balking at interpretations of her unconscious. Although she always remembered the facts of the incest and the sense of privilege she derived from it, she was, until a year and a half before we terminated, unconscious of her anger about it. At that time, Elizabeth began to follow the increasing media coverage of the sexual abuse of children because she had just learned that there had been more sexual abuse in her own family. Johnnie, who had died in a freak accident at age 26, had left behind a wife and two children. His widow later married a man who, it turned out, molested both his stepdaughter and his stepson's daughter, that is, Johnnie's own daughter and granddaughter. Elizabeth's subsequent outrage on behalf of her niece and her grandniece allowed us to probe her rage about what had happened to her.

As Elizabeth recovered her anger and sense of betrayal about the incest, her splitting generally lessened, and her drug and nicotine dependencies disappeared. Nevertheless, the obesity, about which she was unhappy, and her uninterest in unconscious interpretation, held fast all the way to the end. As I write this, I can now link this tenacity to a splitting in the transference–countertransference configuration, in which Elizabeth embraced the manifest, the literal, and the body, and I embraced the latent, the symbolic, and the mind. Neither is it surprising that this split intersected gender as well. During one session, when she was in deep distress about her family's inability or refusal to appreciate her work, she spoke of her "inquiring mind." Together, we then discovered that, of her parents, brother, and three sisters, the only other person in her family who could also be described as having an inquiring mind was her father. If, therefore, her mind inquired, then it followed that she could not be female. For reasons to which I return, we were unable to explore the paradox that women, too, could have inquiring minds.

Desire in the Space of Difference

Let me sum up what I have said so far. Taking a deconstructionist tack, I have said that the core of gender is difference, not essence, and that the relation between masculinity and femininity is culturally conceived, interpersonally negotiated, and intrapsychically experienced. To put this view in developmental terms, one becomes gendered not by learning "a one-dimensional message that (one is) either male or female"; rather, one "absorb(s) the contrast between male and female" (Dimen, 1986, p. 8). In theoretical terms, looking at either masculinity or femininity without looking at the contrast between them encourages us to imagine fixed essences, hard-and-fast polarities. If, however, we enter the space occupied by their difference, we can see more clearly other differences that, although not necessarily related to sex, in fact secretly construct gender (Scott, 1988, p. 38). What I did in that space is examine the gender dualism as it shiftingly intersects other dualisms, any pole which, rigidly clung to, may also signal splits in the self. I have also suggested, by means of a clinical example, that gender identity as we know it can organize and disguise such splitting, and I have implied that a focus on the space between the poles can reveal and help dismantle these splits.

So far, then, the axis of my discussion has been splitting and its interface with the gender polarity. Other, cross-cutting axes introduce other considerations. Take, for example, desire. It, too, is dualistically organized, such that desire is gender syntonic for men but gender dystonic for women. Let me quote myself again (cf. Benjamin, 1988, pp. 85–113):

> Our culture has two patterns for desire, one for males and another for females. The first pattern honors, masculinizes, and makes adult the self experience of "I want." The second demeans, feminizes, and infantilizes the state of being wanted, the felt experience of "I want to be wanted." (Dimen, 1986, p. 7)

This dualism between wanting and wanting to be wanted intersects not only the contrast between masculine and feminine but also that between subject and object, and it results in a primary contradiction that I (1986) termed the *subject-as-object*. Subjects, in our cultural and intrapsychic representations, are men. The subject says "I want." The subject, "man," desires. Because men represent authorship, agency, and adulthood, women as adults are expected to be subjects, too. At the same time, through splitting that occurs equally on cultural and psychological levels, women are also expected to be objects (here, meaning not the intrapsychic representation of persons, as the term is used in psychoanalysis, but "thing," as the vernacular has it). As inanimate things, women are represented to be without desire, to be the targets of the subject's desire. If subjects want, objects are there to be wanted.

Women, then, are expected to be both the subject and the object. The development of femininity is, therefore, a compromise—almost, you might say, a compromise formation. It is the process of learning to be both, to take yourself as an object and to expect others to do so, too, and all the while you know that you are a subject. Elizabeth's case is an extreme version of this common dilemma, an embodiment of a primary sexual contradiction. On the one hand, as a woman, you would want to be a woman, not a child or a man; unwilling to weep on my shoulder, Elizabeth pronounces herself a woman. On the other hand, if being a woman means being both the subject of your own desires and the object of others', and therefore torn or suspended between these two positions—like Elizabeth, who, as a little girl, feared she would have been held responsible for her brother's sexual incursions—then perhaps you would not want to be feminine after all. So Elizabeth stopped time when the incest ceased; often feeling like a 5-year-old girl, she walks with the rolling gait of a sailor, identifies as a heterosexual woman, and generally keeps clear of sexual intimacy.

Hierarchy and Aggression Between Women

Examining the gendering of desire and the contrast subject–object—or, better, subjectivity–objectification—returns to us gender as critiqued because it introduces the particularly critical notion of hierarchy. The contrast power–weakness intersects all the others considered so far. As literary critic Armstrong (1988) describes the ambiguities of the gender hierarchy, "gender refers not only to a polarity within a field of cultural information but also to the asymmetry between the two poles of that opposition" (p. 2)—or to put it less formally and more whimsically, all genders are created equal, but some are more equal than others.

The contrast masculine–feminine, then, interfaces not only with inherently gender-neutral and nonhierarchical polarities. By means of gender hierarchy, which is named "male dominance" or "patriarchy" or "sexism," it also intersects with the duality of domination and subordination as well, as indeed do all polarities, because, according to postmodernism, "binary oppositions are inseparable from implicit or explicit hierarchies" (Flax, 1990, p. 101). Without, however, recapitulating what the last 25 years of gender politics has had to say about the effects of gender hierarchy on women, I would like to consider how this new contrast, power–weakness, can illuminate masculinity as well.

That femininity is not essentially, but only contingently, a compromise between subjectivity and objectification is revealed when we understand that men, too, can be subject-as-object. In fact, this contradiction is what they, like women in the workplace, enter every Monday morning. On the job, most men have to follow someone else's orders with the same alacrity as though they had thought of the orders themselves. There they, too, must be subject-as-object. They escape this contradiction only when they leave; even then, if they are of Third World identity or in some other way stigmatized, they are not safely free of this sort of domination until they return to their own communities or homes. The difference for women is that hierarchy follows them everywhere they go; although most men are "feminized" at work, most women are stigmatized not only at home but also in the community and on the street because they wear the contradiction of subject-as-object on their bodies. It may be, indeed, that the only time they are safe is when they are with other women. Even then, not only the social hierarchies women inhabit but the relational structures of domination and subordination govern them almost as surely. Indeed, hierarchy between women may have kept Elizabeth's treatment from going further than it did. I had hoped that, before she terminated, we would have been able to negotiate the paradox that she, a woman of an active intellectuality, was in a room with me, a woman of like mind, a woman on whose shoulder she could finally permit herself to cry without any threat to her gender, sexual identity, and sense of maturity. There were barriers, however, to the mutual recognition of our common engagement with the dilemma of being the subject-as-object. Although all women are created equal, some, particularly "archaic" mothers (Chasseguet-Smirgel, 1986; Dinnerstein, 1976), are more equal than others. As Shapiro and I (Dimen & Shapiro, 2000) argued elsewhere, trouble arises between women in the analytical situation because

> the juncture of caring and authority in one member of the dyad, that is, the analyst, painfully juxtaposes the most primitive dimensions of the mother/daughter relationship to the complications of femininity's social construction. The profound longing for maternal nurturance conflicts with an equally deep repudiation of women's subjectivity and authority, itself rooted in, simultaneously, infantile love and hate, gender-identity formation, and conventional sexual stereotyping. (p. 15)

Sometimes, in consequence, "a collusive pretense to a sisterly, mutually nurturant relationship" emerges to deny "competition, contempt, envy and devaluation" (p. 15). In particular, the anxiety that comes with aggression between women evokes the dangers of preoedipal maternal destructiveness, dangers that, in turn, incline women to excise aggression from their intimacy and replace it with pseudo-mutuality. This excision not only prevents them from understanding the creative potential of aggression in politics and in analysis (Harris, 1989) but can also threaten them with merging, a common solution to which is splitting (Lindenbaum, 1985).

It is interesting that countertransference anxiety was less of a problem when my superiority to Elizabeth depended on my not being a woman. When I was the actively probing, thinking, and sometimes bullying father to Elizabeth's passively resisting, vegetating, and sometimes helpless daughter, my interpretations permitted her to engage her rage and therefore her ambivalent identification with her father. When I was superior as a woman, however, I became far more dangerous. Neither I nor Elizabeth could give words to the fact that, so often, I seemed to be the better woman: Not only could I think, but I was thin. As winner of both contests, of minds and of bodies, I became the omnipotent preoedipal mother with a monopoly on power and desire. I therefore remained, in Elizabeth's belief, incapable of understanding the shame, despair, and neediness she felt inside her fat. Instead, I was the mother who heaped her children's plates and insisted they eat everything, even when, as an adolescent, Elizabeth begged to be allowed to diet.

To some extent, Elizabeth was right. Like so many women who think of themselves as fat even though they are not, I could, indeed, imagine Elizabeth's anguish, but I could not empathize with her despair and self-hate. Unable to own my ruthless triumph in being the thin, thinking winner, I could neither enter into her feeling of humiliation nor use my aggression in the service of recognizing her own desires to be the woman warrior. Unreleased, my competitiveness became contempt instead, which only now finds expression in my likening of Elizabeth to Jackie Gleason's brilliant television creation, that gentle blowhard, the lower middle-class bus driver, Ralph Kramden. It is, in retrospect, no wonder that Elizabeth presented as a split her plan to terminate her 8-year, once-a-week treatment; now that she no longer had to commute to Manhattan for therapy, she would have time to work on her obesity with a self-help group in the suburbs.

Difference and Transitional Space

I would like to end with some remarks about the transitional paradoxical space between apparent opposites, the space in which I have been playing throughout this chapter. Although the idea of a creative and pleasurable tension within dualism is an increasingly familiar one in feminist theory, its most useful psychoanalytic expression is, I believe, that of Benjamin (1989). The answer to splitting is never simply the recall of the forgotten role of any split but, in her phrase, the tension of holding "the paradox of simultaneity." This paradox is essential to both development and treatment and is a paradox that is potentially pleasurable, as it represents the Winnicottian transitional space where play occurs. Indeed, this pleasurable play was rare for Elizabeth and me, play being laborious when splitting dominates (Winnicott, 1971), when the "inability to 'play with reality' . . . result(s) in using reality as a defense against fantasy" (Bassin, 2000, p. 13).

The pleasure of the tension is, then, intrapsychic as well as intersubjective. Consider what Greenberg and Mitchell (1983) said about Jacobson's (1953) redefinition of the constancy principle:

> Rather than operating in the service of keeping the level of tension as low as possible, it is the function of the constancy principle redefined [by Jacobson], to establish and maintain a constant axis of tension and a certain margin for the biological vacillations around it. (p. 321)

As Greenberg and Mitchell suggested, pleasure paradoxically inheres in the cycle of tension, in its oscillating reduction and increase, not in its reduction alone. Cyclicity, in turn, implies the oscillation between two positions, not an unvarying habitation of one. The pleasure of play, for example, lies in the repeated oscillation between reality and fantasy; indeed, play loses its piquancy when it settles into either reality or fantasy, when, for example, "the nip becomes the bite," to quote Bateson's (1972) famous insight. To my mind, one way to describe Elizabeth's sexuality is in terms of a frightened and pleasureless person, holding onto one's position, an asexual attachment to a heterosexual identity that is never played out, with or against because it serves to defend against an inner world in which nips are bites and, as such, too terrifying to enter.

Within desire, this pleasurable oscillation takes place between want and need. Desire is conventionally defined as wish, emergent in the psyche, and is thereby absolutely distinguished from need, rooted in the drives (Laplanche & Pontalis, 1973, pp. 481–483). I regard this definition, however, as a false dichotomy that intensifies polarization instead of illuminating experience. In contrast, I see the longing that characterizes desire as engaged with both want and need. As I wrote elsewhere,

> merged in infancy as different aspects of desire, need and want separate out as development proceeds. Although they continue unconsciously to be kin to one another, they appear culturally as unequal strangers. Wanting associated with adulthood, active will, and masculinity, is better than need, linked to infancy, passive dependency, and femininity. (Need is, furthermore, frightening, recalling as it does unconscious memories of helpless, total dependence on others for love and care.) Adults therefore try to distance their dependency

needs by regarding their longings for love, tenderness, and care as weak, childish, "womanish." (Dimen, 1989, pp. 41–42)

In other words, adults split. By means of the intersection of the contrast
want–need with adulthood–infancy, activity–passivity, and masculinity–
femininity, they effect what I have termed "the gendered divorce of want from
need," with undeniable, serious consequences for their own well-being. As they
try to want and not to need, they inevitably diminish what they try to preserve:
any appetite for living. Although, then, mental health is normally defined by
the triumph of desire—defined as want over need—I propose a necessary,
creative tension in the space between want and need. How else, for example,
might we negotiate Fairbairn's (1952) paradox of "mature dependence" than to
feel both want and need for the other?

"Difference," as I have been writing of it here, is a paradoxical space that
selfhood itself inhabits. Autonomy and dependence, activity and passivity, heterosexuality and homosexuality, body and mind, selfness and otherness, subjectivity and objectification, superiority and inferiority, want, and need—and I
could go on—these apparent polarities are but different moments of the self,
the passage between which might be regarded as pleasurable, even though when
we leave the preferred polarity—when, for example, we transition from want
to need—we are, as things now stand, extraordinarily uncomfortable. To repeat,
the solution to the problem of splitting is not merely remembering the other
pole but being able to inhabit the space between them, to tolerate and even
enjoy the paradox of simultaneity.

What then, of masculinity and femininity, which do not appear on this
increasingly long list of contrasts? I might have said that they, too, are but
different moments of the self. But I am not sure that they are because, in fact,
I am not sure what they are. I am not arguing, as I once did, that because
masculinity and femininity are less determinate than conventionally thought,
gender need not exist (Dimen, 1982). On the other hand, even though the
ethnographic evidence for the predominance of dual gender systems is very
persuasive (Cucchiari, 1981), the content of gender or the number of genders
in any given system remains cross-culturally variable (Gailey, 1988), suggesting
the desirability of further investigation. I would still make the same case for
the possibility and pleasures of gender multiplicity (Dimen, 1982; see also Goldner, 1991).

Perhaps, then, it would be better to restate this position as a question: If
masculinity and femininity were to be regarded as different moments of the
self, what would each moment mean to a particular self? What is masculinity?
What is femininity? In other words, I question these terms because, although
we can name everything we think they are, on examination their meanings
become uncertain. Therefore, I have used this uncertainty epistemologically; if,
as I am asking in this chapter, we assume nothing about gender other than that

it is a socially and psychologically meaningful term, what meanings can we find for it?

At the same time, I do not take the deconstructionist train all the way to its nihilist last stop of saying that things are only what texts say they are, that there is no ontology. I believe in the reality of gender identity experience and of gender as an organizer in the psyche; as such, gender is variably meaningful, a variability that generates uncertainty, invites inquiry, and offers richness. This "diagnosis" of uncertainty should not, however, be regarded as a failure of method or theory. Instead, it is a sign of what gender is. Gender, as an internally varied experience, is sometimes central and definitive, sometimes marginal and contingent. Consequently, it is fundamentally and inalterably paradoxical (Goldner, 1991). Harris's (1991) phrasing expresses well a conceptualization of gender's ambiguity and complexity with which I agree:

> Gender is neither reified nor simply liminal and evanescent. Rather, in any one person's experience, gender may occupy both positions. Gender may in some contexts be thick and reified, as plausibly real as anything in our character. At other moments, gender may seem porous and insubstantial. Furthermore, there may be multiple genders or embodied selves. For some individuals these gender experiences may feel integrated, ego-syntonic. For others, the gender contradictions and alternatives seem dangerous and frightening and so are maintained as splits in the self, dissociated part-objects. (p. 212)

To put it more figuratively, if life is a sea, then gender is an island. Sometimes people drown in the sea, sometimes they are stranded on land. I am arguing that we need the sea as much as we need the land and, to push this Winnicottian metaphor further, we also need the seashore, where land and water merge (Winnicott, 1971).

In other words, I am suggesting that the notion of transitional space can help us comprehend what our theory has heretofore been able to handle only by splitting. Gender identity, born in the space of difference between masculinity and femininity, always retains the marks of its birth. Therefore, although gender identity has come to be seen in developmental theory as finalizing differentiation, I suggest, counterintuitively, that it does more: At one and the same time gender identity seals the package of self and preserves all that the self must lose. It serves to bridge the archaic depths; the impossible that underlies human creativity (McDougall, 1985, p. 8); and the self, the psychic agency that authors creation. Not only, as Fast claims (1984), does gender identity incline us to look for what we are not in the opposite-sexed other but, alternatingly definitive and liminal, gender identity also permits us to find in ourselves the overinclusiveness we have had to renounce so that we can also recognize it in the other, of whatever gender. This view of gender tracks the progress Fast charts from "gender differentiation" to "overinclusiveness" to gender identity—conceptualizes how access to the overinclusive depths of the self might be conserved even as renunciation entails their loss, and addresses "the capacity to identify with the opposite sex as a fundamental element in the mobilization of sexual desire" (McDougall, 1980, pp. 149–150).

I am ending, then, where I began, on a note of ambiguity because the space of paradox is where psychoanalysis works (Boris, 1986). There are many instances of paradox in the clinical situation. At any given moment, for instance, countertransference may be complementary, concordant, or both (Racker, 1985, pp. 135–137). Gender's habitation of transitional space is another instance. The analyst may be a good mother or a bad one; a pre-Oedipal and an Oedipal father; sometimes a sister, a transference Elizabeth and I explored; and sometimes a brother, a transference that, unfortunately, we did not examine and that did not occur to me at the time. Imprisoned not only within my own gender but also within a sense of femininity that splits aggression from nurturing, I could not imagine then what seems likely now: that my inquiry may have represented to Elizabeth the early violation she suffered at her brother's hands.

There is, as well, a final instance of ambiguity: We are not always of our gender; sometimes, according to the traditional, orthodox position, the analyst's gender is irrelevant. Analysts dwell not only in the paradox of being sometimes female and sometimes male but also in the paradox of feeling and being construed as variably having a gender and being gender free. Thus, we enter the countertransferential counterpart of our patients' experience, a paradox captured by Boris's (1986) exemplification of Bion's approach: "If the 10:00 Patient is one we know to be a married man in his thirties, we know too much, for how are we to attend the four-year-old girl who has just walked in?" (p. 177).

References

Armstrong, N. (1988). The gender bind: Women and the disciplines. *Genders, 3,* 1–23.

Bassin, D. (2000). *Toward the reconciliation of the masculine and feminine in the genital stage.* Unpublished manuscript, Institute for Psychoanalytic Training and Research, New York.

Bateson, G. (1972). *Steps toward an ecology of mind.* New York: Ballantine.

Benjamin, J. (1988). *The bonds of love.* New York: Pantheon Press.

Benjamin, J. (1989, December 9). *Elements of intersubjectivity: Recognition and destruction.* Paper presented at the postdoctoral program in psychotherapy and psychoanalysis, New York University, New York.

Boris, H. N. (1986). Bion revisited. *Contemporary Psychoanalysis, 22,* 159–184.

Chasseguet-Smirgel, J. (1986). Freud and female sexuality: The consideration of some blind spots in the exploration of the "Dark continent." In J. Chasseguet-Smirgel (Ed.), *Sexuality and mind* (pp. 1–28). New York: New York University Press.

Cucchiari, S. (1981). The gender revolution and the transition from bisexual horde to patrilocal band: The origins of gender hierarchy. In S. B. Ortner & H. Whitehead (Eds.), *Sexual meanings* (pp. 31–79). Cambridge, England: Cambridge University Press.

Dimen, M. (1982). Notes for the reconstruction of sexuality. *Social Text, 6,* 22–30.

Dimen, M. (1986). *Surviving sexual contradictions.* New York: Macmillan.

Dimen, M. (1989). Power, sexuality and intimacy. In A. Jaggar & S. Bordo (Eds.), *Gender/body/knowledge* (pp. 34–51). New Brunswick, NJ: Rutgers University Press.

Dimen, M., & Shapiro, S. (2000). *Trouble between women.* Unpublished manuscript, New York, NY.

Dinnerstein, D. (1976). *The mermaid and the minotaur.* New York: Harper & Row.

Fairbairn, W. R. D. (1952). *Psychoanalytic studies of the personality.* London: Routledge & Kegan Paul.

Fast, I. (1984). *Gender identity.* Hillsdale, NJ: Erlbaum.

Flax, J. (1990). *Thinking fragments.* Berkeley: University of California Press.

Gailey, C. (1988). Evolutionary perspectives on gender hierarchy. In B. Hess & M. Ferree (Eds.), *Analyzing gender* (pp. 100–143). Newbury Park, CA: Sage.

Goldner, V. (1991). Toward a critical relational theory of gender. *Psychoanalytic Dialogues, 1,* 249–272.

Greenberg, J., & Mitchell, S. A. (1983). *Object relations in psychoanalytic theory.* Cambridge, MA: Harvard University Press.

Harris, A. (1989). Bringing Artemis to life: A plea for militancy and aggression in feminist peace politics. In A. Harris & Y. King (Eds.), *Rocking the ship of state* (pp. 93–114). Boulder, CO: Westview Press.

Harris, A. (1991). Gender as contradiction. *Psychoanalytic Dialogues, 1,* 197–220.

Jacobson, E. (1953). The affects and their pleasure-unpleasure qualities in relation to the psychic discharge process. In R. M. Lowenstein (Ed.), *Drives, affects, behavior* (pp. 50–70). New York: International Universities Press.

Laplanche, J., & Pontalis, J. B. (1973). *The language of psycho-analysis* (D. N. Smith, Trans.). New York: Norton.

Lindenbaum, J. (1985). The shattering of an illusion: The problem of competition in lesbian relationships. *Feminist Studies, 11*(1), 85–103.

May, R. (1986). Concerning a psychoanalytic view of maleness. *Psychoanalytic Review, 73,* 179–194.

McDougall, J. (1980). *Plea for a measure of abnormality.* New York: International Universities Press.

McDougall, J. (1985). *Theaters of the mind: Illusion and truth on the psychoanalytic stage.* New York: Basic Books.

Racker, H. (1985). *Transference and countertransference.* London: Maresfield Library.

Scott, J. W. (1988). Deconstructing equality-versus-difference: Or, the uses of post-structuralist theory for feminism. *Feminist Studies, 14,* 33–50.

Winnicott, D. W. (1971). *Playing and reality.* New York: Penguin.

COMMENT:

Self, Gender, and the Transitional Space

C. Seth Warren
Stanley B. Messer

In chapter 8 of this volume, we wrote the following:

> We view the self neither as an essential given, as would a positivist, nor as socially or interpersonally constructed, as would those who advocate the concepts of a "multiphrenic," protean, empty, or saturated self. Rather, we think of it as akin to Winnicott's (1951/1975) notion of the "transitional object," which refers neither to the external object as a given, nor to the object as pure fantasy. We suggest that the self, like Winnicott's transitional object, exists in a region between what is real, biologically given, anchored, and coherent and what is created by means of cultural, historical, and interpersonal categories. ... Thus, we seek to place the self in a region that is not totally relativistic but partakes of a sense of inner authenticity and "truth."

These sentences were a response to a query by the editor about whether our position regarding the existence of an essentialist versus a constructed, multiple self was "either–or" or "both–and." In fact, we would characterize our position as "neither–nor," as something between essentialist and constructivist, which can be illuminated by reference to Winnicott's idea about transitional space or transitional objects. We regard it as important to clarify this concept for readers of this volume who are not familiar with psychoanalytic terms because, as it turns out, Muriel Dimen also makes considerable use of it in her chapter, especially as applied to the concept of gender.

Transitional phenomena are neither objective nor subjective but occupy a paradoxical realm between the two that can be sustained only by a recognition that the question as to whether the experience is created or given is not correctly posed (Winnicott, 1953). The interaction of the objective and the subjective creates a new arena that can be referred to as an intermediate area of illusion within which lies people's capacity for culture, creativity, and religion. Here, too, resides the nonessentialist but nonrelativistic meaning we are giving to the concept of self and where, we believe, Dimen's conceptualization of gender rests

235

as well. She also uses the term *gender* in the sense of a paradoxical intermediate zone between apparent polar opposites.

For a reader inclined toward tight operationalization of psychological concepts the notion of transitional space may appear too indeterminate, vague, or even mystical—a kind of psychological ether zone. Although it is true that it bespeaks a reality that is not readily grasped or measured, it can be known through subjective experience, observation, and inferentially, as we tried to show in the case of Henry (see chapter 8). For example, Henry's inability to feel real about himself implies his potential possession of a real self, even if it was not one that he could readily point to or access.

In her chapter, Dimen continues her ongoing project of navigating the problematic waters of gender, self, sexuality, and identity. Her argument takes the form of unraveling the notion of "gender," which in the usual discourse has the straightforward appearance of a nice, familiar round ball. However, the ball turns out to be made of yarn, and as Dimen pursues her analysis more and more strands come apart in our hands, and one begins to wonder if there will be anything left in the end but the unspooled yarn. Although this self-professedly deconstructive project might seem at first glance to be at odds with our own critique of deconstructive discourses on the self, in fact we find ourselves in substantial sympathy with both Dimen's method and her conclusions.

Dimen suggests that before there is gender, there is the experience of difference and the tendency to make a sharp demarcation (a split) between male and female. "At the heart of gender," she writes, "is not 'masculinity' or 'femininity' but the difference between them." She thus disposes of the comforting but deceptive naturalistic or essentialist categories of gender, such reifications being perhaps the inevitable consequence of dualistic thinking. She clarifies further that gender, in this context,

> appears to be less a deterministic category than something resembling a force field. Much like the atom, once thought of as a substance but now construed as a set of interacting forces, so gender looks to consist not of essences but of complex and shifting relations among multiple contrasts or differences.

If "the self" is substituted in this last sentence for "gender," we find that Dimen has given voice to a crucial piece of our own argument, namely, that the self cannot be properly described in terms that are fixed, determinate, and naturalistic. Her critique of gender complements and parallels one pole of our own critique, namely that of the transhistorical, essentialist self.

It also illuminates an interesting aspect of our case of Henry, namely the fluidity of his sense of gender identity. We focused on the way in which he illustrates this nonfixed, nonessentialist sense of gendered self. One of his complaints was that he did not feel like a man. Being a "man" was one more thing he reified and from which he then felt alienated. He spoke of other gender complications. A (mostly) straight woman he met and kissed one night told him, as a compliment, that he kissed like a woman. Another woman, a lesbian with whom he had an intense erotic relationship, once commented that she felt that she "brought out the woman" in him. These experiences were not exactly ego dystonic for him, although they contributed to his sense of not knowing, so to speak, "which bus to get on" (in a dream of his that we report in chapter 8). He also complained that he did not feel like a "manly man," although he tended to make fun of the men he met who seemed to fit that bill ("the only allowable topics of conversation are sports and paving the driveway"). He could be mocking and superior—after all, did not he do the undoable and seduce a lesbian?—yet he was disturbed by his lack of assertiveness, sexual initiative, and strength.

Dimen's thinking deepens one's appreciation of Henry's dilemma, which included the dimension of gender. What does it mean to be a man? What does it mean to feel manly, or not to feel manly? For Henry the "solution" of being a more stereotypically masculine person—itself often a façade covering over problems of dependency, intimacy, and identity—just did not work. One can see how different dimensions of experience (male–female, passive–active, strong–weak, masculine–feminine) are being conflated, how abstractions such as gender are taken to be real things, and how, following Dimen, the operation of splitting is "creating" the overly dichotomous endpoints of gender polarities.

Yet at the same time and to return to the problems of the other pole of a too-fluid concept of self, it seems important to take seriously the feeling that Henry speaks of—that he doesn't feel right, doesn't feel like himself. For him, and perhaps for all of us, gender is real enough to feel alienated from. One might say that one of the real things about gender is that it is something that leaves us uneasy and uncomfortable, uncertain about where we stand in relation to others of the same or different gender, especially idealized others. What would it mean to feel "manly (womanly) enough"? Does anyone actually feel that way? If one felt that way, what would one actually be feeling? Can that feeling be simply "true?" Does it last, or is it always shifting? It keeps eluding us in the final analysis, and yet we suffer from what we understand gender to be. It may be true that matter, composed of the vast empty spaces of atoms, is itself mostly empty space, and yet, when the atoms of our head meet the atoms of the wall, the lump is altogether real.

This dilemma of a naturalistic versus a constructed reality brings to mind a well-known Buddhist story related by Mark Epstein (1998):

> A Tibetan master's son died suddenly from illness. Hearing him weep incon-
> solably, the master's disciples came and confronted him with their surprise.
> "You taught us that all is illusion and that we should not be attached," they
> admonished him. "Why are you weeping and wailing?" The master answered

immediately, "Indeed, all is illusion. But the loss of a child is the most painful illusion of all." (p. 64)

It appears that Dimen, like us, rejects a purely constructivist view of self–gender: "I do not take the deconstructionist train all the way to its nihilist last stop of saying that things are only what texts say they are, that there is no ontology." In particular, we can indicate some of the grounding dimensions of the self: its rootedness in bodily experience, including the perceptual apparatus and the biological horizons of human being; the universality of the sense of development of the self; and the psychological dimensions of existential concerns, such as the ultimate finitude and mortality of the self. We do not view these deterministically; rather, we see them as contexts of being that can be elaborated only in particular historical (social, cultural, familial) contexts, resulting in a self that is indeterminate and yet not constructed. We suggest that it may be necessary to maintain some notion of true selfhood to be in a position to evaluate historical configurations and decide which ones we prefer; that is, to make moral decisions about societies and the kinds of human beings and institutions they produce. Likewise, to do so enables us to maintain some notions of psychological health that are not entirely circumscribed by particular ideologies or discourses.

We are helped here by Dimen's allusion to Benjamin's work on "recognition," for although in that framework what is real is invariably real in a self–other context—and not an objectivist one—recognition requires that something be there to be recognized. The notion of recognition requires a notion of a spontaneous gesture that can be thought of as a truly personal and individual act, not based on internalizations or compliance. This act of self is meaningless without the other to receive it and yet is not bound by the perception of the other (Winnicott, 1960/1965).

Dimen's use of the notion of paradox is also compatible with our own. For us, a central polarity as noted above, and that need remain unresolved, is whether the self is given or made. To force a resolution of this tension is to fall into either the constructivist error of eradicating the given pole or aspects of the self (such as its bodily manifestations, its developmental dimension, and our awareness of its mortality) or the objectivist error of denying the role of context, culture, and history. In this vein, we recall Winnicott's (1953) injunction against asking the question "Was this here or did you make it?" The notion of paradox provides a vehicle for conceptualizing self as neither given nor made but rather a real but indeterminate locus of experience.

Dimen seems to conceptualize the categories of gender in much the same way as we did the categories of self: as moments in a process that is to be viewed as fluid, changing, and nontransparent but as, nonetheless, having an impact, being real, and deeply personal. Dimen concludes, as we do, that Winnicott's notion of transitional space is a way to approach such categories so as to avoid both their reification or their reduction to ephemera. One might extrapolate from her writing that psychological difficulties arise from taking gender categories too literally ("I don't feel like a man"), from being overly stuck in one of the poles of a dichotomy, from all the time having to take sides. Dimen's argument suggests the need of individuals to move into and out of gender experiences, to find moments that are not so differentiated, but either genderless or multiply gendered, and to be able to enjoy the creativity of the self in all its aspects—passive and active, dominant and submissive, penetrating and penetrated, objectifying and being objectified, desiring and being desired. It is in this way that a human being can be most truly real.

References

Epstein, M. (1998). *Going to pieces without falling apart: A Buddhist perspective on wholeness*. New York: Broadway Books.

Winnicott, D. W. (1953). Transitional objects and transitional phenomena. *International Journal of Psycho-Analysis, 34,* 89–97.

Winnicott, D. W. (1965). Ego distortion in terms of true and false self. In *The maturational processes and the facilitating environment* (pp. 140–152). New York: International Universities Press. (Original work published 1960)

CHAPTER 10

The Cognitive Self in Basic Science, Psychopathology, and Psychotherapy

Timothy J. Strauman
Zindel V. Segal

> The zone of mediation where meaning is made is variously called by person-ality psychologists "ego," the "self," the "person." From some perspectives it is one among many functions, all of which together make up the person. From other perspectives it is the very ground of personality itself—it *is* the person. (Kegan, 1982, p. 10)

When William James first published his now-famous observations concern-ing the self as a psychological construct (James, 1890/1948), he scarcely could have predicted how his ideas would inspire a century of conceptual and empirical investigations in behavioral science. James's seminal analysis of the psychological self provided both an astute summary of the construct's philosophical underpinnings and a remarkably fertile set of observations about its nature and vicissitudes. Currently, the self is one of the most ubiquitous topics of investigation within the fields of social, developmental, and clinical psychology. Nonetheless, despite the enormous literature on the self that has emerged over the past decades, it remains in some respects as challenging sci-entifically as James anticipated.

The purpose of this chapter is to examine the heuristic impact of the cog-nitive self on theories of psychopathology and psychotherapy. In doing so, we acknowledge our personal values as researchers and therapists—namely, com-mitment to a scientifically grounded clinical psychology—and challenge our readers to acknowledge their own as they evaluate the ideas presented in this chapter.

Even when James was drafting his authoritative treatise on the nature and origins of the self, a diverse literature already existed describing the self and its psychological characteristics (for a review, see Kegan, 1982). A number of au-thors have traced the evolution of research and theoretical traditions in the psychological study of the self (e.g., Segal, 1988; Strauman & Higgins, 1993).

Despite the diversity of these theories, they share many features: (a) the tendency to view the self as comprising multiple elements or aspects, in terms of content (behavior specific, situation specific, standard specific), time frame (past, present, future), and standpoint (one's own, a significant other's, a generalized other's); (b) recognizing the importance of the origins of the self for understanding its psychological characteristics; and (c) acknowledging the intimate and complex links between self and affect.

Whereas several decades ago neither cognitive nor social psychology seemed to consider the self a major topic, during the past 20 years the self has returned to center stage as a focus of investigation. Indeed, the influence of the "cognitive revolution" (Baars, 1986) on psychological theories of the self has been profound. The reviews of this literature on the self (Higgins & Bargh, 1987; Markus & Wurf, 1987; Segal, 1988; Strauman, 1989a) identify two key premises shared by most investigators in the field. First, it is presumed that the cognitive self actively mediates between the environment and interpersonal behavior and is not simply an epiphenomenon of how the individual responds to interpersonal stimuli, as behaviorally oriented theorists have argued. The cognitive self actively organizes behavior, interprets and responds to the interpersonal context, and regulates the individual's pursuit of emotionally significant goals and standards. Second, most self researchers have appropriated information-processing principles into their models (Kihlstrom & Cantor, 1984). These principles provide useful concepts for such self functions as environment monitoring ("reality testing"), controlled allocation of attentional resources, response selection, and behavior–standard discrepancy reduction. Although it has been argued that exclusive reliance on a computer metaphor may hinder our understanding of the affective and motivational aspects of the self (Sorrentino & Higgins, 1986), the utility of the information-processing perspective for self research is considerable.

It is interesting, however, that some reviewers (e.g., Higgins & Bargh, 1987) have suggested that important questions remain concerning the status of the psychological self from an information-processing perspective. Perhaps the most important issue within contemporary cognitive theories of the self is the extent to which the self is envisioned simply as an "abstraction" in the mind of the investigator (representing a set of independent bits of information or knowledge referring to the individual who "owns" them) versus a unitary cognitive structure "out there" (in the head of the subject) in which the individual elements are organized with a high degree of interrelation. This distinction, which is probably best considered a continuum, carries significant implications for research and, ultimately, for psychotherapy.

As would be expected in an evolving scientific enterprise, the self construct of 1990s behavioral science manifests both strengths and weaknesses. Certainly, the introduction of information-processing concepts provided a degree of rigor and experimental sophistication far beyond what was previously available. In addition, the cognitive *weltanschauung* of present-day behavioral science permits investigators to focus on unobservable processes and hypothetical constructs without incurring the ridicule of behaviorally oriented colleagues (a freedom that psychodynamically oriented clinicians and theoreticians can certainly appreciate).

Possibly the greatest advantage of the cognitive self lies in the body of evidence demonstrating that self-knowledge profoundly influences the entire sequence of psychological events composing social perception and interpersonal behavior. The clinically derived suppositions of Freud, Adler, Sullivan, and others concerning the influence of self-knowledge on an individual's experience, as well as the sociological observations of Cooley, Mead, Sarbin, and more recent theorists concerning the sway of interpersonal forces in shaping the self, have been validated (albeit often in less compelling laboratory contexts).

Nonetheless, it is important to remember that each successive paradigm to arise within behavioral science has had its biases and limitations. As Gergen (1984) and others have pointed out, the information-processing perspective and its counterpart, the computer metaphor, entail assumptions about the nature of mental phenomena that are more appropriate for some features of the self (e.g., memory) than others (e.g., goal-directed action, emotion). Although this point has not been lost within social cognition (e.g., Showers & Cantor, 1985; Sorrentino & Higgins, 1986), it is crucial for self theorists and researchers not to lose sight of other aspects of the essence of the self, that is, the experience of human agency (James's "I"). In many respects, the self literature of the past 20 years bears the unmistakable markings of earlier (particularly behavioral) paradigms; for example, construing the self as "automatically" responding to social stimuli.

The Cognitive Self and Psychopathology

> Once one abandons simpleminded perspectives such as behaviorism or information theory, it becomes obvious that the human higher mental processes are among the most complex and intractable problems known to man. Even the simplest behaviors are the result of enormously complex and abstract causal processes that result, in last analysis, from the central nervous system's ability to structure and restructure its own activity. (Weimer, 1974, p. 177)

One of the most important extensions of the cognitive self in behavioral science is its application to theories of psychopathology. Just as the cognitive revolution in behavioral science fundamentally changed how the psychological self was conceptualized, so it has led to a new generation of clinical theory and intervention. Nowhere has the influence of the cognitive self been more apparent than in the study of depression (Segal, 1988). We cannot present all of the important developments that have occurred in the application of cognitive self theory to the study of psychopathology during the past decades. Instead, we restrict our focus to depression and present three areas in which the cognitive self has been particularly influential: self-esteem, the self-schema, and self-discrepancy.

Depression and Self-Esteem

Of all aspects of the self with potential relation to depression, self-esteem has been the most extensively studied. Clinical, epidemiological, social, and personality researchers have theorized that low self-esteem can both lead to and result from clinical depression. The origins and maintenance of self-esteem are puzzling; nonetheless, the clinical implications of self-esteem are widely acknowledged.

A substantial volume of research indicates that low self-esteem constitutes a significant risk factor for depression. In a series of surveys, Brown and his colleagues have demonstrated that chronic low self-esteem was a common precursor of depression (e.g., Andrews & Brown, 1993; Brown, Andrews, Harris, Adler, & Bridge, 1986). Brown proposed that self-esteem was the most important proximal (immediate) causal locus for the indirect effects of distal vulnerability factors, including childhood loss or abuse experiences, temperament, and socioeconomic factors (Brown et al., 1986). The studies by Brown and his colleagues are particularly important because they demonstrate that for many individuals, low self-esteem preceded the onset of their initial depressive episode.

More recent investigations, using large community samples and sophisticated statistical modeling, have led to similar conclusions. Kendler, Kessler, Neale, Heath, and Eaves (1993) proposed that a confluence of biological and psychological influences determine self-esteem, which in turn manifests a primary causal influence on mood and depressive vulnerability. Low self-esteem was particularly likely to lead to depression in the period following a significant life event. It also has been shown that low self-esteem and negative self-evaluation contribute significantly to the maintenance of depressive episodes and to the likelihood of relapse and recurrence (Beck, Rush, Shaw, & Emery, 1979; Teasdale, 1988). Space limitations preclude a more extensive review of the association between low self-esteem and depression; nonetheless, it is clear that for at least some depressed patients low self-esteem is an important factor in the onset and continuation of depressive episodes.

Social and clinical psychologists have been both "captivated and provoked" (Alloy, Albright, Abramson, & Dykman, 1990) by a striking series of findings from laboratory studies: Whereas nondepressed individuals tend to manifest self-enhancing biases in perception, categorization, interpretation, and memory, under specific circumstances depressed individuals appear to evaluate themselves and comprehend events with a greater degree of accuracy. This phenomenon, termed *depressive realism*, has sparked a good deal of debate regarding its generalizability and clinical significance (Dykman & Abramson, 1990). Does depressive realism occur outside the artificial constraints of the laboratory? Are depressed people suffering because they are more honest with themselves? Should psychotherapy for depression endeavor to reinstate positive biases— that is, to teach people to view themselves in an unrealistically positive manner?

In many respects, depressive realism can be viewed as one manifestation of a more general tendency toward "motivated cognition" in both nondistressed and distressed people (Greenwald & Pratkanis, 1984). Social–cognitive theorists have argued that psychological and physical health depend largely on individuals' beliefs about themselves and their ways of construing events (Scheier & Carver, 1983; Taylor & Brown, 1988). Our view, based on critiques by investigators representing a variety of theoretical perspectives on self and depression (e.g., Bargh, 1989; Coyne & Gotlib, 1983; Higgins & Bargh, 1987; Segal & Shaw, 1986), is that depressive realism should be interpreted in the broadest possible context. Tendencies among depressed individuals to evaluate themselves in a non-self-enhancing manner are likely to be realistic in certain limited circumstances but unrealistic in most others. Thus, depressive self-esteem and self-evaluation are perhaps best characterized cross-situationally as manifestations of bias—the converse of that typically manifested by nondepressed individuals.

Nonetheless, the depressive-realism literature suggests that depression can be difficult to treat in part because low self-esteem is likely to be experienced by the individual as an accurate portrayal of her or his behavior and personal attributes. The weight of evidence supporting the assertion that self-esteem plays a role in the onset and maintenance of depression is impressive. The question is no longer whether such an association exists but rather how self-esteem contributes to the onset and persistence of depressive episodes. Roberts and Monroe (1994) proposed a multidimensional model of self-esteem in depression that was intended to integrate hypotheses from psychodynamic, cognitive, and social–environmental perspectives. Their model emphasized that the relation between self-esteem and depressive vulnerability was more complex than previous theories had postulated; that is, the association is not linear but rather involves additional factors ranging from temperament to current relationships.

According to Roberts and Monroe's (1994) multidimensional approach, self-esteem-based vulnerability to depression depends on three main factors: structural deficits within the self (e.g., few, rigid, or inaccessible self-beliefs); negative self-evaluation and resultant abnormally low self-esteem; and temporal instability of the individual's sense of self-worth, as a function of depressogenic cognitive distortions, negative life events, and the acute impact of negative mood states on the individual's sense of self. This approach illustrates both the complexity of the self (Guidano & Liotti, 1983) and the necessity for integrative theorizing that draws on basic science and the phenomenology of depression (Alloy et al., 1990; Strauman, 1992).

Self-Schemas and Depression

The preponderance of research examining the role of the self in depression has concerned various aspects of information processing, including self-perception, self-representation, and self-evaluation (Bargh, 1989). Undoubtedly the most widely studied cognitive topic linking self and psychopathology over the past several decades is the notion of *self-schemas*. Borrowing from Bartlett's (1932) seminal investigations of how mental structures influenced perception, categorization, and appraisal, and memory, schema researchers have examined the impact of self-relevant cognition on mood and symptomatology.

Although widely used, the schema construct continues to pose significant methodological and theoretical challenges in depression research (for a review of the basic science literature, see Higgins & Bargh, 1987; for a review of the relevance of the self-schema notion to depression, see Segal, 1988). The limitations of currently available experimental methods effectively preclude arrival at final answers to questions such as "Does the self-schema cause depression?" At the same time, contemporary investigations have led to findings that are surprisingly congruent with clinical observation and theory.

According to Segal (1988), the term *schema* refers to organized representations of past reactions and experiences that form a relatively coherent and persisting body of knowledge capable of guiding subsequent perception and appraisals. There are at least two thorny issues in the schema literature that complicate the application of this construct to the diagnosis and treatment of depression. First, a schema cannot be measured directly and must therefore be considered a hypothetical construct, whose value depends on its utility in explaining (in this case) depression. Therefore, assessment of schemas is inherently inferential and inherently difficult. Second, it can be difficult to determine whether schema is the best available explanation for a particular behavior or emotion or whether some other explanation (e.g., habits, attitudes, physiology) is more parsimonious, more likely to lead to effective therapeutic interventions, or both. Fortunately, recent developments in the application of cognitive science techniques to the study of depression have significantly increased the potential clinical utility of the schema concept.

The pioneering work of Aaron Beck (1976; Beck et al., 1979) has done much to popularize the application of cognitive constructs to the conceptualization and treatment of depression. Beck's original observations about thought processes in depressed patients became systematized into a model of depression that focused on three primary cognitive characteristics: a distorted and negative pattern of information processing; the occurrence of repetitive and unintended self-referent thoughts associated with themes of loss; and a negative view of self, world, and future. It was Beck's hypothesis that the various cognitive and symptomatic manifestations of depression were caused by maladaptive underlying cognitive structures that were triggered by stressful life events.

Beck's clinical hypotheses and theoretical model inspired a wealth of basic and applied research examining cognitive aspects of depression. Although differences exist among specific models and conceptualizations, most involve some form of structural construct generally labeled as *schema* or *self-schema*. As above, the self-schema is conceptualized as an organized representation of the individual's prior experiences and associated knowledge (Segal & Ingram, 1994). It is hypothesized to exert a significant influence on information processing by shaping the individual's expectations regarding ongoing and future events and her or his appraisals regarding the meaning of events and interactions. A negative self-schema is presumed to underlie the self-criticism, cognitive distortions, and associated distress observed in depressed patients (Teasdale & Barnard, 1993).

What would it mean for an individual to possess a depressogenic self-schema? On the basis of trends in the literature, a number of factors are likely to obtain given such a hypothesis. Most cognitive models of depressive vulnerability postulate that developmental factors play a significant role in the acquisition of problematic beliefs and belief structures. For example, Hammen (1991) argued that depressogenic self-representations have a predictable developmental history that involves patterns of interactions within the family of origin. Individuals acquire sets of self-beliefs that over time evolve into self-schemas containing highly accessible negative information about the self. Continued and increasing activation of these structures, in turn, will be associated with increasing frequency and intensity of dysphoric states, contributing to the onset and maintenance of depressive episodes. Hammen and her colleagues concluded, on the basis of longitudinal findings, that the negative self-view frequently evident in depression is attributable to pre-existing beliefs about the self; hence, cognitive aspects of depression are not secondary to a more fundamental biological dysfunction.

Similarly, there are numerous studies demonstrating that individuals characterized by negative self-belief structures are more prone to depressogenic cognitive distortions than comparable individuals without evidence for such a self-schema (Spielman & Bargh, 1990). Although there is a notable degree of inconsistency within this literature (i.e., findings involving certain cognitive processes and products have not always been replicated), most observers concur that underlying self-referential belief structures have a strong, frequently unconscious influence on a wide range of thoughts and feelings. These data constitute the aforementioned "flip side" of depressive realism: That is, it would be inaccurate to characterize depression as a disorder of brutal realism. Rather, the self-beliefs of depressed individuals are self-critical and self-denigrating.

Overall, there is substantial evidence that individuals prone to or currently suffering from depression manifest cognitive-processing peculiarities consistent with an underlying depressogenic self-schema (Ingram, Miranda, & Segal, 1998). In the presence of particular conditions, such as depressed mood or a challenging interpersonal interaction, depression-prone individuals show characteristic distortions in attention (noticing a grimace but not a smile among audience members), categorization (deciding that the silence of a conversation partner connotes boredom rather than respectful attention), memory (recalling only frustrations with a spouse rather than a more balanced sampling of interactions), and appraisal (judging one's academic future to be hopeless on the basis of a single disappointing grade).

The importance of the self-schema concept is best demonstrated in the context of a comprehensive diathesis–stress model of vulnerability to depression; that is, underlying depressogenic belief structures typically are inoperative, influencing information processing and self-evaluation only when activated by current circumstances (which presumably resemble important features of the representations themselves, e.g., in terms of mood congruency, interpersonal contingency, or attachment theme). In other words, the individual is not always operating in a depressogenic cognitive mode. However, when such beliefs are activated, they are likely to have a predictable acute and, ultimately, chronic and cumulative negative impact. Furthermore, the individual is not likely to perceive the resultant differences in cognitive processing; instead, she or he will only notice increased distress and associated cognitive products (specific negative thoughts, images, and memories). The greater the extent and accessibility of the underlying cognitive diathesis are, the less severe the circumstances required to activate it will be.

Self-Discrepancy and Vulnerability

Among the self theories postulating that conflict or inconsistency can predispose an individual to distress, models focusing on perceived discrepancies between some current behavior or attribute and important personal standards have received the greatest degree of empirical support. These phenomenologically based models derive their predictive power from the observation that human behavior and emotional experience are highly influenced by whatever goals are active at any moment (Guidano & Liotti, 1983). Carl Rogers (1961) generated a theory of the healthy personality in which discrepancies between the person's self-concept and her or his ideals were minimized. He also pioneered a method for individualized assessment of the self-concept, the Q-sort technique, through which he was able to demonstrate that client-centered therapy significantly reduced within-self inconsistency in addition to achieving symptomatic relief.

Among contemporary investigators, the control-theory perspective on self-regulation proposed by Carver and Scheier (1981) has been particularly influential. Carver and Scheier characterized human behavior as a process of moving toward various kinds of personally significant goal representations guided by a feedback-control system. These authors postulated systems of feedback processes that were hypothesized to determine the affective outcomes of self-regulation. In some instances, the individual is motivated to reduce the discrepancy between her or his present state and some desired state; at other times, she or he is motivated to increase the discrepancy between her or his present state and an undesired state. Individuals are presumed to hold representations of emotionally significant approach and avoidance goals. The process of self-evaluation is said to consist of a continuing, automatic evaluation in which one's current status is compared with the goals that are most salient at that particular moment. Recent extensions of the model, concerning dispositional tendencies for negative versus self-affirming feedback systems, have proven especially relevant to depressive vulnerability.

Another contemporary model of self-regulation is *self-discrepancy theory* (Higgins, 1987), which asserts that the relation between the self-concept and certain self-regulatory standards determines the emotional impact of those self-beliefs. Different patterns of relations among self-beliefs are proposed to have different psychological significance and are associated with distinct emotional states. The theory postulates that people are motivated to ensure that the self-concept is congruent with certain valued end-states, that is, to reach a condition in which their *actual* self (a representation of the attributes they believe they actually possess) matches their *ideal* self-guide (a representation of their own or a significant other's hopes, wishes, or aspirations for them) or their *ought* self-guide (a representation of their own or a significant other's sense of their duties, obligations, or responsibilities).

A series of correlational and experimental studies (for a review, see Strauman & Higgins, 1993) supported the prediction that an actual–ideal discrepancy is associated with dejection-related states because it signifies the absence of positive outcomes (i.e., not actualizing hopes or wishes), whereas an actual–ought discrepancy is associated with agitation-related states because it signifies the (expected) presence of negative outcomes (i.e., punishment or sanction). The model has been validated in clinical populations, indicating that depressed patients are characterized by high levels of actual–ideal discrepancy (Scott & O'Hara, 1993; Strauman, 1989b, 1992). Self-discrepancy theory also has been used to consider treatment-induced structural change within the self-system (Strauman, 1994).

Summary

As can be seen from our selective review, the cognitive perspective on the self has been greatly influential in shaping current theories of psychopathology. Although this review was limited to clinical depression, there are extensive literatures relating cognitive aspects of the self to anxiety disorders, eating disorders, and a number of Axis II disorders (Ewell, Smith, Karmel, & Hart, 1996; McNally, 1996; Waller, 1999). The information-processing perspective that is manifested in the theories reviewed above possesses a number of desirable characteristics.

First, the self literature contains a number of explicit as well as implicit references to theories of normal and abnormal development. As such, this cognitive perspective can be linked with models of emotional regulation, such as theories based on Bowlby's attachment framework. Thus, theories that might otherwise appear devoid of emotional or motivational relevance can be linked directly to emotional processes based on physiological substrates. For example, the acquisition of self-knowledge has been traced by Higgins and others to experiences during early childhood of receiving (or not receiving) positive or negative responses from significant others (e.g., Higgins, 1989).

Second, by virtue of their origins in the psychological laboratory, cognitive theories of the self bring a degree of testability that is often considerably greater than the testability of previous theories of psychopathology. An obvious example of this advantage is the large experimental literature examining the self-schema in depression. Studies with a variety of cognitive priming procedures show that remitted depressives still respond negatively to certain types of emotionally significant stimuli but only during periods of low mood. For example, Segal et al. (1999) examined the nature of cognitive reactivity to mood changes in formerly depressed patients who recovered either through cognitive therapy or pharmacotherapy. Patients completed self-reported ratings of dysfunctional attitudes before and after a negative-mood induction procedure; in response to similar levels of induced sad mood, pharmacotherapy patients showed a significant increase in dysfunctional cognitions, whereas patients in the cognitive therapy group did not. In addition, the extent of dysfunctional thinking endorsed during the transient sad mood, regardless of the treatment received, was predictive of depressive relapse. These findings argue for differential effects of treatment on cognitive reactivity to mood induction and for the link between such reactivity and risk for later depressive relapse. Similarly, recent studies of self-regulation in depressed and anxious patients used autobiographical memory priming procedures to show that individuals with particular problems in self-regulation are more likely to experience subsequent depressive symptoms than individuals without such self-regulation problems (Strauman et al., in press).

Third, the cognitive perspective is particularly useful for making a distinction between conscious and unconscious influences on mood and behavior. Information-processing models can accommodate both the intentional and unintentional effects of an individual's goals on her or his behavior and emotional state. Furthermore, the concepts and methods of cognitive psychology have provided surprising insights regarding the limitations of people's awareness and understanding of their mental processes (e.g., Nisbett & Wilson, 1977). Although from an epistemological standpoint cognitive psychology may not have "solved" the dilemma of subjectivity described so well by James, its methodologies can capture both deliberate and unintended aspects of thought and behavior.

For these reasons, the cognitive self continues to have an enormous impact on the study of psychopathology—from depression and anxiety to schizophrenia. It should be noted as well that the association between cognitive theories of psychopathology and the development of new approaches to psychotherapy over the past 20 years has been bidirectional; that is, much of the recent work examining the role of self-representations and self-schemas in vulnerability to emotional disorders has been inspired, at least in part, by the rise of cognitive–behavioral therapy as a treatment modality for depression. This synergistic approach—in which basic theory leads to clinical innovation, which in turn fosters subsequent theory development—has long been a goal of scientific clinical psychology. Whatever its limitations, the cognitive self offers fertile ground for the application of behavioral science to the study of psychopathology and psychotherapy.

The Cognitive Self: Implications for Psychotherapy

> A human "knowing system" reflects a dynamic equilibrium unfolding through successively more integrated models of self and world. This perspective has some remarkable consequences for the therapeutic approach. (Guidano, 1987, p. 215)

The challenge of psychotherapy, when considered from the cognitive perspective, is to identify interventions that facilitate change in the features of the self that cause or maintain the client's suffering. Among the common themes that surface in descriptions of pathology of the self are disavowal of aspects of the self, discrepancy from standards for the self, and constriction in the facets of the self that are expressed. There is also the implicit belief that an expanded or more coherent sense of self will be related to positive therapeutic outcomes.

A central therapeutic task is to help the patient begin to question his or her model of what a self is and how the idea of the self is often defined by personally relevant categories (me as a success—me as a failure, me as attractive—me as unattractive, me as inferior—me as superior). Reliance on these categories limits a patient's ability to see him- or herself in ways that might support a newer, more adaptive self-construct. Furthermore, assigning meaning to one's experience on the basis of these categories may end up contributing to the perpetuation of the negative emotional states and thereby feed the very problem one is trying to solve.

Cognitive–behavior therapy uses a number of interventions that promote the construction of a new set of beliefs about the self, and their implementation often becomes a focus for the latter half of treatment. The total therapy regime, including the overall treatment rationale, the high treatment structure, and the active and frequent practice of coping responses, leads to repeated experiences in which alternative, less debilitating, schematic models concerning the self, its deficits, effects, and related problematic life situations are synthesized and stored in memory. In other words, during treatment, patients have frequent experiences of approaching problematic situations with a different "view" or "set" concerning the self and related areas. A core skill that the patient learns along the way is the ability to *decenter* or distance him- or herself from his or her current experience. For instance, simple techniques, such as writing down thoughts (memories, interpretations, conclusions, fantasies) and examining them collaboratively with the therapist, encourages patients to adopt a relative rather than an absolute perspective on the validity of their beliefs and to separate feelings from the assumptions and beliefs that accompany them.

Many of the interventions that have become the hallmark of this treatment tradition, along with reducing acute symptomatology, allow the patient to recognize both the antecedents and consequences of self-distortions and fragmentation and to interrupt and reverse this process (Segal & Blatt, 1993). For example, Socratic questioning of belief statements (such as "My situation is hopeless") can facilitate the process of translating personal axioms into tentative hypotheses ("Is that really true?"), thereby setting the stage for a consideration of self-generated alternatives ("Is there another way of looking at this?") and subsequent experimentation. Another technique that facilitates decentering is monitoring automatic thoughts between sessions. A patient might be asked to maintain a record of anxiety-provoking situations and the thoughts and images that emerge. By learning to recognize the thoughts that increase the likelihood of anxiety, the patient can begin to consider alternative, more adaptive responses.

More recently, there has been some interest in the use of mindfulness training as perhaps a more direct way of facilitating this core cognitive change skill (Teasdale, Segal, & Williams, 1995). The essence of the mindful state is to be aware of the present moment, without judging or evaluating it, without reflecting backward on past memories, without looking forward to anticipate the future (as in anxious worry), and without attempting to problem solve or otherwise avoid any unpleasant aspects of the immediate situation. The mindful state is also associated with a lack of elaborative processing—that is, thoughts that are essentially "about" the currently experienced situation, its implications, or further meanings.

Both mindfulness training and cognitive–behavior therapy share the same basic underlying rationale, namely that emotional disturbance can be caused by viewing thoughts as "absolute realities" rather than "mental events." Consistent with that rationale, both treatment approaches lead patients to alternative views of their problems. States of mind (such as those achieved through mindfulness training) in which attention is actively allocated to one's present experience may compete with the more automatic (or mindless) mode of processing associated with escalating ruminative elaborations about the self. Through mindfulness training, individuals acquire the skill habitually to deploy limited processing resources to deal with information related to specific "neutral" objects of attention, such as the breath, or to the contents of moment-by-moment experience.

For example, patients with excessive worry may be instructed during mindfulness training to observe occasions when they worry and to practice bringing their attention back to their breath in the midst of these unsettling experiences. The simple intervention is intended to help patients view their thoughts as mental events rather than absolute realities while realizing that they can let these thoughts occur without continuing to attend to them and elaborating. As a result of habitually redeploying attention in this way, the resources necessary to support self-distortion-enhancing or -maintaining processing cycles are less available (Teasdale & Barnard, 1993). Consequently, from a mindfulness perspective the chances of dysfunctional self-views developing or persisting should be reduced. Data from a recently completed randomized trial suggest that this may be the case for prevention of depressive relapse–recurrence (Teasdale et al., in press).

Another new cognitive approach to understanding and altering the self in psychotherapy is the application of a *self-regulation* perspective on vulnerability to depression and other disorders. In brief, this approach postulates that the ongoing processes of self-evaluation and self-regulation (occurring continuously at both conscious and unconscious levels) can contribute to distress through a number of problematic aspects of the self: extreme standards (e.g., perfectionism), outmoded or maladaptive expectancies of the self or others (e.g., interpersonal patterns based on unfulfilled needs from an earlier relationship), or ineffective developmentally derived tendencies to experience interactions as having particular implications for self-worth (Strauman, 1994). On the basis of principles of social knowledge activation as well as research supporting self-discrepancy theory, investigators are examining whether psychotherapeutic interventions targeting self-regulatory cognition—how each person evaluates him- or herself with respect to important personal goals—can alleviate symptoms and reduce subsequent vulnerability to depression (Strauman et al., in press).

A number of familiar and novel psychotherapeutic interventions are consistent with a self-regulation perspective. For example, many therapists work with patients to help them explicitly identify their goals for themselves (both their ultimate aspirations as well as their responsibilities and obligations). Often this exercise leads to the realization that some goals are extreme, outmoded, or self-defeating. Similarly, psychotherapy for depression and anxiety frequently involves the exploration of patients' expectancies regarding the probable success or failure of their efforts to meet important goals. Also because many depressed individuals find that their daily routines and interactions with others have been significantly eroded, it can be helpful to use behavioral-activation techniques to reawaken their sensitivity to pleasure and reward. Most important, a self-regulation perspective requires that patient and therapist gain an understanding of how the patient's efforts to achieve his or her aspirations or meet his or her obligations go awry. In some cases, goals need to be "let go" or modified; in others, goals need to be broken down into a series of short-term milestones; in still others, patients need assistance learning to compensate for the likelihood that they will never completely fulfill their wishes or responsibilities (e.g., due to personal limitations, financial constraints, and other real-world contingencies).

Conclusion

In the brief space of this chapter, we endeavor to characterize the cognitive view of the self and its implications for psychopathology and psychotherapy. Despite the long history of the self as a psychological construct, the study of psychotherapeutic process and technique from a cognitive perspective is still largely in its infancy. For some of the reasons outlined above, we believe that the cognitive self is a powerful construct both for advancing our knowledge of vulnerability to depression and other disorders and—perhaps more important—for improving the effectiveness of psychotherapy.

The ultimate paradox of the self (Strauman, 1989a), and its ultimate challenge as a theoretical construct, is that it simultaneously represents ("me") and personifies ("I") one's unique past, present, and anticipated future. This paradox has significant implications for our understanding of the self as structure, as process, and as a source of vulnerability to emotional distress. We hope this chapter illuminates our belief that the self construct is a natural locus for inquiry regarding the manner in which an individual's identity, experience, and self-regulatory behaviors may predispose her or him to emotional disorders.

The eventual direction in which this consequential and challenging research area evolves should entail a deliberate effort to more fully appreciate each historical perspective on the self. In reviewing the conceptual and empirical trends within the self literature, it is encouraging to consider the wealth of ideas and observations that have accumulated. If the present volume, with its creative format of dialogue and contrast, is any indication, we anticipate a new era of integration and progress in the psychological study of the self.

References

Alloy, L. B., Albright, J. S., Abramson, L. Y., & Dykman, B. M. (1990). Depressive realism and nondepressive optimistic illusions: The role of the self. In R. Ingram (Ed.), *Contemporary psychological approaches to depression* (pp. 71–86). New York: Plenum Press.

Andrews, B., & Brown, G. W. (1993). Self-esteem and vulnerability to depression: The concurrent validity of interview and questionnaire measures. *Journal of Abnormal Psychology, 102,* 565–572.

Baars, B. J. (1986). *The cognitive revolution in psychology*. New York: Guilford Press.

Bargh, J. A. (1989). Conditional automaticity: Varieties of automatic influence in social perception and cognition. In J. S. Uleman & J. A. Bargh (Eds.), *Unintended thought* (pp. 25–52). New York: Guilford Press.

Bartlett, F. C. (1932). *Remembering*. Cambridge, England: Cambridge University Press.

Beck, A. T. (1976). *Cognitive therapy and the emotional disorders*. New York: Basic Books.

Beck, A. T., Rush, A. J., Shaw, B., & Emery, G. (1979). *Cognitive therapy of depression*. New York: Guilford Press.

Brown, G. W., Andrews, B., Harris, T., Adler, Z., & Bridge, L. (1986). Social support, self-esteem, and depression. *Psychological Medicine, 16,* 813–831.

Carver, C. S., & Scheier, M. F. (1981). *Attention and self-regulation: A control theory approach to human behavior*. New York: Springer-Verlag.

Coyne, J. C., & Gotlib, I. H. (1983). The role of cognition in depression: A critical appraisal. *Psychological Bulletin, 94,* 472–505.

Dykman, B. M., & Abramson, L. Y. (1990). Contributions of basic research to the cognitive theories of depression. *Personality and Social Psychology Bulletin, 16,* 42–57.

Ewell, F., Smith, S., Karmel, M., & Hart, D. (1996). The sense of self and its development: A framework for understanding eating disorders. In L. Smolak & M. Levine (Eds.), *The developmental psychopathology of eating disorders: Implications for research, prevention, and treatment* (pp. 107–133). Mahwah, NJ: Erlbaum.

Gergen, K. J. (1984). Theory of the self: Impasse and evolution. *Advances in Experimental Social Psychology, 17,* 49–115.

Greenwald, A. G., & Pratkanis, A. R. (1984). The self. In R. Wyer & T. Srull (Eds.), *Handbook of social cognition* (Vol. 3, pp. 105–130). Hillsdale, NJ: Erlbaum.

Guidano, V. F. (1987). *Complexity of the self: A developmental approach to psychopathology and therapy.* New York: Guilford Press.

Guidano, V. F., & Liotti, G. (1983). *Cognitive processes and emotional disorders: A structural approach to psychotherapy.* New York: Guilford Press.

Hammen, C. L. (1991). *Depression runs in families.* New York: Springer-Verlag.

Higgins, E. T. (1987). Self-discrepancy: A theory relating self and affect. *Psychological Review, 94,* 319–340.

Higgins, E. T. (1989). Continuities and discontinuities in self-regulatory and self-evaluative processes: A developmental theory relating to self and affect. *Journal of Personality, 57,* 407–444.

Higgins, E. T., & Bargh, J. A. (1987). Social cognition and social perception. *Annual Review of Psychology, 38,* 369–425.

Ingram, R. E., Miranda, J., & Segal, Z. V. (1998). *Cognitive vulnerability to depression.* New York: Guilford Press.

James, W. (1948). *The principles of psychology.* New York: World. (Original work published 1890)

Kegan, R. (1982). *The evolving self: Problem and process in human development.* Cambridge, MA: Harvard University Press.

Kendler, K. S., Kessler, R. D., Neale, M. C., Heath, A. C., & Eaves, L. J. (1993). The prediction of major depression in women: Toward an integrated etiologic model. *Archives of General Psychiatry, 150,* 1139–1148.

Kihlstrom, J. F., & Cantor, N. (1984). Mental representations of the self. In L. Berkowitz (Ed.), *Advances in experimental social psychology* (Vol. 17, pp. 1–47). New York: Academic Press.

Markus, H., & Wurf, E. (1987). The dynamic self-concept: A social psychological perspective. *Annual Review of Psychology, 38,* 299–337.

McNally, R. J. (1996). Cognitive biases in the anxiety disorders. In D. Hope et al. (Eds.), *Nebraska Symposium on Motivation* (Vol. 43, pp. 211–250). Lincoln: University of Nebraska Press.

Nisbett, R. E., & Wilson, T. D. (1977). Telling more than we can know: Verbal reports on mental processes. *Psychological Review, 84,* 231–259.

Roberts, J. E., & Monroe, S. M. (1994). A multidimensional model of self-esteem in depression. *Clinical Psychology Review, 14,* 161–181.

Rogers, C. R. (1961). *On becoming a person.* Boston: Houghton-Mifflin.

Scheier, M. F., & Carver, C. S. (1983). Two sides of the self: One for you and one for me. In J. Suls & A. Greenwald (Eds.), *Psychological perspectives on the self* (pp. 184–201). Hillsdale, NJ: Erlbaum.

Scott, L., & O'Hara, M. (1993). Self-discrepancies in clinically anxious and depressed university students. *Journal of Abnormal Psychology, 40,* 1116–1124.

Segal, Z. V. (1988). Appraisal of the self-schema construct in cognitive models of depression. *Psychological Bulletin, 103,* 147–162.

Segal, Z. V., & Blatt, S. J. (Eds.). (1993). *The self in emotional distress: Cognitive and psychodynamic perspectives.* New York: Guilford Press.

Segal, Z. V., Gemar, M. C., & Williams, S. (1999). Differential cognitive response to a mood challenge following successful cognitive therapy or pharmacotherapy for unipolar depression. *Journal of Abnormal Psychology, 108,* 3–10.

Segal, Z. V., & Ingram, R. E. (1994). Mood priming and construct activation in tests of cognitive vulnerability to depression. *Clinical Psychology Review, 14,* 663–695.

Segal, Z. V., & Shaw, B. F. (1986). Cognition in depression: A reappraisal of Coyne and Gotlib's critique. *Cognitive Therapy and Research, 10,* 671–694.

Showers, C. J., & Cantor, N. (1985). Social cognition: A look at motivated strategies. *Annual Review of Psychology, 36,* 275–305.

Sorrentino, R. M., & Higgins, E. T. (1986). Motivation and cognition: Warming up to synergism. In R. Sorrentino & E. T. Higgins (Eds.), *Handbook of motivation and cognition: Foundations of social behavior* (pp. 3–19). New York: Guilford Press.

Spielman, L. A., & Bargh, J. A. (1990). Does the depressive self-schema really exist? In D. McCann & N. Endler (Eds.), *Depression: New directions in theory, research, and practice* (pp. 111–126). Toronto, Ontario, Canada: Wall & Emerson.

Strauman, T. J. (1989a). The paradox of the self: A psychodynamic/social–cognitive integration. In R. C. Curtis (Ed.), *Self-defeating behaviors: Experimental findings, clinical impressions, and practical implications* (pp. 311–339). New York: Plenum Press.

Strauman, T. J. (1989b). Self-discrepancies in clinical depression and social phobia: Cognitive structures that underlie affective disorders? *Journal of Abnormal Psychology, 98,* 14–22.

Strauman, T. J. (1992). Self-guides, childhood memory, and anxiety and dysphoria: Toward a cognitive model of vulnerability to emotional distress. *Journal of Abnormal Psychology, 101,* 87–95.

Strauman, T. J. (1994). Self-representations and the nature of cognitive change in psychotherapy. *Journal of Psychotherapy Integration, 4,* 3–21.

Strauman, T. J., & Higgins, E. T. (1993). The self construct in social cognition. In Z. V. Segal & S. J. Blatt (Eds.), *The self in emotional distress: Cognitive and psychodynamic perspectives* (pp. 3–40). New York: Guilford Press.

Strauman, T. J., Kolden, G. G., Davis, N., Stromquist, V., Kwapil, L., & Heerey, E. (in press). The impact of treatments for depression on perceived failure in self-regulation. *Cognitive Therapy and Research.*

Taylor, S. E., & Brown, J. D. (1988). Illusion and well-being: A social psychological perspective on mental health. *Psychological Bulletin, 103,* 193–210.

Teasdale, J. D. (1988). Cognitive vulnerability to persistent depression. *Cognition and Emotion, 2,* 247–274.

Teasdale, J. D., & Barnard, P. J. (1993). *Affect, cognition and change: Re-modelling depressive thought.* Hillsdale, NJ: Erlbaum.

Teasdale, J. D., Segal, Z. V., & Williams, J. M. G. (1995). How does cognitive therapy prevent relapse and why should attentional (control) mindfulness training help? *Behaviour Research and Therapy, 33,* 25–39.

Teasdale, J. D., Segal, Z. V., Williams, J. M. G., Ridgeway, V. A., Soulsby, J. M., & Lau, M. A. (in press). Prevention of relapse/recurrence in major depression by mindfulness-based cognitive therapy. *Journal of Consulting and Clinical Psychology.*

Waller, N. G. (1999). Evaluating the structure of personality. In R. Cloninger (Ed.), *Personality and psychopathology* (pp. 155–197). Washington, DC: American Psychiatric Press.

Weimer, W. B. (1974). Overview of a cognitive conspiracy: Reflections on the volume. In W. Weimer & D. Palermo (Eds.), *Cognition and the symbolic processes* (pp. 175–182). Hillsdale, NJ: Erlbaum.

COMMENT:

Comparing and Contrasting the Cognitive and Interpersonal Selves

William P. Henry

The issues raised—conceptual, empirical, heuristic, and political—in comparing and contrasting models of an interpersonal versus cognitive self could easily take up a full-length chapter if not a book. Given the space restrictions, I am necessarily brief (hoping to stimulate a more extended dialogue) and split my time between comparing the two models and commenting on the cognitive model itself, as represented in Timothy Strauman and Zindal Segal's chapter. I first comment on the many similarities between the approaches, and then I discuss how the two models complement one another. Next, I touch on possible conceptual incompatibilities and briefly offer a critique of Strauman and Segal's presentation of the cognitive self. Finally, I discuss avenues of future integration.

Similar Perspectives

While reading Strauman and Segal's chapter and comparing it with my own chapter (11) on the interpersonal self, I was first struck by their similarities. There may be a similar mechanism underlying the process of therapy, a similarity that is certainly not obvious from observing the surface procedures and language of cognitive versus psychodynamic–interpersonal therapy. However, both therapies rely in large part on the idea that dissonance is created as the expected and actual results of therapeutic processes diverge and that this inconsistency causes a "perturbation" in the system that leads to positive change because we are driven to reduce dissonance. In short, both approaches share a common emphasis on change through examining and disconfirming the expectancies individuals have of self and others in interaction as represented by mental schemas of the generalized other.

I do not belabor the points of correspondence because I feel that most readers can readily see the surface similarities between the two approaches to

259

260 WILLIAM P. HENRY

the self. The more interesting questions involve how these similarities came to be and to what extent, if any, the similarities mirror deeper theoretical issues. From one point of view, it is ironic to note that the cognitive position, which grew from a behavioral tradition, can now be seen as almost "mentalistic" (the anathema of traditional behaviorism), making use of unobservable constructs such as self-schemas. In turn, the interpersonal self I describe, with its roots in hypothetical psychodynamics, now emphasizes observable interpersonal behavior, at a relatively low level of inference. In fact, the principle of transactional complementarity is often discussed in the language of base rates, altering response contingencies, and so on.

What has happened? One possibility is that the two positions were actually very similar all along and that this fact is just now being recognized. However, given the truly different views of the human being inherent in the historical origins of the cognitive and interpersonal traditions, I doubt this is the case. Rather, I believe the two chapters represent an emergent and potentially exciting "work in progress" by formerly opposing camps that are moving ever closer together in the present—and for good reason. Given a seeming reduction in automatic political tensions, I think that both traditions are evolving in the same direction because the writers in both areas have begun to tap into the same underlying truths about the self and its development. So, do we now have simply to breach the vestiges of our older tribal languages, or do fundamental issues remain that might impede or prevent integration?

Complementary Perspectives

Despite the similarities between the two models, there is one overarching difference. The interpersonal model of self I describe focuses on the processes of the self in transaction, whereas the model articulated by Strauman and Segal focuses on the conscious cognitive contents of the self. This difference, however, is not necessarily an incompatibility. Indeed, the two approaches may ultimately complement one another synergistically by combining the unique contributions of a process and a content focus. The interpersonal approach may add needed inter- and intrapersonal mechanisms and a fuller understanding of developmental self-etiology to the cognitive approach. On the other hand, the model of the cognitive self may add needed specificity and organization to the mental contents generated by and operated on by the generalized interpersonal theory of process.

One obvious example of this potential theoretical complementarity has to do with the shared idea that individuals cycle through a number of temporary "states," most obviously as related to depressogenic states. Cognitive theory is weak when it comes to explaining the mechanisms behind the origins, maintenance, and shifting of these states. Interpersonal theory contributes the idea of introjection of early interpersonal process to address etiology and the idea that contemporary interpersonal process may cause state shifts by differentially activating various introjects (i.e., self-schemas). Additionally, interpersonal theory proposes that individuals help create the external circumstances that activate "depressogenic self-schemas" by means of the principle of complementarity, which helps explain maintenance. On the other hand, cognitive self-theory may add needed organization, differentiation, and content to this process-based understanding. For example, interpersonal theory does not directly address the self in terms such as possible selves, life goals (except in the abstract sense of seeking attachment and differentiation), types of cognitive distortions that guide interpersonal expectancies, and the specific content of self-statements that would be associated with different introject states.

Fundamental Incompatibilities

There are several potential differences between the approaches that may prove troublesome, and they deserve brief mention. The first difficulty has to do with the long-standing debate over the primacy of affect versus cognition. Both models are relatively weak when it comes to emotion theory per se. It is one thing to say that depression is caused by dysfunctional cognitions, or that affective symptoms are generally embedded in an interpersonal context, and so on. Although it is true that both statements seem to have face validity, there are still problems associated with specifying more exact mechanisms. In this regard, the extent to which adherents to a cognitive model insist on cognitive primacy, particularly as based in conscious cognition, may govern whether the two approaches are ultimately compatible. However, as the interpersonal theory of the self develops, it may or may not even be necessary to take a stance on this fundamental issue, and cognitive theorists may adjust their stance as new knowledge is obtained about the underlying mechanisms and structure of emotions.

The second area of potential incompatibility has to do with the proposed mechanisms represented by the general idea of *active mediation* and how it is to be defined. Strauman and Segal state that

> the cognitive self actively mediates between the environment and interpersonal behavior and is not simply an epiphenomenon of how the individual responds to interpersonal stimuli, as behaviorally oriented theorists have argued. The cognitive self actively organizes behavior, interprets and responds to the interpersonal context, and regulates the individual's pursuit of emotionally significant standards.

On the surface, I would have to agree with this statement as applied to either the cognitive or interpersonal self. Certainly, the interpersonal case formulation model I present in chapter 11 incorporates similar ideas of internal mediational processes that organize and guide behavior. It is interesting, however, that the idea of interpersonal complementarity, which is also a central process, may ironically be considered too "behavioral" or passive in a sense to fit Strauman and Segal's definition of "active" mediation. Ultimately, the idea of complementarity can be traced to and supported by primate research, which does not necessarily involve the type of cognitive processes envisioned by Strauman and Segal (although we may be selling other primates short). Additionally, there is the problem of how to define *epiphenomenon* in systems that are at the moment too incompletely understood. At any rate, I think that these are interesting questions with which neither approach has dealt in any depth. Whether they lead to fundamental incompatibilities remains to be seen.

A Critique of the Cognitive Self

Here, I touch on two critiques. The first critique is of the ideas, theories, and research methodologies related to the cognitive self. In the second critique, I discuss the authors' presentation of their ideas, particularly as they relate to the central focus of this volume—how our theories address, oppose, and integrate a variety of "postmodern challenges" to understanding the self (especially within a therapeutic context).

My first critique belies old wounds resulting from a self-identity as an empiricist finding himself on the politically "wrong" side theoretically during a "we're scientific, you're not" era (that still unfortunately persists in much of academia). At this point in the development of both the cognitive and psychodynamic–interpersonal traditions, I have to argue with Strauman and Segal's suggestion that cognitive theory offers a significant advance over previous perspectives on the self because it brings "a degree of testability which is often considerably greater." These statements may historically have held more water during an earlier era then dominated by an entrenched psychoanalytic establishment that often viewed research at best as irrelevant and unnecessary and at worst a sacrilegious intrusion into their private world of "self-obvious truths."

Insofar as the two approaches to the self might be judged currently on their relative empiricism and ability to generate and test hypotheses, I would like to make the following points. To begin, the intellectual honesty and rigor of attempting to operationalize and test one's theories—make them falsifiable—is certainly to be desired. However, empirical testability is a double-edged sword. Its pursuit per se may produce trivial knowledge and is no guarantee of anything. Nevertheless, in recent years the psychodynamic and interpersonal camps have made increasing attempts to test theory systematically (see Henry, Strupp, Schacht, & Gaston, 1994, for a review) and develop meaningful, stricter operational methods such as those associated with the applications of Benjamin's (1974) structural analysis of social behavior (SASB). I feel that, at present, the empirical methodologies of both approaches are relatively equivalent in their strengths and weaknesses (although these relative strengths and weaknesses might vary between approaches at times). As might be expected, each "side" sometimes produces important findings that advance our understanding, and sometimes produces a rather trivial set of "empirical" results—pro forma statistics with little external meaning of note. In addition, when it comes to the study of etiology and developmental psychopathology, both approaches do and will suffer from the same methodological problems associated with the reliability of retrospective self-reports, the use of paper-and-pencil methods and analogue populations, and so on.

Second, I believe that Strauman and Segal, in their zeal to present the cognitive position, have overstated several important points (and of course this may be a case of the pot calling the kettle black). First and foremost, I would question the suggestion that the cognitive position represents a major paradigm shift. The rise in cognition in social psychology can be traced to the 1920s. The cognitive self as described by Strauman and Segal rests on many, many different historical foundations, and a number of them are similar to the theoretical foundations of the interpersonal self. I think that the model of the cognitive self has added some new labels and language; offered a somewhat new context or perspective from which to view similar self-phenomena; provided a stimulus for concrete, manualized therapy protocols; and infused the clinical field with some "new" research methods (although, to be frank, many of these methods were largely borrowed from existing paradigms in social learning, social cognition, and animal behaviorism). Although all of these things are contributions, I do not think they represent a "paradigm shift"—just a logical continuation and expansion of an existing paradigm (which is the same thing I would say about my own model of the interpersonal self). To draw a tenuous analogy, saying that a person has a wish for autonomy is not a fundamental shift from saying he or she has a fear of control or dependence, although the language casts the phenomena in different contexts.

Finally, I would like to make a few observations about Strauman and Segal's presentation of the cognitive self and the challenges of postmodernism and psychotherapy because I feel that this was unfortunately the weakest part of the chapter. They fail to grapple with the effects that contemporary society may or may not be having on these hypothesized cognitive structures and operations. One problem that immediately comes to mind is how processes such as "matching to standard" and related discrepancy-reducing operations are affected by a postmodern era of ever-increasing, and perhaps equally valent, "standards." How would Gergen's (1991) notions of the "saturated self" be translated into cognitive terms, and with what effects? Cognitive theorists often use the term *information*. We are clearly in a period that has been described as a time of "information explosion." How are "information" and "meaning" conceptually related, and what impact (if any) does this have on the development and understanding of the cognitive self? In short, I think that Strauman and Segal did an admirable job of presenting and critiquing a pre-existing model of the cognitively based understanding of the self, but the links to postmodernism are tenuous and vague. I would like to have seen them address much more directly how they feel their model is unchanging across historical epochs versus affected by changing contemporary conditions, which must, of intellectual necessity, affect at least in some ways any social-learning-based model.

These omissions are particularly noticeable in the section on the implications of the cognitive self for psychotherapy. All I can say is that there was no mention of how postmodern ideas might challenge or affect the conduct of cognitive therapy. All therapies (like religions) likely have constant, unchanging ideas and components as well as those that are adjusted to fit changing social contexts and the needs of the people we are to serve. In today's society the adaptations and developments in analytic theory in the form of object relations, with an emphasis on structural deficits in the self as opposed to interior self-conflicts, make sense and fit well into postmodernism. I would like to hear more about what cognitive theorists think about societal changes as they relate to adjusting psychotherapeutic thinking within a similar overall approach to therapy. Additionally, I would like to have seen actual clinical transcripts and more theoretical justification for statements such as "an expanded or more coherent sense of self will be related to positive therapeutic outcomes."

Toward a Future Integration of Cognitive and Interpersonal Perspectives

I already discussed what I feel are the complementary process and content foci of the two positions, and this is an obvious starting point for integration. I further think that the potentially divisive debate about the relative primacy of cognition versus affect can, and should, be avoided. For the sake of new theory, I find it an artificial (if useful at times) distinction between higher order phenomena. I would replace the cognitive term *information* and attempt to develop a shared language and conceptual structure revolving around the term *meaning*, which I would roughly define as the direct apprehension of environmental stimuli as "knowledge," a primary process that is both unconsciously cognitive and affective in one way and neither in another because it is both.

Before I go any further, I must acknowledge that there are two basic questions regarding integration of the cognitive and interpersonal self models that must be asked: *why* and *how*? As to why, I can only point to an educated intuition that the two approaches are fundamentally compatible and together help fill in various gaps in a manner that leads to a more comprehensive, unified, and useful theory. As to how, I would suggest that a useful first step is to look at where both theories are weak in similar ways and explore whether an integration might address these mutual weaknesses. To me, the obvious starting point involves emotion, as I feel that both models fail to truly integrate in any real models of affect as related to models of self. The cognitive position may have made somewhat more strides in this direction (particularly in terms of depression), but I feel that the best either camp has to offer at the moment involves surface descriptions and vague, implied ties that are still lacking in true depth. The potential value of integration can be seen in Strauman and Segal's recognition that the relation between the self and affect is generally interpersonal in context and in that the literature suggests the relationship involves conflict and inconsistency—areas both addressed from different perspectives by the cognitive and interpersonal traditions.

The area of psychotherapy process and outcome research is another clear avenue for collaboration. I proposed in this volume and elsewhere (Henry & Strupp, 1994) that interpersonal process is a common factor across therapies and involves both direct change (by means of the introjection of therapist-offered process) and indirect change (by means of the activation of various introject states that enhance or impede the momentary process of self-relatedness and openness to change). Critchfield, Henry, Castonguay, and Borkovec (1999) recently completed a study of interpersonal process (measured by SASB) related to outcome in cognitive–behavioral therapy and compared it with previous similar research with dynamic–interpersonal therapy (Henry, Schacht, & Strupp, 1986, 1990). The results suggest that interpersonal process predicts outcome in cognitive–behavioral therapies as well as interpersonal therapies, although there may be some interesting specific differences in the predictors as related to the natures of each therapy. In short, although there is considerable common ground to explore, there are also potential differences between these two major approaches to therapy in regard to how interpersonal process operates. A careful consideration of both the similarities and differences may ultimately help proponents of each approach better understand unique and shared underlying mechanisms—that is, to better understand psychotherapy and self-change in general.

As Mahoney (1991) and others, such as Kuhn (1962), have eloquently stated, science is not just a disembodied set of data judged neutrally on its merits, and such data do not in turn automatically alter beliefs or what we perceive to be the facts. Cognitive theorists and therapists primarily read the cognitive and related literatures, as of course do those who identify with the interpersonal and psychodynamic positions. Rarely seen or heard are the majority of studies that are never published because they fail to support the pre-existing position of the authors or that simply "fail" to show any differences of whatever type (which is a finding). Even more rarely do researchers from different positions challenge themselves and their theories through joint research with those of different persuasions. It is time to do something different.

Volumes such as this one will remain interesting intellectual exercises read by a relative handful of academics and students, unless they inspire action. Action will have to involve specific individuals from both areas coming together out of mutual interest to pursue shared goals. To be frank, there is little in the "system"—be it in our graduate programs that increasingly will consist of training (not education) in a variety of treatment manuals, traditional academia and its politics of "science" and career advancement, research funding dictates, or the current therapeutic zeitgeist being forced by third-party payers—that will encourage this intellectual synergy. Yet I think that the spirit, the desire for this type of collaboration, is present among many and has never been higher.

References

Benjamin, L. S. (1974). Structural analysis of social behavior. *Psychological Review, 81,* 392–425.

Critchfield, K. C., Henry, W. P., Castonguay, L., & Borkovec, T. D. (1999). *Interpersonal process and outcome in cognitive–behavioral psychotherapy.* Unpublished manuscript, University of Utah.

Gergen, K. J. (1991). *The saturated self.* New York: Basic Books.

Henry, W. P., Schacht, T. E., & Strupp, H. H. (1986). Structural analysis of social behavior: Application to a study of interpersonal process in differential psychotherapeutic outcome. *Journal of Consulting and Clinical Psychology, 54,* 27–31.

Henry, W. P., Schacht, T. E., & Strupp, H. H. (1990). Patient and therapist introjects, interpersonal process, and differential psychotherapy outcome. *Journal of Consulting and Clinical Psychology, 58,* 768–774.

Henry, W. P., & Strupp, H. H. (1994). The therapeutic alliance as interpersonal process. In A. O. Horvath & L. S. Greenberg (Eds.), *The working alliance: Theory, research and practice* (pp. 51–84). New York: Wiley.

Henry, W. P., Strupp, H. H., Schacht, T. E., & Gaston, L. (1994). Psychodynamic approaches. In A. E. Bergin & A. L. Garfield (Eds.), *Handbook of psychotherapy and behavior change* (4th ed., pp. 467–508). New York: Wiley.

Kuhn, T. S. (1962). *The structure of scientific revolutions.* Chicago: University of Chicago Press.

Mahoney, M. J. (1991). *Human change processes: The scientific foundations of psychotherapy.* New York: Basic Books.

CHAPTER 11

Defining the Self in an Interpersonal Context

William P. Henry

Every day I get up, and at some point I find myself in front of a mirror, preparing for the day ahead. Like thousands of times before, I stare at something called *myself,* and this visage stares back at me. The reflection and I are in fact one and the same, are we not? Yet on some days, I smile and unconsciously renew an old friendly bond with this image, and on other days, I may feel oddly estranged. Is that *me?* This is an occurrence so common for us all that we scarcely pay it any mind, but it raises important questions— *whom* are we looking at, *what* do we see and feel, and *why?*

Paradoxically, the self looking at its reflection seems to be having an interpersonal encounter. Because only one person is present, who is talking to whom? We are of course talking to ourselves, but this "self" staring into the mirror is an interpersonal construction, a chorus of internalized voices accrued over a lifetime. Some days the voices chant in unison, and on other days they may resemble a rowdy, quarrelsome mob. Like actors in an ancient Greek play, we listen to, interact with, and are shaped by this unseen chorus. Our sense of identity is the phenomenological result, as these commentaries on our every move become our own thoughts—the conscious and unconscious dialogue that creates and maintains the self. We may find ourselves apart from others, but we are never alone.

The purpose of this chapter is to describe a view of the self as strictly the product of interpersonal interactions; their internalized representations; and the result of these representations in terms of emotions, cognitive expectancies, and interpersonal behavior. It includes the notions of the self as multiple and as contextually dependent. I consider the self as not an internally constrained thing but rather an interactive emergent process shaped by external social and contextual factors. I present elements of my own self-related theories as grounded in Lorna Benjamin's (1974) interpersonal circumplex system, the structural analysis of social behavior (SASB), and then place these ideas into a clinical framework by describing a generic interpersonal process model of psychotherapy and related research.

Across the last century, a number of theorists who differ in other ways have all emphasized a core perspective about the self, namely, that the self is largely or completely formed in the developmental cauldron of early interpersonal interactions with central caregivers, as the child seeks to lessen anxiety by attaching to or bonding with these protective, all-powerful figures (see Henry, 1997, for a more complete discussion). Furthermore, this self is typically maintained in a stable fashion across time because of the expectations and resultant repetitive, self-confirming patterns based on these early experiences. Through these interpersonal transactions, (a) we come to treat ourselves as we have been treated; (b) we learn behaviors through identification and imitation (behaviors that define the self to others and, through these others' reactions, to ourselves); and (c) we learn the "conditions of worth"—how we are expected to act, what we are expected to "be" if we are to achieve normal attachment drives and earn our birthright of love, acceptance, and protection.

To truly set the proper foundation for defining how an interpersonal self is a social or contextual construct, we need to ask a fundamental question: Is there a noninterpersonal self as well and, if so, what is it like, and how is it different? Space does not permit an elaborate exploration of this question. Nevertheless, I have come to believe for all intents and purposes that all self-related phenomena or experience must ultimately be seen within an interpersonal framework. I believe that concluding that the self—at least, pragmatically speaking—is purely interpersonal not only involves a crucial theoretical distinction but also contributes an important working principle for clinicians. This core belief provides a unifying heuristic to structure the vast amount of "material" a client provides to us in hopes of some relief from his or her distress. This material may be in the form of childhood recollections, current problems with significant others, in-session behaviors, emotional experiences, regrets, beliefs, expectancies, desires, fears, or goals. The important thing is that all of these may be translated in interpersonal terms into the ultimate clinical currency—an understanding of the client's phenomenology or sense of self. Furthermore, this sense of self may be understood within an operational framework (SASB) accompanied by a set of developmental and maintaining principles anchored to observable behavior.

An Interpersonal Model of the Self Based on the SASB

In this section, I first provide a brief summary of the SASB system (Benjamin, 1974) for those who are unfamiliar with it. I then sketch out the basics of my own theory of the interpersonal self as operationalized by means of the SASB system. These theoretical principles address the categorical distinction between normal and abnormal personality and provide a linked model of developmental psychopathology and adult disorders. Finally, I describe how these principles may be combined to form a structured, operationalized method of interpersonal case formulation (ICF) for clinical and research purposes.

SASB: A Brief Overview

SASB is an interpersonal circumplex system that is based on, but expands, Leary's (1957) original interpersonal circumplex (see Figure 11.1). In SASB, Surface 1 (focus on other) represents transitive actions by one person toward another, whereas Surface 2 (focus on self) describes intransitive or reactive behaviors by an individual. Both surfaces contain the same horizontal affiliation axis which, like Leary's, moves from hostile disaffiliation on the left to friendly affiliation on the right. When the focus is on actions toward another, the vertical interdependence dimension moves from autonomy granting at the top to controlling behavior at the bottom. When the focus is on the self, the reactive interdependence axis moves from autonomy taking or separation at the top to submission at the bottom. Benjamin also added a third surface: the introject, which theoretically represents Surface 1 actions by early significant others transformed to become actions by the self toward the self (e.g., self-acceptance, self-criticism, self-control).

The three-surface circumplex structure enables precise explanation and predictions of both interpersonal and intrapsychic behavior and theoretically links historical and ongoing interpersonal transactions to self-concept and symptom presentation. The explanatory and predictive principles drawn from interpersonal theory include the concepts of introjection, complementarity, and antithesis. *Introjection* refers to Sullivan's (1953) basic postulate that the self is composed of the reflective appraisals of others. The principle of *complementarity* states that interpersonal actions tend to "pull for" responses that are similar on each axis. In the case of SASB, friendliness pulls for friendliness, hostility pulls for hostility, dominance pulls for submission, and autonomy granting pulls for autonomy taking. The adult with a long history of being criticized as a child comes to expect criticism and acts in a manner that pulls for it, creating a self-fulfilling prophecy that confirms a stable introject. Combined, the principles of introjection and complementarity help theoretically to explain how early experiences transform into adult behavioral patterns (adaptive as well as maladaptive) and enable prediction of future behavior. The *antithesis* of a behavior is the opposite of its complement, located directly across from (at 180 degrees to) the complement on the circumplex. In other words, the antithesis is opposite on both the affiliation and interdependence dimensions. Theoretically, responding with antithetical behavior to any given interpersonal action or reaction by another produces the maximum pull for behavior change in the other person.

The SASB system may be used in different methodological ways and at

FIGURE 11.1

The structural analysis of social behavior circumplex system. From The INTREX User's Manual *(p. 6), by L. S. Benjamin, 2000. Copyright 2000 University of Utah. Reprinted with permission.*

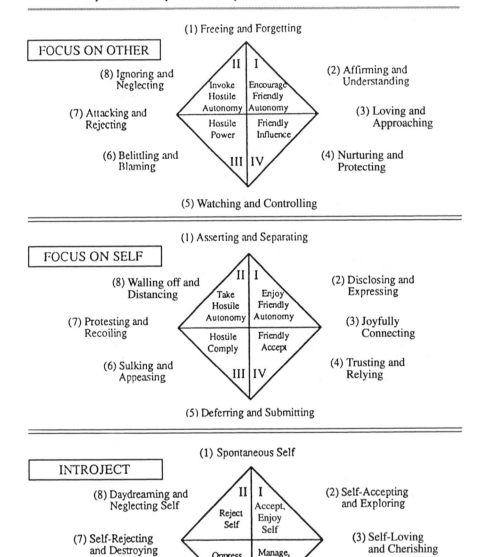

varying levels of measurement specificity. It may be used by independent raters to code ongoing interpersonal processes between or among individuals or to code the interpersonal content of the spoken dialogue. There is also a self-report version, the INTREX Questionnaire (Benjamin, 1983), which allows individuals to make ratings of any relationship (such as a current significant other, mother during childhood, or the introject—how the person acts toward him- or herself). These relationships may further be rated twice—in the perceived best and worst state of the relationship. The SASB system itself, regardless of the use to which it is put, may be used at varying levels of specificity. The full model contains 36 points around each circumplex surface, and the cluster model (the one typically used) collapses these 36 points into eight clusters. The simplest form of the model contains four quadrants on each surface. In short, the SASB system is quite flexible in terms of what can be measured, the perspective of the ratings, and the specificity of the codes.

An Interpersonal Model of Psychopathology: The Etiology of Normal and Abnormal Self Structures

Bowlby (1977, 1988) posited two basic and normative activities of the human infant: attachment seeking and exploration. These were seen as primary motivational forces despite the absence of primary drive reduction (such as food or sex). Once the child's primary attachment needs are satisfied, resulting in what Bowlby termed a *secure base*, the child is free to explore the environment (which has evolutionary survival value) before returning to renew the attachment bond. For the child to attach, a certain degree of availability and affiliation must be offered by the primary caretaker. For the child to explore, the attachment figure must permit some degree of autonomy. Attachment seeking and exploratory behaviors typically alternate in a balanced fashion in healthy infants.

These early experiences, centered on the twin drives of attachment (enmeshment) and exploration (differentiation), form the basis of personality, which may be defined interpersonally as "the mental operations associated with internal representations of self and others in interaction, and made manifest in interpersonal behavior" (Henry, 1994, p. 324; see also Benjamin, 1994). Three basic mechanisms are proposed as hypothetical constructs to explain how a child's early experiences are "copied" to determine these mental representations in interaction: (a) *identification*, which is hypothesized to be the process of acting like significant others through imitation; (b) *internalization*, which is hypothesized to be the process by which an abstract representation of the other forms and serves as a basis for interpersonal expectancies; and (c) *introjection*, which is hypothesized to be the mechanism by which the child comes to treat him- or herself as he or she has been treated by the other. The three SASB surfaces may be seen to correspond with these three proposed processes. Consistent with these hypotheses, Surface 1 actions by others form the basis of the object image identified with and hence may drive actions toward other people; internalized representations shape Surface 2 interpersonal reactions to others; and the introjected actions are measured by Surface 3.

In SASB language and theory, normal personality results when the interpersonal experiences that are transformed by these processes into internal representations come primarily from Clusters 2 (Affirmation), 3 (Active Love), and 4 (Protection). The 2–3–4 baseline (called the *attachment group*; Benjamin, 1994; Henry, 1994) is considered to define normalcy because it corresponds to the successful satisfaction of the basic drives or needs as proposed by attachment theory. That is, the interpersonal behaviors represented by the attachment-group clusters form a balance of moderate friendly enmeshment (permitting bonding) and moderate friendly differentiation (permitting exploration). Individuals with personality disorders do behave within the attachment group clusters at times, but more typically they display behaviors drawn from the *disrupted attachment group* (SASB Clusters 6 [Blame], 7 [Attack], and 8 [Abandonment]). In everyday language, excesses of interpersonal submission (overly enmeshed), distance (overly differentiated) and hostility (overly attacking) are hallmarks of disrupted attachment styles.

The contrasting baseline of manifest interpersonal behavior stemming from the attachment versus disrupted-attachment groups provides a qualitative distinction between normal and abnormal personality. Paradoxically, however, both normal and abnormal personalities are thought to develop from the same universal mechanisms (e.g., the internalization of interactions with important others while trying to satisfy the simultaneous aims of attachment and differentiation). Individuals with both normal and abnormal personalities also share the same basic set of wishes for affirmation, love, and protection and fears of blame, attack, and abandonment. However, individuals raised in an unhealthy interpersonal environment may come to fixate on specific wishes and fears that provide too narrow of a motivational prominence (such as fear of abandonment) for balanced, healthy interpersonal behavior. Because these central organizing wishes and fears are so rigidly fixed, and because interpersonal perception is skewed by toxic internalized representations, the resulting attachment-seeking behaviors are maladaptive. This model provides a general theoretical framework with which to categorize interpersonal problems based on the proposed innate motivational drives and predicts the interpersonal dimensionality of early experience and the interpersonal and intrapsychic dimensionality of presenting complaints or psychiatric disorders (see Florsheim, Henry, & Benjamin, 1996, for a fuller discussion of relational diagnoses based on these principles). In summary, SASB translates developmental experiences, presenting interpersonal complaints, and *Diagnostic and Statistical Manual of Mental Disorders* (e.g., 4th ed. [*DSM–IV*]; American Psychiatric Association [APA], 1994) descriptors (where they contain interpersonal content) into a common language and then theoretically links the past and present by means of the mechanisms of identification, internalization, and introjection.

Application to Psychotherapy and Research

The principle of problem–treatment–outcome congruence (PTO) states that the theoretical meaningfulness of psychotherapy research, as well as the ultimate ability to progressively advance knowledge by aggregating findings across studies, is a function of the congruence among how we define and measure patient problems (P), therapeutic change processes (T), and clinical outcomes (O; Strupp, Schacht, & Henry, 1988; also see Henry, 1996). The interpersonal model of self that was presented is ideally suited to follow this principle because it presents a unified theory and measurement metric (SASB) that spans these three areas. Carefully connecting a patient's problems with treatment interventions is obviously important for psychotherapy, and linking therapeutic processes with clinical outcomes in a direct manner is one of the chief aims of psychotherapy research. Putting it all together—from ideas about the definition and etiology of psychopathology to the results of treatment—is the theoretical goal.

In this section, I briefly present interpersonal case formulation (ICF; Henry, 1997) as a method for systematically arriving at a comprehensive understanding of an individual's interpersonal patterns and self-concept and the mechanisms that create and sustain them. Next, I describe a generic interpersonal model of therapeutic process that may be linked to the ICF. Finally, research methods and selected research findings based on the interpersonal model of self as operationalized by means of SASB are presented.

ICF: Modeling How the Self Is Sustained

The traditional psychiatric nomenclature, *DSM–IV*, places what may be seen as disorders of the self (from the distorted self-perceptions associated with conditions such as depression or eating disorders to the more obviously self-related personality disorders) into categorical diagnoses based on a list of symptomatic descriptors. However, by design, these diagnostic labels do not address the etiology or the sustaining conditions of the problem state; that is, they do not address the process of the problem, and it is these processes—from development to current maintaining factors—that most clinicians seek to understand. ICF was developed to provide a structured, empirically replicable and comprehensive understanding of a patient's presenting problems in interpersonal terms (see Figure 11.2). Compared with traditional psychodynamically based formulation schemes (including object relational–interpersonal variants), it places

FIGURE 11.2

Interpersonal model of cyclic psychopathology. From "Differentiating Normal and Abnormal Personality: An Interpersonal Approach Based on the Structural Analysis of Social Behavior" (p. 330), by W. P. Henry, 1994, in S. Strack and M. Lorr, **Differentiating Normal and Abnormal Personality.** *New York: Springer. Copyright 1994 by Springer. Reprinted with permission.*

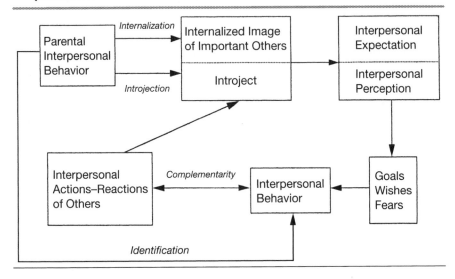

more immediate emphasis on transactional patterns as reflected in observable, conscious interpersonal behaviors.

As can be seen, ICF links categories of interpersonal behavior (including the actual acts of historical and current significant others, expectations of future interpersonal behaviors by others, salient motivational wishes and fears, and resulting acts of the self) to the formation and continued maintenance of the interpersonal self, or introject. These categories (which group conceptually related interpersonal processes) are linked causally through the developmental copy processes discussed earlier (identification, internalization–recapitulation, and introjection) and the ongoing processes of interpersonal complementarity and reintrojection of contemporary transactions with significant others.

Psychotherapy as an Interpersonal Process

The next step in using an SASB-based, PTO-congruent, interpersonal model of the self is to explicate a general model of psychotherapy based on the theories of interpersonal psychopathology and change presented. One possible general model is an interpersonal reformulation of Orlinsky and Howard's (1986) generic model of psychotherapy (see Figure 11.3). This model, which is consistent

FIGURE 11.3

Interpersonal adaptation of the generic process model. From "Process and Outcome in Psychotherapy, by D. E. Orlinsky and K. I. Howard, in S. L. Garfield and A. E. Bergin (Eds.), Handbook of Psychotherapy and Behavior Change (3rd ed.), 1986, New York: Wiley. Copyright 1986 by Wiley. Reprinted with permission.

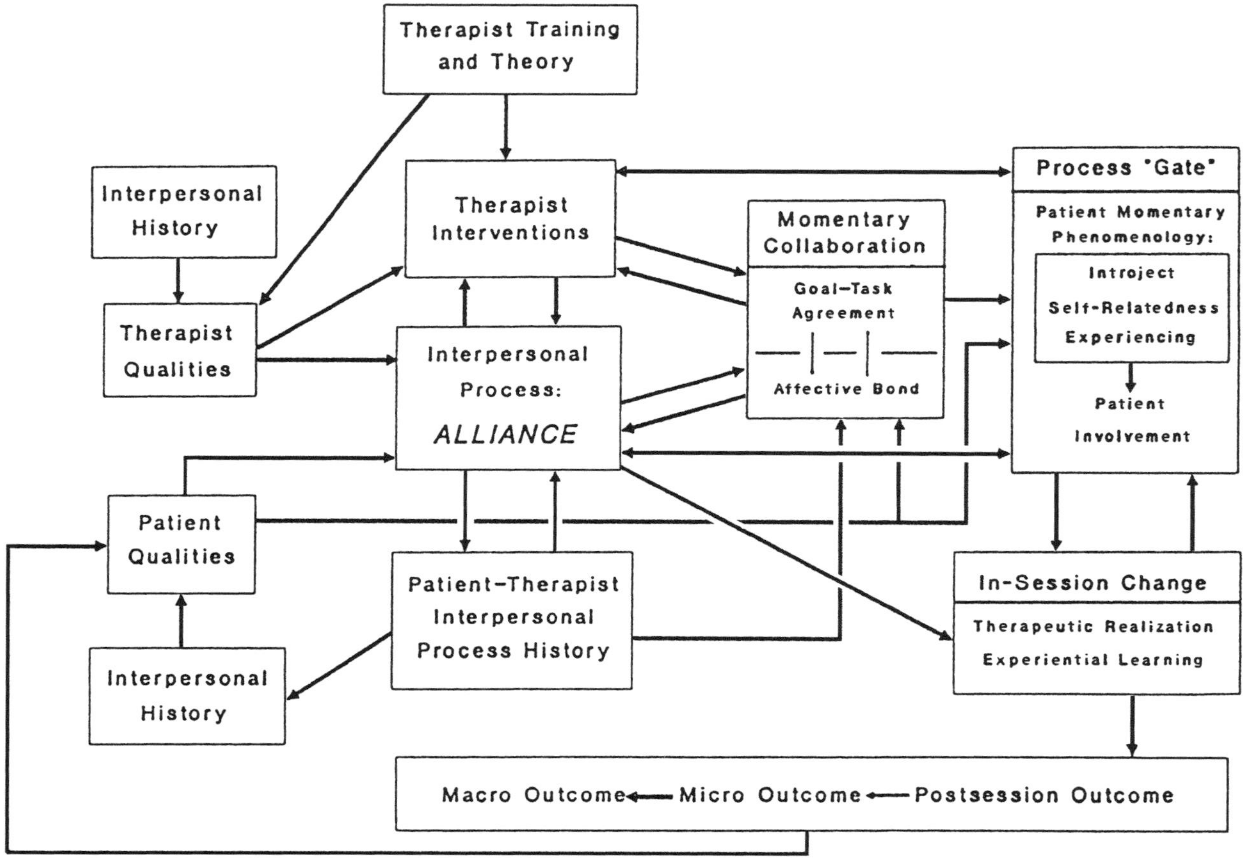

Process "Gate"

Patient Momentary Phenomenology:

Introject
Self-Relatedness
Experiencing

Patient Involvement

In-Session Change

Therapeutic Realization
Experiential Learning

Momentary Collaboration

Goal-Task Agreement

Affective Bond

Therapist Training and Theory

Therapist Interventions

Interpersonal Process: *ALLIANCE*

Patient-Therapist Interpersonal Process History

Interpersonal History

Therapist Qualities

Patient Qualities

Interpersonal History

Macro Outcome ⟵ Micro Outcome ⟵ Postsession Outcome

with all of the theoretical propositions related to the formation and maintenance of the interpersonal self, contains the following core features (see Henry & Strupp, 1994, for a complete overview):

- The interpersonal process in the patient–therapist dyad is the therapeutic relationship or alliance, and the alliance so conceived is a sufficient condition for direct therapeutic change by means of the mechanism of introjection of the therapist-offered process. The function of interpersonal process is a specific mechanism that nonetheless serves as a common factor across therapies.

- This process requires that both patient and therapist possess certain qualities. The therapist must be able to establish the facilitating conditions of a good parent and provide an affiliative balance of enmeshment and differentiation (or teaching–protection and affirmation). To achieve this goal, the therapist must communicate in a straightforward manner that is free of complex messages and free of communications that inadvertently entrench the patient's negative introject by mirroring early pathological interpersonal processes. The ability to provide these conditions is mediated by the therapist's own interpersonal history and current introject state. The quality of the patient's early relationships (in the absence of later ameliorative reintrojection) determines the extent to which his or her introject is rigid and entrenched and hence the degree to which it is malleable by contemporary interpersonal process with the therapist.

- Interpersonal process also serves a mediating role to enhance or reduce the effectiveness of other therapeutic interventions. If the patient has the capacity to form an affectional bond, and if the interpersonal process has been facilitative, then the patient's attachment to the therapist provides a secure base. Just as the secure base allows the infant to explore the environment physically, the therapeutic secure base may allow the patient to explore intrapsychically, try new behaviors, consider alternative construals of the world, and so on.

- Even after a therapeutic secure base has been established, dyadic interpersonal transactions may either facilitate or impede the therapeutic process at any specific time by activating different momentary introject states. For example, therapist process that is unexpectedly accepting might activate a positive introject (SASB Cluster 3–2: Self-Acceptance), furthering openness, whereas an intervention that was simply off the mark might be perceived as abandonment and activate a self-neglecting introject (SASB Cluster 3–8), hampering patient self-relatedness.

- The specific content or goals of therapy are shaped by an understanding of (a) the ICF as it relates to the broader distinctions of attachment and differentiation failure (or excesses/deficits in enmeshment and autonomy) and (b) how these maladaptive patterns relate to the internalized representations of early important figures.

- Theoretically, the patient's interpersonal cyclical maladaptive pattern can be successfully changed by any or all of the following mechanisms: (a) direct reintrojection by means of the therapeutic process, (b) changed perceptions or expectancies of others' behavior that result in different Surface 1 and 2 actions and reactions by the patient (which in turn pull for changed actions and reactions by important others by means of the principle of complementarity), (c) changes in the interpersonal wishes and fears that motivate and organize maladaptive levels of enmeshment and differentiation.

- There are many possible therapeutic techniques through which these change mechanisms may be brought into play. These techniques may theoretically be drawn from any number of different approaches to therapy. For example, behavioral skills training may enhance a patient's ability to enact different interpersonal behaviors resulting in changed patterns of complementarity with others. Cognitive techniques may directly challenge interpersonal perceptions and expectancies that drive a cyclical maladaptive pattern. Psychodynamic techniques, such as transference interpretations, may provide valuable experiential learning and insight that alter rigid expectancies and enable different interpersonal behaviors to be tried outside of therapy.

In their generic model of psychotherapy process, Orlinsky and Howard (1986) placed considerable weight on the concept of patient "self-relatedness," a momentary state of openness versus defensiveness that serves a crucial "gating" function that regulates the patient's ability to assimilate and accommodate therapeutic interventions and to work collaboratively. In an interpersonal version of the generic model, patient self-relatedness is seen in large part as a momentary introject state that is influenced by four factors (see Figure 11.3): the specific content of the therapist's intervention, pre-existing patient qualities (such as defensive structure, interpersonal history), the interpersonal process underlying the intervention, and the state of momentary collaboration. Interpersonal process is hypothesized to be central because it is linked to each factor governing the patient's momentary state of openness to the therapeutic change process. SASB provides a powerful unifying conceptual language and research tool because each of these four factors may be expressed in terms of the SASB model.

Research Applications

The models and theories of the development of the self; the nature of psychopathology, ICF, and intervention; and the generic model of psychotherapy process based on interpersonal theory were all designed to be conceptually consistent and interlinked. SASB has promoted this conceptual integration by providing a concrete heuristic system that operationalizes all of the basic principles associated with a comprehensive theory of the interpersonal self. The SASB system may be used for research on the interpersonal self and its origins in five general ways: (a) independent raters may use the system to precisely describe the ongoing interpersonal process between two or more people in any setting; (b) the interpersonal processes described in the content of dialogue may be rated; (c) the self-report version of SASB, the INTREX Questionnaire (Benjamin, 1983), may be used to measure the interpersonal perceptions of a participant in any relationship (e.g., historical perceptions, such as those relating to the patient's parents, or contemporary ones, such as those relating to a spouse or a sibling) with another in four ways (how the person sees the other as acting toward him or her, how the other reacts to him or her, how the person acts toward the other, and how he or she reacts to the other); (4) the Intrex may also be used to chart an individual's introject (how the self acts toward the self) in best and worst states; and (5) an ICF, intervention strategies, and therapeutic outcome may all be understood and described completely in terms of interpersonal processes and their internal representations.

Measuring Interpersonal Process: An Example

To give the reader a more concrete sense of how the SASB system is used to describe and understand interpersonal process, the following brief exchange from an individual therapy session is presented. The transcript is broken up into *thought units* (any part of speech, usually a sentence or less, that expresses one complete thought), which are used for SASB process analysis and ICF. This passage is taken from the first 15 minutes of the third session of a time-limited (25-session) therapy. Although clearly depressed, the patient's behavior throughout most of the preceding sessions was histrionic, and her affect was shallow. However, in the passage below she began to display deepened negative affect. The passage begins at the end of a long, very self-critical passage during which the patient was berating herself for the manner in which she interacts with her children.

> Patient: I hate it mostly for my kids/. . . see I can't like it for, I can't hate it for me,/ but when I see the way that I react (imitates crying noises) . . . when I see the way that I react to my kids I just hate it,/ because I don't want them to have a nerd for a mom./

> Therapist: Well, the things you're saying I'm not surprised to hear,/ just there I sort of sensed them about you,/ that you, to put it in terms of my own behavior, when I think about you I've wondered now what do I do?/ Do I keep a lot of safety in this process

by not taking her too seriously, any more seriously than she takes herself,/ and keep this manageable so that she can find her own pace with this?/ Or, and I'm really not sure this is a valid distinction,/ but it's what my thoughts have been,/ do I take her as seriously as I want to and take the risk of scaring you away from this./ That may be, I'm sure there are a lot of other choices about how to behave, but it seems very frequently to come down to those two for me./ I'm inclined to do the latter./ The fear that I would have is that that would imply, that would be more scary and threatening and more difficult and more disruptive for you than to sort of so therapy which is the other./ To act like a therapist, say therapeutic things . . . /

Patient: (laughs) Now you sound like [my husband].

This is a case in which the patient's self-critical and self-ignoring introject as reported at the start of therapy did not improve, and in fact deterioration was noted on some measures. This passage was selected as an example of how the therapist (while speaking in a gentle, understanding tone) unwittingly engaged in an interpersonal process that theoretically would confirm the patient's negative self structure.

The patient's interpersonal stance is basically affiliative, and autonomous as she self-discloses with the focus on her self (Cluster 2–2: Disclosing and Expressing), and also self-indicting and blaming on the intrapsychic surface (Cluster 3–6: Self-Indicting and Oppressing). The therapist's response contains a number of complex communications that simultaneously convey different interpersonal processes. The surface form of his process seems friendly, autonomous, and self-disclosing (Cluster 2–2: Disclosing and Expressing) as he speaks in an open manner about his experiences with the patient with the twin affiliative intent of interpretive instruction (Cluster 1–4: Nurturing and Protecting). However, he chooses to comment on the patient's statement in a manner that primarily emphasizes *his* problems with her, ignoring her obvious distress in the service of an extended, confusing intellectualized dialogue with himself ostensibly focused on her (Cluster 1–8: Ignoring and Neglecting). Additionally, he states that he agrees with her assessment of herself (which is very self-critical) and goes on to essentially tell her that he feels he cannot do "real therapy" because she won't be able to tolerate it.

The therapist's response is thus a complex mixture of attempting to nurture and help, while simultaneously blaming and ignoring the patient. This rather rambling, unpredictable mixture of interpersonal processes, coded as SASB Clusters 4, 6, and 8, is one of the most toxic mixes, one that Benjamin (1993) believed to be at the core of serious Axis II diagnoses such as borderline personality disorder (and indeed, this patient manifested many signs of this interpersonal self structure). I find this passage so interesting, for several reasons.

The casual listener might first be struck by the therapist's sincere, soothing, and genuine tone of voice as he attempts to self-disclose in seeming service of the patient. This therapist statement also follows on the heels of the patient's initial contact with deeper layers of emotion and experiencing and thus may be particularly important in the unique history of this dyad. Unfortunately, the patient responds to this complex communication with a complementary complex communication of her own, as predicted by interpersonal theory. She initially smiles and laughs, an affiliative interpersonal gesture that is relatively neutral in terms of the control dimension (Cluster 2–3: Joyfully Connecting) and complements the friendly part of the therapist's complex communication. She then goes on to utter one brief, damning statement, indicating that the therapist sounds just like her husband. Given the context of how she feels about her husband, this statement is rather easily seen to indicate that the therapist "doesn't get it" (like her husband) and also represents a countercriticism toward the therapist. It is interesting that after this exchange, the patient goes on to increase the level of her self-blaming statements, which indicates that this brief process has only entrenched her negative interpersonal self (and likely done so through very similar interpersonal processes that helped create her self-structure historically).

Research Support

1. There is accumulating evidence that the interpersonal self as reflected in the concept of the introject is directly affected by the ongoing therapist-offered interpersonal process in therapy. Well-trained, experienced professional therapists using similar technical strategies tend to engage in markedly different interpersonal processes in their good- and bad-outcome cases with similarly diagnosed patients (Henry, Schacht, & Strupp, 1986). The therapists show surprisingly high levels of hostile and complex process, and this process seems directly linked to introject change, or lack thereof, as predicted by theory (Henry et al., 1986; Henry, Schacht, & Strupp, 1990).

2. The therapists' own introjects have been linked with their tendencies toward problematic interpersonal process (Henry et al., 1990). For example, therapists with hostile, controlling introjects (self-critical) tend to be more critical toward their patients, and their patients in turn make more self-critical statements.

3. There is evidence not only for the intrapsychic processes of the self but also for the principles governing the interpersonal exchanges that reflect, create, and re-create the self. The most im-

portant principle, complementarity, seems to hold true even in therapy. Although therapists are ideally supposed to be able to refrain from complementing negative patient interpersonal behaviors, typically they do not, and often they actually initiate the negative process sequences (Henry et al., 1986, 1990; Hilliard, 1995). Even relatively small amounts of this negative interpersonal complementarity early in therapy seem sufficient to lead to poor outcome in most cases that have been studied.

4. Recently, more comprehensive segments of the interpersonal process model of therapy have been tested for direct and mediational effects on outcome as measured in several ways (Hilliard, Henry, & Strupp, 1999). A three-step path model was constructed that combined: (a) interpersonal history (patient and therapist INTREX self-reports of their relationships with their parents when they were children), (b) interpersonal process early in therapy (as seen from three sources: independent raters and patient and therapist self-reports), and (c) therapeutic outcome (as measured in terms of introject change as well as other global and symptom measures). Both direct and mediational links were found. The patients' interpersonal histories did have a direct effect on outcome (symptom change) and independent mediational effect on outcome by means of interpersonal process. The therapists' interpersonal histories also affected outcome (symptom change and global change ratings), but primarily this was a mediational effect by means of process. Finally, independent ratings of the process were the only source that predicted patient introject change.

5. Although the majority of therapies studied have been psychodynamic–interpersonal (a context within which one might expect interpersonal-process factors to have a particularly strong effect), similar SASB process analyses have recently been used to examine interpersonal process–outcome links in other approaches. Critchfield, Henry, Castonguay, and Borkovec (1999) demonstrated substantially similar effects of interpersonal process on outcome in cognitive–behavior therapy for generalized anxiety disorder. Thus, there is at least some initial evidence supporting the idea that the interpersonal-process model of psychotherapy does represent a common factor or change process across different theoretical approaches to psychotherapy. In turn, this strengthens the case for viewing the psychotherapy as the process of changing the interpersonal self.

Conclusion

The ideas presented about the nature and formation of the interpersonal self potentially incorporate any number of the basic existing theories about the importance of early social learning as well as the maintenance of problem cycles in the present. Paradoxically, the conceptual structure provided by an operationalized interpersonal definition of self provides a coherent theory, while at the same time it leaves open any number of specific interventions in therapy drawn from a number of traditions (e.g., cognitive, behavioral, dynamic, experiential). Furthermore, the present model embodies several ironies: (a) postmodern views of the self (e.g., those concerning multiplicity and contextualism) are explicable within a historical context of interpersonal theories that extend so far back that they do not necessarily demand any new set of theories or psychotherapeutic approaches, and (b) although postmodern intellectual viewpoints often lead to ideas about self-formation that are highly contextual and subjective, these ideas may be easily contained within a broader theoretical framework that is ordered and universally applicable.

The challenges for the future involve unlocking the mechanisms that govern the individually determined differential adoption of the three copy processes as related to specific significant others during development. Why is one person's self structure based almost completely on the introjection of one parent versus the other? Why do we identify with and hence act like certain interpersonal figures while reacting continuously to distorted expectations based on another? These basic issues are, of course, confounded by postmodern concerns of social contextualism and constructionism, the intersubjective relationship among multiple selves, and so on. These are the true postmodern challenges—the unexplored mechanisms through which these phenomena operate within a traditionally conceived model of the interpersonal self. In and of themselves at a surface level, these so-called postmodern challenges constitute primarily a battle against a compelling but simplistic intellectual nihilism as applied to the self. At a deeper level, however, these challenges should force us to dig deeper into the expansion and refinement of our existing interpersonal conceptions of self —into the uncharted territory of the differential mechanisms operating within the framework of general principles.

References

American Psychiatric Association. (1994). *Diagnostic and statistical manual of mental disorders* (4th ed.). Washington, DC: Author.

Benjamin, L. S. (1974). Structural analysis of social behavior. *Psychological Review, 81,* 392–425.

Benjamin, L. S. (1983). *The INTREX user's manual, Parts I and II.* (Available from University of Utah, Department of Psychology, Salt Lake City, UT 84112)

Benjamin, L. S. (1993). *Interpersonal diagnosis and treatment of personality disorders.* New York: Guilford Press.

Benjamin, L. S. (1994). Good defenses make good neighbors. In H. R. Conte & R. Plutchik (Eds.), *Ego defenses: Theory and measurement* (pp. 53–78). New York: Wiley.

Benjamin, L. S. (2000). *The INTREX user's manual.* Salt Lake City: University of Utah.

Bowlby, J. (1977). The making and breaking of affectional bonds: I. Aetiology and psychopathology in the light of attachment theory. *British Journal of Psychiatry, 130,* 201–210.

Bowlby, J. (1988). *A secure base: Parent–child attachment and healthy human development.* New York: Basic Books.

Critchfield, K. C., Henry, W. P., Castonguay, L., & Borkovec, T. D. (1999). *Interpersonal process and outcome in cognitive–behavioral psychotherapy.* Unpublished manuscript, University of Utah, Salt Lake City.

Florsheim, P., Henry, W. P., & Benjamin, L. S. (1996). Integrating individual and interpersonal approaches to diagnosis: The structural analysis of social behavior and attachment theory. In F. W. Kaslow (Ed.), *Handbook of relational diagnosis and dysfunctional family patterns* (pp. 81–101). New York: Wiley.

Henry, W. P. (1994). Differentiating normal and abnormal personality: An interpersonal approach based on the structural analysis of social behavior. In S. Strack & M. Lorr (Eds.), *Differentiating normal and abnormal personality* (pp. 316–340). New York: Springer.

Henry, W. P. (1996). Structural analysis of social behavior as a common metric for programmatic psychopathology and psychotherapy research. *Journal of Consulting and Clinical Psychology, 64,* 1263–1275.

Henry, W. P. (1997). Interpersonal case formulation: Describing and explaining interpersonal patterns using the structural analysis of social behavior. In T. D. Eells (Ed.), *Handbook of psychotherapy case formulation* (pp. 223–259). New York: Guilford Press.

Henry, W. P., Schacht, T. E., & Strupp, H. H. (1986). Structural analysis of social behavior: Application to a study of interpersonal process in differential psychotherapeutic outcome. *Journal of Consulting and Clinical Psychology, 54,* 27–31.

Henry, W. P., Schacht, T. E., & Strupp, H. H. (1990). Patient and therapist introject, interpersonal process, and differential psychotherapy outcome. *Journal of Consulting and Clinical Psychology, 58,* 768–774.

Henry, W. P., & Strupp, H. H. (1994). The therapeutic alliance as interpersonal process. In A. O. Horvath & L. S. Greenberg (Eds.), *The working alliance: Theory, research and practice* (pp. 51–84). New York: Wiley.

Hilliard, R. B. (1995). *Disaffiliative interpersonal process in psychotherapy.* Unpublished doctoral dissertation, Vanderbilt University, Nashville, TN.

Hilliard, R. B., Henry, W. P., & Strupp, H. H. (1999). *An interpersonal model of psychotherapy: Linking patient and therapist developmental history, therapeutic process, and types of outcome.* Unpublished manuscript, Vanderbilt University, Nashville, TN.

Leary, T. (1957). *Interpersonal diagnosis of personality: A functional theory and methodology for personality evaluation.* New York: Ronald Press.

Orlinsky, D. E., & Howard, K. I. (1986). Process and outcome in psychotherapy. In S. L. Garfield & A. E. Bergin (Eds.), *Handbook of psychotherapy and behavior change* (3rd ed., pp. 311–381). New York: Wiley.

Strupp, H. H., Schacht, T. E., & Henry, W. P. (1988). Problem–treatment–outcome congruence: A principle whose time has come. In H. Dahl & H. Kachele (Eds.), *Psychoanalytic process research strategies* (pp. 1–14). New York: Springer.

Sullivan, H. S. (1953). *The interpersonal theory of psychiatry.* New York: Norton.

COMMENT:

What's Interpersonal Is Cognitive and What's Cognitive Is Interpersonal

Timothy J. Strauman
Zindel V. Segal

> It is much easier to *feel* the self than to *define* the self. (Allport, 1961, emphasis added)

William Henry's chapter "Defining the Self in an Interpersonal Context" offers a compelling and refreshingly broad view of the self from an interpersonal perspective. It is an enjoyable task for us to contemplate the ideas presented in his chapter in the context of our own cognitively oriented perspective on the self. In this commentary, we discuss the convergences between cognitive and interpersonal perspectives on the self as behavioral science enters its 3rd century of the study of the self. We focus on the following points: (a) metaphors as starting points for scientific investigation, (b) the emerging correspondence between interpersonal and social–cognitive perspectives on the self, and (c) directions for future research (basic and clinical).

Metaphors and Starting Points

Henry noted that different approaches to the self frequently involve the use of different metaphors for the self. Coming from an interpersonal perspective, he uses the metaphor of the "Greek chorus"—"this 'self' staring into the mirror is an interpersonal construction, a chorus of internalized voices accrued over a lifetime." This metaphor captures succinctly the experiential, identity, and stability–instability dimensions explored by self researchers. Indeed, using such a metaphor as a starting point for investigation brings into relief a number of important issues, many of which are explored (or at least implied) in Henry's chapter. For example, how is it that people maintain a sense of identity across all the different eras and circumstances of their lives? How are people's experiences with others (particularly parents and caregivers) assimilated into their developing selves? Which one of the many different "selves" is really in charge? Which ones should the therapist address?

What is striking to us is not the metaphor itself—the starting point for scientific inquiry—but rather where it has led interpersonally oriented research. To use Henry's own description, the interpersonal approach involves a "view of the self as strictly the product of interpersonal interactions; their internalized representations; and the result of these representations in terms of emotions, cognitive expectancies, and interpersonal behavior." This description is remarkable both because of its comprehensiveness and, more important because it would fit equally well in a chapter on the self from a cognitive perspective. The convergence between interpersonal and social–cognitive perspectives on the self is both inevitable and desirable; that is, the choice of metaphor may have determined how investigators began to seek answers to questions about the self, but over time those investigations have begun to coalesce.

What Is Cognitive Is Interpersonal

Researchers in social cognition—following in the footsteps of the cognitive revolution of the 1960s and 1970s—adopted a different metaphor for the self: the computer. For instance, Kihlstrom and Cantor (1984) declared that

> we define the self as one's mental representation of oneself, no different in principle from mental representations that a person has concerning other ideas, objects, and events and their attributes and implications. In other words, the self is a concept, not unlike other concepts, that is stored in memory as a knowledge structure, not unlike other knowledge structures. (p. 12)

Naturally, this approach made it easier to study certain aspects of selfhood, such as self-knowledge and self-referential information processing, but was not necessarily a good gestalt fit with other aspects of the self.

One particular limitation of the computer metaphor was in the area of self and affect. A number of investigators endeavored to account for the inherent links between self and emotion (as well as psychopathology) using principles of information processing. For instance, Ortony, Clore, and Collins (1988) proposed that "to say that emotions arise from cognition is to say that they are determined by the structure, content, and organization of knowledge representations and the processes that operate on them" (p. 10). However, as argued elsewhere (e.g., Segal, 1988; Strauman & Higgins, 1987, 1988), "cold" information-processing models do not explain the role of the self in vulnerability to psychopathology, both because they are insufficiently sensitive to developmental and interpersonal aspects of the self and because it is extremely difficult to link higher order cognitive processes with the neurophysiology of emotion.

Thus, a major contribution of the interpersonal approach to the self is the ability to account for the affectivity of selfhood. Theorists such as Sullivan (1953), Bowlby (1977), and Benjamin (1993) combined developmental observation with clinical experience to propose models for how the emotional consequences of early relationships with significant others are internalized and form an important component of the self throughout life. Bowlby's model in particular, in which innate needs for nurturance and security drive the young child's acquisition of self-knowledge and internalization of "working models" of significant relations, provides a critical bridge between self and emotion. Henry's recent investigations document an ambitious program of research to refine the interpersonal perspective on the self and build a systematic treatment approach. It is these findings that lead us to propose that what is "cognitive" about the self is inherently interpersonal.

What Is Interpersonal Is Cognitive

Just as cognitive approaches to the self have relative strengths and weaknesses, so interpersonal approaches are better able to capture certain self phenomena than others. One aspect of selfhood that cognitive approaches, in our view, have more successfully addressed is *self as representation*. Interpersonal theorists from Sullivan to the present have incorporated concepts such as expectancies to describe how individuals anticipate specific patterns of interactions with significant others and interpret ambiguous social stimuli in predictable (if not always accurate) ways. The challenge, of course, is to determine both what is represented (content) and how the representations influence perception, affect, and behavior (process). It is here that the cognitive perspective excels and here that behavioral science has much to offer psychotherapy.

In our opinion, the cognitive perspective owes much to the writings of Kelly (1955), whose personal construct theory of personality anticipated many of the best features of contemporary social–cognitive self theory. Kelly proposed that interpersonal expectancies (by which individuals construe both who they are and the meaning of others' behaviors) are fundamental aspects of the self. It is interesting that a number of Kelly's mentors were social psychologists, and Kelly himself acknowledged a formative influence of social constructionism and interpersonal psychiatry on his theorizing. These trends lead us to propose, in concert with Henry's definition, that what is "interpersonal" about the self is inherently cognitive.

Convergences and Unanswered Questions

The fact that convergence can be observed across theorists as different as James, Kelly, Sullivan, Bowlby, and so on—and across research traditions as distinct as social cognition and the interpersonal circumplex—should provide a sense of nurturance and security for self researchers. More important, each tradition offers useful ideas for psychotherapeutic intervention. Two examples follow.

1. If the self is *cognitive*, then much of what is known about social information processing may be applicable to the role of the self in vulnerability to psychopathology. For instance, the tendency for motivationally significant beliefs or attitudes to be activated unconsciously (without the individual's awareness or deliberate intention) should be manifest strongly among self-beliefs. Bargh and Chartrand (1999) demonstrated many such phenomena both in clinical and nonclinical populations and proposed that the role of unintended self-referential cognition is broader than has been conceptualized in many theories of psychopathology.

2. If the self is *interpersonal*, then attending to the expectations of others should activate an individual's sense of self (and lead to a process of self-evaluation with potential positive or negative emotional consequences). Andersen and Berk (1998) reported that actual or imagined interactions with others led to activation of patterns of beliefs (*transference*, in the language of traditional psychotherapy) in direct proportion to the similarity of others with one's parents, partners, friends, and so on.

These examples are only a sample of the richness of cognitive and interpersonal self theory for understanding how psychotherapy works and how to make it work for particular individuals. Nonetheless, there are important unanswered questions with regard to self and psychotherapy. We believe that a combined cognitive–interpersonal perspective on the self can generate testable, clinically relevant hypotheses addressing critical issues such as What is represented within the self? Do self-representations vary according to the developmental stage at which they were acquired? How does the self maintain its stability? Does psychotherapy change the self? If so, how does it change the self?

Do other forms of treatment (e.g., medication) also alter the self? Our hope is that continuing cross-fertilization between social–cognitive and interpersonal theories of the self will lead to more effective interventions and a fuller understanding of what it means to be, possess, and experience the self.

References

Allport, G. W. (1961). *Pattern and growth in personality.* New York: Holt, Rinehart, & Winston.

Andersen, S. M., & Berk, M. S. (1998). Transference in everyday experience: Implications of experimental research for relevant clinical phenomena. *Review of General Psychology, 2,* 81–120.

Bargh, J. A., & Chartrand, T. L. (1999). The unbearable automaticity of being. *American Psychologist, 54,* 462–479.

Benjamin, L. S. (1993). *Interpersonal diagnosis and treatment of personality disorders.* New York: Guilford Press.

Bowlby, J. (1977). The making and breaking of affectional bonds: I. Aetiology and psychopathology in the light of attachment theory. *British Journal of Psychiatry, 130,* 201–210.

Kelly, G. A. (1955). *The psychology of personal constructs.* New York: Norton.

Kihlstrom, J. F., & Cantor, N. (1984). Mental representations of the self. In L. Berkowitz (Ed.), *Advances in experimental social psychology* (Vol. 17, pp. 1–47). New York: Academic Press.

Ortony, A., Clore, G., & Collins, A. (1988). *The cognitive structure of emotions.* New York: Cambridge University Press.

Segal, Z. V. (1988). Appraisal of the self-schema construct in cognitive models of depression. *Psychological Bulletin, 103,* 147–162.

Strauman, T. J., & Higgins, E. T. (1987). Automatic activation of self-discrepancies and emotional syndromes: When cognitive structures influence affect. *Journal of Personality and Social Psychology, 53,* 1004–1014.

Strauman, T. J., & Higgins, E. T. (1988). Self-discrepancies as predictors of vulnerability to distinct syndromes of chronic emotional distress. *Journal of Personality, 56,* 685–707.

Sullivan, H. S. (1953). *The interpersonal theory of psychiatry.* New York: Norton.

CHAPTER 12

Functional Contextualism and the Self

Steven C. Hayes
Jennifer Gregg

The purpose of this chapter is to describe an approach to issues of the self from within a functional contextual framework. *Functional contextualism* is our name for a particular type of pragmatic scientific philosophy rooted in the functional analytic wing of behavioral psychology. So that the reader may understand our approach to the self, we describe what we mean by functional contextualism and lay out a series of empirical concepts on which our analysis is based. Finally, we address the self in the context of this orientation.

A Functional Contextual Approach to Self-Knowledge

A functional contextual approach to the self builds on the traditional behavior-analytic approach to self-knowledge. The traditional position is a fairly straight-forward extension of the core behavior-analysis view of private events. The basic idea is that we know about our ourselves, both in the public and private realms, because such knowledge is systematically taught by the social–verbal com-munity: "Self-knowledge is of social origin. It is only when a person's private world becomes important to others that it is made important to him. It then enters into the control of the behavior called knowing" (Skinner, 1974, p. 31).

Furthermore, once we are aware (in this verbal sense) of what we do, feel, and think, we are also made aware that we are aware. Again, the traditional position is also straightforward, if a bit vague: This is directly taught. Using the example of seeing, Skinner (1988) claimed that "there are no natural contin-gencies for such behavior. We learn to see that we are seeing only because a verbal community arranges for us to do so" (p. 286).

These ideas are core concepts in an approach to the self and, although we agree with their general thrust, we think their vague quality reveals a funda-mental deficit. Explaining the nature of this deficit takes some time, but a good place to begin is Skinner's (1974) claim that "self-knowledge has a special value to the individual himself. A person who has been 'made aware of himself' is in a better position to predict and control his own behavior" (p. 31). If, however, we ask the question "Why would self-knowledge put an individual in a better position to predict and control his or her own behavior?" we discover a core flaw in a traditional functional analytic approach.

To make this case, we first have to deal in a somewhat technical fashion with a modern behavior-analytic approach to language. This gives us the necessary tools to examine the meaning and importance of the self as well as to examine how it is possible to discuss it within a behavior-analytic framework.

If a child of sufficient verbal abilities is trained to point to a particular object given a particular written word—say, *c-a-t*—the child may point to the word given the object without specific training to do so. Additionally, given training in the spoken word *cat*, when presented the written word, the child may now, without additional training, call a cat a "cat" and point to cats on hearing the oral name. These kinds of derived relations lead us to say that the child "understands" the word *cat* and is not merely parroting it.

In this same sense, the core of human verbal knowledge is not unidirectional (event → description); rather, verbal knowledge is bidirectional and combinatorial (event → description leads to description → event). Symbolic interaction with an event can alter the psychological meaning of both the description and the event as a result (Hayes & Wilson, 1994). This ability can greatly assist humans in their endeavor to create and build, but it provides an immediate problem when humans examine their own behavior and history. The bidirectionality of human verbal knowledge means that self-awareness is painful when what is known is painful and, in turn, our responses to pain themselves become painful. For example, suppose a person recalls a trauma, say, an instance of sexual abuse. The original event was aversive, but now the verbal awareness and report of the event are aversive. This requires bidirectionality because classical conditioning and other unidirectional processes do not transfer the functions of the event that precedes to the event that follows. In the same way, the natural responses to aversive events, such as anxiety or anger—or, in our example, sexual arousal—themselves can become aversive. When they are evaluated and labeled, this process may be accelerated. For example, if "bad" events produce anxiety, anxiety itself will soon be "bad."

Three Types of Known Selves

We are ready now to apply this analysis of verbal knowledge to issues of the self. From the outside, *self* can mean many different things, such as an integrated repertoire of behavior, the totality of a history, or a physical organism. We do not deal with these senses here but limit our analysis to senses of self that are verbally known to the individual. The kinds of selves we are speaking about are those referred to by questions such as "Who are you?" or "What are you feeling?" or "what are you like?"

Consistent with a functional contextual approach, our task is twofold: (a) to develop historical accounts that could give rise to particular forms of self-knowledge and (b) to attempt to apply this knowledge to practical ends. We begin with the former task.

It seems to us that self-knowledge, viewed in light of the modern literature on derived stimulus relations, can involve at least three senses of self: a conceptualized self, self as an ongoing process of awareness, and an observing self. Each, we believe, emerges fairly directly from a functional contextual approach to verbal knowledge more generally.

Conceptualized Self

The ability to engage in derived relational responding means that we can derive relations between our ongoing stream of behavior and a variety of categorical concepts. The same verbal abilities that allow us to treat *ball* as a name for a round object allow us to treat *anxiety* as a name for a loose collection of bodily sensations, behavioral predispositions, thoughts, feelings, and contextual circumstances. Thus, verbal ability leads readily to a broad attempt to make sense of oneself and to describe one's own characteristics and attributes.

Verbal analysis is driven in part by coherence and sense making, and when we have derived a coherent set of relations among events we often present these analyses to the social–verbal community, the members of which agree or disagree that we are correct. Making sense and being right produce a very well-known set of effects, however, including the strong cognitive tendency to distort the world to fit our conceptualization of it. This has been shown in a variety of situations (Dawes, 1988, 1994).

The implications of these simple observations are significant as they apply to oneself. They mean that we tend naturally toward (a) a consistent and coherent set of descriptions of our dominant attributes and (b) the tendency to ignore or otherwise resist contradictory evidence and to amplify confirmatory evidence, including the tendency to act in ways that avoid disconfirmation. We term the self that is verbally known through such a process the *conceptualized self*. When we fuse with such a conceptualization—when we treat it as what it claims to be (i.e., who we are), several negative features emerge, including dishonesty and disguised ignorance, rigidity, and defense.

Dishonesty and *disguised ignorance* emerge because we try verbally to make sense of ourselves and to put our own histories and tendencies into verbal networks, despite the fact that we have very limited access to the relevant information and very limited conceptual tools to make sense of what we do recall. The former is a problem of memory, the latter is a problem of scientific knowledge. Scientists simply do not know how to describe a human life in all its richness, complexity, and situational sensitivity, and the average person is hardly a psychological scientist. Our conceptualized selves are therefore based very heavily on whatever lay culture has to say, and even then the input considered is but a tiny fraction of what has actually occurred. Even the most accurate interpretation of "who we are" is a small and fundamentally distorted picture.

Rigidity emerges because when we apply these verbal concepts in systematic ways to ourselves we enter into a verbally established conspiracy to maintain that picture. If a person believes him- or herself to be "kind," there is less room to deal directly with instances of behavior that could more readily be called "cruel." Our conceptualized selves settle into a pattern, and they change only slowly. As this proceeds, behavior becomes less flexible. Singing out loud, dancing with abandon, or skiing down a mountain may be rejected out of hand because "I don't have a good voice" or "I'm just not a dancer" or "I don't like taking risks." If these behaviors were sampled, they might be greatly rewarding, but they are not attempted because they do not fit a conceptual scheme.

Defense refers to the active ways we protect a conceptualized self, even if that conceptualization is quite negative. It is a more extreme form of rigidity, and in some ways it is the most disturbing aspect of the conceptualized self. It is ironic that most people come into therapy wanting to defend their particular conceptualized self. They view their familiar ideas about themselves as one would view dear friends. Clients literally say, "I am who I believe myself to be." These same clients, quite naturally, are often defensive and fearful of the changes that might occur in therapy, and they work to undermine the possibility of change. Even when clients view their conceptualized self as loathsome ("I am bad" or "I will never be loved" or "I can never live a normal life"), those conceptualizations are protected as if a life depended on it.

Ongoing Self-Awareness

Although defending a conceptualized self is inherently dangerous and distorting, self-awareness can be an ally to healthy and civilized life. This is true primarily because much of our socialization about what to do in life is tied to our ongoing process of self-awareness. A good example is emotional talk. Conditions such as anger, anxiety, and sadness are quite varied when one looks at the direct training that gives rise to them, but they are quite similar in their social implications. A person who is not aware of his or her ongoing behavioral states cannot address the individualized and changing circumstances that daily life presents. It is a kind of talk that cuts across many differences and provides a common ground for learning how to be human.

A person who has had a deviant training history that did not give rise to the self as an ongoing process of knowing will have a hard time living a successful life. For example, suppose a young girl has been sexually abused for many years by her father. Suppose during this time expressions of emotion associated with the aversiveness of this experience were reinterpreted, ignored, or denied. For example, the perpetrator might try to convince the child that she actually is not upset when she is, or he might tell her that she is upset because she has done something wrong. With such a history, the person's sense of self-awareness or the process of verbally knowing one's reactions would be weak. In some real sense, this person would be flying blind emotionally until this deficit is corrected (e.g., in the context of a therapeutic relationship that helped the person get in touch with her feelings or, in present terms, develop a sense of self-awareness).

Therapists have spent much of their time working on this exact aspect of self. Sometimes, unfortunately, they confuse this aspect with a conceptualized self. For example, they may try in various ways to get a client to say particular positive things about him- or herself and view that as a sign of success. But even positive verbalizations about oneself, held as a defended category, can cut off experience. What therapy should in part be about is making room for all of the various reactions that occur with regard to a current situation, so that the sense of self-awareness is always supported and strengthened. By staying open, the therapist creates an environment that helps to establish a stronger sense of self-awareness.

The challenge to self-awareness as an ongoing process is experiential avoidance. Organisms naturally tend to escape or avoid aversive events. The bidirectionality of human language means that self-awareness naturally leads humans to attempt to avoid contact with negative aspects of their own history and to avoid their own negative emotions and thoughts associated with such aspects.

There is a growing literature (see Hayes, Wilson, Gifford, Follette, & Strosahl, 1996, for a review) that shows that experiential avoidance can have highly detrimental effects on human functioning. Avoidance strategies have been shown to lead to poorer outcomes when used for depression (DeGenova, Patton, Jurich, & MacDermind, 1994), substance abuse (Cooper, Russell, & George, 1988; Ireland, McMahon, Malow, & Kouzekanani, 1994), and sequelae of child sexual abuse (Leitenberg, Greenwald, & Cado, 1992) than for other coping strategies that do not use avoidance or the suppression of negative emotional content.

There is a growing body of literature in the area of the suppression of thoughts and specific bodily sensations that supports this general point. For example, a number of studies have shown that when individuals are asked to suppress a thought, they later show an increase in this suppressed thought, compared with individuals who were not given the suppression instructions (Clark, Ball, & Pape, 1991; Gold & Wegner, 1995; Wegner, Schneider, Carter, & White, 1987; Wegner, Schneider, Knutson, & McMahon, 1991).

Additional research in this area has demonstrated that individuals who have been asked to suppress a specific thought show rebound effects in contexts that are similar to that in which the thought was suppressed (Wegner et al., 1991). The implications for this finding are apparent: If an individual suppresses a painful thought in one set of circumstances, the suppression will appear to be successful as long as the individual is not subsequently faced with a similar context. When a similar context is eventually encountered, the individual is likely to attribute the reappearance and amplification of the negative thought as a breakdown in his or her ability to successfully suppress, in which case the effort to do so may increase, which would continue the process.

In addition to context, the rebound of suppressed thoughts also has been shown to be related to mood. In one study (Wenzlaff, Wegner, & Klein, 1991), participants were asked to not think about a specific thought while they were in a particular mood. Participants were then assigned to either similar or different mood induction procedures. Participants in both groups showed a rebound effect, but those in the similar-mood induction group had a significantly higher rebound effect than those in the different-mood induction group. Another experiment showed that the suppressed thought is capable of producing the mood that was present during the original suppression phase (Wenzlaff et al., 1991). The implications for this finding with clinical populations is easy to see. If a client has a particular thought while experiencing a very depressed mood, not only will suppression of that thought produce and increase in the to-be-avoided thought, but the thought may come to produce the depression that the original suppression was intended to diminish.

Similar findings to those of the thought-suppression literature have been found in studies of examining somatic sensation. Cioffi and Holloway (1993) used a cold-pressor pain induction procedure and gave participants one of three sets of instructions: (a) think about their room at home, (b) focus on the sensations in their hand, or (c) eliminate thoughts about pain entirely. Participants who were given suppression instructions recovered—according to their discomfort ratings—the slowest, and participants who were given the focus instructions recovered the quickest. Later in the experiment, all participants were asked to rate the unpleasantness of an innocuous vibration. Participants from the suppression condition rated the sensation as more unpleasant than did participants in the other instruction-set conditions. Again, the clinical implications of this finding are very apparent: Not only does this finding point toward the prolongation of negative reports regarding a private sensation when the sensation is suppressed, but also the fact that subsequent innocuous sensations are then rated more unpleasant is of considerable consequence for clients who seldom experience a single negatively evaluated private event.

Thus, self-knowledge, we argue, has both a positive and a negative aspect. On the one hand, it permits self-control and planful life direction. On the other hand, it encourages fusion with a conceptualized self and avoidance of ongoing awareness of that which is painful.

The Observing Self

The final aspect of self is one that is most often ignored, but it is of key importance because it helps provide a solution to the problems presented by the other two forms. It has been termed the *observing self* (Deikman, 1983).

To have the ability to report events verbally in a sophisticated manner, it is necessary to develop a sense of perspective or point of view and to distinguish this from others. Children need to learn to report what has occurred to them- selves or to others and to do so from a given perspective. If asked "what did you eat?" a child must report what he or she ate, not what someone else ate. If a child is asked "what did you do at school?" the child must report what he or she did, not what someone else did. The content of these answers differs, but the context from which the answers are given is always the same. "I", in some meaningful sense, is the location that is left behind when all of the content differences are subtracted out. From this point of view, when a person is asked many questions, the "I" that is consistent in all of the answers is not just a physical organism but also a perspective.

A full sense of self-perspective also seems to require its distinction from something else. For example, a sense of observing from a location or being located behind one's eyes is probably facilitated by appreciating that the view of others is different. The verbal community teaches us to discriminate cognitive and spatial perspectives of this kind in part by establishing perspective-oriented relational frames, such as here versus there, near versus far, or now versus then (see Barnes, Hegarty, & Smeets, 1997, for an extended explanation).

With adequate training, a sense of self as a perspective or psychological locus emerges. This is an extraordinary behavioral phenomenon because once it begins to occur it provides a kind of continuity of experience that could not otherwise occur. For one thing, it is available as an aspect of virtually all verbal knowledge. It is rare indeed (although it can occur) that people cannot locate experience as known by themselves as opposed to experience as known from the perspective of someone else. When a person says "I felt this," it means that the feeling was felt from a particular perspective (i.e., "me") and not from the perspective of some other person.

There is another odd feature of the observing self: For the person engaging in the behavior, it is not truly possible to examine it as an object. Perspective taking is experienceable only in its effects, the feelings associated with it, or as a kind of fleeting afterimage when we attempt to grab it and look at it directly. If we were to see our own perspective (i.e., as an object), from what perspective would we see it? You cannot truly see your perspective and at the same time view from that perspective. To see perspective, perspective must change.

A similar situation may serve as a helpful metaphor in describing this issue. Consider the event of looking from one's eyes. It is impossible truly to look at looking from one's eyes, where the object is the same as looking at the object. If you could leap aside yourself faster than the speed of light, you would see yourself looking (as you might if you took a snapshot), but you would now be doing so from a changed perspective (namely, aside yourself). Your eyes would be elsewhere. No matter where you are, your eyes are there. In the same sense, no matter where you go, you as an observing self goes, too, and this aspect is part of everything that is known, so far as you know. When this aspect is lost (as in extreme drunkenness, fugue states, brain injury, transient global amnesia, etc.), we generally have no memory of what occurred, even if some higher cognitive functions (e.g., reasoning) were maintained.

Experience of the observing self, or self-as-perspective, is inherently transcendent and is at the core of what is meant by spirituality. The *Oxford English Dictionary* (1989) defines *spirit* as an "incorporeal or immaterial being" and as a "being or intelligence distinct from anything physical" (Vol. 16, p. 251). In essence, then, spirit is said to be knowable, but it is nevertheless said to be neither material nor physical. If you look up *matter*, you find that it is related to the word *materia,* which is the origin of the word, for timber or building materials. Matter is the "stuff of which a thing is made" (Vol. 9, p. 479). A *thing* is defined as "that which is or may be an object of perception, thought, or knowledge" (Vol. 27, p. 941). An *object* is a "thing thrown down to the senses or the mind" (1971, Vol. 1, p. 1963). Thus, spirit, in a nutshell, is a private event that cannot be experienced as a thing or an object. Self-as-perspective has the exact properties of spirit so defined because anything requires contact with its limits to be experienced. Self-as-perspective is so central to a sense of continuity of consciousness that the edges of this behavior cannot be consciously known for the person engaging in it. If we were aware of when we were no longer aware, we would (a) still be aware and (b) be aware that we were aware. Thus, it is not possible to consciously contact the limits of self-as-perspective. This is so radically not thinglike that it makes perfectly good sense to distinguish it from "matter," although there is no real reason to do so dualistically. Other than *spirit*, terms such as *pure consciousness, pure awareness*, and *being* are frequently used to describe contact with the observing self.

As a clinical matter, this aspect of self is critical because it provides a domain that is not directly threatened by awareness of negative content and that does not depend on belief for a sense of identity. Thus, the observing self is an area that can be used to moderate the negative features of a conceptualized self, or of an ongoing process of self-awareness. It is important, for our account, that all three emerge naturally from self-knowledge that is based on derived stimulus relations.

An Example of the Clinical Use of the Senses of Self: Acceptance and Commitment Therapy

In a functional contextual approach, the truth of analyses is not determined solely by their coherence but by their utility. This account of self is thus correct only insofar as it leads to useful applied outcomes.

To examine this issue, we focus on acceptance and commitment therapy (ACT) because it has self-consciously been constructed in a fashion consistent with the present account. *ACT* (stated as a word, not as initials) is a behavioral psychotherapy that views the relation between thoughts, feelings, and other private events, and overt behavior as contextually established and maintained. The goal of ACT is to change not the content of private events that occur with overt behavior but the context in which they are related to undesirable behavior. The specific targets of ACT are diminishment of cognitive fusion and experiential avoidance and an augmentation of self-as-perspective and behavioral commitment. In this chapter, we describe only some of the aspects that are relevant to issues of self. For a more detailed version of ACT, see Hayes, Strosahl, and Wilson, 1999, or other references (Hayes & Wilson, 1993, 1994).

To address issues of self, ACT conceptualizes each of the three components of self discussed above as having separate treatment agendas. Each aspect of self, then, is targeted with different techniques.

Targeting the Domination of the Conceptualized Self

As therapists, we have emphasized content entirely too much. We have been too ready to define certain thoughts as rational and others as irrational, certain emotions as good and others as bad. But this kind of categorization is old hat for our clients. It's what they have been doing all their lives. Rather than help them win this war, it would make more sense to help clients distinguish themselves from their conceptualized content, however "good" or "bad." It is better to kill off the ossified conceptualized selves that pop up repeatedly in any verbal organism. Sometimes, clients are very involved with self-related talk and self-related logic. A client might come into therapy with particular beliefs or "insights" about how he or she is and how he or she developed into this or that. These "explanations" usually become integrated into a life story that helps explain why the person is struggling and how that struggling is completely justified and really the only option the person has. This can take the form of a "faulty" childhood that explains low "self-esteem," "self-confidence," and so forth.

To address practical concerns with regard to the conceptualized self, it is necessary to examine the mechanisms that are operating to maintain this conceptualization. First of all, clients come in to therapy with very specific stories about "who they are" and "what they can and can't be" in terms of their identity. These stories are formulated largely by their private experiences and, perhaps more important, by the relationship between those private experiences and their meaning regarding the individual. Clients often engage in what someone working from an ACT perspective would call *cognitive fusion*, by which we mean that the client's thoughts, feelings, bodily sensations, and the like are not experienced as these private events but rather are fused into what the client believes him- or herself to be.

There are many contexts within human culture that foster the maintenance of cognitive fusion. One obvious area is the concept of consistency and its influence on humans' characterizations of themselves. In the name of consistency, humans "buy" particular beliefs about themselves and find private and public events to be proof of the validity of such statements, and they disregard other, contradictory events. Another context that works to maintain this type of fusion with one's beliefs is self-description. To describe oneself, it is necessary to use such statements as "I am a person who," which often leads to the fusing of such statements with a person's conceptualization of him- or herself.

Clients often have come into therapy to gain assistance in changing their self-conceptualizations. This is partly because the linkage between self-conceptualization and successful performance is deeply embedded in popular culture, and clients often seek therapy to learn to eliminate bad and limiting self-beliefs and to induce a higher degree of self-confidence. The ACT therapist introduces the idea that it may be the attachment to a specific conceptualization, rather than the content of the conceptualization, that has caused difficulties for the client.

To address this problem of clients buying their self-conceptualizations and seeking assistance in changing the content of those conceptualizations, a crucial step in ACT is to break down the literal meaning of the statements that compose them. In this phase, private events are not to be eliminated; rather, their meaning in relation to the client is disconnected. This process, called *deliteralization*, is based on the view that the relation between private events and overt behavior is itself contextually situated. Thus, the meaning of a verbal event is derived from its relation with other events in a social–verbal context. In deliteralization, the functions that come from the derived relation between verbal events and other events is lessened, and the direct auditory functions become more dominant.

One way that this process is addressed is that if a word is repeated over and over, the meaning of the word diminishes, and the sound of the word becomes more dominant. For example, one exercise that is used is to have the client repeat the word *milk* over and over. This emphasizes the ability to observe negative thoughts without necessarily believing or disbelieving their meaning because as the client repeats the word the auditory functions surpass the "meaning" functions in the exercise, and the perspective of this being "just a word" is taken by the client.

To illustrate to the client how language facilitates this dyed-in-the-wool thinking of one's self-conceptualizations, an ACT therapist can use the following exercise, called *Pick an Identity*:

> I want you to play a game with me—the identity game. Your job is to reach into my hat and pull out one slip of paper at a time. On each slip of paper, I have written down an identity statement. Some of these statements are things that you have told me in here. Some of the things are things I just bring up to describe characteristics of people. Your job is to pick any four slips of paper, and then I want you to try as hard as you can to imagine that you are the person described by those four slips of paper. So, some of the slips of paper will have messages on them that you have told yourself are true of you, and you might see some slips of paper that have messages that you have not told yourself. Your job is to take both kinds of messages and try as hard as you can to be that person, right here in the room with me, right now. I'm not trying to change what you believe about yourself. So, this is not a trick to stop believing in any of your beliefs about who you are. I'm just interested in seeing what it feels like to actually imagine that you can become the person described by the identity statements. OK?

In the Pick an Identity exercise the therapist places maximum emphasis on helping the client actually "take on" the characteristics on each slip of paper. Ordinarily, clients easily assimilate statements that are negative and that have been used before. They may have more trouble with statements that are positive. The therapist's job is to help the client construct the reality of being this person and then ask questions such as "What does this person think about his or her career, relationships, and family upbringing?" The therapist also asks questions such as "How does this person feel around others in a social gathering?" and "How does this person feel in an intimate situation?" Once this has been done, and the therapist is satisfied the person has really taken on the imaginary identity, then the exercise is repeated, with the client drawing a new set of identity slips. There is not necessarily a moral to this exercise. If the client makes remarks about feeling different under different identity formations, then the therapist may point out that different self-related content tends to produce different reactions. The agenda is not to convince the client that there is a better identity than the one that is currently being held; the mere experience of seeing thoughts as a kind of identity begins to make the point because the person who is aware of these identities is not the identities.

Targeting Barriers to Ongoing Self-Awareness

Another important component of ACT is the fostering of emotional acceptance in the service of behavior change. Clients come to us spending so much of their energy avoiding their undesired thoughts, emotions, and feelings that they have long lost sight of the reasons they have for avoiding them. This is not surprising, given our cultural insistence that people try to not feel what they're feeling. Expressions such as "Stop crying, or I'll give you something to cry about" or "Stop worrying" are not the exception but the rule. Another contextual factor that makes this difficult is the fact that the strategy of avoiding is successful in so many other areas of our life. If we do not want to encounter dangerous events, we may avoid entering a particular area at night by ourselves. This same avoidance, however, often has detrimental effects when what we are trying to avoid is our own private events. This pattern of attempting to avoid what we have already got tends to combine with other elements to remove our directive goals and values from the equation altogether. In ACT, clients are helped to accept what they are experiencing by fostering contact with self-awareness and the observing self. A key intervention designed to help clients discover and loosen their grip on a self that in some sense isn't "them" anyway is the *Two Computers Metaphor*:

> Imagine two computers, sitting side by side, each with an operator in front of them. These are identical machines, and they have the same programs and the same data in them. Now, the way computers work is that if you give them a particular input they are highly likely, given particular software and data, to give a particular output. So suppose we push a key on these two machines and some read-out shows up on both screens. Suppose what comes up is, "Deep down, there's something wrong with me." Now imagine two different situations. In Situation 1, the operator is totally lost in the operation of the computer. It's like being lost in a movie; you're not watching, you're in that movie, so when someone jumps out from behind a door, you jump. It is like that. The operator is sitting right in front of the monitor, nose touching the screen, lost in the read-out and unable to distinguish between the machine and the person operating the machine. The operator has forgotten that there's any distinction. So the screen shows "Deep down there's something wrong with me." Now, from that place—with the operator in the machine—the operator's only choice is to try to reprogram the machine. Who is going to accept that deep down inside there's something wrong with them? That's like saying it would be okay to be eaten by a tiger. In Situation 2, same computer, same programming, everything is the same. The person is sitting back a little, and it is real clear that there is a distinction between the machine and the person. He's the operator of the machine, he's working on the machine, but he is not

the machine. The operator can still see the read-out very clearly, but because there's a distinction between himself and the machine, the read-out doesn't necessarily have to change. He could call over his friends and say "Look at this thing. I type in X, and look what comes out on the screen. Interesting, huh?" It's like that. Your mind has been programmed by all kinds of people. So at one point, Mom comes over and works on the keyboard for a while; a little later Dad comes over. At various times, your husband (or wife), your teachers, your kids, your friends, your work mates—they all spend a little time at the computer. And in certain situations—given the right input—you'll get a certain read-out. You might even believe it to be true. For example, it says on the screen, "Boy! I am really anxious!" It may be accurate. The issue isn't whether the read-out is true or false. The issue is whether there is any distinction between the person and the mental machinery. Is there any distinction between you and the stuff that is in your life?

This exercise allows the client to stand in a place where the content of the private events that compose their self-conceptualizations is not necessarily that which makes up the person or self but rather can be the content that whether positive or negative is held from the context of the observer self.

Targeting the Observing Self

The *Chessboard Metaphor* is a central ACT intervention and another way to connect the client to the distinction between content and the observing self.

It is as if there is a chess board that goes out indefinitely in all directions. It is covered with different colored pieces, black pieces and white pieces. They work together in teams, like in chess—the white pieces fight against the black pieces. You can think of your thoughts and feelings and beliefs as these pieces; they sort of hang out together in teams too. For example, "bad" feelings (like anxiety, depression, resentment) hang out with bad thoughts and memories. Same thing with the "good" ones. So it seems that the way the game is played is that we select which side we want to win. We put the good pieces (like thoughts that are self-confident, feelings of being in control) on one side, and the bad pieces on the other. Then we get up on the back of the white queen and ride to battle, fighting to win the war against anxiety, depression, thoughts about using drugs, whatever. It's a war game. But there's a logical problem here, and that is that from this posture, huge portions of yourself are your own enemy. In other words, if you need to be in this war, there is something wrong with you. And since it appears that you're on the same level as these pieces, they can be as big or even bigger than you are—even though these pieces are in you. So somehow, even though it is not logical, the more you fight, the bigger they get. If it is true that "if you are not willing to have it, you've got it," then as you fight them they get more central to your life, more habitual, more dominating, and more linked to every area of living. The logical idea is that you will knock enough of them off the board that you will eventually dominate them—except your experience tells you that the exact opposite happens. Apparently, the black pieces can't be deliberately knocked off the board. So the battle goes on. You feel hopeless, you have a sense that you can't win, and yet you can't stop fighting. If you're on the back of that white horse, fighting is the only choice you have because the black pieces seem life threatening. Yet living in a war zone is no way to live.

As the client connects to this metaphor, it can be turned to the issue of the self:

Therapist: Now let me ask you to think about this carefully. In this metaphor, suppose you aren't the chess pieces. Who are you?

Client: Am I the player?

Therapist: That's exactly what you've been trying to be, so that is an old idea. The player has a big investment in how this war turns out. Besides, who are you playing against? Some other player? So suppose you're not that either.

Client: Am I the board?

Therapist: It's useful to look at it that way. Without a board, these pieces have no place to be. The board holds them. Like what would happen to your thoughts if you weren't there to be aware that you thought them? The pieces need you. They cannot exist without you, but you contain them, they don't contain you. Notice that if you're the pieces, the game is very important; you've got to win, your life depends on it. But if you're the board, it doesn't matter if the war stops or not. The game may go on, but it doesn't make any difference to the board. As the board, you can see all the pieces, you can hold them, you are in intimate contact with them, and you can watch the war being played out on your consciousness, but it doesn't matter. It takes no effort.

This metaphor allows clients to view their private events, both negative and positive, as pieces to be held rather than as something that necessarily has to be bought or believed. Thus, when a client walks in with thoughts that he or she is a bad person, the therapist can examine whether the client is fighting against those thoughts (piece level) or holding them as thoughts (board level).

Data in Support of the ACT Conceptualization

If the functional analyses laid out above are actually in effect, then it follows that one way to test this would be to examine the outcomes, as well as the processes, obtained by ACT treatments. The data gathered on this treatment over the years indicate that ACT is focused on a generally applicable set of phenomena and thus seems to have a fairly broad effect on a variety of problems of human living. Small but controlled studies have shown ACT to be effective treatment for depression (Zettle, 1985; Zettle & Raines, 1989). Larger randomized controlled trials show that ACT is effective in reducing stress in the workplace (Bond & Bunce, 2000) and in reducing rehospitalization in psychotic patients experiencing hallucinations and delusions (Bach, 2000). Less well-controlled research provides some evidence that ACT is helpful in the treatment of anxiety disorders (Hayes, 1987; Hayes, Afari, McCurry, & Wilson, 1990) and depression in patients with personality disorders (Strosahl, 1991) or parents of children with disabilities (Biglan, 1989). Process research has shown that these changes occur through processes hypothesized for ACT, namely changes in emotional avoidance, acceptance, and cognitive defusion (e.g., Bach, 2000; Bond & Bunce, 2000; Khorakiwala, 1991; McCurry, 1991; Zettle, 1985; Zettle & Hayes, 1986; Zettle & Raines, 1989).

In addition to these data, there are now controlled-effectiveness data indicating that clinicians in a general outpatient setting who are trained in ACT produce better overall outcomes across the range of patients they usually see (Strosahl, Hayes, Bergan, & Romano, 1998). This finding suggests that the generic functional analyses presented in this chapter must be generally true or an effect would not be observed across the outpatient population.

Conclusion

In the examination of an issue such as the self from a functional contextual approach, the task is twofold: to develop historical accounts that could give rise to particular forms of self-knowledge and to attempt to apply this knowledge to practical ends. By breaking down the concept of the self into the observer self, the conceptualized self, and ongoing self-awareness through an examination of the verbal events that compose these constructions, we are able to examine the historical accounts that may lead to them. In the examination of ACT, a psychotherapy designed to target these aspects of self in the change process, we offer an example of the application of this knowledge to practical ends.

References

Bach, P. (2000). *The use of acceptance and commitment therapy to prevent rehospitalization in psychotic patients.* Unpublished doctoral dissertation, University of Nevada, Reno.

Barnes, D., Hegarty, N., & Smeets, P. M. (1997). Relating equivalence relations to equivalence relations: A relational framing model of complex human functioning. *Analysis of Verbal Behavior, 14,* 57–83.

Biglan, A. (1989). A contextual approach to the clinical treatment of parental distress. In G. Singer & L. Irvin (Eds.), *Support for caregiving families: Enabling positive adaptation to disability* (pp. 299–311). Baltimore: Brookes.

Bond, F. W., & Bunce, D. (2000). Mediators of change in emotion-focused and problem-focused worksite stress management interventions. *Journal of Occupational Health Psychology, 51,* 156–163.

Cioffi, D., & Holloway, J. (1993). Delayed costs of suppressed pain. *Journal of Personality and Social Psychology, 64,* 274–282.

Clark, D. M., Ball, S., & Pape, D. (1991). An experimental investigation of thought suppression. *Behaviour Research and Therapy, 29,* 253–257.

Cooper, M. L., Russell, M., & George, W. H. (1988). Coping, expectancies, and alcohol abuse: A test of social learning formulations. *Journal of Abnormal Psychology, 97,* 218–230.

Dawes, R. M. (1988). *Rational choice in an uncertain world.* San Diego, CA: Harcourt Brace Jovanovich.

Dawes, R. M. (1994). *House of cards.* New York: Macmillan.

DeGenova, M. K., Patton, D. M., Jurich, J. A., & MacDermind, S. M. (1994). Ways of coping among HIV-infected individuals. *Journal of Social Psychology, 134,* 655–663.

Deikman, A. J. (1983). The evaluation of spiritual and utopian groups. *Journal of Humanistic Psychology, 23,* 8–18.

Gold, D. B., & Wegner, D. M. (1995). Origins of ruminative thought: Trauma, incompleteness, nondisclosure, and suppression. *Journal of Applied Social Psychology, 25,* 1245–1261.

Hayes, S. C. (1987). A contextual approach to therapeutic change. In N. Jacobson (Ed.), *Psychotherapists in clinical practice: Cognitive and behavioral perspectives* (pp. 327–387). New York: Guilford Press.

Hayes, S. C., Afari, N., McCurry, S., & Wilson, K. G. (1990). *Acceptance and commitment therapy: A working manual for the treatment of emotional avoidance disorders.* Reno, NV: Context Press.

Hayes, S. C., Strosahl, K. D., & Wilson, K. G. (1999). *Acceptance and commitment therapy: An experiential approach to behavior change.* New York: Guilford Press.

Hayes, S. C., & Wilson, K. G. (1993). Some applied implications of a contemporary behavior analytic account of verbal behavior. *Behavior Analyst, 16,* 283–301.

Hayes, S. C., & Wilson, K. G. (1994). Acceptance and commitment therapy: Altering the verbal support for experiential avoidance. *Behavior Analyst, 17,* 289–303.

Hayes, S. C., Wilson, K. W., Gifford, E. V., Follette, V. M., & Strosahl, K. (1996). Emotional avoidance and behavioral disorders: A functional dimensional approach to diagnosis and treatment. *Journal of Consulting and Clinical Psychology, 64,* 1152–1168.

Ireland, S. J., McMahon, R. C., Malow, R. M., & Kouzekanani, K. (1994). Coping style as a predictor of relapse to cocaine abuse. In L. S. Harris (Ed.), *Problems of drug dependence, 1993: Proceedings of the 55th Annual Scientific Meeting* (National Institute of Drug Abuse Monograph Series No. 141, p. 158). Washington, DC: U.S. Government Printing Office.

Khorakiwala, D. (1991). *An analysis of the process of client change in a contextual approach to therapy.* Unpublished doctoral dissertation, University of Nevada, Reno.

Leitenberg, H., Greenwald, E., & Cado, S. (1992). A retrospective study of long-term methods of coping with having been sexually abused during childhood. *Child Abuse and Neglect, 16,* 399–407.

McCurry, S. M. (1991). *Client metaphor use in a contextual form of therapy.* Unpublished doctoral dissertation, University of Nevada, Reno.

Oxford English Dictionary. (1989). Oxford, England: Clarendon Press.

Oxford English Dictionary. (1971). (compact ed.). Oxford, England: Clarendon Press.

Skinner, B. F. (1974). *About behaviorism.* New York: Vintage Books.

Skinner, B. F. (1988). Behaviorism at fifty. In A. C. Catania & S. Harnad (Eds.), *The selection of behavior* (pp. 278–292). New York: Cambridge University Press. (Original work published 1964)

Strosahl, K. (1991). Cognitive and behavioral treatment of the personality disordered patient. In C. Austad & B. Berman (Eds.), *Psychotherapy in managed health care: The optimal use of time and resources* (pp. 185–201). Washington, DC: American Psychological Association.

Strosahl, K. D., Hayes, S. C., Bergan, J., & Romano, P. (1998). Assessing the field effectiveness of acceptance and commitment therapy: An example of the manipulated training research method. *Behavior Therapy, 29,* 35–64.

Wegner, D. M., Schneider, D. J., Carter, S. R., & White, T. L. (1987). Paradoxical effects of thought suppression. *Journal of Personality and Social Psychology, 53,* 5–13.

Wegner, D. M., Schneider, D. J., Knutson, B., & McMahon, S. R. (1991). Polluting the stream of consciousness: The effect of thought suppression of the mind's environment. *Cognitive Therapy and Research, 15,* 141–151.

Wenzlaff, R. M., Wegner, D. M., & Klein, S. B. (1991). The role of thought suppression in the bonding of thought and mood. *Journal of Personality and Social Psychology, 60,* 500–508.

Zettle, R. D. (1985). Cognitive therapy of depression: A conceptual and empirical analysis of component and process issues. *Dissertation Abstracts International, 46,* 669.

Zettle, R. D., & Hayes, S. C. (1986). Dysfunctional control by client verbal behavior: The context of reason giving. *Analysis of Verbal Behavior, 4,* 30–38.

Zettle, R. D., & Raines, J. C. (1989). Group cognitive and contextual therapies in the treatment of depression. *Journal of Clinical Psychology, 45,* 436–445.

COMMENT:

Contextualizing "Functional Contextualism and the Self"

Barry Protter

S peaking as a pluralist and pragmatist in matters psychotherapeutic, I welcome as helpful any therapeutic intervention that has had success in helping patients more effectively cope with what Sullivan called "problems in living." In their chapter, Steven Hayes and Jennifer Gregg suggest several interventions in the direction of what I call "contextualizing the self," understood as a "dereification" (Protter, 1985) of the self. Rorty (1989) generically described this process as a movement of "substituting a tissue of contingent relations or web which stretches backward and forward through past and future time, from a formed, unified present, self-contained substance, something capable of being seen steadily and whole" (p. 41)—or, to say this in another way, seeing the self as action, process, and perspective rather than as a reified thing or structure.

Hayes and Gregg draw almost exclusively from behaviorist traditions, sensibilities, and language, which have historically been user-unfriendly to notions like the self. Indeed, Skinner, to whom Hayes and Gregg often refer as their philosophical progenitor, represents a curious hybrid, much like Freud, in the modernist–postmodernist distinction I make in chapter 13. Skinner's Wittgensteinian insight that meaning is constructed in the field of language games "out there" (the "verbal community") might be described as postmodern in its deconstruction of the hegemonic, Cartesian subjective self. His relentless account of how this meaning is constructed, in terms of stimulus–response (S–R) contingencies, reinforcement schedules, and the like, can be seen as a modernist attempt at a universalistic explanation of human psychology. This universalism is achieved by an atomistic reductionism, broken down in the purported language of psychological reality itself, namely S–R units. The pigeon in various controlled environments becomes the objectivist, scientifically aspiring model–metaphor of framing and studying psychological functioning.

Hayes and Gregg describe, in effect, a self-interpreting self (the "conceptualized self"), a phenomenological self ("ongoing awareness") and an intentional–agentic self (the "observing self"). They suggest different psycho-educational interventions to facilitate knowledge of these different selves. This is done in the service of dereifying the self which, in effect, says to the patient such things as "you are not equal to what you and the culture attribute yourself to be"; "be immediately aware, don't deny"; "you can choose to see experience from different perspectives and not be defined or driven by 'sheer' events/reality"; "the past does not equal the future"; and so on. These kinds of interventions, particularly when used propitiously in therapy, can foster helpful "Gestalt shifts" in the outlook of the self. Indeed, sensibilities from all the schools have been working in this terrain for many years now, including cognitive–behavioral (e.g., Ellis, 1962); psychodynamic (e.g., Schafer, 1976); systems (e.g., Watzlawick, Beaven, & Jackson, 1967) and, probably most pointedly, Gestalt–experiential approaches (e.g., Perls, Hefferline, & Goodman, 1951), which have had a long and rich history in the use of experiential–psychodramatic type interventions to change the "self set" of the individual. Outside of psychotherapy proper, Eastern philosophical influences have long emphasized the illusory and tyrannically possessive nature of the ego self, and Western humanistic–hermeneutic influences, from Heidegger to Sartre, have addressed the ways that the self "mis-objectifies" and "thingifies" itself in the various acts of "bad faith."

To the extent that Hayes and Gregg are suggesting dereifying intervention in the context of these essentially larger humanistic and hermeneutic traditions and sensibilities, this strikes me as, broadly speaking, potentially helpful. It also manifests sound therapeutic wisdom accumulated over many years of reflecting on the self, both therapeutically and extratherapeutically. Hayes and Gregg do this, though, from a narrow behavioristic framework. On the one hand, this may perhaps be seen as radical and exotic to some (particularly those who have been wedded to this framework); indeed, one could applaud Hayes and Gregg for stretching this mechanistic framework to look at matters to which it typically selectively inattends, as the units of meaning (what is a self, what is a context) do not easily accommodate atomistic analysis. To me, though, who operates outside this framework with integratively inspired sensibilities, much of the language that Hayes and Gregg bring to bear in the background explanation of their suggested interventions seems overstretching a limited vocabulary (S–R language) to cover essentially humanist–hermeneutic domains.

Ultimately, I would say that the framework to which Hayes and Gregg appeal suffers because of the limitations regarding a Skinnerian legacy. To my mind, issues of the self can be more fruitfully unpacked by a wider range of domain-appropriate vocabularies (not excluding S–R terms for certain purposes) that can be both hermeneutically accurate and appropriate in terms of proximate focus of concern as well as more pragmatic, by speaking to the patient in the language of the self as it is lived in the cultural horizon of meaning (see, e.g., Bruner, 1990; Woolfolk, 1998). If Hayes and Gregg's implicit purpose in applying an S–R terminology to molar issues of the self is to address larger comparative–pluralistic vistas and communities in psychotherapy, then they would have greater impact by simplifying some of the lingo, which often mystifies what can be embraced in more accessible, psychologically bridging, commonsense terms.

A further note I would make in the direction of contextualizing Hayes and Gregg's contextualization of the self is more practical: What is the larger therapeutic context in which these psychoeducational interventions take place? What purpose do they serve in a flushed-out therapy and when, broadly speaking, would one use them? For whom, for what kinds of problems, to what end? For example, it may be helpful to disengage the "I" from excessive identification–responsibility with the events/attributes in the self's life (what Hayes and Gregg call "cognitive fusion")—but at other times certain patients may need to vigorously re-engage and reown these features of the self (see, e.g., Schafer, 1976). Are the psychointerventions Hayes and Gregg suggest loosely heuristic suggestions, or do they require the fixed narrative–parable text in the manner set forth by them? Although I realize that fully addressing these type issues may be reasonably beyond the scope of Hayes and Gregg's chapter, it would have been edifying for them to at least acknowledge there is a larger and nuanced therapeutic context within which these interventions take place in the service of contextualizing the self.

References

Bruner, J. (1990). *Acts of meaning*. Cambridge, MA: Harvard University Press.

Ellis, A. (1962). *Reason and emotion in psychotherapy*. New York: Stuart.

Perls, F., Hefferline, R., & Goodman, P. (1951). *Gestalt therapy*. New York: Julian Press.

Protter, B. (1985). Toward an emergent psychoanalytic epistemology. *Contemporary Psychoanalysis, 21,* 208–227.

Rorty, R. (1989). *Contingency, irony and solidarity*. Cambridge, England: Cambridge University Press.

Schafer, R. (1976). *A new language for psychoanalysis*. New Haven, CT: Yale University Press.

Watzlawick, P., Beaven, J., & Jackson, D. (1967). *Pragmatics of human communication: Study of interactional patterns, pathologies and paradoxes*. New York: Norton.

Woolfolk, R. (1998). *The cure of souls*. San Francisco: Jossey-Bass.

CHAPTER 13

Knowing the Self in Psychotherapy: Toward a Postmodern Integrative Approach

Barry Protter

My purpose in this chapter is to sketch an epistemic direction for an integrative psychotherapy informed both by features of what I describe as a reconstructive postmodern sensibility and by trends in humanistic post-Freudian, psychodynamic theory and therapy. I consider the process of knowing and accessing the self to be fundamental to the psychotherapeutic effort, and I use it as an organizing principle by conceptualizing what I call the three domains of knowing the self: the *monadic* (embodied from within), the *dyadic* (other related, in between), and the *triadic* (culturally–linguistically situated from without). I focus on three epistemic methodologies that focus on phenomenology and agency, interaction and relationship, and interpretation of meaning and values.

My purview is not to articulate a theory of integrative clinical practice per se but rather to address the systemic operations that would underlie and make such an integrative practice possible. Recent philosophic and conceptual trends can be construed as stimulating renewed imaginative efforts in thinking through the differences (pluralism) and commonalities (integration) in the various therapeutic approaches, in the aftermath of a failed modernist climate of "school psychology" orthodoxy and totality. In the broadest sense, I hope to weave a coherent sensibility that I call "humanistic–hermeneutic pragmatism" and an accompanying theoretical scaffolding organized around these processes of knowing and accessing the self that can accommodate both pluralistic and integrative outlooks, which are, in effect, dialectical offshoots of one another. Such an overarching sensibility would recognize that each therapeutic approach (psychoanalytic, behavioral, cognitive) is epistemically legitimate within the purview of its own perspectives and purposes. Psychotherapeutically speaking, the features of each approach may all be used purely (leading to pluralism) or more integratively, depending on the pragmatics of the therapeutic situation, while being able to be reconfigured along the "self-knowing" dimensions I outline in this chapter.

Matters of Integration

Various writers, in what has become by now a full-fledged integrative psycho-therapy movement, have described different emphases in psychotherapy integration. The various characterizations of such efforts as "theoretical integration," "technical eclecticism," "common factors," and "complementary integration" are somewhat self-explanatory and have been explicated in more detail elsewhere (see Norcross & Goldfried, 1992). Aspects of all these projects of integration would be consistent with the more metatheoretical sensibility I develop in this chapter. In speaking specifically of a postmodern integration in psychotherapy, a central pitfall would be the presumption that some kind of complete therapeutic or theoretical unity might be achieved. This integrative unity could be sought either from "above"—in the sense that one grand theory could super-ordinately encompass many outlooks and perspectives—or from "below," as if some agreed-on neutral clinical observation language could achieve uniformity by just presenting the facts as they are. Such unifying–homogenizing efforts, either from above or below, would only reinstitute modernist, Kantian–positivist trends toward universalism and reductionism. Any umbrella outlook or sensibility that draws from postmodern trends certainly needs to give due epistemic weight and respect to notions of difference and pluralism.

Another important restraint in matters of integration is the recognition that in the process of incorporating a particular psychotherapeutic approach into another, the imported modality would, almost by necessity, take on meaning not only from whence it came but also from the new therapeutic approach and context to where it is transferred (e.g., incorporating a cognitive–behavioral intervention or mindset into an ongoing psychodynamic psychotherapy), usually with one theory or approach taking on a more dominant influence, in the manner of a "home paradigm," so to speak (see Messer, 1992). My home paradigm, by dint of my training and sensibilities, is largely drawn from a humanistic, post-Freudian, relational psychoanalytic outlook (itself a product of earlier integrations). I do not mean by this that I would advocate, for example, that all therapeutic experience and operations ultimately need to go through the "analytic mill" (e.g., seen in the context of the transference–countertransference matrix). Indeed, the sensibility I am suggesting would acknowledge a range of other viable outlooks and interventions, from a problem-centered, technical, goal-oriented one to a more nondirective one that could achieve a host of purposes without being particularly informed by psychoanalytically inspired viewpoints and actions.

Psychodynamic thinking and practice, though, may have some privileged views in regard to certain epistemic and clinical matters. The post-Freudian analytic models, which have comprised a good deal of my clinical training, inform me primarily in the generalized manner of their rich tradition in theory making in the genre of philosophical anthropology. First, even though the "depth" psychology metaphor has become transformed over the years, psychoanalysis continues to theorize about the big questions concerning "what makes people tick." Much of this purview, chastened by earlier modernist overreaching, certainly has influenced the notions of the self described below—a conceptual arena very prominent in a more humanistically transformed psychoanalysis. Second, psychoanalysts, having invented the narrative–conversational structure that we call psychotherapy, developed a finely textured focus on what generally has been called therapeutic process. In recent years, psychoanalytically oriented process description and theory have shed illuminating light on the nature of the mutually constructed in-session participatory interactions (the "knowing processes") of therapist and patient. Indeed, this development, as well as related metatheoretical developments in current post-Freudian psychoanalysis, have pulled from, as well as contributed to, the larger postmodern sensibility that informs my thinking. Psychoanalysis is not unique in this: Almost all the other school psychology traditions—including cognitive, systems, humanistic, and even behavioral—have been bitten by the postmodern bug (e.g., Neimeyer & Mahoney, 1995).

Ultimately, the appeal of developing an integrative-type framework is pragmatic. Surveys have indicated that most practitioners (see Jensen, Bergin, & Greaves, 1990) practice "integratively"; that is, they use several approaches or outlooks in varied combinations and formats, sometimes willy-nilly and unwittingly, sometimes more formally and systematically. This move to integration is no doubt due to a variety of factors. For the modal therapist, pragmatic concerns of being able to have an elastic and epistemic outlook that is comprehensive enough to increase one's capacity to thoughtfully address a wider array of psychological and psychotherapeutic perspectives, challenges, purposes, and solutions (both purely and integratively) are readily understandable. This is particularly underlined in a postmodern marketplace climate that can be characterized, paradoxically, by an "anything goes" mentality amid the diverse pressures (some worthy, some not) of managerial–technical accountability.

Metatheory and the Postmodern Turn

In the heyday of early to later modernism (until, say, around 25 years ago), becoming a therapist meant first and foremost taking a stand in regard to a clear and definite theoretical persuasion. Spanning the field of psychotherapy was rather like being led down a grand hall of corridors, the "Schools of Psychology," each of which offered an all-encompassing scenic view of the human condition, snugly accompanied by a therapeutic methodology aimed to heal and effect change. As a therapist, it was a matter of deciding which corridor to enter and, when securely committed to one path, one rarely looked back. One could also count on being swept along the way by an invigorating ideology proclaiming the true virtues of each approach as it bestowed on the practitioner a kind of moral and epistemological authority. Such disparate nostalgic phrases and terms as "Where id was, there shall ego be," *Walden Two*, "Esalen," and "reprogramming the mind" evoke the flush enthusiasms, approaching utopianism, of this modernist psychotherapy sensibility. Therapists certainly still invest in and jealously guard their identities as analysts, behavioral therapists, family system therapists, and so on. However, there has been an epistemic and cultural sea change in the last quarter century or so that has reached self-conscious recognition, characteristic of developments that have usually been described as postmodern. One might refer to an earlier modernist age in psychotherapy as the age of metapsychology. *Metapsychology* was the term Freud first used to describe his early efforts in positing a scientific groundwork for his instinctually focused psychoanalysis on the basis of late 19th-century physics and biology, using the conceptual language of energy and force. His attempts to do so were subsequently criticized (by Freud himself as well) not only because of their outdated science but also, more important, as a misguided reductionist attempt to collapse a discourse of mentalistic meaning into one of biophysicalistic force. The term *metapsychology* has been somewhat broadened in the recent analytic literature to mean not only reductionistic attempts to explain one thing in terms of something else but also as totalist efforts at explaining everything (Protter, 1996). This is metapsychology as method to, and theory of, universal truth. As a grand narrative description and explanation of the human psychological condition it purports to provide a bedrock foundation and rationale for therapeutic practices by framing the scientific and normative parameters (conceptions of etiology, psychodiagnosis, health, therapeutic action) from which therapeutic discourse is conducted and understood. Epistemically speaking, the universalist assumptions of grand theory represent the view from both nowhere and everywhere; that is, it does not acknowledge itself to be a view or perspective on psychological reality but rather proclaims itself as reality—or, more precisely, proclaims that it represents reality as it is.

Applied to the larger span of psychotherapy, the phrase *modernist metapsychology* corresponds to the grand theoretical underpinnings of the various school psychology systems and the offshoot psychotherapeutic approaches. The postmodern turn in the various psychotherapeutic traditions is tantamount to a heightened critical self-consciousness concerning the very status of this modernist metapsychology and its associated implications. All the other school traditions have, *mutatis mutandis,* roughly shared the same cycle of postmodern fate as has psychoanalysis; initial metapsychology as "foundational ontology" enthusiasm; and subsequent local, pluralistic, and integrative deconstruction of these universalist claims in theory, method, and practice. The particular course of postmodernization in the various schools would require a variety of separate stories and histories beyond the scope of this chapter. However, regardless of whether the core universal theories and methods of the various schools revolve around an "atheoretical" technical–objectivist behaviorism or an "amethodological" self-expressionistic humanism, the modernist, Kantian, top-down or positivist bottom-up aspirations to universalism that marked the various separate traditions have become what the philosophers would describe as problematic.

But to speak contemporaneously of the separate schools as epistemic paradigms of truth, method, and cure does not reflect the postmodern pluralistic–integrative scene in psychotherapy in which the various schools or traditions operate, akin to what Kuhn (1970) described as more or less cohering, sometimes overlapping, disciplinary matrices. A historic overview of the larger span of psychotherapy reveals that, paradoxically, in the midst of a seemingly endless proliferation in psychotherapy systems, approaches, and modalities over the years, third- or fourth-generation integrations of earlier approaches have emerged that are viably contending in the field as newer revitalized and transformed "pure" paradigms. Examples of this are legion, including the explicit wedding of cognitive and behavioral approaches into a cognitive–behavioral paradigm and the implicit incorporation of humanistic and existential sensibilities into many current post-Freudian approaches in theory and practice, signifying a kind of dialectical interplay between pluralism and integration in the evolution of psychotherapy. The fact that the most recent empirical-outcome meta-studies have pretty much consistently debunked the omnibus advantage of any one pure and totalist approach over another across a spectrum of problems (e.g., Lambert, 1992; Seligman, 1995) has only encouraged various efforts at integration, for purposes of greater flexibility and comprehension in the clinician's therapeutic armamentarium.

The term *postmodern* as I use it in this chapter, in the context of psychotherapy, applies to precisely those developments that have taken place as a result of rethinking modernist metapsychology and its Kantian–positivist universalism, referred to above, as well as to related aspects of monadic Cartesianism, which I discuss below in reference to the self. As a general epistemic proposition, *postmodernism* has referred to various critical assaults on notions of truth and rationality that gained currency in the Enlightenment, through the major contemporary strands of modernism. Briefly stated, this postmodern critique problematizes the notion that rationality can provide real, universal, and atemporal standards and guideposts for the grounding of knowledge and the determination of objective principles whereby validity is independent of point of view. As there is no reality, objectivity or truth except my (our) "point of view," or to say it another way, no reference behind the text (language, symbol) but more tact, all judgment may be justified by "another legitimate" perspective.

There is, however, a troubling and unsettling anarchic trajectory of logic in deconstructive postmodern thinking, particularly as it has been appropriated by certain avant garde trends in psychology and psychotherapy. The postmodern position is probably most often associated with a *radical sociotextual* constructivist outlook. The consequences of such a position is that the self is constructed from without by the discursive sociolinguistic processes of the historic culture. The notion of an enduring, unified, private, substantial self, an embodied self of endogenous nature and structure, is an illusory reification according to this view. The self, such as it is (depending on the postmodern theorist), has been variously described as a "symptom," a "rhetorical device," or an "epiphenomenal trace in a linguistic signifying chain." Indeed, the radical sociotextual constructionist position would linguisticize not only the self but also the very legitimacy of psychotherapy as well, out of existence. Psychotherapy, in such an extreme view, could be construed only as the pure exclusive practice of ideology or as a kind of aestheticized semiotic experience that has no significance in regard to matters of real change.

There is another problematic sensibility in certain postmodern directions in psychotherapy, features of which have recently become prominent in sectors of humanistic theory, cognitive therapy, psychoanalysis, and a slew of New Age–popularized therapeutic outlooks as well as a psychotherapy movement to which some have explicitly referred as postmodern therapy (see, e.g., White & Epston, 1990). It has, in effect, incorporated the idealist (antirealist) features of the radical postmodern position (everything is text) by substituting a *subjective* constructivist outlook for the sociotextual constructivist view. Reacting against the same Kantian–positivist universalism, which had come under critical assault for its overvaluation and reification of structure and realism, this view valorizes a kind of authorial pan-subjectivism whereby a supraordinate, disembodied Cartesian self becomes a kind of inventor and "writer" of reality. Only subjective experience, epistemologically and therapeutically, is relevant and of interest. Psychotherapy hence becomes a matter of the self narratively rewriting and creating a new reality. A kind of muddled conflation of these two positions (subjective and social constructivistic) results in an epistemic model of psychotherapy as an insulated, idiographic world of radical difference and pluralism. In this form, the psychotherapy session can be understood only as an ontically unique story and narrative developed by two selves in session, without reference to anything else (e.g., explanatory issues in development–etiology or structure and function, the reality outside the session, the historic reality in the patient's life) because all else is just simply more removed and unreal text and narrative. Indeed, the only theory of relevance, according to this outlook, is the theory that the patient's supraordinate self holds about him- or herself in the authorizing process in the unfolding narrative of the session. There is no way to bridge outside the universe of the session to make systematic or generalized descriptions or explanations, a position that is ultimately riddled with contradictions as well as a host of disclaimed realist assumptions (see, e.g., Held, 1998). Such a position, suffice it to say, offers a transparently problematic episteme for the project of developing anything like a discipline of psychotherapy.

A question presents itself: How can we more fruitfully engage the postmodern critique of Kantian–positivist universalism and yet not end up in one of the overinflated balloons of idealist antirealism (all is self, all is text) that pervade the deconstructive focus of postmodernism? One way, which I call *humanist–hermeneutic pragmatism*, represents a more reconstructive way to cope with the crisis of knowledge and self that marks the postmodern critique (see Protter, 1985, 1989). Humanist–hermeneutic pragmatism pulls sensibilities from the humanist–existential tradition (e.g., Merleau-Ponty, 1962), hermeneutic outlooks (e.g., Gadamer, 1975), and American neopragmatism (e.g., Rorty, 1982). One could say this is a more even-keeled view, in which modulated notions of objectivity and truth are goals to which to aspire in the context of a limited realism. It acknowledges the notion that lurking behind each relativistic-like claim typical of various postmodernisms lie latent appeals to objectivity and realism (see Hacking, 1999; Held, 1998; Merton, 1997). The self is neither sovereign in the radical Cartesian sense, nor insignificant and epiphenomenal in the radical anti-Cartesian sense. Notions of the self embodied in the monadic domain, stressed by a phenomenological–existential tradition that does not ignore the significance of both embodied form and structure as well as matters related to agency and will, stand in pluralistic tension with the interpersonal, dyadic self and the sociolinguistic, triadic self, each of which transfigures the other's tendency to see the self in exclusively universalist terms. The precise emphasis and focus on one of these three domains of knowing the self is partly a pragmatic decision, made in the context of the purposes and goals of theory regarding what needs to be done and accomplished. It is also a hermeneutic matter. By that, I mean that each of the domains of self is presented as a heuristic perspective in what I take to be the "reality" of the self.

Theory and Knowing the Self

Discussions of the self, particularly after postmodernity, often center around issues of enduring structure versus impressionistic situationalism, harkening back to such philosophical precursors as Leibnitz, Descartes, and Hume. Is the self an inner, substantial, and enduring structure or is it on the order of an impressionistic juxtaposition and confluence of events and phenomena "from the outside" that results in the misreading of a self signifying unity, structure, and organization "from the inside"? In contemporary psychoanalysis, this discussion is often co-coordinated with the distinction between what has been called a *one-person* psychology (partaking in what I call the monadic domain) versus a *two-person* psychology (partaking in what I call the dyadic domain). I also refer below to what amounts to a "three-person psychology" (what I call the *triadic* domain of culture–language–history). There is a way of understanding structure versus situation as a continuum of more to less structure as one moves from a monadic to a more "field-dependent" postmodern triadic domain. If one means by *structure* a very slow changing process (Rappaport, 1951), there is a sense that the last two domains can also impose a frame or structure on the self, the dyadic by the more or less enduring hold of the other(s) in relationship, and the triadic by the more or less enduring hold of language and culture from without, the world of values and normativity.

Yet the paradoxical dilemma remains—how does one identify the *who* of the action?—and a puzzling challenge presents itself: How is it that such processes as memory inhere so as to congeal into a sense of sameness and identity in a self? Both spatial and temporal metaphors, issues of continuity and discontinuity, structure and situation, are the yin and yang in understanding the self, best construed along complementary rather than mutually exclusive lines of explanation (see, e.g., for different perspectives, Gergen, 1991; Levin, 1992; Mischel, 1973; Mitchell, 1997; Modell, 1995; Sampson, 1985). The various *domains*, as I call them, touch on these issues, but they are specifically focused on the nature of the epistemic space and time in which various perspectives of the self, pulling from traditions in the human sciences and philosophy, become illuminated in psychotherapy. Each domain entails a kind of knowing process and what I take to be an accompanying "indeterminate structure" or perspective of the self as a corollary feature of this knowing process.

Elsewhere (Protter, 1988a, 1988b), I have elaborated on the interdependence of these knowledge domains, viewing psychoanalytic psychotherapy as existentially contextualized text (Protter, 1985), which connotes the meaning of subjective–agentic experience—apprehended from the contextual, interpersonal field—and understood from a particular perspective, to be read and told in some narrative value-laden form. Perhaps one of the main stories in the epistemological journey of the human sciences in the last century is indeed the point that phenomena are interwoven in this manner, and it was epistemically naive, for example, for the phenomenologists to have felt that all prejudgments, perspectives, and so on, could be bracketed out so as to achieve a purist, "first-person" knowledge. The same types of observations could be made for any of the other modes. Singly, they are problematically described if thought of as exclusive and universal because they all modify and presuppose each other in subtle and complicated ways.

Many of the conceptual debates that have taken place in the field of psychotherapy and, more generally, concerning the psychology of the self, have been attempts to elevate one domain while trumping and deconstructing another. The social construction of the self and the accompanying deconstruction of the exclusive, private, autonomous self is the most extreme instance of this. Close to two generations of analysts now have been arguing about the merits of a well-known version of competing domains, namely, that of a drive structure versus a relationship structure approach to psychoanalysis (Greenberg & Mitchell, 1983). The epistemic stakes amount to what is considered primary versus derivative and epiphenomenal. Does the clinical issue have to do with thwarted–conflicted interpersonal intimacy or with repressed–conflicted drive (sexuality)? What is psychogenetically foundational: the mother–child dyad or the endogenous vicissitudes of drive inside the monadic self? What is attended to and interpreted, the methodology of the therapy, and what is normatively valued all hinge on this issue. Each camp has developed, over the years, finely honed rhetorical skills in explaining one dynamic in terms of another, but the received wisdom is that the interpersonal–relational view has won the day, in yet another blow to the monadic self. But this victory in contemporary psychoanalysis has often been conceptualized in terms of the inadequacy of the Freudian libidinal self of sexualized drive, which is one perspective into the monadic domain of the biophenomenological self. Other monadic issues, such as "felt" embodiment (not the sexualized body of drive), agency and will, and values of privacy have an order of their own that stubbornly resist being collapsed into reconceived dyadic or triadic domains that often smuggle latent universalist assumptions into their viewpoints.

Integrative Praxis and Humanist–Hermeneutic Pragmatism

The goal of achieving something like defining "fundamental similarities and incorporating useful differences amongst the schools" (Beitman, 1992) for the purpose of psychotherapeutic praxis places us in one potentially fruitful path through the post-metapsychology theory-lite world of contemporary psychotherapy. The monadic, dyadic, and triadic domains I discuss as applied to the broader range of integrative and pluralistic psychotherapy is a schematic attempt to think through certain basic similarities and differences in psychotherapy. These three parameters operate on ontological, epistemological, and developmental levels, respectively touching on different fundamental notions about the self and human nature, how one knows others and oneself, and the psychogenesis of the self throughout the course of the life span. For purposes of discussion here, I briefly highlight the differences in the monadic, dyadic, and triadic domains as poles in an epistemic–methodological triad. They can signify, in toto, a broad-based hermeneutic–pragmatic outlook that encompasses a wide range of therapeutic approaches. At different times they play different roles in most courses of psychotherapy: sometimes front and center, sometimes background, often alternatively operating in a figure–ground sense. Purist approaches and methodologies define and delineate their outlook more or less exclusively within one domain and hence construe phenomena consistent with this. More integratively inspired approaches would be more likely to operationally shift, both hermeneutically (view of therapeutic material and the self) and pragmatically (achieving different therapeutic results).

Monadic Domain

The monadic domain operates in a unidirectional field; one might say from subjectivity—the knowing vantage point of the therapist—to objectivity, the knowable mind, behavior, and experiences of the patient's self. Another way of portraying this unidirectional field is conversely: from objectivity—that is, the objective interventions and methodologies, whether they be interpretation, cognitive restructuring, or "bracketed" phenomenologic listening—to subjectivity —that is, the self of the patient who appropriates the intervention. Although different schools would of course characterize the matter in accordance with the school's own metapsychology and theory of therapy, it is the embodied self's experience (mostly affect) and the self's endogenous capacity to be agentically empowered that are ultimately the targets of the intervention which represents core components of an agentic, biophenomenological self.

The monadic domain borrows heavily from the language and sensibilities of not only science and medicine but also education. The therapist is able to direct his or her understanding and interventions from some clearer point of detached objectivity. One might say the monadic approaches are more (although not exclusively) symptom and results oriented in that their claims for objectivity allow for an emphasis on outcome. Therapeutically operating in the monadic domain is often labeled as *positivist*, a kind of dirty word in postmodern circles. Indeed, many practitioners would seek the goal of a positivist-inspired pure-knowledge medical-type model (Berger, 1985) whereby an empirically established theory or therapeutic intervention (or both) could be systematically applied to practice in a technical–prescriptive manner so as to achieve specific results. In the realm of psychotherapy, though, such an aim is rarely or very imperfectly reached.

As alluded to above, modernist positivist metapsychology (particularly as present in psychoanalysis and behavioral psychology) has largely been the story of misfired attempts in prematurely claiming success and closure in these matters. But even in the more modest, contemporary, technical efforts of focused, short-term problem–symptom oriented therapies, as opposed to less directive psychotherapies that have a more open-ended, ambiguous, nonhomogeneous character to the clinical work, the object of the therapist's technical input—

namely, another self (the patient)—needs to appropriate the intervention in the course of psychotherapy. This self-appropriation is achieved in the "epistemic" service of facilitating greater clarity and in the curative service of making personal change in a lived life.

Achieving clarity is a result of self-interpretation. Whether the therapy is based on a stimulus–response (S–R) behavioral model or a drive–structure psychoanalytic model, in some fundamental sense the self, whether implicitly or explicitly, is being "explained" therapeutically (Woolfolk, 1998). In a post-modern climate, one might add, such explanations have a less ideological, dogmatic, and exclusive flavor. Making personal change in psychotherapy is always implicated in a thick nexus of the meaning, purpose, and value of a human life, the ends to which change is being effected. Also within each psychotherapy approach, in which the person's self is being explained and changed in some way, lies a prescriptive layer of ideal notions about health and normality. The context of meanings, values, and ends to which desired therapeutic change in one's life is placed can be more or less openly discussed depending on the purposes and purview of the therapy. The technical "means approaches" focused on narrowly defined and agreed-on goals (e.g., mastering a particular anxiety) may shift and transform the desired ends during the course of therapy, which potentially opens up a larger discourse for discussion. A more inclusive, hermeneutically conceived model of psychotherapy encompasses issues of technical causality–explanation appropriated within the epistemic space, whether in the foreground or background, of a self in a world of meaning, purposes, and values.

Dyadic Domain

Therapy in a more fully realized dyadic domain is immersed in a bidirectional field from subjectivity to subjectivity. All monadically inspired approaches, inasmuch as psychotherapy is a two-person endeavor, pull in some manner from the dyadic domain. This is captured by the broad-based notion of the therapeutic alliance and its family constellation of like-minded terms, a host of well-established process and outcome relationship variables (e.g., therapeutic warmth and congruence), and widely acknowledged "placebogenic" factors of therapist-to-patient influence such as occur, for example, in monadically oriented hypnotherapy practices.

Dyadic approaches are more fully intersubjective: Any intervention in the therapy must primarily take into account the meaning and nature of the interaction between subjectivities that were the occasion for the intervention. Although enlightened monadically oriented practice would acknowledge participant–observational factors in praxis as an adjustment parameter toward the realization of some greater objectivity, dyadic approaches more fully make the claim that such factors constitute the very nature of the work. The significance of the therapeutic material can be fully unpacked only by accessing the subjective states (conscious and unconscious) of patient and therapist and how these subjective states are mutually influenced and constructed during the course of therapy. This kind of interpersonal knowing presupposes as central the notion of the *interactive relational self*, a self constituted by "relational units" that are shaped and organized and ultimately derived from the interactivity with other selves in different relational contexts. The self-interacting-with-others-in-the-world may revolve around such issues as safety, security, self-esteem, or individualism. Whatever the "stuff" of the interplay with the other is, it is the sheer ontic alterity of the other (Taylor, 1987)—the otherness of the other— in his or her difference from this self that is positioning and constructive of a self that is centrally informative of character and personality. The presence of this other "within" or "outside" the self can also be understood as a major decentering factor toward the postmodern deconstruction of the universally conceived monadic, private self of insularity. The self is, in effect, always psychically negotiating and differentiating itself from other selves. How much of the self-with-others is taken in or internalized as structural disposition in the form of self–other schemas (as affective, cognitive, or actional dispositions), to be potentially enacted with future others, is a matter that has separated more drive-structured object relationalists from more field-oriented interpersonalists.

Many psychotherapies may embrace the importance and centrality of the interactive–relationist self but focus their intervention not inside but outside the therapeutic frame. Some have argued that what separates the former approaches from the latter is precisely what demarcates a psychotherapeutic sensibility from a psychoanalytic one. In psychoanalytic terms, transference has been the concept to most centrally bridge the entree to the dyadic domain, but in the Freudian lineage, as it is related to the psychoanalytic situation, *transference* is largely a unidirectional term that focuses on what the patient does to the analyst against the backdrop of a blank-screen therapist. The emphasis is on the patient's displaced distortion of the analyst and the analyst's understanding of the patient by means of these distortions. A more open, participatory–interactive focus in post-Freudian analytic work has set the tone for such notions as transference–countertransference and cotransference matrices (e.g., Aron, 1996; Hoffman, 1983; Racker, 1968; Sandler, 1976). These approaches have greatly enriched our views of character and personality and enhanced our understanding of the two-party psychotherapy process.

As characterologic presentations both manifest and alter themselves in an intersubjective matrix of shifting experiences and enacted behavioral patterns that are importantly lived through and enacted, the cutting edge of post-Freudian relational approaches emphasize the process subtleties and intricacies of the continually shifting bidirectional field. This process can be only evanescently, and often only retrospectively, "caught" and understood in narrative terms. Mitchell (1997) demarcated a broad spectrum of contemporary dyadic analytic approaches according to the objectivity of the analyst's stance, achieved by appealing to more unmediated knowable features of a monadic self that can stand outside the interpersonal field so as to grant a greater degree of epistemic authority to the therapist. He compared the object-relations stance with the more radical interpersonalist stances, which can be said to occupy a more fully realized logical extension of the dyadic domain. Although the challenging epistemic demands of dialogical openness in more cutting-edge contemporary interpersonal work have made widely acknowledged advances over earlier dogmatic approaches—which have often been valorized in a postmodern sensibility of ambiguity and uncertainty—they also situate psychoanalysis on a slippery slope of "flattened interactionism" (Protter, 1996). Issues of objectivity in regard to systems of validation and therapeutic outcome can become clouded in the dizzying swirl and infinite regress of process (see, e.g., Bader, 1998). Some would argue that the nuanced meaning of the process interactions are less important than the correctively new experience of an authenticated and democratized relationship with the other.

Triadic Domain

The world of language–culture–history—which has variously been referred to by Popper (1972) as "World 3," Lacan (1988) as "the symbolic order," Wittgenstein (1953) as "forms of life and language games," Geertz (1983) as "the symbolic trafficking of culture," Kuhn (1970) as "paradigms," and Foucault (1982) as "discourses" or "*systemes*"—speaks to the constitutive nature of the sociolinguistic dimension. The triadic domain represents both the shared sociolinguistic world of practices, norms, and conventions that presupposes the very possibility of intersubjective communication and meaning and the long and powerful reach of the sundry socialization processes that delineate narratives of the self throughout the cultural horizon. These narratives include the clinical presentation of patients in psychotherapy who tell stories of how a self lives and conducts a life as well as the manner in which the therapist retells this story to him- or herself and the patient. Psychotherapy as an institution is shaped by the culture, and psychotherapy has been a shaping force in the articulation of modern culture. The hermeneutic world of values and virtues highlights the triadic dimension in psychotherapy praxis. This is expressed in generalized health and humanistic values shared by virtually all approaches to psychotherapy as well as in the differing sensibilities and emphases in the various schools. The categories of the "social" and the "cultural," of course, have been a prominent influence in psychology, psychotherapy, and psychoanalysis. The most recent emphasis on the social construction of the self has proceeded apace in such areas as gender (Bem, 1993; Goldner, 1991), character (Roland, 1988; Schweder, 1991), emotion (Harre, 1986), psychodiagnosis (Kleinman, 1988; Showalter, 1997), and folk-cultural psychology (Bruner, 1990; Shotter, 1993), in addition to more broad-based pronouncements concerning the fate of the postmodern self (Cushman, 1995; Gergen, 1991; Sampson, 1988). Within psychoanalysis proper, Lacan and his followers have championed the decentering effects of the symbolic order on the self. How the sociocultural–historical field has affected individual personality and psychology has been the province of the neo-Freudian culturalists. Such theorists as Fromm (1964) and other post-Freudian thinkers, notably in the Frankfurt school tradition of critical theory, have attempted to wed a sociohistorical emancipatory narrative to an individual psychoanalytical one by embracing one or another grand narrative explanation of the repressive or thwarting effect of the larger social order on human experience.

The emphasis on the normative–prescriptive dimension of psychotherapy is the most completely postmodernist–historicist position and, taken in the exclusionary extreme, as indicated above views psychotherapy as pure ideology. "Hermeneutic data" are not only theory and method laden but also value laden. Values in turn are constituted and shaped by larger cultural–historical units. Theories (e.g., about the self) are radically intertwined and situated not just in the contextual–interpersonal field in the session but in a larger cultural–historical field encompassing therapist, therapy, and patient. Indeed, it is the ethos and values of modern selfhood—how we lead our lives and their purpose, meaning, and significance—that has come under the most critical scrutiny in a certain strand of "revisionist" postmodern thinking. In what has been described as "modern anthropocentrism," the self simultaneously assumes an inflated but ultimately depleted significance. With the loss of shared worlds and communities that produce a texture of meanings, goals, and purposes, more burden is placed on the self. In an instrumentalist, "disenchanted world" the self needs to inflate itself and organize around such individualistic ideologies as self-actualization and the pursuit of personal gratification as a kind of compensation for what it has lost (Cushman, 1995; Smith, 1994). The modern, individual self "defines its moral universe as so many strategies of self fulfillment" (Bellah et al., 1985, p. 48), devoid of larger transcendent values or, in Taylor's (1991) words, "horizons of significance." Such an individualist view conceives of

> the life course without referent to any social or historical context—every life crisis, not just that of adolescence, is a crisis of separation–individuation, but what the ever freer and more autonomous self is free for grows more obscure. Thinking about the life course in this way may exacerbate rather than resolve the problem of the meaning of the individual life. (Bellah et al., 1985, p. 82)

Some recent writers in psychotherapy (e.g., Doherty, 1995; Wallach & Wallach, 1983) have taken critical positions against the ethos of self-interest utilitarianism in its "avirtuous" and "amoral" stance. From the perspective of some recent neo-Aristotelian philosophers, psychotherapy and its intrinsic goals of happiness and fulfillment are self-contradictory notions unless they also are understood as latent appeals to a certain process of virtue creation that takes place in the triadic domain. This has a psychophilosophical lineage that goes back to the Stoics (Gewirth, 1998; Nussbaum, 1994).

My point here is not to offer a solution to this postmodern crisis, or even necessarily to agree with the analysis of it in all its forms (other postmodernists would revel in a "freer" and less engaged, more "protean" self), but to underline the critical movement involved in historically situating the self—which is, after all, the focus and raison d'etre of modern therapeutic culture—and making it problematic; that is, to take what is accepted as a naturalized state of affairs (the self and its cultural–moral life in contemporary culture) and to thematize it and radically place it in a historically contingent, normative–prescriptive context, which is epistemically just about where the sociolinguistic self is located. This self of the triadic domain has been variously described in terms, from afar, as a cultural and historical "type" (e.g., Lasch's narcissistic character, Reiff's psychological man) or, up close, as a kind of Goffmanesque (Goffman, 1961) presentation of self located at the joints of the "demand characteristics" of the social practice or game. Other writers, in a more monadically oriented humanistic vein, have emphasized the authorial features of the triadic self. Achieving the self is a process of meaning-making as a kind of "narrative quest" (MacIntyre, 1981), which takes place in the context of an individuating and agonistic relationship with a culture or tradition.

Symptoms, Character, and Philosophy of Life

A helpful distinction in psychotherapy is between the therapeutic narratives and methodologies that focus on (a) symptoms or problems; (b) character, personality, or core schemas; and (c) philosophy of life and ideology. These areas are interrelated but distinctive in important ways. People go to therapists implicitly and explicitly for help with any of the above.

The relationship between symptoms (or focal problems) and character is certainly more multifaceted than was conceptualized in earlier debates between the behaviorists and analysts of the 1950s through the 1970s. Symptoms can be "caused" by larger or underlying character or personality patterns. Symptoms can also cause large-scale personality adaptations. The two can be comorbidly associated or be, in effect, independent of each other. Any person of course who presents him- or herself to a therapist with a symptomatic problem does so, as is true of any individual, with a complicated set of personality patterns and adjustments in the self's life situation. The older view, which has since been rebutted empirically and conceptually, that removing the symptom in a larger characterological picture results only in a displacement to another symptomatic manifestation, was based on a kind of crude energic–hydraulic psychodynamic outlook. Some of the most noted success stories in psychotherapy have focused on specialized problems (e.g., certain anxiety disorders, sexual dysfunction), and the increasing use of specialized therapeutic modules or approaches to certain syndromes or diagnostic presentations attests to this. The narrative tools and methodologies of cognitive–behavioral-inspired viewpoints have been most successful in this and related areas of focus, which have emphasized the sensibility of mastery and problem-solving outlooks and skills and largely focus on the monadic domain of the self. The "personal theory as personal science" viewpoint (Mahoney, 1980) is heuristically descriptive of a sensibility that fosters a rational, open-minded, scientific outlook that can be used to view the problem–symptom object of one's own psychological experience—a kind of scientific, open-minded, self-observation or "observing ego."

Character, personality, and core schemas have been the province of psychodynamic and humanistic—and, more recently, cognitive—approaches that implicitly incorporate dynamic and humanistic sensibilities. Exploratory therapists generally map the larger network of meanings and relationships in the individual's life. Sometimes symptoms, or problematic traits and patterns, may be in the foreground or background or not particularly there at all. Sometimes they are able to be formulated by one or both partners in the therapy, sometimes not. In the former case, if more narrowly focused therapeutic approaches targeting symptoms are not working, it is usually clinically advisable to look to more core schema issues that may be relevant. In the latter case, often the individual self may have more vague complaints or inchoately want more satisfaction out of a life. Indeed, the therapist may need to spell things out before the issues are formulated in terms of problems to be changed. It may also be that what was labeled a symptom or problem to be changed may be a red herring or a communication about a different state of affairs in the life of the self, seen differently in a larger clinical picture. The relational therapists, as indicated above, who operate largely in the dyadic domain, have written extensively on an essentially interpersonal "spelling-out" process involved in psychotherapy, viewing individual personality as interpersonal relations. A variety of integrative therapists have emphasized the benefits of a complementary-stage use of facilitative clarificatory procedures followed by action-oriented interventions to translate insight into instigation of new behaviors (Prochaska & DiClemente, 1992; Wachtel, 1997). Conversely, others have used biobehavioral interventions at the initiation of therapy that can offer a measure of symptomatic relief (Beitman, 1992; Rhoads, 1988) to remove impediments to more clarificatory process. Certainly, the Cartesian bifurcation of a cognitively weighted insight and a behaviorally weighted action has been the occasion of much nonproductive competition between various approaches. Insight—or, better stated, internal cognitive–affective shifts—can be facilitated by actions-in-the-world. Synergistic reverberations of these two poles, insight and action, can make for dramatic change.

A third reason people seek therapy is what I have termed *philosophy of life* or *ideological* reasons. In the process of examining a life—or, for that matter, even focusing on a specific problem—psychotherapists may offer a philosophy of life or an ideological belief system. In the most general sense, the values of a psychotherapeutic sensibility—the therapeutic culture—aspects of which have been criticized and lampooned by the media and other critics, have been embraced by many sectors of society. Core philosophical values inhere in these sensibilities and include a range of humanistic and hermeneutic perspectives that can be traced back to Plato, Augustine, and Judeo–Christian influences (Fromm, 1964; London, 1986). The importance of a caring, healing relationship in the service of enlightenment and change is primary among these values.

In the more narrow sense, schools or therapeutic outlooks have had specific appeal because of their encompassing worldviews and sensibilities (see, e.g., Frank, 1973; Messer, 1992; Schafer, 1983). The modernist euphoria described above is the extreme ideological instance of this; one thinks of the mystique and fervor of earlier psychoanalytic sects and societies. It is still not unusual today, at least in the community in which I live, for a contemporary practicing analyst, for example, to have 80% of his practice be composed of other analytically oriented therapists in training. This is not necessarily bad or good. Indeed, the development of psychotherapy technique and theory goes on productively in pure-school approaches, as it does in more integrative outlooks. Certainly, strong identifications with "community-of-healers"-oriented approaches—as, for example, 12-step-inspired therapeutic programs—have arguably provided some of the most effective—in their sheer impact—transformative philosophy-of-life narratives in the history of psychotherapy. Often philosophy-of-life approaches have a wide appeal because of their response to wider extant sensibilities in the culture, such as earlier liberating psychoanalytic views in the context of a Victorian repressive society, or humanistic psychology outlooks as reactions to a technical instrumentalist age. Currently, one could argue, for example, that the ascendance of New Age views, which speak of "transcendence," "spirit," "mythos," and so on, has an ideological appeal to an inchoate urge to go beyond the modern self. A cautionary note with regard to the notion of "therapy as philosophy of life" needs to emphasize the ever-present possibility of narrowness (there is only one right way), banality (everything becomes the same—e.g., the cult of the inner child) and, more pernicious, diagnostic blindness (the philosophy of life may obscure in some way other problems that need to be addressed differently). Integratively inspired approaches, which can come in all stripes and varieties, may import various philosophy-of-life sensibilities in one shape or another but generally keep a steady eye on pragmatically related issues.

Illuminating the Domains Therapeutically

I suggested that the knowing domains operate as separate though inter-related psychoepistemic heuristic avenues to the biophenomenological self, the interactive–relational self, and the sociolinguistic self in a wide spectrum of psychotherapeutic approaches. In Table 13.1, I schematize and make some brief comments about various features of these domains in regard to therapeutic modes of action, attributes, and goals associated with these modes.

By *therapeutic illumination,* I mean the reorganizing and reconstructing of a self's experiences by a spelling-out process of exposure–disclosure and rework-ing in the therapy. In a generic sense, exposure–disclosure has largely been associated with a movement toward personal change in approaches as different as psychoanalysis and behavioral therapy. Bringing into the light of day, facing the reality of, and more clearly elucidating the fears, inhibitions, conflicts, lim-itations, needs, and relational patterns of the self in an impactful way—whether affectively, cognitively, or actively—is an essential step in psychotherapy. Fur-thermore, the process of achieving this, whether it be in the form of discovering and reowning a split-off part of the self, or in exposing one's self in a thera-peutically structured manner to a known source of avoidance fears, may be sufficient to facilitate the self toward a self-corrective course of change. Often, for change to be consolidated further therapeutic reworking needs to occur—that is, a practice, or rehearsal, a working through, or a repetitive playing over, of themes and issues earlier brought to light. This can be done in a directive or a nondirective manner, in session or outside of the session, depending on many of the issues mentioned above.

In the monadic domain, therapeutic illumination is most often associated with a kind of generic emphasis on expressive–actional modes. Catharsis has been an important therapeutic feature in such varied approaches as psychoan-alytic, Gestalt–existential, and behavioral. Catharsis has had a kind of "steam kettle" or psychodramatic connotation of a crude affective spilling out. By *expressive–actional*, though, I mean to connote a broader category in which one's inner sense of being becomes known to oneself through an act of expressive-ness. This centrally involves the "felt embodied sense"—or, in more common lingo, the world of affects–feelings–moods. Although the embodied subjective world is in essential and crucial ways a site for the interpersonal construction of emotions in dyadic relationships, and is shaped as well by larger triadic social constructive factors, emotions first and foremost emanate from, and are con-cretely incarnated in, the embodied self. This expressiveness may also be in the form of action in the world as "trial and experimental" behavior, or it may pull

TABLE 13.1

Features of the Therapeutic Domains

DOMAIN	FIELD OF KNOWING	SELF	THERAPEUTIC ILLUMINATIONS	ATTRIBUTES–GOALS
Monadic	Unidirectional	Biophenomenological consciousness	Expressive–active modes	Self-regulation, inner attunement, will and agency
Dyadic	Bidirectional	Interpersonal–interactive other-consciousness	Relationship–collaborative modes	Relatedness, collaboration, intimacy
Triadic	From without	Sociolinguistic self-consciousness	Interpretive–valuational modes	Meaning, reflexivity, valuation

from the imaginal capacity in the projection of choiceful possibilities understood as an opening up to a sense of futurity.

The regulation of and attunement to this world of "embodied sense" which, as research increasingly indicates, includes a host of biodispositional factors (temperament, activity level, etc.), has been in recent years bioarchitecturally mapped out by the efforts of psycho–neuro–hormonal investigators (see, e.g., Ledoux, 1996; Pert, 1996). Their efforts have placed in clearer perspective both the mind–body splits (cortex–limbic system gap) and interconnections (neuropeptide effects on brain interactions with internal organs, the gut, and the immune system) that roughly translate into therapeutic issues centering on such matters as affective discharge and control (earlier, the monadic aim of "renunciatory" classical analysis), and inner-affective attunement, the purview of a range of sensibilities in self-meditative and holistic biopsychological approaches. The area of psychopharmacology, arguably the most pervasive component in integrative psychotherapy (as it is incorporated within some form of "talking" therapy) has become an important biointervention in certain instances in which the felt embodied sense of self may need to be retuned in some manner. In addition to the general ameliorative impact such interventions may have, they can productively facilitate further work in therapy.

As Kierkegaard stated long ago in a different context, the expression of existential choice—that is, a choice that matters in the personal change of a lived life—does not happen in abstract cerebration but is a result of the capacity of the agency or will of a self to be passionately engaged. An important line of academic therapy research has repeatedly indicated that therapeutic change is propelled only if the individual experiences a significant affective component (Bergin & Garfield, 1994). Indeed, a self-selection of patients on the criteria of "I can't stand it anymore—I've emotionally had it—something has to change" is the best guarantee of psychotherapy success, whatever the approach. Furthermore, many people would state that in a larger sense, the matter of finding a voice, or seizing a sense of authorship of one's life, is most fully and authentically enacted by affectively embracing the felt embodied sense. The line of psychological thinkers who have commented on the notion of an expression of a "true self" usually grounds itself in some manner in the "wisdom of the body."

Many people would argue that relationship factors are the most crucial in the therapeutic enterprise. A line of important research has consistently indicated that the support and caring of, and collaboration between, therapist and patient are key factors in therapeutic outcome (Lambert, 1992). The good-enough therapist necessarily operates in the dyadic domain by providing a kind of safe steady-state human relational contact with the other, whatever the nature of the role of the therapist (therapeutic and working alliance, benign positive transference, mirroring self–object, authentic encounter). The therapeutic relationship also provides a self–other medium of exposure–disclosure and reworking from which to access, elucidate, and edify the psychological issues and factors (past and present fears, conflicts, delimitations, insecurities) that are delineated in self–other matrices and patterns. Some approaches presuppose a necessarily existing therapeutic alliance that can be narrowed in the direction of a contractual arrangement to cognitively–behaviorally target certain problems. Other approaches, often with a character–relational scope, attend to and therapeutically play out a host of relational factors that cluster around, and often get in the way of, the therapeutic alliance. The relationship can become the axis in which key experiences are constructively relived and correctively re-experienced (e.g., disconfirming a fear, or expectation, from a self–other perspective), which may, in some manner, facilitate the expressionistic process of the self referred to earlier.

The particulars of the intepetative slant and narrative bent on the therapeutic work—the triadic domain of the therapist's school interpretive community—seems to be less of a significant factor in therapeutic-outcome research (Lambert, 1992). Few would disagree, though, that, more generically, clarity of meaning, formulation of experience, and the nature of the story we tell ourselves and others—the narrative dimension—is essential in psychotherapy. Indeed, this is often seen as the sine qua non of therapy, and it is the only medium, certainly, in which we can "talk about" therapy. Roughly speaking, this domain may be said to represent a more fully realized sense of self-consciousness, a self capable of observing itself in the larger symbolic order (and as well, as indicated above, a self that may get definitionally immersed in the culture), as opposed to, respectively, consciousness and other-consciousness of monadic and dyadic domains.

All systems of psychotherapy are interpretive–valuational, including the focus of the cognitive–behaviorist who, in instructing his client to make a journal of trigger stressor anxieties that precipitate a problematic behavior, is interpretively carving out the phenomena of therapeutic relevance and value. There is probably an agreed-on finite list of psychological truths that noncontroversially would enter the narratives of a variety of therapies—certainly, those of many integrative therapies. The importance of learning, attachment, self-deception, and latent process and biodispositional factors comes to mind. Conducting narrative psychotherapy, though, as indicated above, is not simply the reflection of expertise in specialized psychological knowledge and principles. Some would argue (Bruner, 1990; Woolfolk, 1998) that psychotherapy is a folk-cultural activity in which the therapist's expertise is one of an astute reader and instructor in the shared conventional wisdom of the commonsense psychological and interpersonal relationship culture. The "common sense," of course, is often not shared by all and can be explicitly valuational. Think of the cluster and intersection of psychological issues and values revealed in the narrative unfolding of a besieged middle-class woman with children, undergoing a divorce and attempting—however ambivalently—to be successful in the contemporary world about which she is trying to get clear. She sees (in a thought experiment) two similarly trained therapists, one an admirer of Pat Robertson, the other an admirer of Simone de Beauvoir. The narrative of the two therapies might very well be read and rewritten in radically different ways. Indeed, most often the triadic domain of values and virtues operates silently though pervasively in the work; it makes itself known, sometimes dramatically, when there is a clash or conflict of value domains in therapist and patient.

The Case of Tony Soprano

There is no "pure" generic psychotherapy. Psychotherapists practice from all sorts of perspectives and methodologies. Patients in turn select therapists for a whole host of variables. These include the nature and kind of problems to be treated and, with increasingly sophisticated consumers, a specific preference for therapists' theories and approaches. Certainly, the interpersonal feel of the initial therapist–patient encounters is vital in selecting and sustaining a choice. Of course, systemic economic matters, such as managed-care policy, are centrally determinant in the types of choices available to psychotherapy clients.

I have chosen to very briefly illustrate some of the epistemic parameters mentioned above in a widely known, fictionalized account of what might be described as a generic, vaguely integrative, "out-of-pocket" psychotherapy, namely, that of Tony Soprano, the lead character of the Emmy-award-winning HBO series *The Sopranos*. Tony Soprano, a second-generation Italian American, is a successful underworld crime figure who with his own crew is engaged in assorted acts of embezzlement, thievery, often-brutal intimidation and, occasionally, murder. Yet these acts are done in a manner and style representative of a "Mafia" in transition, more white-collar oriented and less rigidly codified than in earlier "Godfather"-type characterizations. The program is really a series of shifting vignettes between the straight upper-middle class New Jersey suburban world of various mundane but often hot-button domestic issues and conflicts—such as applying to college, a mother with senility and dementia going to a nursing home, a distant father–son relationship—and Tony's immersion in the ruthless underworld climate of organized crime as well as all points between.

Early in the series Tony, who has a minor public reputation as a crime figure but who characteristically splits his work and domestic, suburban life as he presents to the rest of the world (including his family), seeks out psychological help because he experiences some anxiety symptoms consistent with panic disorder. He is referred to a therapist, Dr. Melfi, who also happens to be an Italian American and lives in the same community of successful business and professional people as Tony does. This ongoing psychotherapy is portrayed in very brief vignettes that run like a leitmotif throughout the series. What transpires in the generic psychotherapy is in some ways probably typical, in other ways clearly not so. Tony, after describing his anxious symptoms and other related experiences, is offered monadic procedures, namely medication (his therapist is a psychiatrist). It could just as well be one of a number of cognitive–behavioral treatment protocols; both of these procedures have pretty good outcome results (often when integrated with one another) in successfully targeting problematic affect, and concerning increased mastery of coping skills in regard to self-state regulation. It would appear that the anxious symptoms improve somewhat, and Tony finds himself continuing to utilize therapy, warily and guardedly, as a kind of impersonalized ventilation vehicle, expressing mostly angers and frustrations in his periodic visits although at times attempting to exercise his "alpha male" prerogatives by sexualizing the relationship. Some level of therapeutic alliance is able to support the general continuity of the work.

What emerges fitfully (at least as portrayed in the therapy sessions—the viewer of course has a smoother filmic narrative of episodes of Tony's actual life) is, minus the crime underworld identity (which for the most part is tacitly not discussed in the therapy), a profile of interpersonal self–other patterns, clinically typical of an angry, at times explosive, impulsive–narcissistic character who is very capable of displaying at times an appealing, boyish, not unlikable charm and warmth. His character, one readily infers, was formed in large part by dysfunctional, poor parenting, personified by a severely narcissistic, at times malevolent mother (at least as portrayed in later life). The therapist, in addition to the earlier biobehavioral intervention, operates in what one would imagine is a largely monadic, intrapsychic psychodynamic manner (although clearly accessing dyadic character patterns), offering modulated commentary in regard to Tony's feeling states and his defenses (e.g., his needs to deny and insulate himself from his mother's coldness) intuitively picking up on his affective states interspersed with psychoeducational information that is conveyed to the patient about the operation of feelings and interpersonal relationships. Not much of this relatively stable course of the therapy is portrayed as explicitly making anything of the dyadic relationship inside the treatment. Then catastrophe occurs: The triadic domain of the therapy—namely, the radically disjunctive value lifestyle worlds of the patient and the therapist—forcefully intrudes into the psychotherapy, blowing it apart. Tony suddenly needs to abandon treatment because he fears that some underworld cohorts, who have some knowledge that Tony is in therapy, may be determined to try to harm or kill Dr. Melfi because of concerns that she may be betraying confidentiality, fueled as well by concerns that inasmuch as Tony is in therapy, he might well be "losing it." Tony precipitously demands that Dr. Melfi, in effect, get out of town and ditch her practice, which she is forced to do by relocating and practicing out of a motel. While these fearful concerns that Tony has "blow over," pandemonium breaks loose as well in the internal life of Dr. Melfi. She is now consulting her own therapist, terrified, overwhelmed, and furious, as well as confused about what has occurred. After a period of time, she resumes therapy with Tony, contacting him after she had refused to see him when he made an earlier request. Meanwhile Dr. Melfi dismisses queries from her own therapist that she might somehow be attracted to or excited by Tony, stubbornly insisting that she is abandoning Tony in some way (expressed in her dreams), and the psychotherapy resumes. Tony's underworld life episodically breaks through in varying ways, despite Dr. Melfi's efforts to more explicitly keep it in the background, in the guise of not "being judgmental." Some degree of "neutrality" is gallantly attempted to be struck by Dr. Melfi, now more centrally impinging on ethical value-laden issues in the midst of powerful interpersonally generated emotions, not the least of which is the fearful outburst of looming danger in the thicket of intertwining dyadic and triadic domains. As the second season of the series ends, Dr. Melfi becomes more real both in acknowledging her own feeling in the treatment of Mr. Soprano and in some critical comments directed at Tony's life style. The "therapeutic outcome" is yet unclear.

This fictional psychotherapy is, of course, anything but generic, but it serves to portray the tension between the interviewer and the at-times-separate modes of operation of the various domains, particularly portrayed in a graphic manner with respect to the triadic domain, which more often operates in a more silent, naturalized manner in psychotherapy. In respect to the case example above, there is no necessary interrelationship of panic disorder symptoms, narcissistic–explosive character, and criminal underworld lifestyle and values. Any of the other foci can be bracketed out for pragmatic purposes. Sometimes we may pay a toll for such exclusion; in the case of Tony, one could say that the triadic value issue should have been explicitly aired out in the sessions, Tony's guardedness notwithstanding. Something on the order of "If I help you be less anxious, will that make you a better criminal?" might have been an interesting—and, one might add, courageous—line of inquiry, although it is likely that if it had, the treatment would have dramatically ended. My point here is not to explore why other therapeutic options were not taken in this fictitious treatment but to highlight that there is another level of inquiry here—more graphically displayed in this example—just as more commonly one might miss crucially formative dyadic issues of personality and character by exclusive and dogmatic focus on symptom-alteration psychotechnology. Many therapies proceed from a monadic to an interpersonal spelling-out process in the dyadic realm (inside and outside session), from which often emerges a more subtle realization of value-laden issues. More often though, the triadic domain of values shifts over the course of therapies rather than in a single therapy. When one thinks of the big value-laden, normative issues that have emerged since psychotherapy appeared on the scene a century ago—such as gender identity issues, sexual orientation, and the triumph of the individual consumer self—one realizes that they have all represented larger cultural shifts that have only gradually become absorbed into psychotherapy modes and ideals.

Conclusion

In an integrative–pluralistic psychotherapeutic climate, a world of many perspectives—including the interrelationship of these views, utilization of experiences, methodologies, and narratives—is pulled from three psychoepistemic domains, resulting in the rather unique enterprise we call psychotherapy, a hybrid tension of explanatory, descriptive, and prescriptive discourse. One of these domains may be emphasized in the foreground, while others play background roles; pragmatic considerations are always present. Reconstructive postmodern sensibilities are leery of a world of only one view—what in the present context may be called *domain hegemony*, apropos of modernist metapsychological universalization. Although each domain can rhetorically deconstruct the purview of the others virtually out of existence and reconstrue the phenomena exclusively in terms of its own perspective, each domain has an order of its own that cannot be reduced to some other order. Future efforts toward the project of enriching integrative psychotherapy might be fruitfully directed at further understanding the nature and interaction of these psychoepistemic domains in the operations of psychotherapy.

References

Aron, L. (1996). *A meeting of minds: Mutuality in psychoanalysis.* Hillsdale, NJ: Analytic Press.

Bader, M. J. (1998). Postmodern epistemology: The problem of validation and the retreat from therapeutics in psychoanalysis. *Psychoanalytic Dialogues, 8,* 1–32.

Beitman, B. (1992). Integrating the fundamental similarities and useful differences among the schools. In J. Norcross & M. Goldfried (Eds.), *Handbook of psychotherapy integration* (pp. 202–231). New York: Basic Books.

Bellah, R., Madsen, R., Sullivan, S., Swidler, A., & Tipton, S. M. (1985). *Habits of the heart.* Berkeley: University of California Press.

Bem, S. (1993). *The lenses of gender.* New Haven, CT: Yale University Press.

Berger, L. (1985). *Psychoanalytic theory and clinical relevance.* Hillsdale, NJ: Analytic Press.

Bergin, A., & Garfield, S. (Eds.). (1994). *Handbook of psychotherapy and behavioral change* (4th ed.). New York: Wiley.

Bruner, J. (1990). *Acts of meaning*. Cambridge, MA: Harvard University Press.

Cushman, P. (1995). *Constructing the self, constructing America: A cultural history of psychotherapy*. Reading, MA: Addison-Wesley.

Doherty, W. (1995). *Soul searching: Why psychotherapy must promote moral responsibility*. New York: Basic Books.

Foucault, M. (1982). *Archeology of knowledge*. New York: Pantheon.

Frank, J. (1973). *Persuasion and healing: A comparative study of psychotherapy*. Baltimore: Johns Hopkins University Press.

Fromm, E. (1964). *The heart of man*. New York: Harper & Row.

Gadamer, H. (1975). *Truth and method* (G. Bunden & J. Cuming, Eds. & Trans.). Cambridge, England: Cambridge University Press.

Geertz, C. (1983). *Local knowledge: Further essays in interpretation anthropology*. New York: Basic Books.

Gergen, K. (1991). *The saturated self*. New York: Basic Books.

Gewirth, A. (1998). *Self-fulfillment*. Princeton, NJ: Princeton University Press.

Goffman, I. (1961). *Presentation of self in everyday life*. New York: Doubleday.

Goldner, V. (1991). Toward a critical relational theory of gender. *Psychoanalytic Dialogues, 1,* 249–272.

Greenberg, J., & Mitchell, S. (1983). *Object relations in psychoanalysis*. Cambridge, MA: Harvard University Press.

Hacking, I. (1999). *The social construction of what?* Cambridge, MA: Harvard University Press.

Harre, R. (Ed.). (1986). *The social construction of emotions*. London: Basil Blackwell.

Held, B. (1998). *Back to reality*. New York: Norton.

Hoffman, L. (1983). A reflexive stance for family therapy. In S. McNanee & K. Gergen (Eds.), *Therapy as a social construction* (pp. 7–24). San Francisco: Sage.

Jensen, J., Bergin, A., & Greaves, D. (1990). The meaning of eclecticism: New surveys and analysis of components. *Professional Psychology Review and Practice, 21,* 124–130.

Kleinman, A. (1988). *Rethinking psychiatry: From cultural category to personal experience*. New York: Free Press.

Kuhn, T. (1970). *The structure of scientific revolution* (2nd ed.). Chicago: University of Chicago Press.

Lacan, N. (1988). *The seminars of J. Lacan, Book 1* (S. Miller, Ed. & Trans.). New York: Norton.

Lambert, M. (1992). Psychotherapy outcome research: Implications for integrative and eclectic therapists. In J. Norcross & M. Goldfried (Eds.), *Handbook of psychotherapy integration* (pp. 94–130). New York: Basic Books.

Ledoux, J. (1996). *The emotional brain.* New York: Simon & Schuster.

Levin, J. (1992). *Theories of the self.* Washington, DC: Hemisphere.

London, P. (1986). *Modes and morals of psychotherapy* (2nd ed.). New York: Rinehart & Holt.

Mahoney, M. (1980). Psychotherapy and the structure of personal revolutions. In M. Mahoney (Ed.), *Psychotherapy process* (pp. 157–180). New York: Plenum Press.

MacIntyre, A. (1981). *After virtue.* South Bend, IN: University of Notre Dame Press.

Merleau-Ponty, M. (1962). *The phenomenology of perception* (C. Smith, Trans.). New York: Routledge & Kegan Paul.

Merton, T. (1997). *The last word.* London: Oxford University Press.

Messer, S. (1992). A critical examination of belief structures in integrative and eclectic psychotherapy. In J. Norcross & M. Goldfried (Eds.), *Handbook of psychotherapy integration* (pp. 130–169). New York: Basic Books.

Mischel, W. (1973). Toward a cognitive social learning reconceptualization of personality. *Psychological Review, 80,* 252–283.

Mitchell, S. (1997). *Influence and autonomy.* Hillsdale, NJ: Analytic Press.

Modell, A. (1989). *Psychoanalysis in a new context.* New York: Basic Books.

Modell, A. (1995). *The private self.* Cambridge, MA: Harvard University Press.

Neimeyer, R., & Mahoney, M. (1995). *Constructivism in psychotherapy.* Washington, DC: American Psychological Association.

Norcross, J., & Goldfried, M. (Eds.). (1992). *Handbook of psychotherapy integration.* New York: Basic Books.

Nussbaum, M. (1994). *The therapy of desire: Theory and practice in hellenistic ethics.* Princeton, NJ: Princeton University Press.

Pert, C. (1996). *Molecules of emotion.* New York: Scribner.

Popper, K. (1972). *Objective knowing: An evolutionary approach.* London: Oxford University Press.

Prochaska, J., & DiClemente, C. (1992). The transtheoretical approach. In J. Norcross & M. Goldfried (Eds.), *Handbook of psychotherapy integration* (pp. 300–335). New York: Basic Books.

Protter, B. (1985). Toward an emergent psychoanalytic epistemology. *Contemporary Psychoanalysis, 21,* 208–227.

Protter, B. (1988a). Some reflections on the nature of the psychoanalytic process. *Contemporary Psychoanalysis, 23,* 142–155.

Protter, B. (1988b). Ways of knowing: Some epistemic considerations for an autonomous theory of psychoanalytic praxis. *Contemporary Psychoanalysis, 24,* 498–526.

Protter, B. (1989, May). *The bridge between hermeneutics and science: Remarks on Grunbaum's presentations*. Paper presented to the meeting of the American Academy of Psychoanalysis, New York.

Protter, B. (1996). Classical, modern and postmodern psychology: Epistemy and transformation. *Psychoanalytic Dialogues, 6,* 533–562.

Racker, H. (1968). *Transference and countertransference*. New York: International Universities Press.

Rappaport, D. (1951). *Organization and pathology of thought*. New York: Columbia University Press.

Rhoads, J. (1988). Combination and synthesism in psychotherapies. *Annals of Psychotherapy, 18,* 280–289.

Roland, A. (1988). *In search of self in India and Japan: Towards a cross-cultural psychology*. Princeton, NJ: Princeton University Press.

Rorty, R. (1982). *Consequences of pragmatism*. Minneapolis: University of Minnesota Press.

Sampson, E. (1985). The decentralization of identity: Toward a revitalized concept of personal and social order. *American Psychologist, 40,* 1203–1211.

Sandler, J. (1976). Countertransference and role responsiveness. *International Review of Psychoanalysis,* 43–47.

Schafer, R. (1983). *The analytic attitude*. New York: Basic Books.

Schweder, R. (1991). *Thinking through cultures: Expeditions in cultural psychology*. Cambridge, MA: Harvard University Press.

Seligman, M. E. P. (1995). The effectiveness of psychiatry: The *Consumer Reports* Study. *American Psychologist, 50,* 965–974.

Shotter, J. (1993). *Cultural politics of everyday life*. Toronto, Ontario, Canada: University of Toronto Press.

Showalter, E. (1997). *Hystories*. New York: Columbia University Press.

Smith, M. (1994). Selfhood at risk: Postmodern perils. *American Psychologist, 49,* 1–16.

Taylor, C. (1991). *The ethos of authenticity*. Cambridge, MA: Harvard University Press.

Taylor, M. (1987). *Alterity*. Chicago: University of Chicago Press.

Wachtel, P. (1997). *Psychoanalysis and behavior therapy and the relational world integrations*. Washington, DC: American Psychological Association.

Wallach, M., & Wallach, L. (1983). *Psychology's sanction for selfishness: The error of egoism in theory and therapy*. New York: Freeman.

White, M., & Epston, D. (1990). *Narrative means to therapeutic ends*. New York: Norton.

Wittgenstein, L. (1953). *Philosophical investigations* (G. E. Anscombe, Trans.). New York: Macmillan.

Woolfolk, R. (1998). *The cure of souls*. San Francisco: Jossey-Bass.

COMMENT:

Postmodernism and the Goals of Scientific Analysis

Steven C. Hayes

Jennifer Gregg

Postmodernism is not exactly dead, but what is emerging in many corners of discourse and knowledge is quite different from the heyday of postmodern thinking. Barry Protter attempts to carve out a pragmatic postmodern position that is true to core aspects of postmodernism but is reconstructive, not deconstructive. This is something that can be done, and it is all to the good, but he needs to be more clear about how that shift can happen. When he is, we suspect that his own substantive analysis may change.

It is not enough to say, as Protter does, that deconstructive postmodernism is extreme, or anarchic, or troublesome to the project of developing a discipline of psychotherapy. That is true enough but, to be consistent, a critique of deconstructive postmodernism from within postmodernism needs to be based on a postmodern critique. Similarly, it is not enough merely to laud pluralism, or hermeneutics, or the value of self as conceived of within a reconstructive postmodern position. To take that approach is to embrace a kind of "truth by appealing example," all the while hiding one's own purposes, or one's own history and thus the contextual nature of the example itself. Pragmatists from Pierce and James forward have succumbed to this temptation (it is the tack taken in, e.g., James's [1936] *The Varieties of Religious Experience*), but it is a bad practice that has harmed pragmatism repeatedly as an intellectual tradition.

To use a word that postmodernists hate, there is one thing that is foundational in any contextualistic, pragmatic analysis: the goals of the analyst (Hayes, 1993; Pepper, 1942). Goals are foundational not in the modern, positivistic sense of truth being based on reality, mechanisms, or reductive processes; rather, they are foundational because they are the means by which a pragmatic truth criterion can be mounted. Goals and purposes are local, and situational, but they nevertheless *are*. They cannot be justified or explained. To be a successful pragmatist you have to own up to them, otherwise you simply hide them inside the appealing examples that are necessarily offered as a substitute. Additionally, when you do own up to them the pragmatic truth criterion (one form or another of successful working) can finally be applied.

Goals put the excesses of postmodernism back into context. In an absolute sense, it is correct to point out that science is no more true than blowing one's nose. There is no assumption of "capital-T" Truth within a contextualistic, pragmatic, or postmodern viewpoint. Truth is always local and contextually situated. But if one wishes to, say, feed hungry people, then there is a differential value between knowing how to grow insect-resistant crops as compared with knowing how to blow a good "honker." Conversely, if one wishes to clear out a congested head, the truth value of these two bits of knowledge may be reversed.

The excesses of postmodernism came about because an appreciation of the contextual nature of knowledge suddenly revealed the arbitrary nature of the seemingly rock-solid foundation assumptions of modernity. It initially came as an awesome shock. Postmodernists became stuck on that shock of revelation and tried to recapture it in setting after setting, ad nauseam. What was often missed was the source of that revelation itself: an appreciation for the situated and especially the purposive nature of knowing.

It is this issue that makes possible Protter's pragmatic middle way. We need not deconstruct if it does not serve our purposes to do so. To travel this road with integrity, however, Protter needs to be clearer about his goals. To make this point, we examine Protter's three-part distinction among monadic, dyadic, and triadic epistemic domains.

We hardly need point out that Protter's very analysis is a triadic exercise. Whatever monadic biophenomenal experiences there are that might have participated in his analysis are largely unstated, although they undoubtedly could be examined. The interpersonal knowing of the dyadic domain also is vague, although in the text there does seem to be a sense of interaction between Protter and his teachers. The reader is largely left out of that domain, and the dyadic interaction that is obvious (that between Protter, as a writer, and his readers) is simply too lean for guidance. Protter's chapter is, dominantly, a triadic narrative, a story: about therapy, postmodernism, psychoanalytic thinking, and the domain of ideas.

How are we to evaluate this narrative? We could do so from the point of view of the goals of the reader or those of the writer. For present purposes, those of the writer seem most relevant, but here we have a problem: Protter does not clearly state what the goals are.

This is why there is a sense of disconnectedness in his analysis of deconstructive and reconstructive postmodernism. After laying out the excesses of deconstructive postmodernism, he essentially says, "but we can still be postmodernists and do better." The question is "Better for what?" He provides examples of the advantages of his kind of postmodernism, but the question still remains "Better for what?" He proceeds to a detailed analysis of epistemic domains that he hopes is a better analysis, but the question still remains "Better for what?"

Reading between the lines reveals that Protter seems to want an analysis that integrates multiple strands of thinking from multiple traditions all roughly related to the topic of self and that illuminates the content and process of psychotherapy as it deals with that topic. Stated another way, Protter seems to be after a kind of personal coherence—a sense of multiple participants in a larger whole.

This may be wrong, but if so, we can surely be forgiven because it is left to us to guess. If our guess is correct, we would be reassured because this general goal is a very common one for contextualists and pragmatists (in Hayes, 1993, such analysts are called "descriptive contextualists").

In view against this goal, we have few complaints. Protter seems happy with the analysis, and we can sense that some personal coherence has been achieved. We can share in the sense somewhat, especially because of the amazing number of connections Protter draws to various strands of thinking.

Although Protter's analysis seems to strike a level of personal coherence for him, it draws out an interesting comparison to an analysis that we make in our chapter (12). The differences are apparent as well, and the intention here is not to evaluatively compare the two chapters but rather to investigate the seeming overlap that exists between portions of Protter's analysis with our own. We briefly lay out where the overlap between the two analyses exists, in an effort to examine if the two different stories told here may be onto something that is shared. We then address what we see as the fundamental difference and discuss why this might be important.

The analysis we put forth in this volume, like Protter's, involves a three-part system. These parts are considered as divisions of self: the observing self, the conceptualized self, and ongoing self-awareness. The observing self is viewed as the conscious, psychological context in which various content is known. We argue that the observing self is important in therapy because from this aspect of self, thoughts and feelings can be fully acceptable because they are separate from the person who is noticing them. The conceptualized self is seen as the attempt to make sense of oneself verbally and to define or describe one's characteristics and attributes according to some coherent conception of what and who we are in the world. Finally, self-awareness is the ongoing process of making contact with and describing psychological content that is appearing at any given time.

In examining these three divisions of the self in the context of Protter's chapter, it seems to us that there are some useful comparisons to be made.

First, the concept of the monadic self shares many properties with our concept of an observing self, in that both attempt to talk about an experiential sense of knowing that is essentially nonlinguistic in form. Similarly, a conceptualized self maps onto Protter's triadic self. In essence, the triadic form of knowing self laid out by Protter relates to the domain of how interacting with others in the socioverbal community affects the conceptualization of oneself and others. Finally, there is a degree of overlap between the idea of dyadic knowing of the self and the experiential basis of ongoing self-awareness. In dyadic knowing, the interaction with others provides a context for the definition and construction of emotion and other psychological events. In our conception of the self as ongoing self-awareness, the ability to discriminate and report one's private events is developed dominantly through dyadic social interaction.

There are also differences, however. All of our categories are psychological, although their sources lie in manipulable aspects of other domains. Similarly, we do not include the purely nonverbal experience in the monadic domain pointed to by Protter; our observing self is verbal not by content but by process. These and other differences, it seems to us, arise because the goals of the analyses are different. Protter's analysis, as noted above, appears to have as its goal personal coherence, whereas our analysis has the goal of relating a conception of self to concrete things that might be done in psychotherapy and similar fields of application. In our analysis, the observing self and ongoing self-awareness are viewed as allies in therapy, to be supported by establishing a special social–verbal community in treatment, whereas the conceptualized self is largely an interference and is to be undermined by that same social–verbal community. Protter's analysis, on the other hand, does not specify pathways for intervention on the part of the therapist. It is not necessary that the events that Protter believes give rise to these divisions are manipulable by anyone. That is a problem, however, if the analytic goal is personal coherence.

We may be wrong about Protter's goals. Perhaps he wants an analysis that also tells him and others how to achieve client goals in therapy. If that is the purpose, his analysis seems to fall short, primarily because it says so little about how clinicians might proceed to change specific events.

In an abstract sense, there are general problems with both goals from the point of view of progressive postmodernism. A personal sense of coherence is easy to contact and easy to keep in context but relatively hard to share. How do we know when the strands have all been pulled together, and how can we show this to others? There is an opposite problem with the goal of making a therapeutic difference: We can share it, but it tends to become decontextualized, as is shown so clearly by the technical drift of some therapy traditions. Protter's chapter seems to instantiate the problems and benefits of coherence goals in postmodern, pragmatic thinking. As readers, we are entertained. As clinicians with practical problems to solve, we are left wondering.

References

Hayes, S. C. (1993). Analytic goals and the varieties of scientific contextualism. In S. C. Hayes, L. J. Hayes, H. W. Reese, & T. R. Sarbin (Eds.), *Varieties of scientific contextualism* (pp. 11–27). Reno, NV: Context Press.

James, W. (1936). *The varieties of religious experience.* New York: Modern Library.

Pepper, S. C. (1942). *World hypotheses: A study in evidence.* Berkeley: University of California Press.

CHAPTER 14

A Final Note: Meditations on "Both/And"

J. Christopher Muran

M any of the contributors to this volume have been in agreement with regard to the notion of the self, voicing postmodern views of the self as multiple, relational, and contextually embedded. The differences that did emerge from the dialogue seem to be largely about emphasis and nuance. It is interesting that a number of the contributors resisted taking a radical postmodern position of rejecting any sense of structure or integral organization. They struggled to negotiate the paradox of the self as both multiple and unified. Mardi Horowitz's chapter (chapter 3) and William Whelton and Leslie Greenberg's chapter (chapter 4), for example, emphasize process and the momentary identification of how various states of mind or self-states are interrelated and at the same time maintain the conception of underlying schemas or schemes (see also Fast, 1998). Stuart Pizer (chapter 5) and, to a lesser extent, Lewis Aron (chapter 6) elaborate on the idea of the self involving a dialectic between multiple, discontinuous and integral, continuous (see also Bromberg, 1998; Mitchell, 1993; and Modell, 1993).

This is a long-standing struggle. More than 100 years ago, William James (1890/1981) described the paradox of multiple states of consciousness and a unified sense of personal identity. According to him, our stream of thought, which is different in each instant, is subjectively synthesized to create a sense of continuity and objectively synthesized to create a sense of unity and identity. In so doing, he described the self as reflexive, as ongoingly oscillating between the subjective "I" and the objective "me." In this volume, this is a conception elaborated on by Sheldon Bach (chapter 2), in terms of oscillating states of subjective and objective self-awareness (see Fast, 1998; Modell, 1993), as well as by Aron (chapter 6) in his application of self-reflexivity to understanding the psychoanalytic situation (see Auerbach & Blatt, 1996; Fonagy & Target, 1996). In this final chapter, my aim is to address this paradox and present a perspective that is both integrative and elaborative. It seems only fitting to finish this book on such a note.

Process and Structure: Relational Configurations of the Self

Elsewhere (Muran, 1997), I have attempted to emphasize process, with consideration of structure, and to account for the self-as-dialectic, self as both multiple and integral, by articulating a model that provides a relational conception of the self grounded in contemporary theories of cognition and emotion. Accordingly, the self is considered with regard to four relational configurations.

First, there is the continuous interplay between the self's various processes and structures. With this I am invoking the operational and representational aspects of the self that are described in the interpersonal literature (e.g., Barnett, 1980; Sullivan, 1953, 1964; Wolstein, 1974) and have been greatly influenced by Mead and James (see Introduction to this volume). The former refers to the various cognitive and interpersonal operations that establish and protect the representational side. This is the self as I, the self as subject. In addition to describing the self in relation to the outside world, this is the self in relation to the self, that is, how the I relates to the me. In terms of the self-in-relation-to-other, it would include what has been termed "cognitive distortions" (Beck, Ellis), "security operations" (Sullivan), and "defense mechanisms" (Anna Freud), or what Horowitz termed in chapter 3 "defensive control processes." In terms of the self-in-relation-to-the-self, it would include the processes involved in "experiential avoidance," as described by Whelton and Greenberg (chapter 4) as well as by Steven Hayes and Jennifer Gregg (chapter 12), and in dissociation (and the idea of splitting off aspects of the self), as described by Bach (chapter 2) and Pizer (chapter 5) in this volume (see also Ferenczi, 1931; and Winnicott, 1965, for seminal examples).

The latter, the representational side of the self, consists of memory stores or knowledge domains that include internalized self-assessments and expectations regarding others that inform the individual how to relate to others and that form the basis for what Sullivan called the "me–you" patterns of the self. This is the self as me, self-as-object. It represents the multiple discrete experiences of the self. Theoretically, there may be as many "me's" as there are different interactions in one's life. Alternatively, these can be considered *interpersonal schemas* (Safran, 1998) or generalized representations of self–other relationships that are abstracted on the basis of interactions with significant others to increase the likelihood of maintaining relationships with those others and that are hierarchically organized by different orders of abstraction and generality. For example, one's general sense of oneself as a lover is based on more specific relationship patterns, including various expectations of others as love interests, which in turn are based on even more specific relationship experiences. Thus, the second relational configuration in this conception of the self is the implicit and intrinsic relation between self and other in its representational content.

This conception follows in the footsteps of Fairbairn (1952), Bowlby (1969), Laing (1972), and Daniel Stern (1985), in addition to Sullivan (1953), who suggested that what are internalized or represented are relationship patterns—the whole, and not the isolated elements.

Along the lines of the thinking of Jean Piaget (1970) and the emotion theorist Howard Leventhal (1984), these interpersonal schemas are also considered cognitive–affective structures that develop from birth (Greenberg & Safran, 1987; Safran & Greenberg, 1991). Accordingly, the newborn infant engages in immediate, perceptual–motor appraisals of the environment. These appraisals evoke innate expressive–motor responses that serve adaptive functions and form the core for the development of subsequent emotional experience. Although the infant is born with expressive–motor responses prior to any learning, these responses subsequently become elaborated through a process of learning. From birth, the infant develops memory stores that consist of specific expressive–motor responses, physiological arousal, associated images, and relevant eliciting stimuli. These memory stores serve as the primary templates for emotional experience that are developed and elaborated over time into subtle and idiosyncratic variations. They serve a communicative function in that they continually orient the individual to the environment and the environment to the individual. For example, the tensing of muscles associated with fear prepares the individual to escape from danger, and the facial patterning associated with fear can serve as a signal to another to come assist.

It also seems important to understand interpersonal schemas as emerging from a more complex system. The 1980s were marked by the emergence of connectionist, distributed processing and neural network models of the mind, models based on a brain metaphor, which challenged the schema conception that was derived from an information-processing model and computer metaphor (see Cilliers, 1998; Dennett, 1991). This involved a greater appreciation of the human brain in understanding self experience because of its own structural complexity and its capability to deal with complexity, including its ability to self-organize internal structure. It also involved a rejection of traditional notions of representations for notions of distributed representations, according to which information is encoded in distributed form in a complex system of interconnected elements that can be understood only as a whole. As an example, Rummelhart, Smolensky, McClelland, and Hinton (1986) conceptualized schemas not as representational objects but as emergent properties (see also Stinson & Palmer, 1991). These properties emerge from an interaction of large numbers of simpler elements, a network of neuronlike units with connections weighted so that activation of a part of the network produces an activation pattern that functions like a schema. As Rummelhart et al. (1986) noted,

> one important difference between our interpretation of schemata and the more conventional ones is that in the conventional story, schemata are stored in

memory. Indeed, they are the major content of memory. In our case, nothing stored corresponds very closely to a schema. What is stored is a set of connection strengths which, when activated, have implicitly in them the ability to generate states that correspond to instantiated schemata. (pp. 20–21)

Efforts, such as Pizer's (chapter 5) application of Edelman's (1987) neural model (with its link to evolutionary theory) to the self, should not supplant but rather elaborate on the schema concept.

With the activation of a particular interpersonal schema, there emerges a corresponding experience, a particular state of mind or self-state (Horowitz, chapter 3; Whelton & Greenberg, chapter 4). Self-states are the experiential products of the various processes and structures of the self. They reflect the presence or activation of an underlying interpersonal schema. In other words, they can be understood as "the crystallization of different" interpersonal schemas (Slavin & Kriegman, 1992, p. 204). They may be understood as automatic thoughts or images (in cognitive terms) and immediate feeling states of sadness, anger, fear, and so on. They may be out of awareness, but they can come into awareness through attention. In addition, different self-states can activate different interpersonal schemas, resulting in a cycling through different experiential states of mind. The transition points or boundaries between these self-states vary in terms of seamlessness but are often marked by changes in vocal quality, facial expression, focus and content of verbal reports, emotional involvement, and so on. The transitions among the various self-states that an individual experiences characterize the third relational configuration in this self conception.

What accounts for the illusory sense of continuity and singular identity is dissociation and our self-organizing and integral capacities. As Bach and Bromberg, among others, have described, dissociation is basic to optimal functioning, to feeling "like one self while being many" (Bromberg, 1993, p. 166). Pizer (chapter 5) makes the useful distinction between dissociation as a healthy process of selectively focusing attention and dissociation as an unhealthy process of severing connections between memory stores or schemas, an organization of unlinked interpersonal schemas. Greatly influenced by Winnicott (1965) and Davies and Frawley (1994) in this regard, he describes the latter as a result of "traumatic overload" that leads to "breaches of communication, the demolition of bridges between the mind's islands of associated" interpersonal schemas and disrupts the sense of continuity and unity. Thus, the more conspicuous and abrupt the transitions between self-states, the more problematic the dissociative process.

Finally, it is important to note, as a number have in other ways (e.g., Kiesler, 1983; Sullivan, 1964), that there is an ongoing reciprocal relationship between the self-states of one person in a dyadic interaction and those of the other; this is the fourth relational configuration. For example, sadness from one would evoke sympathy and closeness from another, and anger would evoke defensiveness and distance. As individuals cycle through various self-states in an interpersonal interaction, there should be subtle movements and fluctuations in intimacy and varying degrees of relatedness. Sullivan (1953) described this by his theorem of reciprocal emotion. Infant researchers, such as Beebe and Lachmann (1992), have described this in terms of the ways in which the subjective or affective states of mother and child are interpersonally communicated and mutually regulated. The reciprocal relationship in a dyadic interaction is based on the conception that an interpersonal schema shapes one's perception of the interpersonal world and leads to cognitive processes and interpersonal behaviors, which in turn shape the environment in a manner that confirms the schema; thus, a self-perpetuating cycle emerges (Safran, 1998). For example, an individual who generally expects others to be essentially hostile and attacking might tend to act in a defensively hostile and aggressive manner, which would invariably provoke the response from others that is expected. Mitchell (1988) described this self-perpetuating cycle in terms of his notion of the "relational matrix."

Discovery and Construction: Implications for the Psychotherapy Process

The various relational aspects of human experience just outlined have a number of important implications for clinical practice. I articulate a few. One is the importance of facilitating awareness of patients' operational selves in dialectic relation to their representational selves, that is, self-as-subject in relation to self-as-object. This suggests the importance of working in the here and now and attending to in-session process, to the emergence and transitions of various self-states. Following in the operationism that is fundamental to both the behavioral and the interpersonal traditions,[1] careful attention is paid to what is manifest and to the details of self experience. The operative emphasis here is on functional analysis (Hayes & Gregg, chapter 12) or detailed inquiry (Sullivan, 1954). It is a respect, even a reverence, for particularity. It was basic to the credo "to the things" of phenomenologists, such as Husserl (1931), and became a technical principle of humanistic psychotherapies (Whelton & Greenberg, chapter 4). It was essential to artists, such as Mies van der Rohe, who said "God is in the details," and Vladimir Nabokov, who wrote, "Caress the detail, the divine detail" (see D. B. Stern, 1997).

---

[1]Rogers's (1951) ideas regarding the psychotherapeutic process were also greatly influenced by operationism, which dominated the intellectual milieu characterizing American thought in the early 20th century.

Although most clinicians from most orientations would agree with the importance of paying careful attention to patient experience in session, in practice this seems to be lost for a variety of reasons. In some instances, this can be attributed to a lack of appreciation of what this means; in others, it can be attributed to therapists' own anxieties that lead them to assume they are a lot closer "to the things" than they really are. Simply put, though, therapists' efforts should be directed toward inviting and orienting patients to look at their immediate experience and especially calling their attention to the transition points of their experience as it emerges in the here and now. What is therapeutic, therefore, is not simply increasing the patient's retrospective awareness of intrapersonal or interpersonal patterns—which is increasing awareness of the self-as-object—but increasing the patient's immediate awareness of how he or she engages in such patterns, which involves increasing awareness of the self-as-subject in relation to self-as-object. This involves increasing one's immediate awareness of self as agent of one's own experience and behavior, of the subjective "I" processes that mediate the objective "me" patterns.

In a sense, an important therapeutic aim is to expand conscious awareness in patients with respect to the details of their experience. In the words of Kierkegaard (1849/1944), the idea here is "the more consciousness, the more self" (p. 128). In recent years there has been increasing discussion in a variety of orientations of the applicability of the Eastern notion of mindfulness to the clinical situation (e.g., Epstein, 1995, 1998; Linehan, 1993; Safran & Muran, 2000; Teasdale, Segal, & Williams, 1995). The term *mindfulness* means a form of awakening, a state of psychological freedom, a disciplined self-observation that involves a bare attention to our experience of mind and body at successive moments of perception, without attachment to any particular point of view and without becoming stuck in unconscious prejudices (Epstein, 1995; Goleman, 1980; Kabat-Zinn, 1994; Martin, 1998); the operative emphasis is on awareness with acceptance. Although there has been some discussion of comparable notions in the psychotherapy literature, relatively little has actually been said about developing the capacity to move easily between self-as-subject and self-as-object.[2]

---

[2]For example, in the psychoanalytic literature (see chapter 6), there has been the long-standing notion of the split between the experiencing ego and the observing ego (Sterba, 1934) and the idea of psychological mindedness and recent discussions of mentalization (Main, 1991), reflective functioning (Fonagy & Target, 1996), and self-reflexivity (Auerbach & Blatt, 1996). In the cognitive–behavior literature, there is the notion of *decentering*, which involves stepping outside of and observing one's immediate experience, thus introducing a gap between reality and reality as one construes it (Safran & Segal, 1990; see Strauman & Segal, chapter 10) and, in the humanistic literature, there is the idea of *detachment*, which involves the adoption of a phenomenological stance toward one's experience and the expansion of attentional space (Bohart, 1983).

The introduction of mindfulness into these discussions might help enrich clinical theory and practice.[3]

From the perspective of multiple selves, psychotherapy involves a process of discovering who within the patient is speaking. In practical terms, this means therapists should try to focus on the concrete and specific in the here and now.[4] They should continually try to track patients' self-states and pay particular attention to the transition points, to the boundaries of each state, to when there are shifts from one experience to another. As described earlier, these are often marked by vocal, verbal, or gestural shifts, such as the softening of one's voice, the abrupt change of a topic, the emergence of a misplaced smile, or the diverting of one's eyes. In paying close attention to their own states, therapists may be clued in or oriented to what the patient may be experiencing. For example, a therapist may be emotionally attuned or connected to a patient who is experiencing sadness and then may lose that attunement and feel disconnected as the patient shifts away from such a self-state out of some implicit fear. In another example, a depressed patient who is stuck in a state of despair and helplessness may elicit from the therapist a powerful urge to help and save the patient, performance anxiety, or even a comparable experience of despair and helplessness. Although these examples describe the impact of patient self-states on the therapist, such interactions should not be understood as unidirectional.[5]

This brings us to another, perhaps self-evident, implication of this relational conception, which is the importance of the therapeutic relationship as a context for bringing the operational and representational selves into relief. The idea behind this is essentially twofold: first, that we are always embedded in an interpersonal field that exerts a great influence on the emergence of a self-state that we experience in a given moment (D. B. Stern, 1997), and second, that greater self-definition can be achieved only by defining the edges of one self in relation to another self—in this case, the patient in relation to the therapist

---

[3] In fact, the Zen tradition makes the radical suggestion the more consciousness, the less self, in which selfhood is considered a reified construct that interferes with our relation to nature.

[4] The emphasis on the here and now does not mean that past events or events currently taking place outside of therapy are not significant. It is important to bear in mind, however, that whatever events the patient is speaking about are being related to or processed in the moment.

[5] This is certainly not to say that this awareness cannot be cultivated otherwise. Patients are able to report extrasession behavior patterns, examine them in detail with their therapists, and then go outside of the therapy situation to discover their subjective processes in relation to the objective patterns. This happens quite frequently and spontaneously, and in a sense self-monitoring homework exercises, as described in the cognitive–behavioral literature, can be considered facilitative of this.

(Ehrenberg, 1992). In a Hegelian sense, I cannot know myself in isolation; I need another self to become aware of my own selfhood (Hegel, 1807/1969). The therapeutic relationship provides a laboratory of sorts in which the subjective and objective aspects of the patient's self can be more sharply or clearly defined in relation to the subjective and objective aspects of the therapist's self. Thus, the therapeutic aim to cultivate mindfulness in patients with respect to the details their own experience invariably involves therapists becoming mindful of corresponding details of their own experience. It suggests that with every therapeutic encounter, therapists must courageously confront themselves and expand their awareness of themselves in relation to yet another individual. The therapeutic process should, therefore, involve change for both participants.

This idea also invokes intersubjectivity, not only in terms of how the self states of patient and therapist mutually regulate themselves but also in terms of the clinical significance of mutual recognition of respective subjectivities, the awareness of the other as both separate subject, as well as object in one's own world (Aron, chapter 6; Safran & Muran, chapter 7; Benjamin, 1990). How mutual recognition is achieved from the perspective of multiple selves involves a process of figuring out who is speaking to whom in a given moment (Bromberg, 1998; Mitchell, 1993). Which patient self is communicating to which therapist self? Who within the patient is speaking, and who within the therapist is listening, and vice versa (see also Davies, 1996)? As Pizer metaphorically puts it in chapter 5 of this volume, it is through dialogue between a patient's dissociated self and a therapist's self that a bridge can be built between that dissociated self and other selves within the patient's self-system.

Mutual recognition also involves an intersubjective negotiation (Benjamin, 1990; Mitchell, 1993; Pizer, 1992). Pizer, for example, suggests that therapists in their interventions and patients in their responses are recurrently saying to each other, "no, you can't make this of me. But you can make that of me" (p. 218). In chapter 7, following Edward Bordin's (1979) definition of the therapeutic alliance, Jeremy Safran and I describe the psychotherapeutic process as an ongoing negotiation between patient and therapist about the tasks and goals of treatment, which taps into fundamental dilemmas of human existence, such as the negotiation of one's desires with those of another, the struggle to experience oneself as a subject while at the same time recognizing the subjectivity of the other, and the tension between the need for self-definition versus the need for relatedness. An important part of the negotiation process is one highlighted by Safran in his commentary on chapter 6 of this volume: the role of the power imbalance in the relationship between patient and therapist. Aron (1996) described this in terms of the asymmetrical versus mutual dimensions of the therapeutic relationship (see also Burke, 1992). Irwin Hoffman (1998) emphasized that the therapist's gestures toward mutuality, those that are spontaneous and personally responsive, must always be understood in the context of his or her assigned role of authority. Safran invoked Jessica Benjamin (1990), who was influenced by Hegel and Winnicott, to suggest that the process toward mutual recognition in psychotherapy is tempered by the patient's investment to not divest the therapist of his or her authority.

In practical terms, Safran and I (1995, 1996, 1998, 2000) have outlined a number of specific guiding principles regarding the process of elucidating the relational configurations in the psychotherapeutic process. We have organized them under the general principle of *metacommunication,* a term borrowed from Donald Kiesler (1996). What is meant by this principle is communicating not only about communication in the interpersonal sense (i.e., about the two individual selves in the psychotherapy situation), which is Kiesler's definition, but also about communication in the intrapersonal sense (i.e., about the multiple selves within an individual self). Thus, an ongoing dialectic is conducted between exploring the me–you relation and the I–me relation. In effect, we are talking about three dimensions—the patient's I–me experience, the therapist's I–me experience, and the me–you experience of their relationship—that operate in parallel process. Metacommunication is an attempt to bring awareness to bear on the relational processes as they unfold. It can be thought of as "mindfulness in action" (Safran & Muran, 2000).

Unlike traditional notions of transference interpretations, in which the therapist offers conjectures as to the meaning of a current interaction, metacommunication attempts to decrease the degree of inference and is grounded in an immediate experience (patient's or therapist's) of some specific aspect of the therapeutic relationship. It is a process that can begin with questions about patients' perceptions of their self states ("What's happening for you right now?"), about the interpersonal field ("What's going on here between us?"), or about their therapist's self states ("I wonder if you have any thoughts about what's going on for me right now?") as well as observations about patients' self states ("You seem anxious to me right now. Am I reading you right?"), about the field ("It seems like we're engaged in some kind of game of cat and mouse. Does that fit with your sense?"), or self-disclosures about one's own self states ("I'm aware of feeling defensive right now.").[6] It is important for any of these interventions to be made in a spirit of collaborative inquiry. They should be presented with skillful tentativeness and with emphasis on one's own subjectivity. This is in recognition that therapists' understanding of themselves and their patients is always partial at best, always evolving, and always embedded in the complex interactive matrix within which they exist (Protter, chapter 13; Hoff-

---

[6]With respect to exploratory questions, not many have talked about the art of asking a good question, but one of the better definitions of this is asking a question to which one does not know the answer (D. B. Stern, 1997). It is a real question to which the answer comes as a surprise to both patient and therapist.

man, 1998; Mitchell, 1993; D. B. Stern, 1997). If therapists become aware at all, it is always in reflection and from another vantage point. Metacommunication is the effort to look back at a recently unfolded relational process from another vantage point. But "because we are always caught in the grip of the field, the upshot for clinical purposes is that we face the endless task of trying to see the field and climb out of it—and into another one, for there is nowhere else to go" (D. B. Stern, 1997, p. 158).

By metacommunication, then, the therapeutic aim takes on the form of a contextualized exploration in the sense of what cultural anthropologist Clifford Geertz (1973) referred to as a "thick description." Accordingly, the therapeutic process involves an intimate and infinite process of exactly detailing the complex specifics of relational experience. In this regard I am reminded of Darlene Ehrenberg's (1992) notion of working at the "intimate edge" of the ever-shifting interface between patient and therapist:

> In effect, the "intimate edge" is not simply at the boundary between self and other, the point of developing interpersonal intimacy and awareness of interpersonal possibility in the relationship; it is also at the boundary of self-awareness. It is a point of expanding self-discovery, at which one can become more "intimate" with one's own experience through the evolving relationship with the other, and then more intimate with the other as one becomes more attuned to oneself. Because of this kind of dialectical interplay, the "intimate edge" becomes the "growing edge" of the relationship. (pp. 34–35)

Thus far the discussion of clinical implications has suggested a process of change that emphasizes the discovery of self experience and expansion of self-awareness in the context of the therapeutic relationship. It is important to recognize that the psychotherapeutic process in a paradoxical sense is not only discovery oriented but also constructive. As Mitchell (1993) described,

> there is no stream of experience separable from experience as accessed by someone (either oneself or someone else) at a specific time, for a particular purpose, in a specific context. Thus, experience is constructed on a moment-by-moment basis. At any given point, the patient can only report a particular construction of his experience, which may overlook or obliterate many other important constructions of his experience (which the [therapist] might be more in touch with). At any given point, the [therapist] can offer only his own construction of some aspects of the patient's experience, a construction of a construction. (p. 60)

Accordingly, self experience does not simply flow forth without impediment but is actually channeled by the efforts of the individual to communicate and the other to understand. Thus, the course it takes is a social one involving co-construction. For example, the therapist's own experience, and his or her articulation of that, which includes his or her theoretical orientation and interpersonal history (Aron, 1999; Schafer, 1983; Spence, 1982), has an enormous impact on the patient's experience and articulation, and, of course, this is a bidirectional and iterative process.

In a sense, the psychotherapeutic process can be likened to the postmodern method of *deconstruction* (Derrida, 1978). The term is a hybrid of *destruction* and *construction* and in effect represents an effort to construct by destructing. It suggests the paradoxical idea of tearing something apart while at the same time creating something new (Lovlie, 1992). The deconstruction of the self results in a rejection of a substantialized or essentialized conception of self at the center of the world—the death of the modern self—for a relational conception of self—the birth of a postmodern self that exists in intricate relation to others in the world.

Sublime and Mundane: A Clinical Illustration

The challenge of presenting a theoretical formulation is to clarify its implications with regard to clinical material, to exemplify the sublime ideas with the mundane details of a particular psychotherapeutic process. In the following clinical vignette, my hope is to illustrate some of the principles articulated above, with special attention given to therapeutic metacommunication and working with the details of self experience in the context of the therapeutic relationship.

Valerie, age 29, is a partner in a small business with her two considerably older brothers. They inherited the business from their father, who died from cancer several years earlier. Valerie described her parents as both self-involved and neglectful of her, although in very different ways. In many ways, her own needs and desires were superseded by those of her parents. She described her father, although gentle in manner, as self-absorbed in his pursuit of personal interests. She described her mother, in contrast, as a very imposing and demanding woman, who could turn nasty if her demands were not met. When Valerie was 5, her father revealed that he was having an affair, but he did not leave home for another 8 years. She characterized those years as those in which she was "standing vigil," as she anxiously waited for his eventual departure. The years following his departure were marked by hysterical and suicidal gestures by her mother during which Valerie was thrown into the role of caretaker. In fact, before her adolescence, she learned to become quite self-reliant—to be her own caretaker, in a sense—because of her parents' self-involvement. For example, she remembered taking responsibility for preparing her own meals as early as age 6. Valerie completed high school and college early and then moved to live and work in Madrid for several years. She returned home in her late 20s, abandoning a love relationship in Spain, to help her father in his business when his health was beginning to fail. Of all his children, her father depended on her to take care of his medical needs. His eventual death marked the onset of her depression. Her mother has over the years become increasingly infirm and dependent on Valerie for her medical needs as well.

She entered treatment in a severe depression that had debilitated her both mentally (she had great difficulty concentrating) and physically (she had great difficulty maintaining a working schedule). In the early stages of therapy, she described herself as in a perpetual state of confusion. She would often begin sessions in a half-humorous and half-poignant manner, which would confuse me and which became a marker that something was amiss; for example, she once settled herself in her chair, turned to me with a smile on her face, and laughingly said, "Oh sure, just look at me. I don't get it. I'm just confused all the time. I don't get it." I responded, "Well, let's start with the 'Oh sure, just look at me.' What's that all about?" Valerie responded, "Like you're all focused to start, and I don't even know what planet I'm on." When I asked her to elaborate, she went on to describe how she gets confused by some of her reactions and to wonder why (specifically) she had an "outburst" at the end of the last session ("It was probably one of those things that went over your head, but in my mind it was a big outburst"). I had not remembered any outburst and so asked for more detail. Valerie then went on to describe the end of the previous session, which I had punctuated with "to be continued." The expression sent her into a panic, as she experienced it as "Here, now take your problems and go away, go work on them on your own." She had jokingly blurted out halfway out the door, "Yeah right, like you really want to." This was her so-called outburst.

Prior to this encounter, Valerie had been discussing the experience of feeling ignored by one of her brothers. She had also had a dream in which I was portrayed as impatiently waiting for her to leave me alone. When I had previously asked her if she experienced me as ignoring her or as impatient with her, she could not link the experience to anything particular that I had done. In this instance, when I raised it again and wondered aloud about what I had specifically done to provoke this experience, she responded, "Well, it's based on something, but you didn't do anything terrible." I chose to focus Valerie on the "something" that she was picking up on, rather than focus on her characteristic tendency to dismiss, forgive, and attribute the blame to herself, which we had explored before in some detail. In the ensuing exploration, I invited Valerie to explore my subjectivity, to speculate on what might have been going on for me when I ended the previous session ("So what do you imagine was going on for me?"). In response, Valerie elaborated on her sense that I was feeling a bit overwhelmed by her dependency and experiencing her as "too much" to handle and tolerate. She then disclosed her fear of being too dependent on me and her fundamental fear of being abandoned by me. As a result of these fears, she was exquisitely sensitive to my movements toward and away from her. She revealed that sometimes she experienced my "careful" approach to her as gentle and caring and other times as cautious and fearful of her. This revelation stirred me to explore my experience further and to begin to identify my subtle reactions to and anxieties about Valerie and what she needed from me. It helped me become more aware of how much she scared me at times, how much I felt wary of her dependency needs.

I subsequently disclosed moments in sessions with her in which I felt anxious and guarded toward her as junctures to begin to explore what was going on between us and to discern our respective subjectivities. These disclosures helped orient our focus to the concrete and specific of the here and now and ground our awareness of our actions and self-states, facilitating the experience of mindfulness, in a sense, for both of us. Earlier in treatment, Valerie had responded to my transgressions with extended periods (sometimes days) of confusion and despair. These disclosures helped her to become more aware of and vocal about her discontents with me, quicker and clearer in recognizing what she did not want from me and, ultimately, what she did want from me. Of course, this process included me being mindful of my own desires with respect to her needs.

For example, when she would enter one of her self-states of confusion and despair, she would frequently try to contact me by telephone (sometimes at the most inopportune times) but then would not be able to articulate what she wanted. The challenge I faced in these instances was to somehow try to create an optimal space for exploration and expression in an abbreviated amount of time and without visual cues. In this regard, as I learned by my mistakes, it was important for me (and for her) to attend to the extent to which I resented the intrusion and the extent to which I could hear her in the given moment. Sometimes this led to me asking her to call me at another, appointed time or to wait until our next session: Simple, but not easy. Valerie appreciated knowing where I stood. It helped her recognize and express her own needs. It helped her move from a diffuse state of confusion and upset marked by occasional "outbursts" to a more differentiated state in which she could more readily discern her desires in contrast to mine. So it became an important, never-ending task to try to figure out where I stood. It was impossible to always or absolutely know, but it was a process—an ongoing collaboration and negotiation between the two of us (Aron, chapter 6; Pizer, chapter 5; Safran & Muran, chapter 7; also Benjamin, 1990; Mitchell, 1993).

So much could be said about this brief vignette (and this therapeutic relationship), and in so many different ways. Nevertheless, my hope was to illustrate the complexities and dialectical process of becoming aware of one's own subjective states and those of another. As a number have noted (e.g., Ehrenberg, 1992), greater intimacy with oneself, meaning the I–me dimension, is reciprocally related to greater intimacy with another, meaning the me–you dimension. From a multiple-selves perspective, Valerie would slip from a hypervigilant state, in which she paid exquisite attention to my position vis-à-vis her, into a dissociative self-state of confusion and futility when I would be neglectful by an act of either commission (e.g., asking the "wrong" question) or omission (e.g., being nonresponsive). When faced with her futility, I often found myself feeling ineffectual and hopeless. In response, sometimes I would anxiously or angrily move away from this state and would commit another neglectful act (e.g., by imposing a sense of hope, sometimes a disingenuous assurance). When I was able to become mindful of this hopeless state, I was more able to meet Valerie where she was. As she described, in my efforts to face and stay with my despair, she felt there was room for her to hope and to begin to talk about her specific fears and expectations.

In a simple sense, this is about figuring out who is speaking to whom—from where was Valerie talking, and from where was I listening, and vice versa. In a more complicated sense, this exemplifies working with the details of self experience, where the task is to recognize the myriad self-states—hers and mine—in continuous exchange and transition; to recognize the various subjective or operational processes in which we engaged; her security operations as they encountered mine; and to elucidate and at the same time challenge underlying interpersonal schemas—explicitly hers, but I certainly expanded my awareness about my beliefs and expectations (as well as my subjective processes) in this process. By this perspective, Kierkegaard's dictum "The more consciousness, the more self" could be extended to include "the more other" as well. I often think that the critical ingredients to this type of intimate work —for both therapist and patient—comes down to curiosity and courage (Singer, 1977; D. B. Stern, 1997) because it involves so much of self as well as other.

Patient and Therapist: Implications for Psychotherapy Research

Although this book is primarily concerned with the practice of psychotherapy, the ideas presented within do have important implications as well for psychotherapy research, and these deserve some mention. But first there is the question of whether empirical research, with its positivist orientation toward searching for an objective truth, has any place in a postmodern dialogue. It can, in the sense that it is treated as yet another discourse, a system of statements that constructs an object, and that it has its own truth claim among many truth claims. It does not have any privileged status or hold any absolute claim on the truth. In such a sense, it should have its place among the many discourses about psychotherapy. What is more, the postmodern sensibility not only places the empirical research discourse into perspective, but it also has much to say about the nature of this discourse, with its emphasis, for example, on process, context specificity, and idiographic analysis, which is evident in the research ideas that follow.

With this said, let me highlight a few research implications from the relational conception of the self that I have outlined in this chapter. Let me begin and frame this discussion with two thought-provoking statements from Allen Bergin and Sol Garfield, whose *Handbook of Psychotherapy and Behavior Change*, now in its fourth edition (1994), has served over the years as the standard reference in the field of psychotherapy research:

> There has been a noticeable increase in the quantity and quality of research evaluating outcome in psychotherapy. Most of this research has focused on comparing different forms of psychotherapy, and the results have generally been positive. There would appear to be a greatly diminished need for such research in the future. On the other hand, our knowledge of the variables that make for positive change as a result of psychotherapy is still quite limited (Garfield, 1990). As a result, there is at present a greater awareness of the need for high-quality process research to enlarge our understanding of the actual therapeutic process. It is readily apparent the key players in this process, the client and the therapist, are of some importance in how this process develops and in the outcomes secured. *Clearly, it is time for us to discard the uniformity myths in the field of psychotherapy, and to focus much more on the qualities and behaviors of the participants as they are manifested in the interactions we call psychotherapy. . . . (Garfield, 1981, pp. 305–306).* (Garfield, 1997, p. 42, emphasis in original)

> It has become clear to me that we cycle through the same issues over and over again. Although we have improved precision and sophistication, we also have continuing frustration in our effort to embrace, conceptualize, and understand what it means to be a human being in a relationship, particularly in a therapeutic relationship. (Bergin, 1997, p. 87)

Bergin and Garfield made these statements as part of a special series of articles regarding the relative neglect of the therapist as a variable for empirical investigation. It seems that the psychotherapy research field has perpetuated a myth of uniformity with respect to therapists (Kiesler, 1966, 1973), predominantly focusing instead on therapeutic interventions and Intervention × Patient interactions. The therapist's contribution has not received adequate attention.

In a fairly comprehensive review of the research regarding the therapist variable, Larry Beutler, Paulo Machado, and Susan Neufeldt (1994) organized the literature around two dimensions: (a) from objective to subjective characteristics and (b) from cross-situational to therapy specific. Their review included research on (a) objective characteristics that are cross-situational, such as age, sex, and ethnicity; (b) objective characteristics that are therapy specific, such as professional background, therapeutic styles, and therapeutic interventions;

(c) subjective characteristics that are cross-situational, such as personality, coping style, emotional well-being, values, attitudes, and beliefs; and (d) subjective characteristics that are therapy specific, such as philosophical orientation, expectancies, social influence attributes, and the therapeutic relationship.

With respect to the therapeutic relationship, there has been a proliferation of research in the field during the past 20 years that has shed light on therapist contributions to the quality of the relationship to the patient and has demonstrated its predictive validity. Much of the research demonstrating the predictive relation of patient–therapist interactions to overall change has been based on measures derived from various idiosyncratic definitions of the therapeutic alliance (e.g., Gaston, 1990; Horvath & Symonds, 1991) and tended toward a global distinction between good and poor alliance, failing to articulate the specific interpersonal behaviors of patient and therapist that constitute a good versus poor alliance. There is also a growing body of research that measures patient and therapist interactions on circumplex models of interpersonal behavior, which organize interpersonal behavior along two dimensions of affiliation and power (Coady, 1989; Henry, Schacht, & Strupp, 1986; Kiesler & Watkins, 1989; Samstag, 1998; Weinstock-Savoy, 1986; see Henry, chapter 11), but this research has failed to produce much beyond equating hostile interactions and complex communications with negative process—a finding that provides limited, and not-so-novel, information to the practicing clinician.

Recently, there has also been increasing consideration of individual differences in therapist contribution. In a series of studies from the Penn Psychotherapy Project, Lester Luborsky, Paul Crits-Christoph, and their colleagues (Crits-Christoph et al., 1991; Crits-Christoph & Mintz, 1991; Luborsky et al., 1986; Luborsky, McLellan, Diguer, Woody, & Seligman, 1997; Luborsky, McLellan, Woody, O'Brien, & Auerbach, 1985) have examined therapist performance as measured by the outcomes of their caseloads and therapist qualities associated with performance. Likewise, Lisa Najavits and Hans Strupp (1994) conducted a similar analysis of data from the Vanderbilt II Study. The results generally demonstrated that individual therapist differences were moderately related to outcome.

To be more precise, what seems to be most absent from the literature is attention to the therapist's in-session subjective experience, that is, in interaction with the patient. A few efforts at studying therapist countertransference have been made (e.g., Holmqvist & Armelius, 1996; Najavits et al., 1995), but these seem to have been done at a global level of analysis that does not yield practical information for the clinician. There has been an initiative by Franz Caspar (1997) directed toward elucidating how therapists process information, form hypotheses, and make clinical judgments in session and, although this endeavor promises to provide a rich, detailed description of what goes on in a therapist's mind, it misses the affective dimension of experience—what it feels like to be with the patient in an intimate encounter. Given the relational model that I have described, which suggests the mutual regulation and recognition of patient and therapist self-states, it seems critical to develop and apply methods that elucidate the therapist's unfolding experience to the psychotherapy process. Of course, this can be understood only in relation to the patient's unfolding experience.

Largely in response to the criticism that psychotherapy research has generally yielded information that has been of limited use to practicing clinicians (e.g., the finding that a particular brand of therapy is effective for the average patient is of little value to a practicing clinician who is confronted with the question of how to proceed with the specific patient who is at this moment in front of her; see Talley, Strupp, & Butler, 1994), there have been important developments in the field that have involved intensive and systematic analyses, which have yielded idiographic, context-sensitive information relevant to the here-and-now particularities of specific cases. Leslie Greenberg and his colleagues (Greenberg, 1986; Greenberg & Foerster, 1996; Rice & Greenberg, 1984; see Whelton & Greenberg, chapter 4), for example, have made an important contribution by suggesting a research strategy called *task analysis,* in which recurring patterns of psychotherapy process that consistently lead to change are operationally defined, such as the resolution of splits in patient self-experience. Horowitz (1987; see also chapter 3), by his configurational-analysis approach, similarly provides a means for mapping and thus sensitizing clinicians to the regularities in the manner in which a particular patient cycles between states of mind: that is, different characteristic ways of processing, reacting to, and defending against difficult self-experiences. Greatly influenced by their contributions, Safran and I (1996; see also chapter 7) have attempted to model the sequential patterns of patient–therapist interactions associated with the resolution of therapeutic alliance ruptures. One of the central features of the research paradigm exemplified by these contributions is the attempt to find some middle ground or straddle between traditional research strategies that buy generalizability at the expense of clinical meaningfulness and case study approaches that capture the richness of the clinical situation at the expense of generalizability. More specifically, these contributions represent an attempt to marry a discovery-oriented, qualitative, idiographic, intensive analytic orientation with a confirmatory, quantitative, nomothetic, extensive analytic orientation.[7]

---

[7]See Russell (1994) and the special section titled Psychotherapy Change Process Research, in L. S. Greenberg & F. L. Newman (Guest Eds.), *Journal of Consulting and Clinical Psychology, 64* (1996), for recent examples of this developing research paradigm as well as Rice and Greenberg (1984) for early examples. See also Toukmanian and Rennie (1992) and Stiles (1991) for methodological advances toward quantifying qualitative research.

Although I consider these to be important advances, the therapist's experience remains inadequately addressed. In Greenberg's view, the therapist seems to simply (though sensitively) direct the process toward self-awareness and synthesis. In Horowitz's view, the therapist seems essentially to be an interpreter of the patient's self-states. The emphasis is on observation and not much on participation. The absence of the therapist's experience in these visions of therapeutic process was not lost by both Bach and Pizer in their commentaries in this volume. To a lesser extent, this criticism can be made of Safran and myself. Although we well recognize and discuss extensively the role of therapist experience (Safran & Muran, 2000), our research on rupture resolution thus far has concentrated on patient self-states and therapist facilitative interventions. What seems necessary to shed light on the various self-states and subjective processes through which the therapist progresses in the resolution process is an iterative process between theory-driven hypothesizing and intensive investigation involving observation and interview of therapists. For example, we began in a preliminary way a few years back a process of exploring the therapist's subjective experience in rupture resolution by using the interpersonal-process recall approach (Batchelder, Jilton, Safran, & Muran, 1994; see Elliott, 1986; Wiseman, 1992), by conducting semistructured interviews of the therapists regarding videotaped sessions that included rupture resolution events as indicated by patient and therapist postsession reports. Work as such seems critical to move us beyond theoretical propositions and prescriptives of therapist subjective states that are necessary in certain change events, such as rupture resolution. For example, there seems to be a great deal of consensus in the clinical literature that some degree of openness or receptivity is necessary (see Safran & Muran, 2000, for a review), but how does a therapist move from a closed or fixed state of mind characteristic of a vicious cycle, enactment, or impasse to one that is open or fluid—how does a therapist shift out of being fully immersed in a defensive position to one that is slightly but significantly less so? Much work is needed in this regard.

In an article titled "Simplicity and Complexity in Psychotherapy Research," Robert Elliott and Cheryl Anderson (1994) articulated the fundamental dilemma faced in psychotherapy research: On the one hand, we recognize psychotherapy as a complex process, involving myriad subtle and not-so-subtle communications between patient and therapist; on the other hand, we follow simplifying assumptions and apply simple methods toward simple goals, as part of our positivist research tradition. Elliott and Anderson extolled the virtues of both positions and suggested a compromise position in which the search for order or simplification is balanced by an equal respect for the complexities of psychotherapy. They argued for maintaining a dialectical tension between the opposing desires for simplicity and complexity. This is the challenge we face.

Both/And

In this chapter, I have presented a mosaic of issues, challenges, and formulations. I have argued for a self that is multiple, relational, and contextual. I have appreciated the most local of detailed analysis. I have proposed a relational conception of the self that maintains a balance between process and structure and have described an intersubjective model for psychotherapy oriented toward discovery and construction (consistent with a number of positions put forth in this volume as well as elsewhere). I have tried to translate what these lofty ideas mean in practical terms with a clinical illustration that depicted some details from a psychotherapy process. Finally, I turned my attention to psychotherapy research and suggested an important initiative that should serve the operationalization of the complex interactions between patient and therapist. So it seems that in one moment, I fully embrace postmodernism; in another, I resist it and am thoroughly modern; and in yet another moment, I am both. Do I contradict myself?

In his postmodern discourse, Jacques Derrida (1978) argued that binary oppositions, such as self–other, in which one term (*self*) is always given a more privileged position than its opposite (*other*), are typical of modern ideologies and "con" the reader (or observer) into believing that one side of the dichotomy has greater value than the other (see Foucault, 1967, and Sampson, 1993, for related arguments). Derrida recommended that instead we adopt the logic of "both–and" rather than the logic of "either–or" that is characteristic of modernism. When considering any phenomenon, we should take as our object of study both what it is taken to be and what it appears to exclude to better understand it.

> Derrida argues that in whatever we take to be immediate and present there is always already absence, difference and deferral. If presence always contains absence, there cannot be a neatly drawn line of opposition between these two notions. It is not that presence and absence are opposites, not that there is *either* presence *or* absence, but rather that there is an inevitable defining of the one through the other: there is *both* presence *and* absence. (Sampson, 1989, p. 12, emphasis in original)

There is both figure and ground, subject and object, multiplicity and unity, process and structure, discovery and construction, complexity and simplicity, or patient and therapist. I think this logic can also be turned on postmodernism itself, in that it cannot be fully understood without consideration of modernism. As noted in my introduction to this book, modernism and postmodernism are intrinsically tied to each other. They are not opposite sides of a dichotomy but inseparable components of a system, neither of which makes sense without the other.[8] The goal of deconstruction is to reveal contradictions and tensions, not to resolve them. So as Muriel Dimen describes in chapter 9, self-experience is composed of complex and shifting relations among multiple contradictions or differences. In line with Stuart Pizer (chapter 5), selfhood is understood as paradoxical. We transition between different polarities—such as modern and postmodern in my case—which are but different self-states.

Do I contradict myself?
Very well, then, I contradict myself,
(I am large, I contain multitudes.)
(Walt Whitman, 1855/1950, Sec. 51)

References

Aron, L. (1996). *A meeting of minds: Mutuality in psychoanalysis.* Hillsdale, NJ: Analytic Press.

Aron, L. (1999). Clinical choices and the relational matrix. *Psychoanalytic Dialogues, 9,* 1–29.

Auerbach, J., & Blatt, S. (1996). Self-representation in severe psychopathology: The role of reflexive self-awareness. *Psychoanalytic Psychology, 13,* 297–341.

Barnett, J. (1980). Interpersonal processes, cognition, and the analysis of character. *Contemporary Psychoanalysis, 16,* 397–416.

Batchelder, S., Jilton, R., Safran, J. D., & Muran, J. C. (1994, June). *An application of interpersonal process recall to alliance rupture resolution events.* Paper presented at the annual meeting of the Society for Psychotherapy Research, York, England.

Beebe, B., & Lachmann, F. (1992). The contribution of mother–infant mutual influence to the origins of self- and object representations. In N. J. Skolnick & S. C. Warshaw (Eds.), *Relational perspectives in psychoanalysis* (pp. 83–118). Hillsdale, NJ: Analytic Press.

Benjamin, J. (1990). An outline of intersubjectivity: The development of recognition. *Psychoanalytic Psychology, 7,* 33–46.

Bergin, A. E. (1997). Neglect of the therapist and the human dimensions of change: A commentary. *Clinical Psychology: Science & Practice, 4,* 83–89.

Bergin, A. E., & Garfield, S. L. (Eds.). (1994). *Handbook of psychotherapy and behavior change* (4th ed.). New York: Wiley.

Beutler, L. E., Machado, P. P., & Neufeldt, S. A. (1994). Therapist variables. In A. E.

[8]This logic invokes for me Hegel's (1807/1969) notion of negation and his idea of two selves in dialectic opposition to each, where the existence of one is very much dependent on the other.

Bergin & S. L. Garfield (Eds.), *Handbook of psychotherapy and behavior change* (4th ed., pp. 229–269). New York: Wiley.

Bohart, A. (1983, May). *Detachment: A variable common to many psychotherapies.* Paper presented at the annual meeting of the Western Psychological Association, San Francisco, CA.

Bordin, E. (1979). The generalizability of the psychoanalytic concept of the working alliance. *Psychotherapy: Theory, Research, and Practice, 16,* 252–260.

Bowlby, J. (1969). *Attachment and loss: Vol. 1. Attachment.* New York: Basic Books.

Bromberg, P. M. (1993). Shadow and substance: A relational perspective on clinical process. *Psychoanalytical Psychology, 10,* 147–168.

Bromberg, P. M. (1998). *Standing in the spaces.* Hillsdale, NJ: Analytic Press.

Burke, W. (1992). Countertransference disclosure and the asymmetry/mutuality dilemma. *Psychoanalytic Dialogues, 2,* 241–271.

Caspar, F. (1997). What goes on in a psychotherapist's mind? *Psychotherapy Research, 7,* 105–126.

Cilliers, P. (1998). *Complexity and postmodernism: Understanding complex systems.* New York: Routledge.

Coady, N. (1989). The association between client and therapist interpersonal processes and outcomes in psychodynamic psychotherapy. *Research on Social Work Practice, 1,* 122–138.

Crits-Christoph, P., Baranacki, K., Kurcias, J. S., Beck, A. T., Caroll, K., Perry, K., Luborsky, L., McLellan, A. T., Woody, G. E., Thompson, L., Gallagher, D., & Zitrin, C. (1991). Meta-analysis of therapist effects in psychotherapy outcome studies. *Psychotherapy Research, 1,* 81–91.

Crits-Christoph, P., & Mintz, L. (1991). Implications of therapist effects for the design and analysis of comparison studies of psychotherapies. *Journal of Consulting and Clinical Psychology, 59,* 20–26.

Davies, J. M. (1996). Linking the "pre-analytic" with the post-classical: Integration, dissociation, and the multiplicity of unconscious processes. *Contemporary Psychoanalysis, 32,* 553–576.

Davies, J. M., & Frawley, M. (1994). *Treating the adult survivor of childhood sexual abuse: Psychoanalytic perspectives.* New York: Basic Books.

Dennett, D. C. (1991). *Consciousness explained.* Boston: Little, Brown.

Derrida, J. (1978). *Writing and difference* (A. Bass, Trans.). Chicago: University of Chicago Press.

Edelman, G. (1987). *Neural Darwinism: The theory of neuronal group selection.* New York: Basic Books.

Ehrenberg, D. (1992). *The intimate edge.* New York: Norton.

Elliott, R. (1986). Interpersonal process recall (IPR) as a psychotherapy process research method. In L. S. Greenberg & W. M. Pinsof (Eds.), *The psychotherapeutic process: A research handbook* (pp. 503–528). New York: Guilford Press.

Elliott, R., & Anderson, C. (1994). Simplicity and complexity in psychotherapy research. In R. L. Russell (Ed.), *Reassessing psychotherapy research* (pp. 65–113). New York: Guilford Press.

Epstein, M. (1995). *Thoughts without a thinker.* New York: Basic Books.

Epstein, M. (1998). *Going to pieces without falling apart.* New York: Broadway.

Fairbairn, W. R. D. (1952). *Psychoanalytic studies of the personality.* London: Tavistock.

Fast, I. (1998). *Selving: A relational theory of self organization.* Hillsdale, NJ: Analytic Press.

Ferenczi, S. (1931). Child analysis in the analysis of adults. In M. Balint (Ed.) & E. Mosbacher (Trans.), *Final contributions to the theory and technique of psychoanalysis* (pp. 126–142). London: Karnac.

Fonagy, P., & Target, M. (1996). Playing with reality: I. Theory of mind and the normal development of psychic reality. *International Journal of Psycho-Analysis, 77,* 217–233.

Foucault, M. (1967). *Madness and civilization.* London: Tavistock.

Garfield, S. L. (1981). Evaluating the psychotherapies. *Behavior Therapy, 12,* 295–307.

Garfield, S. L. (1997). The therapist as a neglected variable in psychotherapy research. *Clinical Psychology: Science and Practice, 4,* 40–43.

Gaston, L. (1990). The concept of the alliance and its role in psychotherapy: Theoretical and empirical considerations. *Psychotherapy: Theory, Research, and Practice, 27,* 143–153.

Geertz, C. (1973). *The interpretation of cultures: Selected essays.* New York: Basic Books.

Goleman, D. (1980). A map for inner space. In R. N. Walsh & F. Vaughan (Eds.), *Beyond ego* (pp. 141–150). Los Angeles: Tarcher.

Greenberg, L. S. (1986). Change process research. *Journal of Consulting and Clinical Psychology, 54,* 411.

Greenberg, L. S., & Foerster, F. S. (1996). Task analysis exemplified: The process of resolving unfinished business. *Journal of Consulting and Clinical Psychology, 64,* 439–446.

Greenberg, L. S., & Safran, J. D. (1987). *Emotion in psychotherapy.* New York: Guilford Press.

Hegel, G. W. F. (1969). *Phenomenology of spirit.* New York: Oxford University Press. (Original work published 1807)

Henry, W. P., Schacht, T. E., & Strupp, H. H. (1986). Structural analysis of social behavior: Application to a study of interpersonal process in differential psychotherapeutic outcome. *Journal of Consulting & Clinical Psychology, 54,* 27–31.

Hoffman, I. Z. (1998). *Ritual and spontaneity in the psychoanalytic process: A dialectical–constructivist view.* Hillsdale, NJ: Analytic Press.

Holmqvist, R., & Armelius, B.-A. (1996). Sources of therapist's countertransference feelings. *Psychotherapy Research, 6,* 70–78.

Horowitz, M. J. (1987). *States of mind* (2nd ed.). New York: Plenum Press.

Horvath, A. O., & Symonds, B. D. (1991). Relation between working alliance and outcome in psychotherapy: A meta-analysis. *Journal of Counseling Psychology, 38,* 139–149.

Husserl, E. (1931). *The Cartesian meditations* (D. Cairns, Trans.). The Hague, The Netherlands: Martinus Nijhoff.

James, W. (1981). *The principles of psychology.* Cambridge, MA: Harvard University Press. (Original work published 1890)

Kabat-Zinn, J. (1994). *Wherever you go, there you are.* New York: Hyperion.

Kierkegaard, S. (1944). *The sickness unto death.* Princeton, NJ: Princeton University Press. (Original work published 1849)

Kiesler, D. J. (1966). Some myths of psychotherapy research and the search for a paradigm. *Psychological Bulletin, 65,* 110–136.

Kiesler, D. J. (1973). *The process of psychotherapy: Empirical foundations and systems of analysis.* Chicago: Aldine.

Kiesler, D. J. (1983). The 1982 interpersonal circle: A taxonomy for complementarity in human transactions. *Psychological Review, 90,* 185–214.

Kiesler, D. J. (1996). *Contemporary interpersonal theory and research: Personality, psychopathology, and psychotherapy.* New York: Wiley.

Kiesler, D., & Watkins, K. (1989). Interpersonal complementarity and the therapeutic alliance: A study of relationship in psychotherapy. *Psychotherapy: Theory, Research, and Practice, 26,* 183–194.

Laing, R. D. (1972). *The politics of family.* New York: Vintage Books.

Leventhal, H. (1984). A perceptual–motor theory of emotion. In L. Berkowitz (Ed.), *Advances in experimental social psychology* (pp. 117–182). New York: Academic Press.

Linehan, M. (1993). *Cognitive–behavioral treatment of personality disorder.* New York: Guilford Press.

Lovlie, L. (1992). Postmodernism and subjectivity. In S. Kvale (Ed.), *Psychology and postmodernism* (pp. 119–134). London: Sage.

Luborsky, L., Crits-Christoph, P., McLellan, T., Woody, G., Piper, W., Imber, S., & Liberman, B. (1986). Do therapists vary much in their success? Findings from four outcome studies. *American Journal of Orthopsychiatry, 56,* 501–512.

Luborsky, L., McLellan, A. T., Diguer, L., Woody, G., & Seligman, D. A. (1997). The psychotherapist matters: Comparison of outcomes across twenty-two therapists and seven patient samples. *Clinical Psychology: Science & Practice, 4,* 53–65.

Luborsky, L., McLellan, A. T., Woody, G. E., O'Brien, C. P., & Auerbach, A. (1985).

Therapist success and its determinants. *Archives of General Psychiatry, 32,* 995–1008.

Main, M. (1991). Metacognitive knowledge, metacognitive monitoring, and singular (coherent) vs. multiple (incoherent) model of attachment: Findings and directions for future research. In C. M. Parkes, J. Stevenson-Hinds, & P. Marris (Eds.), *Attachment across the life cycle* (pp. 127–159). London: Tavistock/Routledge.

Martin, J. R. (1998). Mindfulness: A proposed common factor. *Journal of Psychotherapy Integration, 7,* 291–312.

Mitchell, S. A. (1988). *Relational concepts in psychoanalysis.* Cambridge, MA: Harvard University Press.

Mitchell, S. A. (1993). *Hope and dread in psychoanalysis.* New York: Basic Books.

Modell, A. H. (1993). *The private self.* Cambridge, MA: Harvard University Press.

Muran, J. C. (1997). Multiple selves and depression. *In-Session: Psychotherapy in Practice, 3,* 53–64.

Najavits, L., Griffin, M., Luborsky, L., Frank, A., Weiss, R., Liese, B., Thompson, H., Nakayama, E., Siqueland, L., Daley, D., & Onken, L. (1995). Therapists' emotional reactions to substance abusers: A new questionnaire and initial findings. *Psychotherapy: Theory, Research, Practice, and Training, 32,* 669–677.

Najavits, L., & Strupp, H. H. (1994). Differences in the effectiveness of psychodynamic therapists: A process-outcome study. *Psychotherapy: Theory, Research, Practice, and Training, 31,* 114–123.

Piaget, J. (1970). *Structuralism.* New York: Basic Books.

Pizer, S. A. (1992). The negotiation of paradox in the analytic process. *Psychoanalytic Dialogues, 2,* 215–240.

Rice, L. N., & Greenberg, L. S. (Eds.). (1984). *Patterns of change.* New York: Guilford Press.

Rogers, C. (1951). *Client-centered therapy.* New York: Houghton Mifflin.

Rummelhart, D. E., Smolensky, P., McClelland, J. L., & Hinton, G. E. (1986). Schemata and sequential thought processes in PDP models. In J. L. McClelland & D. E. Rummelhart (Eds.), *Parallel distributed processing: Explorations in the microstructure of cognition* (Vol. 2, pp. 7–57). Cambridge, MA: MIT Press.

Russell, R. L. (Ed.). (1994). *Reassessing psychotherapy research* (pp. 65–113). New York: Guilford Press.

Safran, J. D. (1998). *Widening the scope of cognitive therapy.* Northvale, NJ: Aronson.

Safran, J. D., & Greenberg, L. S. (Eds.). (1991). *Emotion, psychotherapy, and change.* New York: Guilford Press.

Safran, J. D., & Muran, J. C. (1995). Resolving therapeutic alliance ruptures: Diversity and integration. *In-Session: Psychotherapy in Practice, 1,* 81–82.

Safran, J. D., & Muran, J. C. (1996). The resolution of ruptures in the therapeutic alliance. *Journal of Consulting and Clinical Psychology, 64,* 447–458.

Safran, J. D., & Muran, J. C. (Eds.). (1998). *The therapeutic alliance in brief psychotherapy*. Washington, DC: American Psychological Association.

Safran, J. D., & Muran, J. C. (2000). *Negotiating the therapeutic alliance: A relational treatment guide*. New York: Guilford Press.

Safran, J. D., & Segal, Z. V. (1990). *Interpersonal process in cognitive therapy*. New York: Basic Books.

Sampson, E. (1989). The deconstruction of the self. In J. Shotter & K. Gergen (Eds.), *Texts of identity* (pp. 1–19). London: Sage.

Sampson, E. (1993). *Celebrating the other: A dialogic account of human nature*. Boulder, CO: Westview Press.

Samstag, L. W. (1998). *Difficult dyads and unsuccessful treatments: A comparison of dropout, poor, and good outcome groups in brief psychotherapy*. Unpublished doctoral dissertation, City University of New York, New York.

Schafer, R. (1983). *The analytic attitude*. New York: Basic Books.

Singer, E. (1977). *Key concepts in psychotherapy*. Northvale, NJ: Aronson.

Slavin, M., & Kriegman, D. (1992). *The adaptive design of the human psyche*. New York: Guilford Press.

Spence, D. P. (1982). *Narrative truth and historical truth: Meaning and interpretation in psychoanalysis*. New York: Norton.

Stern, D. B. (1997). *Unformulated experience*. Hillsdale, NJ: Analytic Press.

Stern, D. N. (1985). *The interpersonal world of the infant*. New York: Basic Books.

Sterba, R. (1934). The fate of the ego in analytic therapy. *International Journal of Psychoanalysis, 15,* 117–126.

Stiles, W. (1991, June). *Quality control in qualitative research*. Paper presented at the annual meeting of the Society for Psychotherapy Research, Lyon, France.

Stinson, C., & Palmer, S. (1991). Parallel distributed processing models of person schemas and psychopathologies. In M. J. Horowitz (Ed.), *Person schemas and maladaptive interpersonal patterns* (pp. 339–378). Chicago: University of Chicago Press.

Sullivan, H. S. (1953). *The interpersonal theory of psychiatry*. New York: Norton.

Sullivan, H. S. (1954). *The psychiatric interview*. New York: Norton.

Sullivan, H. S. (1964). *The fusion of psychiatry and the social sciences*. New York: Norton.

Talley, P. F., Strupp, H. H., & Butler, S. F. (1994). *Psychotherapy research and practice: Bridging the gap*. New York: Basic Books.

Teasdale, J. D., Segal, Z., & Williams, M. D. (1995). How does cognitive therapy prevent depressive relapse and why should attentional control (mindfulness) training help? *Behaviour Research and Therapy, 33,* 25–39.

Toukmanian, S. G., & Rennie, D. L. (Eds.). (1992). *Psychotherapy process research*. Newbury Park, CA: Sage.

Weinstock-Savoy, D. E. (1986). *The relationship of therapist and patient interpersonal styles to outcome in brief dynamic psychotherapy.* Unpublished doctoral dissertation, Boston University, Boston.

Whitman, W. (1950). Leaves of grass and selected poems. New York: Random House. (Original work published 1855)

Winnicott, D. W. (1965). *The maturational process and the facilitating environment.* New York: International Universities Press.

Wiseman, H. (1992). Conceptually based interpersonal process recall of change events. In S. G. Toukmanian & R. L. Rennie (Eds.), *Psychotherapy process research* (pp. 51–77). Newbury Park, CA: Sage.

Wolstein, B. (1974). "I" processes and "me" patterns. *Contemporary Psychoanalysis, 10,* 347–357.

Author Index

Numbers in italics refer to listings in reference sections.

Subject Index

Messer, Stanley B., 33
  commentary on, 211–217
Metacommunication, 355–356
Metaphor, use of, 285–286, 317–319
  brain metaphor, 349
  chessboard metaphor, 303–304
  computer metaphor, 242–243, 286, 349
  internal board of directors metaphor, 108
  island metaphor, 116, 123
  two computers metaphor, 302–303
Metapsychology, 316–317
Mindfulness, 252–253, 352–355, 359–360
Mind object, 206
Mirroring, transitional, 113
Mitchell, S., 24, 29, 31, 115, 198, 229, 325, 356
Modell, A., 18–19, 120
Modernism, 3–8, 315–316, 329, 365–366
Modernity, 193–195
Modulation, in states of mind, 67
Monadic domain, of self-knowing, 320, 322–323, 344
Monroe, S. M., 245–246
Mood, in states of mind, 67
Mother, as conductor, 112–113, 125–126, 131
Motherhood, distorted view of, 137–138
Mother paradox, 114–115, 124, 132
Motivated cognition, 245
Multiculturalism, 6n4
Multiphrenia, 196
Multiple or mixed model, of self, 48–49.
  See also Selves, multiple
Multiple personality disorders, 57–58, 94
Muran, J. Christopher, 31, 33–34, 348, 354–355, 363–364
  commentary on, 187–191
Mutual analysis, 140
Mutual definition, of selfhood and gender identity, 220–221
Mutual influence, 144–145
Mutual recognition, 354–355
Mutual regulation, 160

Nachtraglichkeit, 52, 124

Naive patient fallacy, 149
Naming, of states of mind, 68
Narcissism, 83–84, 199
Narrative dimension, 333–334
Narrative identity, 93–94
Negotiation, intersubjectivity as, 162–163, 166–167, 354–355
Neopragmatism, 5n1
Neufeldt, S., 361–362
Neuronal group selection theory, 118–121

Object relationships, and paradox, 114–118
Object relations perspective, 11, 13, 264
Oedipal stage, 140–141
Ogden, T., 22–23, 26, 139–140
Operationism, 351
Oscillating function, 141
Oscillation, in desire, 229–230
Other, the, 47–48, 56–57, 69–70, 99, 131, 161. *See also* Intersubjectivity; Self

Paradox, 132–134, 216, 232, 238, 254–255
  father's lap paradox, 116, 133
  mature dependence paradox, 230
  mother paradox, 230
  simultaneity paradox, 229
  tolerance of, 112–118, 120, 124
Parapraxes, 127
Passivity, and activity, 221–222
Penn Psychotherapy Project, 362
Personality, field theory of, 12–13
Personality structure, and attractor state, 90
Perspectivism, 7
Phenomena, in configurational analysis, 70–71
Philosophy of life, focus on, 327, 329–330
Pick an identity exercise, 301
Pizer, Stuart A., 23, 26, 31, 33, 162–163, 347, 350, 354, 364, 366
  commentary on, 131–135
Pluralism, 5–6, 313